GLOBALIZATION AND LOCAL ADAPTATION IN INTERNATIONAL TRADE LAW

The Asia Pacific Legal Culture and Globalization series explores intersecting themes that revolve around the impact of globalization in countries on the Asia Pacific Rim and examines the significance of legal culture as a mediator of that impact. The emphasis is on a broad understanding of legal culture that extends beyond traditional legal institutions and actors to normative frameworks and the legal consciousness of ordinary people. Books in the series reflect international scholarship from a wide variety of disciplines, including law, political science, economics, sociology, and history.

GLOBALIZATION AND LOCAL ADAPTATION IN INTERNATIONAL TRADE LAW

Edited by Pitman B. Potter and Ljiljana Biukovic

UBCPress · Vancouver · Toronto

20 19 18 17 16 15 14 13 12 11   5 4 3 2 1

Printed in Canada on FSC-certified ancient-forest-free paper
(100% post-consumer recycled) that is processed chlorine- and acid-free.

Library and Archives Canada Cataloguing in Publication

Globalization and local adaptation in international trade law /
edited by Pitman B. Potter and Ljiljana Biukovic.

(Asia Pacific legal culture and globalization, 1925-0320)
Includes bibliographical references and index.
ISBN 978-0-7748-1903-9 (bound); ISBN 978-0-7748-1904-6 (pbk.)

1. Foreign trade regulation – Pacific Area. 2. Pacific Area – Commercial policy.
3. Dispute resolution (Law) – Pacific Area. 4. Globalization – Economic aspects –
Pacific Area. I. Potter, Pitman B. II. Biukovic, Ljiljana. III. Series: Asia Pacific legal
culture and globalization (Series)

KNC842.G56 2011   343.51'087   C2010-907162-X

e-book ISBNs: 978-0-7748-1905-3 (pdf); 978-0-7748-1906-0 (epub)

Canadä

UBC Press gratefully acknowledges the financial support for our publishing program
of the Government of Canada (through the Canada Book Fund), the Canada Council
for the Arts, and the British Columbia Arts Council.

Printed and bound in Canada by Friesens
Set in Futura Condensed and Warnock by Artegraphica Design Co. Ltd.
Text design: Irma Rodriguez
Copy editor: Francis Chow
Indexer: Dianne Tiefensee

UBC Press
The University of British Columbia
2029 West Mall
Vancouver, BC V6T 1Z2
www.ubcpress.ca

Contents

Part 2: Local Implementation of Global Standards

Part 3: Case Studies on Dispute Resolution

Preface

This volume offers a range of essays exploring the interplay between international trade standards and local practices. The volume is organized to highlight normative and organizational dimensions of the relationship between global regulatory standards and local performance. We begin with a selection of essays on concepts and methods (Part 1). Pitman Potter's introductory essay on selective adaptation and institutional capacity suggests that these particular paradigms offer useful approaches for understanding normative and organizational aspects of local implementation of international trade standards. The research presented here and the underlying project from which it is derived give significant attention to these normative and organizational perspectives in examining the conditions that affect local implementation of international trade standards. Ljiljana Biukovic's examination of global competition governance illustrates the effects of normative conflict in the implementation of international standards, while Emma E. Buchtel's methodological essay examines the role of normative discourse in cross-cultural conflict resolution. These essays are aimed at sharpening appreciation for the theoretical implications of local knowledge as an essential dimension of the processes of assimilation and transplantation that are so often assumed to accompany processes of globalization. As each of these authors suggests, expectations about globalization and convergence of regulatory norms are likely to go unfulfilled unless the resiliency of local legal and political culture is factored into the analysis of treaty compliance.

Informed by these conceptual and methodological perspectives, Part 2 of this volume then presents a range of case study examples of normative and institutional dynamics in the local implementation of international regulatory standards. International trade standards are explored more specifically in successive chapters addressing the role of local conditions in international contracting (Yoshitaka Wada), labour mobility within the North American Free Trade Agreement (NAFTA) (Kathrine Richardson), new developments in intellectual property law in China (Liao Zhigang), competition policy (Richard Schwindt and Devin McDaniels), and local implementation of World Trade Organization (WTO) transparency standards (Pitman Potter). Each of these essays addresses a salient issue in the international trade regime and examines the dynamics of local application. In these case studies, we discover the complexity of processes and outcomes by which international trade standards are localized. Normative and organizational dimensions addressed in these essays reveal that local compliance with international trade standards is not simply a matter of political will, but neither can it be attributed to singular factors of normative affinity or organizational performance. Rather, elements of selective adaptation and institutional capacity can be seen to operate in tandem to influence the reception and implementation of international rule regimes.

In light of the importance of dispute resolution both as a litmus test for the universality of rule regimes and underlying norms and as a context within which rules and norms are contested, Part 3 addresses local adaptation of international standards in relation to dispute resolution. The essays cover topics ranging from corporate dispute resolution in Japan (Maomi Iwase), international dispute resolution practice in China (Wang Shuliang), education on alternative dispute resolution (ADR) in Japan (Mayumi Saegusa and Julian Dierkes), and a comparative review of the performance of China and Canada under the WTO's TRIPS Agreement (Wenwei Guan). Each essay focuses on the resiliency of local norms and practices, which are an essential component of the dynamics of selective adaptation and institutional capacity. In the context of selective adaptation, it is precisely such resiliency, and the durability of community norms that it represents, that drives local interpretive communities to rely on local norms in the interpretation and implementation of international standards. And in the context of institutional capacity, it is precisely the influence of local conditions on organizational performance that affects local efforts to implement international trade standards in the absence of normative conflicts.

We hope that this collection of essays offers a range of useful case studies on the normative and organizational dimensions of local implementation of international trade standards. This research was made possible through the Major Collaborative Research Initiatives (MCRI) program of the Social Sciences and Humanities Research Council (SSHRC) of Canada, for which the editors are deeply grateful. We are indebted to each of the contributors to this volume for their commitment of time, energy, and ideas to this project. We would also like to thank the Institute of Asian Research and the Faculty of Law at the University of British Columbia for steadfast support and encouragement in connection with this project. Many student research assistants (including those whose essays in this volume formed part of their doctoral research) contributed to this project, including Harry Chao Wang, Matthew Levine, Stephen Rukavina, Ajinkya Tulpule, Karen Slaughter, Frank Huang, Anna Turinov, Nao Kashiwagi, Hayane Dahmen, and Wendy Zhu. We would like especially to thank Megan Coyle, Assistant at the UBC Law Faculty's Centre for Asian Legal Studies, and Rozalia Mate, Project Manager at the Institute of Asian Research, for their ongoing administrative assistance in support of this volume. Thanks also to Dr. Richard Schwindt for assistance in designing the formulae discussed in the Introduction to this volume.

Abbreviations

ACCJ	American Chamber of Commerce in Japan
ADR	alternative dispute resolution
AML	*Antimonopoly Law*
APDR	Asia Pacific Dispute Resolution project
APEC	Asia-Pacific Economic Cooperation
CBPS	Customs and Border Protection Service (US)
CBSA	Canadian Border Services Agency
CCP	*Code of Civil Procedure* (Japan)
CCPIT	China Council for the Promotion of International Trade
CIC	Citizenship and Immigration Canada
CIETAC	China International Economic and Trade Arbitration Commission
CIPE	Center for International Private Enterprise (US)
CLRC	Central Labour Relations Commission (Japan)
CMAC	China Maritime Arbitration Commission
COC	Chinese Olympic Committee
CPC	Chinese Communist Party
DFAIT	Department of Foreign Affairs and International Trade (Canada)
DHS	Department of Homeland Security (US)
ECJ	European Court of Justice
FTC	Free Trade Commission (US)
GATS	*General Agreement on Trade in Services*

GATT	*General Agreement on Tariffs and Trade*
GSP	Generalized System of Preferences
IIRIRA	*Illegal Immigration Reform and Immigrant Responsibility Act* (US)
IOC	International Olympic Committee
IP	intellectual property
IPR	intellectual property rights
JAA	Japan Association of Arbitrators
JCAA	Japan Commercial Arbitration Association
JCCA	Japan Credit Counseling Association
JCSTAD	Japan Center for Settlement of Traffic Accident Disputes
JFBA	Japan Federation of Bar Associations
JFTC	Japan Fair Trade Commission
JIC	Japan Investment Council
JIPAC	Japan Intellectual Property Arbitration Center
JSE	Japan Shipping Exchange, Inc.
LCCA	*Law for Conciliation of Civil Affairs* (Japan)
MITI	Ministry of International Trade and Industry
NAFTA	*North American Free Trade Agreement*
NCAC	National Consumer Affairs Center of Japan
OECD	Organisation for Economic Co-operation and Development
PCT	*Patent Cooperation Treaty*
SCAP	Supreme Command of Allied Powers
SSC	Special Survey Committee (Japan)
SSI	Structural Impediments Initiative (Japan)
TEC	*Treaty Establishing the European Community*
TEWG	Temporary Entry Working Group (NAFTA)
TN	Treaty NAFTA
TOMAC	Tokyo Maritime Arbitration Commission
TRIPS	Trade-Related Aspects of Intellectual Property Rights
UNCITRAL	United Nations Commission on International Trade Law
UNCTAD	United Nations Conference on Trade and Development
UNDP	United Nations Development Programme
UNIDROIT	International Institute for the Unification of Private Law
USAID	US Agency for International Development
USOC	United States Olympic Committee
VANOC	Vancouver Organizing Committee
WIPO	World Intellectual Property Organization
WTO	World Trade Organization

PART 1

CONCEPTS AND METHODS

Introduction
Selective Adaptation, Institutional Capacity, and the Reception of International Law under Conditions of Globalization

PITMAN B. POTTER

Legal behaviour is strongly influenced by norms of legal and political culture[1] and by the institutional context within which these norms are operationalized.[2] Cultural norms are reflected in rules, including formal laws and regulations and informal procedures and practices. The distinction between rules and the cultural norms they represent becomes especially important when rules particular to one cultural group are used by another without a corresponding assimilation of underlying norms. Local implementation of non-local rules is also affected by the institutional context. Under current conditions of globalization, normative tensions are present as liberal rules of governance generally associated with Europe and North America are disseminated to other areas characterized by local norms that are often in conflict with norms of liberalism. International trade regulation is of special importance, where concerns over compliance with international standards often reflect misplaced expectations about the enforceability of rules without agreement on underlying norms. In the context of globalization, economic and political power has allowed trade standards associated with liberal democratic capitalism to be imposed on societies outside the European tradition, but has had less effect in displacing local cultural norms. Better understanding of local implementation of international trade standards requires a deeper appreciation of the normative and structural contexts for legal performance. This introductory essay presents an approach to understanding trade compliance in light of normative factors of selective adaptation and the structural dynamics of institutional capacity, drawing on conceptual and methodological perspectives developed through the course of the Asia Pacific Dispute Resolution (APDR) project of the Institute of Asian Research at the University of British Columbia.

Globalization and the Unification of Trade Standards

Treaty compliance is an important example of the reception of international law. Treaty compliance involves dynamics of interpretation and implementation of international legal standards. In cases where treaties involve rules grounded in non-local norms, interpretation involves a dynamic of selective adaptation by which non-local rules are interpreted according to local norms of legal and political culture. As well, to the extent that reception includes performance, dynamics of structural relationships are also important and are revealed through the paradigm of institutional capacity.

Current conditions of globalization have supported the steady entrenchment of principles of trade liberalization associated with the *General Agreement on Tariffs and Trade* (GATT) and the World Trade Organization (WTO). Of particular importance is the influence of principles of market liberalization, privatization, and fiscal austerity associated with the so-called Washington Consensus. Seen initially as a remedy for economic problems in Latin America,[3] the principles of the Washington Consensus have been expanded to Asia as well, as an antidote to "crony capitalism" and other perceived ills in the economies of the developing world.[4] Although associated most immediately with neoclassical economics, the principles of the Washington Consensus drew more fundamentally on norms of liberalism that call for the diminished presence of government in market regulation. Although this perspective is undergoing active reconsideration,[5] the ideological dimensions of globalization contribute to its capacity to bring about historically unprecedented cultural and institutional change.[6]

Power imbalances between developed and developing economies in particular have strengthened the dissemination and imposition of norms of governance and regulation associated with liberal industrial states in the West, particularly the United States. China's accession to the WTO, the Asia-Pacific Economic Cooperation (APEC) trade liberalization process, the annual process of G8 summitry, and annual reporting on human rights conditions in developing economies by the United States all suggest the intention and capacity of liberal industrial states to disseminate their preferred norms of governance around the world. International regulatory systems associated with the GATT and the WTO also serve as vehicles for global economic integration.[7] Based on regulatory norms of transparency and the rule of law that are considered requirements for economic growth,[8] principles of government restraint are entrenched in regulatory regimes for international trade and investment associated with the WTO.[9]

Ideological features of globalization and their expression through institutional regimes of governance have particular consequences. Although liberal norms of global business regulation may well be aimed generally at broad goals of economic growth and development, they also support the economic and political interests of the post-industrial states. For just as states deploy and manipulate international economic organizations to suit their own policy imperatives,[10] so also do both states and private actors strive to build political and popular support for particular institutional and normative regimes through the deployment and manipulation of ideas. Antonio Gramsci's ideas about "cultural hegemony" raise important questions about the interests being served by the rhetoric of globalization.[11] Thus, trade liberalization, market reform, and market access agreements entrench regulatory principles that are presented as universal but that also support particular political and commercial interests.[12]

In a very important sense, globalization embodies an expansion of geographical imagination,[13] reflecting a process by which the socioeconomic and political preferences that inform certain law and governance rules in a particular region are exported and imposed across the globe.[14] This is made possible by the political, economic, and ideological dominance of the post-industrial capitalist states. Political dominance is achieved through international organizations such as the WTO, where disparities of bargaining capital entrench the interests of post-industrial capitalism.[15] Economic dominance is supported by nearly overwhelming bargaining power, based on territorial control over consumer markets in Europe and North America preserved through tariff measures and anti-dumping provisions.[16] Ideological dominance is achieved through education and training systems based largely at European and North American universities that disseminate norms and values of liberalism. Legal training programs supported by the United Nations Development Programme, the Canadian International Development Agency, the European Union, and the Ford Foundation, for example, suggest continued linkages between the education of elites from developing economies and the dissemination of liberal values.[17]

The development of international commercial law augments these initiatives, such that the cross-border transit of goods is now governed largely by the WTO's multilateral trade liberalization rules. Contemporary international commercial law imposes the particular historical experiences and material preferences of a few powerful trading economies upon the global community, often to the disadvantage of developing economies.[18] As a result, market liberalization principles imposed on the global political economy remain partial and distorted in favour of the governance principles of the post-industrial states, with little attention paid to local perspectives and conditions in developing economies.[19] Halting and incomplete efforts to provide support for developing economies through, for example, the Generalized System of Preferences, have largely given way to the resilient power of "voluntary export restraints" and anti-dumping regimes enforced by fully industrialized economies to inhibit market access.[20]

Challenges for institutional response in the area of global financial flows are also evident, such that territorial and jurisdictional limitations present historically unprecedented challenges to the regulation of transnational capital. The historical relationship between private banking and state expenditures, expressed, for example, in the expansion of the Rothschild financial empire through support for the French king's apparently insatiable appetite for military adventure, was restricted largely to national territory – not least because this imposed a limit on the lender's access to security.[21] Today, by contrast, international lending and investment are facilitated by organizations, processes, and norms tailored to the needs of global capital.[22] Banking and investment firms have the financial and technological capacity to establish themselves around the world and to direct capital flows without regard to national boundaries, supported by WTO-affiliated agreements on trade-related investment and trade in services that limit the capacity of states to restrict such activities.[23] Supporting the organizational and procedural dynamics of financial globalization is a framework of liberal norms and values extolling principles of market autonomy and the supremacy of private property. Bilateral and multilateral investment agreements that entrench principles of national treatment are aimed primarily at securing market access for a relatively narrow band of firms with global capabilities and interests.[24]

Institutional responses to the transnational flow of information also reflect the impact of material and ideological features of globalization, and suggest significant departures from the past. International intellectual property (IP) regimes purport to protect private ownership of proprietary technologies for transmission of information, as well as the information itself, by imposing on member economies obligations to conform their national IP legislation to international standards.[25] Some argue that this privileges a narrow band of knowledge economies and information providers and works to stifle innovation and growth in developing economies.[26] Moreover, although international regimes support unified standards of protection of private interests in knowledge, no parallel system exists to protect public interests, and so the regulation of electronic commerce (both means and content) remains largely dispersed among conflicting national systems.[27] As a result, purveyors of information internationally can be assured that their private interests in the content of expression and the means of transmission are well defended, while remaining relatively free of global regulatory oversight that might protect public interests in both content and means of expression. Thus, institutional responses to globalization of information permit largely unrestricted flows of entertainment and media products, with little accountability for content and responsible access.[28]

Institutional responses to these newly emergent material and ideological dimensions of globalization reflect the extent to which state sovereignty is challenged.[29] By locating the subjects of exchange and the exchanges themselves outside particular jurisdictional boundaries, material features of globalization challenge the state's capacity to regulate these activities. For despite calls for multinational regulation, state governance remains subject to the limitations of jurisdictional boundaries – whether in the realm of exchanges of goods and services (e.g., customs and tariff administration), transactions in capital (e.g., financial disclosure and taxation rules), exchanges of information (e.g., media and Internet regulations), or travel by people (e.g., immigration regimes). To the extent that this challenges closely held beliefs about territorial integrity, the state's capacity and willingness to enforce its sovereign powers over global enterprises is further undermined. The state also faces direct opposition to its efforts to regulate the conduct of global business, where the mobility of capital operates as a disincentive to public interest regulation. Although there is debate over the possible correlations between lax regulation and international investment flows, the discourses of the "race to the bottom" and the concomitant call for renewed state activism[30] reflect concerns with diminishing state sovereignty in the face of material dimensions of globalization.

Some suggest that these historical changes, and the apparent imbalances in purpose and effect associated with them, have generally deleterious effects on developing economies, whose comparative advantages and negotiating powers are weak.[31] Certainly, governments for whom foreign investment is either a key element in local development or a key contributor to the co-optation of elite priorities face increasing challenges to the protection of public goods within their jurisdictions.[32] And yet, it is public goods, such as education and health care, that are essential to developing the human capital that enables developing economies to benefit from the global economy.[33] The emergence of local industries aimed at supplying goods to local consumers is hampered by investment liberalization policies that discourage, if not ban outright, policy efforts aimed at nurturing local industries, and by trade liberalization policies that require local market openings while permitting protectionist anti-dumping barriers in potentially lucrative markets elsewhere.[34] International mobility of capital inhibits local efforts aimed at protection of labour and environmental conditions, which are seen to justify capital flight.[35] The state's capacity to prevent the domination of foreign media and culture is undermined by the prospect of trade sanctions aimed at securing market access for information and entertainment industries,[36] while efforts to stimulate local technologies are constrained by international intellectual property regimes.[37] And finally, efforts to promote internationalization of local labour forces, with ancillary benefits of foreign exchange remittances, opportunities for technical training and education, and the potential for expanding commercial and social networks, face increasingly contested immigration policies.[38]

Although the exegesis of and justifications for globalization reveal elements of material and ideological dynamics, the effects of globalization on local socioeconomic and political conditions remain obscure.[39] Certainly the expansion of market reach, growing diversity in goods and services, developing information infrastructure, expanded transboundary transportation, and accelerating privatization and deregulation programs can all be expected to affect local societies around the globe.[40] Although material effects may seem obvious at first, a closer look suggests significant local variation as well as significant regional contributions to the flows of goods, capital, information, and people. Thus, the penetration of foreign-branded goods has given rise to important elements of consumer differentiation locally as well as local imitation and variation in design, function, features, and appearance.[41] Increased availability of international capital locally, despite encouraging institutions and processes for management and oversight that mirror those of capital-exporting economies, have also permitted local approaches commensurate with local conditions.[42] Transnational information flows, whether through technology transfer, media publication, or entertainment, reveal a constant dynamic of local adaptation as well as regional competition.[43]

The ideological effects of globalization on local cultures are even less clear. There is no shortage of liberal commentators who conclude that changes in ideological perspective are the basis for changes in material conditions – in particular that adoption of liberal approaches to minimal governance and free market triumphalism are the basis for material prosperity.[44] Yet, the empirical evidence remains conflicted. Certainly, globalization has permitted broader exchanges of ideas about product competition and consumer selection, the character and purpose of financial and monetary practices, the content and uses of information, and the identity and worth of human beings. Causal linkages between the spread of liberalism associated with globalization and changes in local norms and values cannot be assumed, however, and we certainly cannot be confident that ideological perspectives associated with liberalism are, or can become, dominant in the local context.[45]

Expectations that material features of globalization will drive changes in local value systems reflect questionable assumptions about the superiority of liberalism and the contingency and weakness of alternative cultural arrangements. Assumptions about the inherent superiority of liberalism are tied to natural law norms on the supremacy of the individual and resulting limits on the authority of state and community.[46] Much of this is expressed in discourses about "civil society," whose beneficial conditions are seen to be the result of the withdrawal of the state.[47] Assumptions about the contingency and indeterminacy of local culture are evident in liberal responses to policy efforts to protect local culture through, for example, restrictions on foreign ownership of publishing media.[48] Assumptions about the power to change culture through material change are driven by enlightenment theories that inspired colonialism (and, incidentally, drove Marxist and Maoist ideas about social transformation).[49]

An alternative approach would be to examine local conditions on their own terms and frame expectations accordingly. Roberto Unger has proposed that the influence of ideas on local communities depends on a dynamic of "reception," which is grounded in the capacity of ideas to resonate with existing values.[50] This suggests that the influences of globalization locally will depend significantly on the possibilities for complementarity with local norms. This in turn would seem to require a more fundamental understanding of local conditions or, to use Geertz's famous phrase, a mastery of "local knowledge."[51]

Thus, understanding globalization raises questions about conceptualization, observation, and expectation. Conceptualizing globalization must take into account historical perspectives in order to account more fully for the particularities of current experience. Observing globalization requires examination of material and ideological dimensions and appreciation of the institutional implications. Expectations about globalization should embrace a cautious skepticism about potential effects on local communities and should be accompanied by a patient sensitivity to the myriad of possible outcomes. One solution to the dilemma lies in research on local cultures and their responses to conditions of globalization. This is the approach taken in this volume, with specific attention to questions of treaty compliance.

Local Reception: The Influence of Selective Adaptation and Institutional Capacity

In contrast to expectations about convergence that suggest development towards a globally unified system of institutional practices,[52] local implementation may be seen as a product of normative and structural factors. Normative dynamics of *selective adaptation* explain variations in compliance with non-local standards by reference to different levels of normative consensus. Structural dynamics of *institutional capacity* depict the ways in which relational factors of institutional purpose, location, orientation, and cohesion affect local implementation of non-local rule regimes.

Selective Adaptation

Selective adaptation describes a range of localized responses to external regulatory standards. In the absence of absolute normative consensus, selective adaptation suggests a spectrum of possibilities for implementation of non-local standards, based on varying degrees of conformity among local and non-local norms. Our research suggests that selective adaptation informs the processes by which implementation of non-local rule regimes is mediated by the influence of local norms.[53] Selective adaptation is made possible by the role of "interpretive communities" in the reception of international rule regimes.[54] Thus, government officials, socioeconomic and professional elites, and other privileged groups all exercise the authority of political position, specialized knowledge, and/or socioeconomic status to interpret non-local standards for application locally. In the course of this process, these interpretive communities express their own normative preferences, and in so doing selectively adapt non-local standards to local conditions. This process of interpretation reflects dynamics of perception, complementarity, and legitimacy.[55] We may conceive of selective adaptation by reference to the following formula:

$$SA = \frac{Rule\ Regime}{(N = Nf\,\mathrm{var}\,N1) \times [(P = Pf\,\mathrm{var}\,P1) + (C = Of\,\mathrm{var}\,O1) + Jn)]}.$$

Thus, selective adaptation (*SA*) may be seen as a function of a particular rule regime in light of the relationship between local and non-local norms attached to particular rule regimes, as affected by factors of local perception (*P*) on interpretation of both the rule and the underlying norm; the extent of complementarity (*C*) between the adapted rule and underlying norms (*O*), and existing rules and norms in the local economy; and the broader question of legitimation (*J*). The rule/norm relationship (*N*) thus involves a rule regime disseminated through processes of globalization, as qualified by the possibility of normative difference between the global and the local, which in turn is affected by factors of perception, complementarity, and legitimacy.

Perception influences understanding about foreign rule regimes and local norms and practices, and the relationships among them.[56] Perceptions about purpose, content, and effect of foreign and local institutional arrangements affect the processes and results of selective adaptation. For example, even where local institutional arrangements for political, social, and economic relations appear to have followed international models and organizational forms, local interpretation of international perspectives on federalism and local governance, multiculturalism and local society, and development and local economic relations are likely to hinge on the content and accuracy of perceptions about non-local institutional rules and practices, and about the norms that inform local systems. The interpretation and application of non-local rules in light of local norms thus depends on perceptions about both. This means, for example, that perception of what is required by WTO regimes for transparency and rule of law may well vary across (and within) different societies, ranging from simple commitments to publish formal laws and regulations[57] to more expansive notions about participation in rule making and the need for appeals processes to restrain state regulatory oversight.

Drawn from principles of nuclear physics, *complementarity* describes a circumstance by which apparently contradictory phenomena can be combined in ways that preserve essential characteristics of each component and yet allow for them to operate together in a mutually reinforcing and effective manner.[58] Complementarity may influence the extent to which norms and practices of local cultural communities can engage in mutually effective ways with institutional rules and processes associated with outside systems. Complementarity may inform the relationship between local accommodation and resistance to international standards in light of local conditions and needs. Thus, the extent to which WTO processes for trade dispute resolution have tended to privilege consensual or compulsory mechanisms[59] may be seen as either more or less complementary to local dispute resolution systems that reveal greater or lesser preferences for binding decision making. Local interpretation of international perspectives on federalism and local governance, multiculturalism and local society, and development and local economic relations may depend on complementarity between international and local forms and processes.[60] Factors of complementarity also arise around questions of compliance with international standards, informing the relationship between local accommodation and resistance to international standards in light of local conditions and needs.

Legitimacy concerns the extent to which members of local communities support the purposes and consequences of selective adaptation.[61] Thus, local interpretation of international perspectives on federalism and local governance, multiculturalism and local society, and development and local economic relations will depend on the legitimacy accorded to the processes and outcomes of the perspectives themselves and the legitimacy of local approaches to interpretation and application. Although the forms and requirements of legitimacy may vary, it remains essential to the effectiveness of selectively adapted governance practices. Legitimacy may derive from any variety of factors, including patterns of sociocultural relations, ideology, or local socioeconomic or political interest. Legitimacy may play a significant role in local implementation of trade disciplines on national treatment or intellectual property, where external pressures for market access or protection of ideas may be seen locally as intrusions on sovereignty and local autonomy. Thus, perception, complementarity, and legitimacy all affect the potential for integrating trade standards at the local level.

Institutional Capacity

Institutional capacity refers to the ability of institutions to perform their assigned tasks. Institutional capacity has been examined from relational perspectives that focus on issues of responsibility between organizations and their constituencies, efficiency in performance and the use of resources, and accountability to varying sources of authority.[62] Functional perspectives have also been applied to the question of institutional capacity, in such areas as access to information, effectiveness and methods of communication, organizational symmetry, and ability to enforce rules and directives.[63] No matter how useful these approaches may be in the abstract, however, actual institutional performance remains contingent on domestic political and socioeconomic conditions.[64] Local conditions of rapid socioeconomic and political transformation in Asia pose particular challenges for institutional capacity, inviting attention to structural relationship questions of institutional purpose, location, orientation, and cohesion.

Examined by reference to factor analysis, institutional capacity can be expressed through the following formula:

$$IC = \frac{Institutional\ Goal}{\left(U = \dfrac{1}{(1-u)}\right)(S = Sn)(A = Ar\ var\ As)\left(D = \dfrac{1}{(1-d)}\right)}.$$

Thus, institutional capacity (*IC*) may be seen as a function of a particular institutional goal being affected by factors of institutional purpose (*U*) concerning the institutional goal; the effects of location (*S*) on understanding of the institutional goal; the effects of institutional orientation (*A*) as to how the goal is to be pursued; and the extent of institutional cohesion (*D*) in organizational structure and behaviour.

Institutional purpose may be seen as a factor of uniformity and diversity, and reveals the ways in which the goals of institutions vary with local material and ideological contexts, the availability and nature of financial, human, and other resources, and the various limitations that attend institutional performance. Institutional purpose plays a significant role in determining the capacity of institutions to respond to socioeconomic change. Institutional purpose concerns the goals of institutional behaviour, and the way these reflect consensus and conflict among communities in which institutions operate. Thus, the capacity of local governance institutions to integrate international standards on trade regulation depends on the degree of clarity and consensus regarding policy objectives. For example, in the intellectual property area, differences among policy actors regarding the purpose of intellectual property rights (IPR) measures (for example, encouraging local innovation versus simply complying with externally imposed rules) have a significant effect on institutional behaviour.[65]

Institutional location is a product of varying degrees of distance from centres of governmental power and conformity, and reflects in particular the question of balancing central authority with decentralization of social and economic development initiatives.[66] Economies in Asia have long traditions of tension between local and central authorities. Although scholarly discourses have come increasingly to accept the application of federalist principles to local circumstances in many Asian economies, this discussion has often been marginalized in established policy discourse. In the process of bargaining that accompanies the allocation of resources and the distribution of costs and benefits of policy initiatives, rigid adherence to contested ideals of unitary authority limits the ability of regulatory arrangements at both local and national levels to provide even limited autonomy in support of predictability and stability in socioeconomic and political relations. Institutional location affects trade regulation; for example, questions about agricultural subsidies may differ significantly when implemented in globalized urban areas as opposed to rural areas.

Institutional orientation may be seen as a factor of the difference between the orientation of regulatory institutions and the behavioural orientation of the societies in which the institutions operate. Orientation refers to the priorities and habitual practices that inform institutional performance. For governance institutions in Asia, orientation involves particularly the tension between formal and informal modes of operation. This is especially sensitive under conditions where local social norms may privilege informal mechanisms for decision making, dispute resolution, and resource allocation. The resiliency of informal relational networks has called attention to the potential re-emergence of civil society dynamics in many economies across Asia, but the potential role of informal institutions is challenged by the continued insistence on the part of modernizing governments on maintaining formal organizational systems to defend ideological orthodoxy and enforce political loyalty. The tension between statist ethics of formal institutionalism and the pervasive local informal arrangements that it strives to control tends to divert resources from institutional performance and undermines institutional capacity. This is particularly important where the informal orientation of local social and economic practices differs significantly from the formalism associated with the regulatory culture of the central government.[67] Contested approaches to recognition and enforcement of international trade standards are important examples of institutional orientation.[68]

Institutional cohesion involves the willingness of individuals within institutions to comply with edicts from organizational and extra-organizational leaders, and to enforce institutional goals. Institutional cohesion may be seen as a product of the relationship between an ideal of cohesive performance and empirical indicators of behaviour by officials within organizations that departs from the organizational norm. Compliance concerns the recognition and enforcement of norms.[69] Conflicts arise when the norms of particular organizations differ from those of the individuals within these organizations – such as where norms of public policy that drive organizational priorities require subordination of the parochial interests of individual officials within the organization. The dilemma of corruption is but one example of the challenge to discipline and subordinate the individual norms of officials to the organizational norms of institutions. Ongoing efforts at bureaucratic reform face difficulties in subordinating the individual interests of officials to organizational norms. In the context of implementation of international trade standards at the local level, institutional cohesion often reflects issues of human resource management and administrative discipline.

Thus, selective adaptation addresses the relationship between rule regimes and underlying norms, whereas institutional capacity addresses the functioning of regulatory institutions and hence raises the issue of structural relationships that may affect performance even without tension between imported rule regimes and underlying norms. Institutional capacity helps build understanding of local and structural relationships among regulatory institutions, as an indicator of performance of non-local rule regimes. Institutional capacity helps build understanding of local compliance with international standards, even where acceptance of international standards and assimilation of underlying norms is relatively coterminous. It helps build understanding that compliance with international standards is more than simply a matter of political will, but rather a matter of structural relationships among regulatory institutions. In the cross-cultural context of globalization, institutional capacity helps meet the need for cross-cultural understanding of relationships between institutional constraints and rule compliance.

Conclusion

Local interpretation and implementation of international trade standards is an issue of significant importance and discord. Conflicting perspectives about the reasons for compliance with international trade rules, ranging from a focus on political will to questions about resistance to neocolonial domination, often tend to obscure understanding. The alternatives presented by normative and institutional analyses are compelling, not only because of their potential to build understanding but also because of their potential to manage and reduce the incidence of disputes. The paradigms of selective adaptation and institutional capacity explain much about the normative and institutional dimensions of local compliance with international trade standards. The particularities of local norms and local institutional conditions may tend to support conditions of "legitimate non-uniform compliance," which are distinct from "willful noncompliance." Such an approach may augment the academic and policy research discourse associated with cultural essentialism, institutional determinism, and behavioural law and economics that is currently used to explain international treaty compliance in a cross-cultural context. The paradigms of selective adaptation and institutional capacity offer exciting prospects for understanding the critical issue of local compliance with international trade standards. It is hoped that future research results will further scholarly discovery, support informed policy making, and strengthen international understanding about trade compliance, and thereby reduce and prevent disputes and facilitate more effective international cooperation.

NOTES

1 Amitai Etzioni, "Social Norms: Internalization, Persuasion, and History" (2000) 1 Law and Society Review 157; Hans Kelsen, *General Theory of Norms*, trans. M. Hartney (Oxford: Clarendon Press, 1991).

2 Douglass North, *Institutions, Institutional Change and Economic Performance* (Cambridge, UK: Cambridge University Press, 1990).

3 John Williamson, "Appendix: Our Agenda and the Washington Consensus" in Pedro-Pablo Kuczynski and John Williamson, eds., *After the Washington Consensus: Restarting Growth and Reform in Latin America* (Washington, DC: Institute for International Economics, 2002) 323; Joseph E. Stiglitz, *Globalization and Its Discontents* (New York: W.W. Norton, 2002).

4 Jude Howell and Jenny Pearce, *Civil Society and Development: A Critical Exploration* (Boulder, CO, and London: Lynne Rienner, 2002), ch. 4.

5 Cal Clark and K.C. Roy, *Comparing Development Patterns in Asia* (Boulder, CO, and London: Lynne Rienner, 1997), ch. 6; Joel Rocamora, "A Clash of Ideologies: International Capitalism and the State in the Wake of the Asian Crisis" in Joseph S. Tulchin, ed., *Democratic Governance and Social Inequality* (Boulder, CO, and London: Lynne Rienner, 2002) 75; Pedro-Pablo Kuczynski, "Reforming the State" in Kuczynski and Williamson, *supra* note 3, 33.

6 Fredric Jameson and Masao Miyoshi, eds., *The Cultures of Globalization* (Durham, NC: Duke University Press, 1998); Farhand Rajahee, *Globalization on Trial: The Human Condition and the Information Civilization* (Ottawa: International Development Research Council, 2000); John Tomlinson, *Globalization and Culture* (Oxford: Polity, 1999).

7 Bernard Hoekman, Aaditya Mattoo, and Philip English, eds., *Development, Trade and the WTO Part V – Technology and Intellectual Property* (Washington, DC: World Bank, 2002).

8 Katharina Pistor and Philip A. Wellons, eds., *The Role of Law and Legal Institutions in Asian Economic Development 1960-1995* (Oxford: Oxford University Press, 1999).

9 John S. Wilson, "Standards, Regulation, and Trade: WTO Rules and Developing Country Concerns" in Hoekman *et al.*, *supra* note 7, 428.

10 Joel P. Trachtman, "The Theory of the Firm and the Theory of the International Economic Organisation: Toward a Comparative Institutional Analysis" (1997) 17 Northwestern Journal of International Law and Business 470.

11 Antonio Gramsci, *Selections from the Prison Notebooks*, ed. and trans. Quintin Hoare and Geoffrey Howell Smith (New York: International Publishers, 1971); Edward Greer, "Antonio Gramsci and 'Legal Hegemony'" in David Kairys, ed., *The Politics of Law: A Progressive Critique* (New York: Pantheon, 1982) 304; Alan Hunt, *Explorations in Law and Society: Toward a Constitutive Theory of Law* (New York: Routledge, 1993).

12 John Braithwaite and Peter Drahos, *Global Business Regulation* (New York: Cambridge University Press, 2000).

13 See especially c. 2 in Nicholas K. Bromley, *Law, Space, and the Geographies of Power* (New York and London: Guilford, 2001).

14 Susan S. Silbey, "'Let Them Eat Cake': Globalization, Postmodern Colonialism, and the Possibilities of Justice" (1997) 31 Law and Society Review 207.

15 Christopher Arup, *The New World Trade Organization Agreements: Globalizing Law through Services and Intellectual Property* (Cambridge: Cambridge University Press, 2000) at 45-49.

16 Robert Feenstra, "How Costly Is Protectionism?" in Philip King, ed., *International Economics and International Economic Policy: A Reader* (Boston: Irwin McGraw-Hill, 2000) 3; Paul Krugman, "Is Free Trade Passe?" in King, *ibid.* at 19.

17 James A. Gardner, *Legal Imperialism: American Lawyers and Foreign Aid in Latin America* (Madison: University of Wisconsin Press, 1980).

18 See generally Michael J. Trebilcock and Robert Howse, *The Regulation of International Trade*, 2d ed. (London and New York: Routledge, 1999) at 367ff.

19 Stiglitz, *supra* note 3.

20 Trebilcock and Howse, *supra* note 18; John H. Jackson, "The Great 1994 Sovereignty Debate: United States Acceptance and Implementation of the Uruguay Round Results" (1997) 36 Columbia Journal of Transnational Law 157.

21 Ron Chernow, *The Death of the Banker: The Decline and Fall of the Great Financial Dynasties and the Triumph of the Small Investor* (New York: Vintage, 1997).

22 Hal S. Scott and Philip A. Wellons, *International Finance: Transactions, Policy, and Regulation* (Westbury, NY: Westview, 1995) at 14ff.

23 Lawrence H. Summers, "Building an International Architecture for the 21st Century" in King, *supra* note 16, 428.

24 Stephen Young and Thomas Brewer, "Multilateral Investment Rules, Multinationals and the Global Economy" in Nicholas A. Phelps and Jeremy Alden, eds., *Foreign Direct Investment and the Global Economy: Corporate and Institutional Dynamics of Global-Localization* (London: Stationery Office, 1999) 13; Tony Clarke and Maude Barlow, *MAI: The Multilateral Agreement on Investment and the Threat to Canadian Sovereignty* (Toronto: Stoddart, 1997).

25 Hoekman *et al.*, *supra* note 7.

26 Keith Mascus, "Intellectual Property Protection: Is It Being Taken Too Far?" in John M. Curtis and Dan Ciuriak, eds., *Trade Policy Research 2003* (Ottawa: Minister of Public Works and Government Services, 2003) 185.

27 Richard T. Pfohl, "Jurisdiction and Procedural Issues" in Alan M. Gahtan, Martin P.J. Kratz, and J. Fraser Mann, eds., *Electronic Commerce: A Practitioner's Guide* (Toronto: Thomson-Carswell, 2003) 22.1.

28 Barbara Trent, "Media and Capitalist Culture" in Jameson and Miyoshi, *supra* note 6, 230; Caren Irr, "Who Owns Our Culture? Intellectual Property, Human Rights, and Globalization" in Mahmood Monshipouri, Neil Englehart, Andrew J. Nathan, and Kavita Philip, eds., *Constructing Human Rights in the Age of Globalization* (Armonk, NY, and London: M.E. Sharpe, 2003) 3.

29 David Held, Anthony McGrew, David Goldblatt, and Jonathan Perraton, *Global Transformations: Politics, Economics and Culture* (Stanford, CA: Stanford University Press, 1999); Susan Strange, *The Retreat of the State: The Diffusion of Power in the World Economy* (Cambridge, UK: Cambridge University Press, 1996); Saskia Sassen, *Losing Control? Sovereignty in an Age of Globalization* (New York: Columbia University Press, 1993); cf. Jackson, *supra* note 20.

30 Peter B. Evans, Dietrich Rueschemeyer, and Theda Skocpol, eds., *Bringing the State Back In* (Cambridge, UK: Cambridge University Press, 1985); Katherine V.W. Stone, "Labour and the Global Economy: Four Approaches to Transnational Labour Regulation" (1995) 16 Michigan Journal of International Law 987.

31 Francis Adams, Satya Dev Gupta, and Kidane Mengisteab, eds., *Globalization and the Dilemmas of the State in the South* (New York: St. Martin's Press, 1999).

32 Clark and Roy, *supra* note 5; Bernard Hoekman and Kamal Saggi, "Multilateral Disciplines and National Investment Policies" in Hoekman *et al.*, *supra* note 7, 439.

33 V.N. Balasubramanyam and Mohammed A. Salisu, "Foreign Direct Investment and Globalization" in Sajal Lahiri, ed., *Regionalism and Globalization: Theory and Practice* (London and New York: Routledge, 2001) 199.

34 Trebilcock and Howse, *supra* note 18.

35 Joan Martinez-Alier, "'Environmental Justice' (Local and Global)" in Jameson and Miyoshi, *supra* note 6, 312; Kavita Philip, "Reflections on the Intersections of Environment, Development, and Human Rights in the Context of Globalization" in Monshipouri *et al.*, *supra* note 28, 55.

36 Ivan Bernier, *Cultural Goods and Services in International Trade Law* (Ottawa: Centre for Trade Policy and Law, 1997).

37 Trebilcock and Howse, *supra* note 18.

38 Douglas Klusmeyer, "Introduction" in T. Alexander Aleinikoff and Douglas Klusmeyer, eds., *From Migrants to Citizens: Membership in a Changing World* (Washington, DC: Carnegie Endowment for International Peace, 2000) 25; Linda Bosniak, "Critical Reflections on 'Citizenship' as a Progressive Aspiration" in Joanne Canaghan, Richard Michael Fischl, and Karl Klare, eds., *Labour Law in an Era of Globalization: Transformative Practices and Possibilities* (Toronto: Oxford University Press, 2002) 339.

39 Dan Ciuriak and Charles M. Gastle, "The Social Dimensions of Globalization: Some Commentaries on Social Choice and Convergence" in Curtis and Ciuriak, *supra* note 26, 199.

40 Wolfgang Michalski, Riel Miller, and Barrie Stevens, "Economic Flexibility and Societal Cohesion in the Twenty-First Century: An Overview of the Issues and Key

Points of the Discussion" in *Societal Cohesion and the Globalising Economy: What Does the Future Hold?* (Paris: OECD, 1997) 11.

41 James L. Watson, ed., *Golden Arches East: McDonald's in East Asia* (Stanford, CA: Stanford University Press, 1997); Yuko Aoyama, "Localization Advantages for Multinational Firms: Views from the Japanese Electronics Industry in Europe" in Phelps and Alden, *supra* note 24, 103.

42 Pitman B. Potter, "Legal Reform in China: Institutions, Culture, and Selective Adaptation" (2004) 28 Law and Social Inquiry 465.

43 Michel Oksenberg, Pitman B. Potter, and William B. Abnett, *Advancing Intellectual Property Rights: Information Technologies and the Course of Economic Development in China* (Stanford, CA: Institute for International Studies, Stanford University, 1998); Richard King and Timothy J. Craig, eds., *Global Goes Local: Popular Culture in Asia* (Vancouver and Toronto: UBC Press, 2002); Perry Link, Richard P. Madsen, and Paul G. Pickowicz, eds., *Popular China: Unofficial Culture in a Globalizing Society* (Lanham, MD: Rowman and Littlefield, 2002).

44 Thomas L. Friedman, *The Lexus and the Olive Tree* (New York: Farrar, Straus, Giroux, 1999); David Landes, *The Wealth and Poverty of Nations: Why Some Are So Rich and Some So Poor* (New York: W.W. Norton, 1998).

45 Jeffrey N. Wasserstrom, "Big Macs Mean Different Things in Boston and Beijing" *Straits Times* (24 June 2003), http://iw.newsbank.com.

46 Pitman B. Potter, "Property: Questioning Efficiency, Liberty and Imperialism" in Nicholas Mercuro and Warren J. Samuels, eds., *The Fundamental Interrelationships between Government and Property* (Stamford, CT: JAI Press, 1999) 177.

47 Howell and Pearce, *supra* note 4.

48 Heritage Canada, News Release, "Ottawa and Washington Agree on Access to the Canadian Advertising Services Market" (26 May 1999); *Canada: Certain Measures Concerning Periodicals – Request for the Establishment of a Panel by the United States* (24 May 1996), WTO Doc. WT/DS31/2.

49 Jonathan Spence, *To Change China: Western Advisors in China 1620-1960* (Boston: Little Brown, 1969).

50 Roberto Mangebeira Unger, *Knowledge and Politics* (New York: Free Press, 1975).

51 Clifford Geertz, *Local Knowledge: Further Essays in Interpretive Anthropology* (New York: Basic Books, 1983).

52 Ugo Mattei, *Comparative Law and Economics* (Ann Arbor: University of Michigan Press, 1997).

53 Pitman B. Potter, "Globalization and Economic Regulation in China: Selective Adaptation of Globalized Norms and Practices" (2003) 2 Washington University Global Studies Law Review 119; Potter, "Legal Reform in China," *supra* note 42.

54 Stanley Fish, *Is There a Text in This Class: The Authority of Interpretive Communities* (Cambridge, MA: Harvard University Press, 1980).

55 Pitman B. Potter, "Selective Adaptation and Institutional Capacity: Perspectives on Human Rights in China" (2006) 61 International Journal 389.

56 Unger, *supra* note 50; Etzioni, *supra* note 1 at 157-78.

57 Pistor and Wellons, *supra* note 8.

58 Niels H.D. Bohr, *Essays, 1958-1962, on Atomic Physics and Human Knowledge* (New York: Interscience Publishers, 1963); Richard Rhodes, *The Making of the Atomic Bomb* (New York: Simon and Schuster, 1986); Okifira Seliktar, "Identifying a Society's Belief System" in Margaret Herman, ed., *Political Psychology* (San Francisco: Jossey-Bass, 1986) 320.
59 Michael K. Young, "Dispute Resolution in the Uruguay Round: Lawyers Triumph over Diplomats" (1995) 29 International Lawyer 389.
60 Pitman B. Potter, "Governance of the Periphery: Balancing Local Autonomy and National Unity" (2006) 19 Columbia Journal of Asian Law 293; David Kennedy, "Receiving the International" (1994) 10 Connecticut Journal of International Law 1.
61 Max Weber, *Economy and Society,* ed. Guenther Roth and Claus Wittich (Berkeley and Los Angeles: University of California Press, 1978); Richard W. Wilson, *Compliance Ideologies: Rethinking Political Culture* (Cambridge, UK: Cambridge University Press, 1992); Nicholas Rose, "Governing Liberty" in Richard V. Ericson and Nico Stehr, eds., *Governing Modern Societies* (Toronto: University of Toronto Press, 2000) 141; F. Scharpf, "Interdependence and Democratic Legitimation" in Susan J. Pharr and Robert D. Putnam, eds., *Disaffected Democracies: What's Troubling the Trilateral Countries* (Princeton, NJ: Princeton University Press, 2000) 101.
62 H.V. Savitch, "Global Challenge and Institutional Capacity: Or, How We Can Refit Local Administration for the Next Century" (1998) 30 Administration and Society 248.
63 William Blomquist and Elinor Ostrom, "Institutional Capacity and the Resolution of the Commons Dilemma" in Michael D. McGinnis, ed., *Polycentric Governance and Development: Readings from the Workshop in Political Theory and Policy Analysis* (Ann Arbor: University of Michigan Press, 1999) 60.
64 P. Healey, "Building Institutional Capacity through Collaborative Approaches to Urban Planning" (1998) 30 Environment and Planning 1531; Lisa L. Martin and Beth A. Simmons, "Theories and Empirical Studies of International Institutions" (1998) 52 International Organization 729.
65 Oksenberg *et al., supra* note 43.
66 James S. Wunsch, "Institutional Analysis and Decentralization: Developing an Analytical Model for Effective Third World Administrative Reform" in McGinnis, *supra* note 63, 243.
67 Thomas Gold, Doug Guthrie, and David Wank, eds., *Social Connections in China* (Cambridge, UK: Cambridge University Press, 2002).
68 Pitman B. Potter, "China and the International Legal System: Challenges of Participation" (2007) 191 The China Quarterly 669.
69 Etzioni, *supra* note 1.

Global Competition Governance
A Step towards Constitutionalization of the WTO

LJILJANA BIUKOVIC

Since the establishment of the World Trade Organization (WTO), there has been considerable discussion among scholars as to whether the trade regime can, or inevitably will, become a new framework for universalizing substantive international law.[1] The *General Agreement on Tariffs and Trade* (GATT)[2] system of international trade law advanced the core principle of wealth maximization through trade liberalization and nondiscrimination by trade actors. Its successor, the WTO system,[3] has moved into the area of linkage between systems of substantive law, such as environmental, labour, intellectual property, investment, and competition law, and the trade regime.

Brian Fitzgerald states that the universalizing process is already occurring in international trade law because the trade regime universalizes the norms attached to the core principle, which starts from the premise that every state in the world wants to maximize wealth and build outward through substantive extensions.[4] Some scholars claim that it is occurring because "the relevant markets" and business practices that influence competition spill across national boundaries.[5] Finally, others suggest that the universalizing process is occurring at the regional level, where numerous regional trade agreements, such as the North American Free Trade Agreement (NAFTA),[6] the *Treaty Establishing the European Community* (TEC),[7] and MERCOSUR,[8] include competition principles and rules in addition to the rules on cross-border trade.[9]

This essay argues that the process of universalizing competition law depends on local identification, interpretation, and application of the norms of international trade and competition. It starts with an analysis of the problem related to identification of norms of international trade and definition of a system of international trade law as a coherent system. It then proceeds to scrutinize the normative underpinnings of global competition law as formulated by various international organizations, including the WTO. Finally, it analyzes the objectives of national competition law or drafts of such law in both China and Japan. This is done by utilizing the concept of selective adaptation. Selective adaptation argues that the level of compliance with foreign rules and norms in a specific jurisdiction depends on three factors: (1) an understanding of the jurisdiction's rules, local norms, and practices; (2) the extent to which members of the local community support reception of foreign norms; and (3) the level at which the international norm and a local norm are complementary or capable of coexisting and operating together in a non-conflicting way despite their potential for substantively contradicting each other (factors of perception, legitimacy, and complementarity).[10]

Trade and Competition in the Context of Global Governance

Despite the connection between trade and competition, it is obvious that trade policy and competition policy seek to facilitate economic development in different ways. Although both attempt to promote competition by removing its impediments, trade policy focuses on removing government-created barriers to competition, whereas competition policy focuses on removing barriers created by private parties.[11] In addition, says Hudec, trade policy focuses exclusively on competition in international markets whereas competition policy focuses primarily on competition in domestic markets.[12]

There have been a number of failed attempts to achieve internationally harmonized competition laws. Waller argues that competition represents a very important set of public values embodied in the concepts of national sovereignty, governmental systems, ideologies, and the economic philosophies of every country.[13] He recounts several unsuccessful attempts to create harmonized international competition laws. He notes the attempt by the League of Nations to explore the system of controlling cartels; the International Trade Organization's set of rules on the substance and enforcement of competition law included in the *Havana Charter;* the Organisation for Economic Co-operation and Development's *Recommendation of the Council Concerning Co-operation between Member Countries on Anticompetitive*

Practices Affecting International Trade[14] and *Recommendation of the Council Concerning Effective Action against Hard Core Cartels;*[15] the United Nations Conference on Trade and Development's *Set of Multilaterally Agreed Equitable Principles and Rules for Control of Restrictive Business Practices;*[16] and, finally, the Doha Round negotiations of the WTO as ill-fated attempts to create an internationalized system that would be highly inconsistent with the concept of national sovereignty and the rights of individual states to enforce and carry out their national competition rules.

The 1999 Working Group on the Interaction between Trade and Competition Policy emphasized that the basic principles relevant to competition policy are also the basic principles of international trade – the principles of national treatment (or treating foreigners and locals equally), most-favoured nation treatment (treating any nation as a "most favoured" nation), and transparency.[17] All of these were incorporated in the 1947 GATT founding document and the subsequent WTO agreements (the *General Agreement on Trade in Services,* hereinafter GATS,[18] and the *Agreement on Trade-Related Aspects of Intellectual Property Rights* (hereinafter TRIPS Agreement[19]).[20] For example, Article IX of GATS acknowledges that anti-competitive business practices may restrain and restrict trade.[21] Article 8(2) of the TRIPS Agreement recognizes that some measures may be needed to prevent the abuse of intellectual property rights by rights holders and to prevent practices that may unreasonably restrain trade or adversely affect the international transfer of technology.[22] Moreover, Article 40 deals with the control of anti-competitive practices in contractual licences.

In contrast to Waller, other authors, such as Antonio Perez[23] and Eleanor Fox,[24] feel that the recent Doha Declaration[25] has made it possible to include competition issues in the current negotiations. An excerpt from the Declaration reads:

> Recognizing the case for a multilateral framework to enhance the contribution of competition policy to international trade and development, and the need for enhanced technical assistance and capacity-building in this area as referred to in paragraph 24, we agree that negotiations will take place after the Fifth Session of the Ministerial Conference on the basis of a decision to be taken, by explicit consensus, at the Session on modalities of negotiation.[26]

The 1997 annual report of the WTO secretariat seems to confirm the predictions of Perez and Fox by stating that "the issue is not whether competition policy questions will be dealt with in the WTO context, but how and, in particular, in how coherent a framework this will be done."[27] Thus, the interesting questions are: (1) To what extent is substantive competition law capable of achieving full universality? and (2) To what extent is cultural diversity capable of impeding the transfer of global substantive law?

A Global Market Regulated by National Laws: What Difference Does It Make?

It has been increasingly emphasized that although the marketplace has become global, the laws regulating it remain national.[28] In addition, it has been said that to maximize market efficiency at the global level, it appears necessary to harmonize (or perhaps globalize) competition laws. Efficient, transparent, and harmonized competition laws could enhance foreign direct investment, reduce government intervention, and potentially even block corruption.[29]

It has been estimated that by 2002 more than ninety countries had adopted competition laws.[30] Sixty percent of the world's competition laws were adopted by developing countries during the 1990s.[31] This was often due to these countries' accession to trade agreements (regional or bilateral) with other, usually developed, countries. Or it was due to the need to respond to requirements for regulatory reform imposed by international financial institutions, such as the World Bank. Adoption of competition laws was sometimes also due to the development of pro-competition consciousness and attempts of national governments to start fundamental economic reforms.[32] According to data from the Organisation for Economic Co-operation and Development (OECD), at least sixty developing countries are still struggling with the adoption of competition laws.[33]

Despite the fact that harmonization of competition laws is desirable, there are at least ninety countries with different competition or antitrust laws.[34] These laws deal with a range of anti-competitive practices, including price fixing and other cartel arrangements, abuse of a dominant position (or monopolization), mergers that limit competition, and agreements between suppliers and distributors ("vertical agreements"). This means, for example, that there are differences in substantive law and also divergent procedural requirements for the multiplicity of merger reporting regimes, and this presents a significant challenge for lawyers and businesspeople around the world working on merger and acquisition deals. Thus, it is possible that an international merger may have to be reviewed in more than ninety jurisdictions by at least ninety different competition authorities.[35]

The high costs incurred by businesses due to duplicative or conflicting enforcement policies is only one of the problems resulting from the existence of numerous different national competition laws. Other problems include the limited ability of national competition authorities to fully protect their citizens from transnational anti-competitive conduct, the possibility of disagreements or conflicts between states arising from antitrust enforcement, and the variety and seriousness of restrictive market access practices.[36]

Further harmonization of competition rules has been delayed because of the lack of consensus between the most active partners in the global market – the European Union (EU) and the United States – regarding the matrix of harmonization. This has ultimately resulted in a lack of global integration.

The European Commission (EC) has proposed that member states of the WTO negotiate a binding competition code. In brief, the Commission's proposal is that a WTO treaty would:

- oblige member states to enact or maintain domestic competition legislation that would include at least core rules such as those prohibiting the abuse of dominant position or cartels
- require the enforcement of the WTO competition legislation based on the principles of nondiscrimination and transparency
- provide for cooperation between competition authorities
- aim for the gradual convergence of national practice.[37]

Notwithstanding the efforts of the EU and some other WTO members from the developed world, the General Council of the WTO decided in July 2004 that competition would not be discussed any further during the Doha Round.[38] The decision to take competition issues off the WTO negotiating table was partly due to constant protests from developing countries. These countries felt that an international treaty on competition would not be beneficial for their economies. The most vocal opponents were Malaysia, India, China, and Hong Kong. First, they argued that the creation of some sort of central competition law-making authority would erode their state sovereignty. Second, it would unnecessarily open their markets to stronger and much more experienced foreign competitors, yet it would not facilitate easier access to foreign markets for them. Third, it would reverse the regulatory priority list in developing economies. Finally, the developing countries rejected international attempts to create a widely accepted global competition law ("one size fits all"), arguing rightly that each country needs to tailor its competition laws to its own specific set of circumstances.

At present, countries drafting competition laws or reforming their existing competition laws are relying on two models – the EU and the US.

Since the WTO multilateral competition framework has not been accepted, most of the developing countries are now even discussing competition policy under the umbrella of regional initiatives such as the Asia-Pacific Economic Cooperation (APEC)[39] or international organizations such as the UN Conference on Trade and Development (UNCTAD)[40] or the OECD.[41]

The possibility of the export of the EU competition model and the extraterritorial application of EU competition laws worries the United States as much as the export of the US competition model and the extraterritorial application of US legislation worries the EU.[42] Until the *Woodpulp* case in the 1980s, the EC had not been interested in the policy of extraterritoriality of its competition law.[43] It had been more concerned with establishing the internal common market and protecting its four freedoms (free movement of people, goods, services/establishment, and capital) from obstacles imposed by its member states. Since *Woodpulp*, however, the EC has adopted American-style extraterritorial enforcement of its own competition rules.

Needless to say, the United States is trying to play a leading role by exporting its competition law through a number of government and nongovernmental agencies, such as the Center for International Private Enterprise (CIPE), which is affiliated with the US Chamber of Commerce, and the US Agency for International Development (USAID), which provides financial and technical assistance to countries in transition. For example, in the past ten years, the US antitrust agencies funded by USAID developed a program of international technical assistance that involved sending resident advisors on short-term missions to transition countries (not only in Central and Eastern Europe but also in Asia), and organizing regional conferences and internships in the US for personnel from transition countries.[44]

The utilization of extraterritoriality by both the EU and the US leads to a type of convergence between the two actors on the general principles of extraterritoriality.[45] In other words, extraterritoriality has worked as an option of soft convergence of competition laws, reducing the importance of international comity concerns.[46] This process of convergence and extraterritoriality of EU and US antitrust laws may be the most effective means of harmonizing competition law and/or creating a global competition law. The problem with a convergence approach through soft harmonization, however, is that it appears to be too slow. In addition, the final result of convergence is not easy to predict. Finally, the extraterritorial application of EU or US domestic competition law to the jurisdiction of other states violates the concept of state sovereignty.[47]

"Competition Culture"

David Gerber states that competition is an abstract concept, a cultural construct where "one can 'see' something called competition only where one's language, training and experience give that concept meaning."[48] Hiroshi Iyori argues that competition laws operate in the context of different social or cultural values.[49]

In 1999, Dr. Wolfgang Pape, at the time with the European Commission, predicted that the sociocultural divergence among WTO contracting parties, including both members and non-member potential candidates, would be a serious impediment to the establishment of common competition rules within the WTO.[50] He suggested that differences between cultures underlie differences in attitude and differences in the structure of ownership and capitalism. These differences ultimately inform the development of different competition policies. Despite the fact that globalization has partially reduced these differences, they should still not be ignored.[51]

In February 2004, the OECD Global Forum on Competition identified the lack of a "competition culture" as one of the major obstacles faced by competition authorities in promoting competition and in achieving greater economic development.[52] The OECD report defined "competition culture" narrowly as the particular political process or the political support necessary to enhance economic development by the use of competition in markets. It thus focused on competition and government authorities and their respective actions, such as the allocation of financial resources, the training of personnel, and the building of an adequate institutional structure for investigating and enforcing competition policy and laws. It also referred to the adequacy (or inadequacy) of powers conferred on competition authorities, powers that allow them to take action independent of government. In the broader context, however, "competition culture" refers to more than just political and financial support for competition. It also refers to awareness among economic actors and the general public of the rules of competition.[53]

These narrow and broad definitions of competition culture are interdependent. Public awareness of the rules of competition greatly depends on adequate advocacy by competition and government authorities. At the same time, public consciousness about competition could inform further government regulatory actions. Thus, the successful creation of a competition culture depends on the existence of financial, political, and human resources, all of which are necessary to facilitate the adaptation of institutions, training of individuals, and establishment of an appropriate legal framework. The lack of these resources is the major impediment to the growth of a competition culture in developing countries.[54]

Pape suggests that EU law can be considered a successful example of how cultural differences in the perception of competition can be coordinated within a workable framework built around a common belief in principles of competition (as presented in the TEC) and respect for competition authorities (primarily the EC but also national competition authorities).[55] EU competition policy has been developed from the basic provisions of the TEC (Articles 81-89[56]) into a complex body of secondary legislation (regulations, directives, and decisions) and European Court of Justice (ECJ) cases on antitrust activities, state aid, and mergers. One of the major objectives of the European Union, as specified in Article 3(g) of the TEC, is to establish a system that would ensure that competition within the internal market has not been distorted.[57] Achieving this objective requires not only a simple regulatory convergence but also a process of building national competition authorities that are coordinated (by the EC and the ECJ) in interpretation and application of the common rules. In addition, the EU provides significant financial and technical resources to support member states in creating the appropriate competition framework.

The recent attempts to decentralize EU competition law, by decentralizing enforcement powers and placing them under the jurisdiction of national courts and competition authorities, illustrate the difficulties of harmonization or convergence of competition policies. Even in the case of a relatively highly harmonized and integrated single market, with a long tradition of balancing diversity of national and community competition rules and cultures, the problem of subsidiarity, or cooperation between different competition authorities and clarification of those authorities' substantive competencies, is still a challenge for the EU. The EU is constantly searching for methods to respond to this challenge, however.

Normative Underpinnings of a Global Competition Law: A Case of Selective Adaptation

What could constitute the normative underpinnings of a global competition law formulated under the umbrella of the WTO agreements? Certainly, such normative underpinnings would derive from trade policy norms. Arguably, the dominant idea behind WTO-led trade liberalization is market access – that is, the idea of promoting open markets by ensuring that restrictive business practices and national competition laws do not impede free trade.

It is commonly accepted that the purpose of competition law is to facilitate the functioning of an efficient and fair market. Perception of the norms of efficiency and fairness is therefore crucial. The paradigm of selective adaptation suggests, however, that the internationally conceptualized norms of efficiency and fairness would be unavoidably contextualized to local legal and political culture. In other words, local conditions determine national priorities regarding competition policy. National competition policy then informs competition laws, which in turn determine the rules and disciplines imposed by government on private actors to ensure that the market is competitive.[58] Competition policy, however, usually includes a broader set of measures and instruments, and their underlying objectives and values could (and should) differ and include more than just economic efficiency and fair competition.

Economic efficiency is the paramount norm of both international trade and competition law. Efficiency can be perceived differently at domestic and international levels, however. Domestic competition laws usually define economic efficiency in the context of efficient resource allocation within the national market and the maximization of national welfare,[59] whereas at the international level, efficiency is perceived in the context of export efficiency or market access possibilities for foreign companies.

Economic efficiency is articulated as an important (if not the most important) objective in a number of international templates and national competition laws. In other words, countries rarely differ in what they articulate as the most important competition law objectives and how they define efficiency. For example, the Pacific Economic Cooperation Council determined in its Principles that "the ultimate goal of this competition framework is to promote the process of competition ... in order to achieve greater overall economic efficiency and an increased average standard of living in domestic economies and the APEC region as a whole."[60]

The *Treaty of Rome* states that establishing a common market and an economic and monetary union is the primary objective of the Union,[61] and that ensuring that competition is not distorted[62] is one of the most important conditions for the functioning of a common market. In other words, besides economic efficiency and fairness, the central objectives of EC competition law are the establishment and maintenance of the single internal market, economic growth, and social cohesion.[63] In contrast, Gerber argues that since the late 1970s and the rise of the law and economics movement, economic efficiency has become the only legitimate objective of competition law in the United States.[64]

Iyori suggests that besides economic efficiency and fairness in competition and consumer welfare, other values and objectives should be included in the competition normative framework. He gives an example of the Japanese statute that considers the protection of business opportunities of small enterprises and reduction of government controls as central objectives of competition law.[65] It is noteworthy that the Japanese *Anti-Monopoly Act* of 1947 was modelled on the US antitrust legislation, but it has not been successful in advancing the Japanese economy from a *zaibatsu*-dominated system towards a demonopolized system of fair competition. On the other hand, the normative framework of the Japanese act is consistent with the norms of "communitarian capitalism," which has been pursued by the Japanese government for decades and which informs Japanese competition policy in general. According to those norms, the state performs a very important role in economic and social redistribution of wealth, and the objective of redistribution comes before the objective of economic efficiency.[66]

The latest draft of the Chinese *Anti-Monopoly Law*, often referred to as the "economic constitution" of China, primarily emphasizes the objective of safeguarding fair competition, but it omits direct reference to economic efficiency.[67] It also includes the objectives of protecting the public interest and consumer rights, and ensuring the healthy development of a socialist market economy. No other competition law in the world is committed to the creation and maintenance of a socialist market economy. Most countries provide for the protection of the legitimate rights of consumers in their consumer protection legislation. The creation and maintenance of a socialist market economy has been the official commitment of the Chinese government since late 1992, however, and it is consistent with the Chinese belief in the evolution of state economic management and competition policy.[68]

Whereas efficiency is a core economic concept, with a relatively clear objective to minimize waste or to get the most out of resources,[69] the concept of fairness appears to be much more dependent on local culture. In the context of the US anti-dumping law, which prompted the enactment of competition laws in most countries, including members of the EU, fairness means equality of entry into a business endeavour.[70] It may, however, mean something else in other countries or in another context. For example, in the context of a developing country concerned that an agreement on competition would mean giving multinational firms greater access to its national market with no reciprocal access for its own firms to the markets of developed countries, fairness could mean the opportunity for all countries to share in economic wealth.[71]

In other words, there are significant sociocultural differences between countries that are relevant to how those countries perceive competition policy and competition law.

Conclusion: On Possibilities for the Development of Global Competition Rules

As previously mentioned, many authors argue that there are overwhelming obstacles to the realization of a global competition law system.[72] Some argue that countries should opt for convergence through regulatory interaction supplemented by extraterritorial competition law enforcement by using either the US or the EC approach.[73] In addition, it appears evident that any form of regulatory convergence mandates the development of a specific competition culture in some countries that already have a very different competition culture or no competition culture at all. The importance of a culture of competition for successful convergence of competition policies has been emphasized not only by the OECD but also by the WTO Working Group on the Interaction between Trade and Competition Policy.[74] These organizations believe that the existence and development of a culture of competition depends on the existence of appropriate independent institutions that can promote a competition culture among economic actors and the public at large.

The theory of selective adaptation suggests that even when norms associated with global competition law have been incorporated locally, those norms will not necessarily be received or interpreted in a harmonious way. Norms of economic efficiency and fairness (founded on the liberal norm of a market economy) have been considered in different contexts in societies such as China and Japan. The interpretation and enforcement of the norms of efficiency and fairness have been deeply affected by local competition policy and, in particular, local political, economic, legal, and social culture. The international norms have been selectively adapted to fit local institutions, traditions, and policy goals. As a result, the central problem related to adoption of global competition policy remains how to identify norms of international trade and competition that will enable harmonious interaction between the globalized system of liberal norms on competition and local norms and values.

NOTES

1 See, *e.g.*, Brian F. Fitzgerald, "Trade-Based Constitutionalism: The Framework for Universalizing Substantive International Law?" (1996/97) 5 University of Miami

Yearbook of International Law 111, or Richard Steinberg, "Judicial Lawmaking at the WTO: Discursive, Constitutional and Political Constraints" (2004) 98 American Journal of International Law 247.

2 *General Agreement on Tariffs and Trade,* 30 October 1947, 55 U.N.T.S. 187, Can. T.S. 1947 No. 27 (entered into force 1 January 1948) [GATT].

3 The World Trade Organization was established on 1 January 1995 in Geneva as the successor to the GATT. See *Marrakesh Agreement Establishing the World Trade Organization,* 15 April 1994, 1867 U.N.T.S. 3, 33 I.L.M. 1144.

4 Fitzgerald, *supra* note 1 at 129.

5 Edward M. Graham, "Internationalizing Competition Policy: An Assessment of the Two Main Alternatives" (Winter 2003) The Antitrust Bulletin 947.

6 *North American Free Trade Agreement between the Government of Canada, the Government of Mexico, and the Government of the United States,* 17 December 1992, Can. T.S. 1994 No. 2, 32 I.L.M. 289 (entered into force 1 January 1994) [NAFTA]. Chapter 15 of NAFTA contains obligations requiring the Parties to adopt or maintain competition laws and cooperate in their enforcement. See, in particular, Article 1501.

7 "Consolidated Version of the *Treaty Establishing the European Community*" (24 December 2002) C 325 Official Journal of the European Communities 33 [TEC]. Commonly called the *Treaty of Rome,* it was signed in Rome in 1957 and came into force in 1958.

8 MERCOSUR, or the "Common Market of the Southern Cone," formed in 1991 by Argentina, Brazil, Paraguay, and Uruguay, with Chile and Bolivia as associate members (*Treaty of Asuncion,* 26 March 1991, 30 I.L.M. 1041), approved its *Protocol on the Protection of Competition in MERCOSUR* (the *Fortaleza Protocol*) on 17 December 1996. The *Fortaleza Protocol* prohibits all concerted agreements that impede, restrict, or distort competition or free access to markets; or abuse a dominant position within MERCOSUR; and affect trade between the member states (c. II). It also establishes the Commission and the Technical Committee of the Defense of Competition as the enforcement institutions (c. IV). The text of the *Protocol* is available at http://www.sice.oas.org/Trade/MRCSR/MRCSRTOC.ASP.

9 In addition, Damien Geradin, in his report to the World Bank, lists several Central African, Latin American, and Caribbean regional trade agreements, such as the 1964 *Brazzaville Treaty* and the 1973 *Treaty Establishing the Caribbean Community* (CARICOM), as examples of trade treaties comprising competition rules. See Damien Geradin, *Competition Law and Regional Economic Integration,* World Bank Working Paper No. 35 (Washington, DC: World Bank, 2004) at 34.

10 Pitman Potter, "Legal Reform in China: Institutions, Culture, and Selective Adaptation" (2004) 29 Law and Social Inquiry 465.

11 Robert Hudec, "Private Anticompetitive Behaviour in World Markets: A WTO Perspective" (Winter 2003) The Antitrust Bulletin 1045 at 1048.

12 *Ibid.* at 1047.

13 Spencer Weber Waller, "Neo-Realism and the International Harmonization of Law: Lessons from Antitrust" (1994) 42 University of Kansas Law Review 557.

14 OECD, *Recommendation of the Council Concerning Co-operation between Member Countries on Anticompetitive Practices Affecting International Trade,* OECD Paris 856th Sess., C(95)130/final (27 July 1995).

15 OECD, *Recommendation of the Council Concerning Effective Action against Hard Core Cartels,* OECD Paris 921st Sess., C(95)130/final (25 March 1998).

16 UN Doc. TD/RBP/CONF/10/Rev.2 (1980), available in 19 I.L.M. 813 (1980).

17 WTO, Working Group on the Interaction between Trade and Competition Policy, *The Fundamental WTO Principles of National Treatment, Most-Favoured-Nation Treatment and Transparency,* WTO Doc. WT/WGTCP/W/114 (14 April 1999).

18 *General Agreement on Trade in Services,* 15 April 1994, *Marrakesh Agreement Establishing the World Trade Organization,* Annex 1B, 1869 U.N.T.S. 183; 33 I.L.M. 1167 [GATS].

19 *Agreement on Trade-Related Aspects of Intellectual Property Rights,* 15 April 1994, *Marrakesh Agreement Establishing the World Trade Organization,* Annex 1C, 1869 U.N.T.S. 299, 33 I.L.M. 1197 [TRIPS Agreement].

20 The principle of national treatment is set out in GATT art. II, GATS art. XVII, and TRIPS Agreement art. 3. The principle of most-favoured-nation treatment is contained in GATT art. I, GATS art. II, and TRIPS Agreement art. 4. Finally, the principle of transparency is set out in GATT art. X, GATS art. III, and TRIPS Agreement art. 63.

21 GATS art. IX: Business Practices

> 1. Members recognize that certain business practices of service suppliers, other than those falling under Article VIII, may restrain competition and thereby restrict trade in services.
> 2. Each Member shall, at the request of any other Member, enter into consultations with a view to eliminating practices referred to in paragraph 1. The Member addressed shall accord full and sympathetic consideration to such a request and shall cooperate through the supply of publicly available non-confidential information of relevance to the matter in question. The Member addressed shall also provide other information available to the requesting Member, subject to its domestic law and to the conclusion of satisfactory agreement concerning the safeguarding of its confidentiality by the requesting Member.

22 TRIPS Agreement, *supra* note 19, art. 8(2).

23 Antonio F. Perez, "International Antitrust at the Crossroads: The End of Antitrust History or the Clash of Competition Policy Civilization" (2002) 33 Law and Policy in International Business 527.

24 Eleanor M. Fox, "Can We Solve the Antitrust Problems of Globalization by Extraterritoriality and Cooperation? Sufficiency and Legitimacy" (2003) 48 The Antitrust Bulletin 355.

25 WTO, *Ministerial Declaration, Fourth Ministerial Conference,* WTO Doc. WT/MIN(01)/DEC/1 (14 November 2001) [Doha Declaration].

26 *Ibid.* at para. 23.

27 World Trade Organization, "Special Topic: Trade and Competition" in *WTO Annual Report 1997*, vol. 1 (Geneva: WTO, 1997) 30 at 32.

28 An overview of national competition laws is available at http://www.global competitionforum.org/gcfover.htm. Texts of all competition statutes are provided in English.

29 Mark Dutz, *Competition Policy Issues in Developing and Transition Markets*, OECD Global Forum on Competition, Paris, 14-15 February 2002.

30 Yves Devellennes and Georgios Kiriazis, "The Creation of an International Competition Network" (2002) 1 EU Competition Policy Newsletter 25.

31 International Competition Policy Advisory Committee, *Final Report to the Attorney General and Assistant Attorney General for Antitrust* (Washington, DC: US Department of Justice, 2000) at 51 and 181.

32 Geradin, *supra* note 9 at 13.

33 *Ibid.*

34 J. William Rowley, Q.C., "IBA Facilitates Global Competition Law Convergence," online: Global Competition Forum <http://www.globalcompetitionforum.org/draft%20IBA%20Facilitates%20Convergence%20article.pdf>.

35 The Global Competition Forum website covers competition laws and procedures from 126 countries, indicating those with already enacted laws and those in the process of adoption of competition laws. For example, by 22 July 2004, only fourteen countries in Africa had adopted national competition laws, while ten countries were in the process of adoption. See "Africa" at http://www.globalcompetitionforum.org/africa.htm#top.

36 Daniel Tarullo, "Norms and Institutions in Global Competition Policy" (2000) 94 American Journal of International Law 478. But see Frank M.K. Wijckmans, "Internationalization of Competition Policy: Observations from a European Practitioner's Perspective" (Winter 2003) The Antitrust Bulletin 1037. Wijckmans argues that the consequences of the lack of substantive harmonization should not be dramatized and that from the practitioner's perspective, it is more important to harmonize certain procedural aspects of competition laws, particularly the one dealing with aspects of merger review. *Ibid.* at 1042.

37 *Communication from the European Community and Its Member States, to Members of the World Trade Organization*, WTO Doc. WT/WGTCP/W/115 (25 May 1999).

38 WTO, *Decision Adopted by the General Council on 1 August 2004*, WTO Doha Work Programme, WTO Doc. WT/L/579 (2 August 2004) at 3: "Relationship between Trade and Investment, Interaction between Trade and Competition Policy and Transparency in Government Procurement: the Council agrees that these issues, mentioned in the Doha Ministerial Declaration in paragraphs 20-22, 23-25 and 26 respectively, will not form part of the Work Programme set out in that Declaration and therefore no work towards negotiations on any of these issues will take place within the WTO during the Doha Round." The decision is available at http://www.wto.org/english/tratop_e/dda_e/draft_text_gc_dg_31july04_e.htm.

39 APEC, *Principles to Enhance Competition and Regulatory Reform* (1999), online: OECD <http://www.oecd.org/dataoecd/48/52/2371601.doc>.

40 UNCTAD, *Model Law on Competition*, UN Doc. TB/RBP/Conf. 5/7 (2000), online: UNCTAD <http://www.unctad.org/en/docs/tdrbpconf5d7.en.pdf>. The most recent version of the Model Law was published in 2003.

41 OECD–World Bank, "A Framework for the Design and Implementation of Competition Law and Policy," online: OECD <http://www.oecd.org/document/24/0,2340, en_2649_37463_1916760_1_1_1_37463,00.html>.

42 See, *e.g.*, Sharon E. Foster, "While America Slept: The Harmonization of Competition Laws Based upon the European Union Model" (2001) 15 Emory International Law Review 46.

43 A number of Finnish, Swedish, American, and Canadian wood pulp producers established outside the EC created a price cartel. Their restrictive practices affected about two-thirds of the total shipments and 60 percent of the consumption of wood pulp in the EC. In December 1984, the Commission issued a decision finding several infringements of former art. 85 (now art. 81) of the *Treaty of Rome* by the said agreements and concerted practices, and imposed fines. The Commission held that the EC had jurisdiction to apply its competition rules to an undertaking outside the Community because the producers involved were exporting and selling directly to customers in the EC or were doing business within the Community through branches, subsidiaries, or other agents. Several companies appealed the Commission's decision. The European Court of Justice (ECJ) confirmed the Commission's decision. It held that in order to establish the application of the EC competition rules (former art. 85, now art. 81), the crucial factor is the place where the agreement, decision, or concerted practice is implemented, not the place where it is concluded. An agreement, decision, or concerted practice is implemented where it has effect on the competitive behaviour of the undertakings party to it. See ECJ Joined Cases 89, 104, 114, 116-17, and 125-29/85 *Ahlstrom (Woodpulp)*, [1988] ECR 5193.

44 See US Federal Trade Commission and US Department of Justice, Antitrust Division, *The United States Experience in Competition Law Technical Assistance: A Ten Year Perspective*, OECD Global Forum on Competition, CCNM/GF/COMP/WD 20 (6 February 2002), online: OECD <http://www.oecd.org/dataoecd/37/61/1833990. pdf>.

45 Charles W. Smitherman III, "The Future of Global Competition Governance: Lessons from the Transatlantic" (2004) 19 American University International Law Review 770 at 854-55.

46 William Sugden, "Global Antitrust and the Evolution of International Standard" (2002) 35 Vanderbilt Journal of Transnational Law 989 at 1013.

47 Ricky Rivers, "General Electric/Honeywell Merger: European Commission Antitrust Decision Strikes a Sour Note" (2003) 9 ILSA Journal of International and Comparative Law 525 at 530.

48 David G. Gerber, *Law and Competition in Twentieth Century Europe* (Oxford: Oxford University Press, 1998) at 10.

49 Hiroshi Iyori, *Competition Culture and the Aims of Competition Law*, in R. Zäch, ed., *Towards WTO Competition Rules: Key Issues and Comments on the WTO Report (1998) on Trade and Competition* (The Hague: Kluwer Law International, 1999) 127 at 132.

50 Wolfgang Pape, "Socio-Cultural Differences and International Competition Law" (1999) 5 European Law Journal 438.

51 *Ibid.* at 439.

52 Centre for Cooperation with Non Members, Directorate for Financial, Fiscal and Enterprise Affairs, *Session II of the Global Forum on Competition*, OECD doc. CCNM/GF/COMP(2003)6 (12-13 February 2004), online: OECD <http://www.olis.oecd.org/olis/2003doc.nsf/0/3ecf5129ef7ea69ac1256dcc0058fd90/$FILE/JT00152334.DOC>.

53 Sally Southey, "Building a Competition Culture," online: Canadian Competition Bureau <http://cb-bc.gc.ca/epic/internet/incb-bc.nsf/en/ct02476e.html>.

54 WTO, Working Group on the Interaction between Trade and Competition Policy, *WTO Regional Workshop on Competition Policy, Economic Development and the Multilateral Trading System: Overview of the Issues and Options for the Future, Cape Town, 22-24 February 2001*, WTO Doc. WTO/AIR/1564 (6 June 2001) at 12, 15, and 19 [*WTO Cape Town*].

55 Pape, *supra* note 50 at 441.

56 In brief, arts. 81-89 of the *Treaty of Rome* defined the major substantive competition law for the European Community. Article 81(1), formerly art. 85(1), prohibits certain agreements between the "undertakings," decisions by associations of undertakings, and concerted practices. Article (81)(2), formerly art. 85(2), states that all prohibited agreements or decisions are automatically void. Article 81(3), formerly art. 85(3), provides for exceptions from these prohibitions under certain conditions. Article 83, formerly art. 87, defines the jurisdiction of the EC institutions to regulate competition policy by adopting regulations and directives. Articles 86-89 (formerly arts. 90-94) cover the status of public undertakings and state aid.

57 *Treaty of Rome, supra* note 7.

58 Bernard Hoekman and Petros Mavroidis, *Economic Development, Competition Policy and WTO*, World Bank Working Paper No. 2917 (Washington, DC: World Bank, 2002) at 8.

59 *Ibid.* at 4.

60 Pacific Economic Cooperation Council, *supra* note 39 at 6.

61 Article 2 of the *Treaty of Rome.*

62 See art. 3(g) of the *Treaty of Rome.*

63 *Treaty of Rome*, art. 2: "The Community shall have as its task, by establishing a common market and an economic and monetary union and by implementing common policies or activities referred to in Articles 3 and 4, to promote throughout the Community a harmonious, balanced and sustainable development of economic activities, a high level of employment and of social protection, equality between men and women, sustainable and non-inflationary growth, a high degree of competitiveness and convergence of economic performance, a high level of protection and improvement of the quality of the environment, the raising of the standard of living and quality of life, and economic and social cohesion and solidarity among Member States." See David Gerber, "Constructing Competition Law in China: The Potential Value of European and US Experience" (2004) 3 Washington University Global Studies Law Review 315.

64 *Ibid.* at 318 and 326.
65 Iyori, *supra* note 49 at 132; see also art. 1, Law No. 54 of 1947 (*Act Concerning Prohibition of Private Monopolization and Maintenance of Fair Trade*).
66 Marie Anchordoguy, *Whatever Happened to the Japanese Miracle?* Working Paper No. 80 (San Francisco: Japan Policy Research Institute, 2001).
67 China does not have a comprehensive competition law but rather a patchwork of laws, regulations, and measures that have not been consistently enforced. In 1993, the *Anti-Unfair Competition Law* was enacted, followed by the 1998 *Price Law, Foreign Trade Law,* and various provincial and city regulations, such as the 1994 *Beijing's Anti-Unfair Competition Law.* See more on the Chinese competition regulation at http://www.globalcompetitionforum.org/asia.htm#china.
68 Edward E. Epstein, "China's New Competition Law" in *Law Lectures for Practitioners* (Hong Kong: Hong Kong Law Journal, 1994) 310; see also Nathan Bush, "Chinese Competition Policy: It Takes More Than a Law" (May 2005), online: *China Business Review* <http://www.chinabusinessreview.com/public/0505/bush.html>.
69 Edward M. Graham and J. David Richardson, eds., *Global Competition Policy* (Washington, DC: Institute for International Economics, 1997) at 8.
70 *Ibid.* at 9.
71 Joseph E. Stiglitz, *Globalization and Its Discontents* (New York: W.W. Norton, 2002) at 78.
72 See, *e.g.,* Pape, *supra* note 50; Smitherman, *supra* note 45.
73 Smitherman, *supra* note 45 at 880; see also Gerber, *supra* note 48.
74 See *WTO Cape Town, supra* note 54.

Methodology and Current Research Directions in Cross-Cultural Conflict Resolution

EMMA E. BUCHTEL

Exactly how cultural differences should be addressed during conflict resolution negotiations is a matter of contention. Conflict resolution theorists have not yet devised a definitive way to deal with "the culture question." Although most theorists seem to agree that culture must be addressed, questions of exactly how important it is and how to take it into account are still hotly debated. Whether or not we fully understand how to handle cultural differences, however, we must be aware of their presence. As the theory of selective adaptation suggests, cultural differences are always lying in wait for the unwary negotiator.

This essay will review the recent cross-cultural conflict resolution literature. It will specifically examine (1) how selective adaptation affects conflict resolution, and (2) how the issue of cultural differences has been dealt with in the discipline of conflict resolution. First, we will discuss why it has been only recently that culture has been recognized as important in conflict resolution. Second, we will use several anecdotes to illustrate how culture can invisibly interfere with negotiations. Third, applying culture-specific knowledge will be compared and contrasted with taking a "culture-general sensitivity" approach. Finally, we will address the question of whether current conflict resolution methodologies advantage the culture that produced them, and the related issue of whether different methodologies should be used.

This essay will show that cultural differences do influence the process and success of conflict resolution in areas such as international trade law. How can cultural knowledge be helpfully applied in the future? Should we go so far as to actually change methods of trade dispute resolution to accommodate cultural differences? By showing how conflict resolution practitioners have answered such questions, we hope to provide readers with new and valuable insights into how to apply the theory of selective adaptation to cross-cultural conflict resolution in general, and in specific areas such as trade dispute resolution.

Culture in Conflict Resolution: Resistance and Acceptance

Is attention to cultural differences necessary for conflict resolution? Until recently, culture has barely been mentioned in the negotiation and conflict resolution literature.[1] For example, the popular negotiation handbook *Getting to YES*[2] does not discuss culture at all, except in a brief note in the second edition that simply warns readers to "look out for culture."[3]

Why has discussion of culture been avoided? One important reason is that talking about culture can be seen as counterproductive since it emphasizes differences between groups rather than similarities. As described by Avruch and Black, theorists and practitioners initially dealt with culture by "relegating [it] to the background and taking it to be, in effect, an obstacle to be set aside ... because it merely masks underlying common ... human nature."[4] Drawing attention to differences might prevent parties from seeing their underlying similarities, thus exacerbating conflict. A second reason was that theorists were specifically seeking conflict resolution methodologies that were universal and neutral. For example, John Burton, founder of the influential "interactive conflict resolution" mediation technique, argued that "culture should not influence the problem-solving process, which needs to cut across cultures in a culturally neutral manner."[5] If the goal is to treat all cultures equally, then conflict resolution techniques should aim to "rise above" culture. Finally, in the area of international diplomacy, a quasi-solution to cross-cultural communication had already been found in the form of an "international diplomatic culture." Diplomats were usually trained in a European-style set of assumptions and communication techniques. This common training and education enabled them to assume a kind of common culture among diplomats.[6] With the negative aspects of introducing culture outweighing the need to introduce it, culture was simply ignored.

In today's world, more and more negotiations are being carried out by politicians, businesspeople, and others who are certainly not trained diplomats.[7] As the European-trained diplomatic corps becomes less dominant and as small-scale cross-cultural disputes between businesses and individuals increase, the smoothing effects of a common diplomatic culture fade from sight. Cultural differences may begin playing a larger role in failed negotiations.

Importantly, the role of cultural differences in failed negotiations may not be apparent to the participants. As Douglas P. Fry and C. Brooks Fry explain it, "an implication of conflict being a cultural phenomenon is that the culturally typical ways of perceiving and responding to conflict remain in some ways invisible to the members of any given society as unquestioned assumptions within their social universe."[8] Today's negotiators and diplomats are unlikely, therefore, to be aware of the way their culture influences their perceptions. As anthropologist Clyde Kluckhohn remarked, "It would hardly be fish who discovered the existence of water."[9] As a result of this invisibility, culture can deeply affect our perception of conflicts, consequences, and solutions without our being aware of its effect. Culture can also make the perceptions of different cultures seem baffling. Cultural differences can easily appear to be negative and irrational traits, rather than points of view reasoned from unfamiliar bases. Negative reactions to cultural differences, or even simple incomprehension of the other side's point of view, are an obvious barrier to conflict resolution.

In its deepest sense, culture is more than different practices or values: it is a reality-constructing aspect of our minds. Studies in cultural psychology have shown that culture not only affects the "content" we think about but also the "process" by which we think about that content. In other words, our culture can affect both what we see and how we think about it.[10] The far-reaching implications of this idea are best articulated by E.T. Hall: "People from different cultures not only speak different languages but ... inhabit different sensory worlds. Selective screening of sensory data admits some things while filtering out others, so that experience as it is perceived through one set of culturally patterned sensory screens is quite different from experience perceived through another."[11] When applied to conflict resolution, culture has the potential power to affect what is perceived to be the content of a conflict, and what is perceived to be the best method to resolve a conflict.[12]

Acknowledgement of the importance of culture in conflict resolution has been slow to develop. But "nowadays," says Avruch, "any self-respecting curriculum in ADR or conflict resolution without at least a 'module' devoted to culture would be considered deficient."[13] Yet, are the problems culture causes important enough that we should risk drawing attention to differences instead of similarities? Are the problems important enough to risk changing the methods we use in different cultures? To answer these questions, we will first show that culture does have an important effect on conflict resolution. In the following section, we will see examples of how this "thick" description of culture can help us reveal reasons for unsuccessful resolutions.

How Culture Affects Conflict Resolution

The invisibility of culture can cause problems at many levels. Both mediators and the conflicting parties can be unaware of how they are affected by their own cultures. For example, cultural blinders can cause a mediator to miss solutions that are not obvious from his or her cultural perspective. Substantially different understandings between parties of the expected tactics of negotiation, what agreement means, what the ultimate goals of conflict resolution are, and what constitutes a well-supported legal decision can lead to failed or contentious agreements.

Culture can influence the kind of solution a mediator suggests. One's culture can act like a filter, allowing some options in and screening others out. Thus, culture can affect the ability of mediators to perceive the best solution for the people involved.[14] For example, LeBaron and Zumeta describe how a mediator in a divorce case did not take seriously the suggestion that the divorcing couple send their child to a grandmother in Hong Kong because that was a marginal solution in the mediator's own culture. Only later did she realize that in the eyes of the divorcing couple, it was the best option for all involved.[15] In another situation, initial blindness to alternative solutions actually caused a mediator's actions to exacerbate conflict. The mediator, who came from a legal background, assumed that contract signing was a natural conclusion to a conflict resolution session. Instead, his predominantly African American clients found that the idea of signing a written contract made him seem distrustful, suggesting that their word was not good enough. This led to future problems with compliance.[16] By unconsciously assuming that others hold the same perception of solutions, we may inadvertently block the achievement of resolution.

Similarly, different assumptions about what it means to be in negotiation can lead to continuing or even escalating conflict. For example, expecting that negotiation is defined by the give-and-take of graduated compromise (which is often assumed, in the words of Madeline Albright, to be "the very nature ... of negotiations"[17]) may in fact lead negotiators to grief. Raymond Cohen suggests that the idea that negotiation is about "give and take" may literally not translate. He argues that a major reason the 1991-2000 Syrian-Israeli talks failed was because of cultural differences reflected in translations of key words, such as "negotiate." The English word "negotiate" implies trade and mutual compromise. This translates fairly easily into Hebrew, which uses a word (*masa umatan*)[18] that implies a similar spirit of trade and noble compromise. In Arabic, however, "negotiation" is translated into a word (*mufawadat*) that implies respectful and high-minded discussion about principles. It in no way implies bargaining or trading. In Arabic, "bargaining" refers to the squabbling marketplace, and it would be insulting to use that word to describe what statesmen do in discussing matters of national importance.[19]

Unsurprisingly, Syrian President Hafez al-Assad found Israel's attempts at "bargaining" to be offensive and indicative that the Israelis "[did] not seek a genuine peace between equals."[20] On the other side, the Israelis thought that "Assad was unwilling to adopt the minimal conditions of sane political give and take."[21] Similar problems occurred with the words "concession," "compromise," "peace," and so on. Although the negotiations took place in English, this merely "masked deep semantic disparities."[22] Cultural differences were invisible to the participants, who did not imagine that the other side could have a different definition of "negotiating." Cohen suggests that "there is no easy answer for this profound problem,"[23] and concludes that a solution can be found only if the semantic issues are openly discussed.

Another example of cultural dissonance can be found in the area of agreement: what does it mean to nod your head, to initial an agreement, to sign a contract? Several authors have described cultural differences in the very nature of what it means to agree, depending on different tendencies towards "contract-centred" versus "relationship-centred" ways of conceptualizing negotiations. These differences imply that even if one appears to have come to an amicable agreement with another party, the result of that agreement may still be up in the air. Cohen suggests that "high-context" cultures, in which relationships and face are much more important than in "low-context" cultures, may "subordinate accuracy to approval."[24] This can sometimes result in "promises being given that cannot be kept and arrangements being agreed to in the full knowledge that they are unlikely to be implemented."[25] In other words, a party may agree to something that cannot be realized, believing that this would be better for the relationship than refusing agreement. With the greater good in mind of saving face for the other, or preserving the image of a relationship, or even with the hope that somehow a future solution may be found, a high-context group may engage in what – to a low-context group – may appear to be simply lying.

Whether a contract is negotiated in "good faith" or "good will" is another reflection of contract- versus relationship-centred ideas of negotiation, respectively. A contract negotiated in "good will" assumes that both parties are beginning a relationship, and that future difficulties will be worked out flexibly. There is also an emphasis on trust, as though the parties were friends. But "good will" may be in conflict with "good faith." "Good faith" assumes that parties are bound by the specific terms of a contract.[26] An agreement made in "good will" may mean that the agreement is merely "a provisional step in a never-ending journey, yet another move in an open-ended relationship."[27]

For example, a conflict between American Motors and the Chinese government over the fulfillment of a joint-venture contract, known as the "Beijing Jeep dispute," was rooted in differences between the specific language in the contract and the Chinese side's expectations.[28] The contract appeared to state that premade Jeep parts would be imported and assembled in China, but the Chinese side was under the impression that American Motors would help develop a Chinese Jeep as well.[29] American Motors believed that "its obligation ran to the letter of the agreement," while "the Chinese viewed the joint-venture contract ... as an expression of a broader commitment to mutual assistance."[30] When American Motors refused to go beyond its contract and the Chinese side began having trouble converting money, a successfully negotiated settlement still resulted in distrust and divergent views of what had caused the problem. American Motors emerged "convinced that the Chinese side could not be trusted to honour its agreements."[31] On the other side, Beijing Automotive Works was "doubtful from the outset about [American Motors'] commitment to their welfare, [and] had these views confirmed through the course of the dispute."[32] Conflict over the meaning of the contract led to mistrust on both sides and irreparable damage to the relationship.

As the Beijing Jeep dispute illustrates, the greater the expectation that similarity will exist, the greater the disappointment and frustration when cultural differences reappear. In the January-February 2003 *China Business Review,* two American trade lawyers based in Beijing grimly described Chinese administrative officials' seeming inability – or unwillingness – to follow World Trade Organization (WTO) norms.[33] According to Patrick

Norton and Kermit Almstedt, Chinese investigations often followed the letter, but certainly not the spirit, of WTO rules. Among other problems, they particularly objected to the fact that decisions were not transparent.[34] For example, Norton and Almstedt stated that the final decisions arrived at by Chinese investigators typically did not explain the logical path taken to arrive at the judgment. Also, evidence was not cited or, when it was cited, was often contradictory to the judgment; the definitions used were also unclear.[35] To Norton and Almstedt, "WTO procedures are premised on transparency."[36] The procedures should allow parties to verify that the decision has been made fairly. Transparency is also important because it gives review panels a clear picture of the reasoning process that led to the decision. Yet, this fundamental norm was missing from Chinese administrative decisions – despite the fact that notices, questionnaires, and hearings all appeared to have been held in accordance with WTO procedures.

Lack of transparency was only one of many problems that led foreign parties to conclude that the investigation itself was essentially a sham, with decisions "resulting less from the persuasiveness of the evidence than from the political clout of opposing domestic interests."[37] Norton and Almstedt argue that the disconnect between WTO-like form and the final decision was rooted in Chinese traditions of dispute resolution, traditions that are quite different from those that led to "Western concepts of the 'rule of law.'"[38] For China to embrace these foreign norms will take much more time than simply implementing foreign procedures did.

Using Knowledge of Cultural Differences: Stereotyping or Sensitivity?

Hopefully, the examples given above have shown why culture must be taken into account when trying to understand cross-cultural dispute resolution. But how should cultural knowledge be taught and used? What can we do to make sure mediators perceive a reality similar to that of the parties they are assisting?

One method is for the mediators and parties in a negotiation to gain specific knowledge about typical aspects of their culture and the culture of their counterparts. This information can then be used to better understand behaviour. For example, the Cushner and Brislin "cultural assimilator" focuses on learning not only that there are many different explanations for the same behaviour but that the best explanation is dependent on the specific culture that the behaviour took place in (for example, "Japanese value conformity over individualism"[39] or "Indonesians associate the left hand with dirtiness, and one should not touch others with the left hand"[40]).

Extensive research by Jeanne Brett on "national negotiating styles" also gives specific suggestions for the kinds of cultural differences to look out for.[41] Assuming a situation in which negotiators from different countries are trying to come to an agreement without the help of a third party, she gives advice about how to discuss issues over use of time, direct or indirect communication, hierarchical or egalitarian power, and the importance or lack of importance of self-interests.[42]

Brett, however, advocates going beyond information about national culture when one is interacting with individuals: "When negotiating cross-culturally, it is important to know more than the likely negotiation values and norms held by people from the other culture. One should also try to learn how likely it is [that] the individual with whom you are negotiating subscribes to those values and norms."[43] This piece of advice demonstrates one of the problems associated with applying knowledge of cultural differences. The concept of culture can be subject to many forms of misuse and abuse, including either simplification or overcomplication of cultural differences, confusing culture and ethnicity, assuming within-group homogeneity, and so on.[44] The potential for harm in the application of cultural stereotypes cannot be dismissed, and the debate about how to ethically use cultural descriptions is ongoing.[45]

Often, one's initial introduction to cultural differences is in the form of "The Japanese value conformity." While absorbing these statements can make one more aware of cultural differences, they can too easily be reified into the kinds of stereotypes we most want to avoid. Searching to sidestep this problem, some practitioners have suggested general ways of increasing cultural awareness that may help one avoid culture-specific knowledge almost entirely. For example, LeBaron suggests a series of methods that mediators could use to increase personal "cultural fluency" or "cultural competence,"[46] rather than stressing the need for mediators to learn cultural facts. Although in *Bridging Cultural Conflicts* she does introduce some common types of cultural differences from a "bird's-eye view" (such as communitarian versus individualist, low-context versus high-context communication),[47] she also specifically states that "cultural competence does not mean having an encyclopedic knowledge of myriad cultural groups to apply in specific circumstances."[48] Instead, she emphasizes developing a spirit of openness and inquiry and avoiding judgments. LeBaron also stresses using techniques of self-exploration to "keep awareness attuned, help us question our givens when they exclude other people or ideas, broaden our experience beyond our familiar favorite channels, and generally keep us present to our choices and ways of seeing."[49] "As a spirit of inquiry infuses mediation processes," LeBaron proposes, "they are more likely to be sites of change and improved relationships."[50]

This method may be the best medicine for dealing with cultural differences, one that does not have undesirable side effects such as stereotyping. The only caveat has to do with the question of how easily these methods can be accepted and learned. Arguably, acquiring a "spirit of inquiry" may be more difficult for many than acquiring bits of information such as "Japanese value conformity." The rewards, however, may be worth the attempt.

Bringing Culture into the Picture: The Methodology

A selective adaptation perspective focuses on how structural elements, such as laws and institutions, will shift meaning in a new culture. The foregoing examples illustrate how a lack of awareness of these underlying changes can lead to surprises and frustration. They also illustrate that the structures themselves, when transported to a different culture, will sometimes simply not work as intended (*e.g.,* contracts, negotiation tactics, informal agreements, and even legal proceedings). Is this reason to change the structures themselves? In the context of conflict resolution, should the methodology used be consciously shifted to better reflect local norms? And what do we do when we need to take several different local norms into account? Would such "structural relativism" simply lead to chaos?

As described by Avruch and Black, a major goal of conflict resolution theorists has been to create a "universally valid set of dispute resolution techniques."[51] In order to create techniques that could be used anywhere and "anywhen," theorists attempted to take culture entirely out of the picture. They did not want to create a technique that would work only in a limited number of cultural contexts. An emphasis on culture when developing dispute resolution theory, therefore, seemed backward-looking and problematic.

Attempts to create "culture-free" methods of conflict resolution have been accused, however, of unconsciously injecting culture into "universal" theories even as they emphasize ignoring culture.[52] For example, Avruch and Black describe how a popular model of dispute resolution – getting rid of the irrelevant "strata" of emotions, relationships, and so on to reach a stage where the desituationalized problem can be "efficiently" and "rationally" dealt with – was dependent on a uniquely "middle-class white American folk model" of the self.[53] In this model, it was possible to separate the "person" and the "emotions" and deal separately with each. To some African

Americans, however, the idea of separating emotions from self was seen as an unreasonable and "white" way of solving a problem.[54] Without being aware of it, the Euro-American authors of the theory had created a method that worked best for Euro-Americans. As Avruch comments, "Where practice is situated, there is theory derived. And for negotiation – as, indeed, for conflict resolution in general – the practice overwhelmingly has been culturally situated within a North American, male, white, and middle-class world."[55] These theories, therefore, might need to be changed in order to be useful in other cultures – especially when they are used between cultures; otherwise, they may accidentally create "home-court advantages" for those from the theory's culture of origin.[56]

While agreeing that culture needs to be paid attention to, some theorists argue that their methods are still useful cross-culturally and do not give advantage to any one culture in particular. Roger Fisher's popular methods of negotiation, for example, are based on John Burton's theories of universal basic needs. These basic needs are alleged to underlie conflicts in any culture.

Similarly, in *Interactive Conflict Resolution* (ICR), Ronald J. Fisher describes a large body of third-party mediation techniques that are largely based on interactive, analytic problem solving between parties. These techniques are also based on Burton's theories.[57] As opposed to *Getting to YES*, however, Fisher's book often mentions cultural sensitivity. In the conclusion, he devotes time to the question of cross-cultural applicability of these methods. While emphasizing that "rather than assuming the cultural generalizability of ICR based on limited experience, scholar-practitioners should take the cultural question much more seriously," Fisher also describes the conflict resolution workshop as creating a "metaculture" with its own values and premises.[58] With appropriate cultural sensitivity employed by a third-party mediator and an emphasis on understanding how people from different cultures might react to the metaculture differently, it may be possible to transfer this metaculture cross-culturally.[59]

Fisher describes Burton's defence of the analytic problem-solving method as follows:

> Burton ... acknowledges that cultures deal with conflict differently and that cultural differences can be important substantive issues in intergroup conflict. However ... culture should not influence the problem-solving process, which needs to cut across cultures in a culturally neutral manner ... conflict resolution seeks a generic process that is based on universal abilities of

logical analysis and problem solving, thus not favoring one culture over another. Although third parties need to be sensitive to cultural aspects, culture as such is not important in analysis and resolution.[60]

In other words, cultural differences in ways of dealing with and perceiving conflict should be dealt with in the same way as other differences of perception in the problem-solving process. They should be dealt with as aspects of the conflict that also need to be brought out into the open and discussed within the general system of open communication and understanding of the "other side." The process is supposed to be inherently unbiased; in particular, logical analysis and problem solving are not supposed to favour one culture over another.

ICR also assumes that open, direct communication and neutral mediators are a necessary part of the conflict resolution metaculture. But what if one side's culture allows it to more easily accept these metacultural values? Raymond Cohen suggests that the ICR way of thinking is an "incongruous" and "ethnocentric supposition."[61] He suggests that negotiation may fail spectacularly when the engaged parties are from cultures that differ widely in communication patterns or understandings of the meaning of "negotiation." Instead, he proposes that culturally experienced mediators, using specific cultural knowledge, can best facilitate negotiation between two groups from different cultures. A mediator's duty should expand from a "Model T" mediator – who is expected to be neutral and impartial while "assisting communication and inventing alternative options"[62] – to a "Model C" mediator – who adds to those duties "interpretation, face-protection, and coordination."[63] Building on examples of cross-cultural negotiation and mediation attempts that failed or worked in the past, Cohen reasons that an "interpretive" third party is absolutely necessary for two groups to come to an agreement. This is because of cultural differences in expectations, understandings of negotiation, and the different needs that are so intrinsic as to be invisible to the parties and thus inexpressible in negotiation.[64] This third party may be called upon to play very different roles for each of the two groups, reflecting each group's cultural understanding of what a mediator is.[65] The third party may also act as a face-saving buffer between groups who would find "open, honest communication" about conflict (which is seen as one of the "first principles" of ICR[66]) to be painfully out of touch with their communication norms.[67]

Benjamin Broome's methodology blends Fisher and Cohen, suggesting a somewhat invariant "Third Culture" (or metaculture), but one based on an understanding that direct communication may not be possible. He instead emphasizes the more emotional value of relational empathy.[68] Broome suggests that the mediator should encourage participants to have the goal of incrementally increasing their understanding of the other party's point of view. Similar to Fisher and Burton, he suggests that mediators should aim to create a third culture, with norms that integrate and overcome the norms that each party is individually comfortable with. He suggests that parties should not try to attain the unrealistic goal of getting rid of "prior understandings" (prejudices). Instead, they should present these "prior understandings" to the other party, and through a system of feedback, change, and re-presentation, "integrate" them with the understandings of the other.[69] He also suggests that attempts to "see behind" the "verbal and nonverbal expressions of the other" might be impossible because of "blinders produced by the different perspectives brought to the situation."[70] Instead, he emphasizes the process of creating new meanings and understandings of a situation through the third culture of a conflict resolution workshop. This can help participants arrive at new meanings of the conflict situation and lead to the "development of stronger ties."[71]

A case study of Broome's methods provides insight into how this "somewhat invariant" methodology works when placed in a new cultural context. In a description of his two and a half years of work on the Cyprus Greek-Turk conflict, Broome comes across as a careful, caring mediator, willing to modify his preferred methods of conflict resolution depending on the cultural situation.[72] In the Cyprus case, he was worried about cultural differences between the Turkish and Greek parties. He was also worried about differences between his culture and the Mediterranean culture of Cyprus. When facilitating cross-cultural meetings, he had to make several adjustments to ensure that the more expressive Greek Cypriots did not talk too much. He also had to act as an emotional interpreter, explaining to the Greek side that "the lack of an enthusiastic response from the Turkish Cypriots might not mean they are not interested in an idea."[73] Or he would have to explain to the Turkish side that "the behavior of the Greek Cypriots may not have been meant as strongly as it appeared to them."[74] Similarly, Broome had to adjust his expectations with regard to "starting on time," and accept that seemingly overextended socializing time was in fact useful to the mediation process.

Broome makes it quite clear that he was constantly concerned about whether his methodologies were appropriate to the cultural context. He feels that other mediators should also be mindful of this concern: "I have seen too many trainers and mediators simply bring in the programs they had developed for use in their own cultural context and try to implement these without modification with local groups. This not only results in approaches that do not work well, but also can do damage that may not show up until well after the outsiders are safely back in their own environment."[75] In his own case, however, Broome felt somewhat trapped between the desire to "introduce new ideas that help break destructive cultural patterns" and the desire to make sure his methodology was appropriate for the situation.[76] "There is a fine line between cultural imperialism and the introduction of appropriate methodology," he commented, "and it is not always easy to make the best decisions about how far to go in adapting one's process to the local culture."[77] As a result, he kept mainly to his planned agenda, although he "carefully evaluat[ed] the entire process at each step of the way and ask[ed] the participants many questions about appropriateness."[78] His choice to mainly use his familiar methodology may also have been influenced by his years of experience at applying it in many different contexts. This experience enabled him to make proper intuitive decisions at certain crucial points, which he explicitly states is a necessary skill for mediators.[79]

Analyzing: A Culture-Neutral Conflict Resolution Strategy?

Although he is more willing than Fisher and Burton to allow culture to change the actual choice of resolution methodology, Broome still remains in favour of being conservative with his changes, explaining that it is his duty to implement new methods of conflict resolution. Radically changing methods, he implies, would lead to incompetent mediators; total "structural relativism" would result in ineffective nonsense. But is his method equally advantageous for all cultures? Broome's "metaculture" seems analytically influenced. It is instructive, then, to look at a method of conflict resolution that is quite different from those described above. LeBaron's methods are different in that they expressly build upon emotional and intuitive reasoning, as opposed to the analytical reasoning favoured by previous theorists. Moreover, she insists that the suggestions she gives are merely suggestions. She expects that in different situations different methods will be used.

Burton's belief that "logical analysis" is a "universal ability"[80] may basically be true, but it does not take into account cultural differences in *preference for* and *values about* using logical analysis. It also does not consider whether logical analysis may be a limited way to solve problems. In research on the preferred foci and goals of mediators in the state of Georgia, it was found that male mediators (and especially those who were also attorneys) focused less on "balancing emotional and material needs" of the client than female mediators. Female mediators also concentrated more on nonverbal body language and emotions.[81] This implies that focusing on simple logical analysis may not always be appropriate or satisfying for the parties to a negotiation. Also, research in cultural psychology has suggested that there are differences in ways of perceiving and reasoning between cultures (relational/ intuitive versus analytical). In various studies done in Japan, Korea, Malaysia, and the United States, East Asians have been shown to be more holistic and context-minded than Caucasian Western participants.[82] This suggests that neutral mediators and analytical forms of conflict resolution may indeed lead to home-court advantage for some participants, perhaps reflected in the degree of comfort felt during mediation.

Is analytical problem solving the best way to solve problems? Openness to a more holistic approach could be a better way to resolve conflict. The "analytic/holistic" theme is a common one in disciplines other than cultural psychology. For example, Mary Clark suggests that there are two world views, or gestalts, through which it is possible to look at the world. The first is the "billiard ball" gestalt, in which everything is seen on a flat plane and cause and effect are linear and predictable. The second, borrowing an image from Indian mythology, is the "Indra's net" gestalt. The intersections of the net are each marked with a jewel that reflects all the other jewels. Any action affecting one part of the net affects all the other parts of the net. Clark argues that the Indra's net gestalt reveals the complexity and interconnectedness of human experience, and if this gestalt were reflected in conflict resolution methodology, we would have more satisfying results.[83]

LeBaron's methods of "dynamic engagement" are an appropriate foil to the analytic models of Fisher and Burton. "Analysis and logic alone cannot guide us through difficult conflicts, so tied are they to our cultural common sense," she begins. "Instead we must engage relationally with those involved to invent and live into new ways of relating."[84] In exploring and bridging conflicts, a series of practices suggested for the personal, interpersonal, and intergroup levels are meant to utilize "intuitive and imaginative," "emotional," "somatic," and "connected or spiritual" ways of knowing.[85] These practices use activities such as developing metaphors, creating images, and envisioning ideal futures in order to create greater mutual understanding between sides and less negativity in relationships. The practices are not meant to be "comprehensive ... nor definitive" but reflect her "perceptions about what is often missing from the books and the training courses about resolving conflict."[86] The methods, however, may be particularly useful in situations where the primary sources of conflict are expressed in relational or spiritual ways. For example, many of her suggestions are coincidentally reflected in the advice given by experts for dealing with the claim of the New Zealand Maori that the presence of a *taniwha* god made the government's desired construction of a new road impossible.[87]

LeBaron also makes it clear that she expects her methods to be used more as "touchstones," or ways to "stimulate imagination and ideas about the ways particular conflicts in specific cultural contexts may be addressed."[88] In other words, the specific practices and stages of "dynamic engagement" are not meant to be transferred wholesale to another country or context. Instead, they are meant to be inspirational, to promote the process of creating new culturally appropriate methods for dealing with conflict.

Imposing Your Own Solution: Is Cultural Sensitivity Necessary for the Powerful?

Political or economic power enables one to force culturally inappropriate solutions on the less powerful. But does this merely cause surface changes and sacrifice long-term advantages for, at best, short-term benefits? As selective adaptation suggests, forcing a culture to adopt a foreign system may lead to unexpected complications. Yet, how can we convince the powerful that it is in their self-interest to accommodate cultural differences?

When the powerful can force changes on others, the short-term gain may be more tempting than gains that can be had in the long term. An example of this are the techniques of US negotiator Charlene Barshefsky,[89] who "bridged" US-China disagreements on the proper position of intellectual property rights in China by making her requirements exceptionally clear (establishing that "direct communication" was going to be the only way to negotiate). She then used the threat of a trade war to push the Chinese side into an agreement that satisfied her country's requirements. Although the Chinese government appears to have fulfilled its promises so far, the US's ultimate goal of a huge reduction in pirated software may not be reached. Did Barshefsky's refusal to back down on her own principles lead to an agreement that was incompatible with the realities of Chinese society?[90] W. Alford argues that US pressure on the Chinese central government does nothing to help change the awareness and perception of intellectual property rights among average Chinese citizens.[91] Instead, such pressure has mainly led to worsening human rights abuses, which, he argues, will ultimately prevent China from developing sustainable protection of intellectual property rights.[92]

Philmer Bluehouse, coordinator of the Navajo Peacemaking Program, has described how in the mid-1970s traditional methods of conflict resolution were disrupted by the Euro-American legal system. In the past, police officers had seen themselves in the traditional role of a "warrior leader" who gives wise guidance, but in the mid-1970s they were pressured to become "the officer who was only interested in establishing probable cause." The evidence-focused, court-driven police force interrupted the traditional role of a Navajo Peacemaker.[93] Serving as an officer during this time, Bluehouse "discover[ed] the power of the maxim 'Use your discretion' when ranking officers did not want to be bothered by complex situations."[94] In other words, when the rules were too much in conflict with local norms, they were simply ignored. An efficient local system of dealing with conflicts had been partially disrupted by a legal system imposed from above. An incomplete integration was achieved only by surreptitiously blocking the government's interference. Recently, Bluehouse has revived traditional Peacemaker knowledge and is developing ways to appropriately integrate it with the Euro-American legal system.

The assumption of cultural similarity may be inefficient in the long term, even when it seems expedient in the short term. Hopefully, we can convince the powerful that cultural sensitivity is ultimately a more productive approach.

Conclusion

We have looked at how a lack of awareness of cultural differences can lead to inefficient or harmful outcomes. We have also discussed different methods of teaching cultural sensitivity and different methods that can be employed by mediators. We have argued that a new "holistic" approach to conflict resolution may be the best way to deal with cultural differences. Finally, we come to two simple questions. Is a combination of many methodologies the best way to approach conflict resolution? And how far should negotiators go in adjusting to cultures?

In international relations, conflict resolution methods such as ICR are almost always used *in addition to* more formal methods of coming to agreements, such as formal negotiation.[95] This suggests the possibility of combining methods of conflict resolution. For example, analytical methods and those drawing more on intuitive ways of thinking might be used together, possibly in combination with formal diplomatic efforts. Also, both specific and nonspecific cultural awareness could be used concurrently in order to gain a better understanding of a particular situation. Foreign and indigenous methods of conflict resolution could be valuably mixed, perhaps in different stages of a conflict resolution workshop. Even the commonly pitted-against-each-other intuitive and analytical ways of thinking could be seen as paired ways of gaining understanding of the other. As Broome states, the goal of conflict resolution could be "an affective *and* cognitive assimilation of the other's values, meanings, symbols, intentions, etc."[96]

Knowing how conflict resolution methods are themselves selectively adapted may also be essential for success at conflict resolution. If parties go into a conflict resolution session with differing concepts of how the process works and what its goals are, problems may be compounded, not ameliorated, as expectations are broken. "Mediation theory," says Cohen, "assumes that players in a bargaining game play by the same rules. However, they may not even be playing the same game."[97] Like WTO rules, conflict resolution methods can also change their meaning when brought into another culture. This adds another layer of complexity that mediators of all types must struggle with. It is hoped that this review will serve to spark some ideas about how conflict resolution practitioners and theorists can be made aware of these potential differences and overcome them. As we develop ideas about how best to manage the selective adaptation of conflict resolution, we hope these ideas can shed light on how to deal with selective adaptation of human rights and international trade norms.

Many questions remain unanswered. What are the relative strengths and weaknesses of using generalized knowledge about cultures? Does such knowledge lead to harmful stereotypes? Or does it enable us to act culturally appropriately? In the same way that methodologies such as ICR might give a home-court advantage to cultures used to "direct communication," would LeBaron's "dynamic engagement" model advantage people from cultures where interpersonal and intuitive interactions are not so uncomfortable? How can we convince powerful states and groups that they would benefit by taking culture into account? Is more research, more theorizing, or more quiet meditation called for in order to answer these questions? We hope for a bit of each. We also hope that combining methodologies and being aware of cultural differences will ensure that cross-cultural conflict resolution and cross-cultural interactions are never again a "dialog of the deaf."[98]

NOTES

1 Kevin Avruch, "Culture and Negotiation Pedagogy" (2000) 16 Negotiation Journal 339; Michelle LeBaron, *Conflict and Culture: A Literature Review and Bibliography*, rev. ed. (Victoria, BC: University of Victoria, Institute for Dispute Resolution, 2001); Anthony Wanis-St. John, "Thinking Globally and Acting Locally" (2003) 19 Negotiation Journal 371.

2 Roger Fisher, William Ury, and Bruce Patton, *Getting to YES: Negotiating Agreement without Giving In* (New York: Houghton Mifflin, 1991).

3 Avruch, *supra* note 1 at 340.

4 Kevin Avruch and Peter W. Black, "Conflict Resolution in Intercultural Settings: Problems and Prospects" in Denis Sandole and Hugo van der Merwe, eds., *Conflict Resolution Theory and Practice: Integration and Application* (Manchester, UK: Manchester University Press, 1993) 131 at 131.

5 John Burton, *Conflict: Resolution and Prevention* (New York: St. Martin's Press, 1990), quoted in Ronald J. Fisher, *Interactive Conflict Resolution* (Syracuse, NY: Syracuse University Press, 1997) at 261.

6 *E.g.,* William Zartman, "A Skeptic's View" in Guy Faure and Jeffrey Z. Rubin, eds., *Culture and Negotiation* (Thousand Oaks, CA: Sage Publications, 1993) 17.

7 Kevin Avruch, *Culture and Conflict Resolution* (Washington, DC: United States Institute of Peace, 1998) at 47; Raymond Cohen, "Cultural Aspects of International Mediation" in Jacob Bercovitch, ed., *Resolving International Conflicts: The Theory and Practice of Mediation* (Boulder, CO: Lynne Rienner Publishers, 1996) 107 at 111.

8 Douglas P. Fry and C. Brooks Fry, "Culture and Conflict-Resolution Models: Exploring Alternatives to Violence" in Douglas P. Fry and Kaj Bjorkqvist, eds., *Cultural Variation in Conflict Resolution: Alternatives to Violence* (Hillsdale, NJ: Lawrence Erlbaum Associates, 1997) 9.

9 Clyde Kluckhohn, *Mirror for Man: The Relation of Anthropology to Modern Life* (New York: Fawcett, 1949) at 11.

10 See, *e.g.,* Richard Nisbett, *The Geography of Thought: How Asians and Westerners Think Differently and Why* (New York: Free Press, 2004).

11 Edward T. Hall, *The Hidden Dimension* (Garden City, NY: Doubleday, 1969) at 2, quoted in Cohen, *supra* note 7 at 110.

12 Michelle LeBaron and Zena D. Zumeta, "Windows on Diversity: Lawyers, Culture, and Mediation Practice" (2003) 20 Conflict Resolution Quarterly 463.

13 Kevin Avruch, "Type I and Type II Errors in Culturally Sensitive Conflict Resolution Practice" 20 Conflict Resolution Quarterly 351 at 353.

14 LeBaron and Zumeta, *supra* note 12.

15 *Ibid.* at 465.

16 *Ibid.* at 467.

17 Raymond Cohen, "Resolving Conflict across Languages" (2001) 17 Negotiation Journal 17 at 28.

18 *Ibid.* at 26.

19 *Ibid.*

20 *Ibid.* at 28.

21 *Ibid.*

22 *Ibid.* at 32.

23 *Ibid.*

24 Raymond Cohen, *Negotiating across Cultures: International Communication in an Interdependent World,* rev. ed. (Washington, DC: United States Institute of Peace, 1997) at 201.

25 *Ibid.*

26 *Ibid.* at 199.

27 *Ibid.* at 201.

28 Michael Donnelly and Pitman B. Potter, *Cultural Aspects of Trade Dispute Resolution in Japan and China* (Vancouver: Asia Pacific Foundation of Canada, 1996) at 32-34.

29 *Ibid.* at 32.

30 *Ibid.* at 32-33.

31 *Ibid.* at 33.

32 *Ibid.*

33 Patrick M. Norton and Kermit Almstedt, "China Joins the Trade Wars" *China Business Review* (January-February 2003) 22.

34 *Ibid.* at 26.

35 *Ibid.*

36 *Ibid.*

37 *Ibid.*

38 *Ibid.* at 29.

39 Kenneth Cushner and Richard W. Brislin, *Intercultural Interactions: A Practical Guide,* 2d ed. (Thousand Oaks, CA: Sage Publications, 1996) at 58.

40 *Ibid.* at 60.

41 Jeanne Brett, *Negotiating Globally: How to Negotiate Deals, Resolve Disputes, and Make Decisions across Cultural Borders,* 2d ed. (San Francisco: Jossey-Bass, 2001); Jeanne Brett, Wendi Adair, Alain Lempereur, Tetsushi Okumura, Peter Shikhirev, Catherine Tinsley, and Anne Lytle, "Culture and Joint Gains in Negotiation" (2004) 14 Negotiation Journal 61.

42 Brett, *supra* note 41; Brett *et al., supra* note 41.

43 Brett *et al., supra* note 41 at 79.

44 Avruch, *supra* note 1; Michelle LeBaron, *Bridging Cultural Conflicts: A New Approach for a Changing World* (San Francisco: Jossey-Bass, 2003).

45 See James K. Sebenius, "Caveats for Cross-Border Negotiators" (2002) 18 Negotiation Journal 121, and Avruch, *supra* note 13, for more discussion.

46 LeBaron, *supra* note 44; LeBaron and Zumeta, *supra* note 12.

47 LeBaron, *supra* note 44 at 53-82.

48 LeBaron and Zumeta, *supra* note 12 at 465.

49 LeBaron, *supra* note 44 at 171.

50 LeBaron and Zumeta, *supra* note 12 at 466.

51 Avruch and Black, *supra* note 4 at 131.

52 LeBaron, *supra* note 1, at 40; Carrie Menkel-Meadow, "Negotiating with Lawyers, Men, and Things: The Contextual Approach Still Matters" (2001) 17 Negotiation Journal 257.

53 Kevin Avruch, Peter W. Black, and Joseph A. Scimecca, eds., *Conflict Resolution: Cross-Cultural Perspectives* (New York: Greenwood Press, 1991).

54 Thomas Kochman, *Black and White Styles in Conflict* (Chicago: University of Chicago Press, 1981), cited in Kevin Avruch, "Introduction: Culture and Conflict Resolution" in Avruch *et al., supra* note 53.

55 Avruch, *supra* note 1 at 343.

56 *Ibid.*

57 Fisher, *supra* note 5.

58 *Ibid.* at 264.

59 *Ibid.* Fisher also argues, with Burton, that nonviolent "problem solving" is not actually very culturally biased towards the West at all. In fact, "its processes are often more compatible with conflict management approaches in other cultures, particularly Third World and indigenous ones": *ibid.* at 263.

60 *Ibid.* at 261.

61 Cohen, *supra* note 7 at 125.

62 *Ibid.* at 109.

63 *Ibid.* at 124.

64 *Ibid.* at 111.

65 *Ibid.* at 113.

66 Fisher, *supra* note 5 at 268.

67 Cohen, *supra* note 7 at 113.

68 Benjamin Broome, "Managing Differences in Conflict Resolution" in D.J. Sandole and H. van der Merwe, eds., *Conflict Resolution Theory and Practice: Integration and Application* (Manchester: Manchester University Press) 95.

69 *Ibid.* at 106.

70 *Ibid.*

71 *Ibid.*

72 Benjamin Broome and John S. Murray, "Improving Third-Party Decisions at Choice Points: A Cyprus Case Study" (2002) 18 Negotiation Journal 75.

73 *Ibid.* at 84.

74 *Ibid.*

75 *Ibid.* at 85.

76 *Ibid.*

77 *Ibid.*

78 *Ibid.*

79 *Ibid.* at 77 and 90.

80 Fisher, *supra* note 5 at 261.

81 Margaret S. Herrman, N.L. Hollett, D.G. Eaker, and J. Gale, "Mediator Reflections on Practice: Connecting Select Demographics and Preferred Orientations" (2003) 20 Conflict Resolution Quarterly 403 at 423.

82 Jeffrey Sanchez-Burks, "Protestant Relational Ideology and (In)attention to Relational Cues in Work Settings" (2002) 83 Journal of Personality and Social Psychology 919; Jeffrey Sanchez-Burks, Fiona Lee, Incheol Choi, Shuming Zhao, Jasook Koo, and Richard Nisbett, "Conversing across Cultures: East-West Communication Styles in Work and Non-Work Contexts" (2003) 85 Journal of Personality and Social

Psychology 363; Jeffrey Sanchez-Burks, Richard E. Nisbett, and Oscar Ybarra, "Cultural Styles, Relationship Schemas, and Prejudice against Out-Groups" (2000) 79 Journal of Personality and Social Psychology 174; Ara Norenzayan, Richard E. Nisbett, Edward E. Smith, and Beom Jun Kim, "Cultural Preferences for Formal Versus Intuitive Reasoning" (2002) 26 Cognitive Science 653.

83 Mary E. Clark, *In Search of Human Nature* (London: Routledge, 2002).

84 LeBaron, *supra* note 44 at 138.

85 *Ibid.* at 170.

86 *Ibid.* at 171.

87 Ian Macduff, "What Would You Do – with a *Taniwha* at the Table?" (2003) 19 Negotiation Journal 195; Ian Macduff, "Part II: What Would You Do – with a *Taniwha* at the Table?" (2003) 19 Negotiation Journal 291.

88 LeBaron, *supra* note 44 at 140.

89 Rebecca G. Hulse and James K. Sebenius, "Sequencing, Acoustic Separation, and 3-D Negotiation of Complex Barriers: Charlene Barshefsky and IP Rights in China" (2003) 8 International Negotiation 311.

90 William P. Alford, "Making the World Safe for What? Intellectual Property Rights, Human Rights and Foreign Economic Policy in the Post-European Cold War World" (1996-97) 29 International Law and Politics 135.

91 *Ibid.* at 142.

92 William P. Alford, *To Steal a Book Is an Elegant Offense: Intellectual Property Law in Chinese Civilization* (Stanford, CA: Stanford University Press, 1997) at 4.

93 Philmer Bluehouse, "Is It 'Peacemakers Teaching?' or Is It 'Teaching Peacemakers'?" (2003) 20 Conflict Resolution Quarterly 495 at 495-500.

94 *Ibid.* at 496.

95 Fisher, *supra* note 5 at 60.

96 Broome, *supra* note 68 at 101.

97 Cohen, *supra* note 7 at 125.

98 *Ibid.* at 150, as stated by Henry Kissinger.

PART 2

LOCAL IMPLEMENTATION OF GLOBAL STANDARDS

Globalization and Local Culture in Contracts
Japanese Companies in Thailand

YOSHITAKA WADA

Under the flag of "globalization," almost all Asian countries are now trying to adapt to the Western model of financial and business transactions. Legal and dispute resolution systems are expected to serve as a foundational framework in which each business transaction takes place. Law, as a standardized universal system of rules, is believed to enhance transparency and ensure the safety of business transactions. Legal scholars throughout Asia have carefully studied the legal systems of Western countries and have made efforts to reform and modernize their own local legal systems.

When examining the impact of globalization in the field of law and dispute resolution, however, we should take into account other factors, such as cultural diversity, specific social structure, people's patterns of behaviour, and so on. Legal and dispute resolution systems do not work in a vacuum; rather, they operate within concrete cultural and social settings. Even if we transplant the same Western model, it can operate differently in different situations and is influenced by local power structures, economic situations, and cultural belief systems. Adopting a universal system does not mean simply transplanting the system from one society to another. To be effective in societies in which other modes of social ordering and dispute resolution are embedded, a transplanted system of laws always requires subtle rearrangements with autonomous transformations. This means that even if Asian countries accept and adopt the common global system of law, they are inevitably faced with conflicts caused by cultural and social diversity.

To some Asian countries, the Western concept of the "rule of law" is itself completely new. In fact, the distribution of power between government and the legal system is ambiguous in some parts of Asia. Moreover, the dispute resolution mechanism embedded in the local social structure is often still the default or preferred method of dispute resolution. In this situation, introduction of the Western model of a universal legal system often leads to superficial changes only, and ad hoc negotiation among a multiple rule system is required.[1]

Even in some parts of Asia where the Western system of law was introduced long ago and where there is experience with ordering of society based on that system, how it functions in the society is very different from how it functions in Western countries. Japan, for example, has a long history of ordering society through a transplanted capitalistic legal system. Japanese business practices and dispute resolution techniques have their own characteristics, however, which have sometimes provoked conflict in international transactions and have been criticized by Western countries. Despite this, the behaviour of Japanese companies has features that are deeply rooted in its culture.

In order to understand the meaning of the term "globalization" in the field of law and dispute resolution in Asian countries, we must scrutinize the functioning of the legal system within the context of its specific social and economic settings. For example, we must examine how everyday social and business transactions take place under the shadow of both the law and local rules, how conflicts are settled when a contract is breached, and under what circumstances local people and businesses use or avoid official litigation.

From this point of view, it is essential to understand the complex relationships between the formal legal system and the informal local mode of dispute resolution. One simple way to understand this issue is to assume that increases in formal litigation are directly proportional to the decline of informal alternative modes of dispute resolution.[2] According to this hypothesis, as a society becomes more complex and urbanized, people prefer a formal court over local methods of dispute resolution. In urban industrialized settings, relationships among people tend to become more impersonal, temporal, and diffuse. As a result, local community and primary groups, such as kinship or neighbourhood, lose the power to control people's behaviour and to settle disputes. Instead, people take a formal approach in order to settle disputes. In short, industrialization and urbanization cause the decline of informal modes of dispute resolution and the concurrent development of a formal legal system.

Although this view is correct in a broad sense, it is too simplistic and partial to be applied to the problem of globalization and localism in Asian countries. It is unrealistic to suppose that local modes of dispute resolution and social ordering will automatically lose power as a result of the introduction of a Western-style legal system. There must be a much more complex relationship between the introduction of a formal legal system in the context of informal local modes of dispute resolution.

This essay examines this complex relationship between a formal legal system and informal modes of dispute resolution by analyzing the behaviour of Japanese companies during the 1997 Asian Financial Crisis.

The Gap between Contract Law and Everyday Contractual Behaviour

The Limits of the Classical Understanding of the Contract

The classical understanding of the contract is based on ideas about the law and human relations drawn from philosophical ideas developed during the Enlightenment. The classical understanding considers freedom and autonomy to be the most important components of a contract. People are free to decide whether they will enter into contractual relations or not, and no one is to intervene in this decision, not even the state. When entering into contractual relations, both parties reach an agreement consisting of clauses that bind both parties and enable them to predict the future. This enables people to undertake transactions without worrying about any risk arising from uncertainty and ambiguity. This classical understanding of the contract is too simplistic and too idealistic for complex modern societies, however.

First, the parties to a contract may not have complete freedom to make decisions and may not even be individuals. For example, a party to a contract can be a large organization, where the intentions of many people are merged and often expressed through the process of entering into a contract. Even if both parties are individuals, they do not always have complete freedom to make decisions because differences in negotiating power can often be found in the contractual relationship (*e.g.*, landlord-tenant or doctor-patient relationship). In these cases, a party is free to negotiate only to a certain degree. That is, even before entering into contractual negotiations, parties may not be able to free themselves from the social, cultural, and organizational constraints to which they are subject. There is often no autonomous individual enjoying "freedom of contract" in the real world. That is why the law or the courts sometimes have to intervene and take into account ideas of substantive justice. In Japan, for example, we have the

Landlord-Tenant Act and a variety of consumer protection acts, which em-
power the weaker party to a contract.[3] In addition, courts may also try to
correct the underlying inequality between the parties through interpretation of the contract.

Second, many contracts take place in the context of long-term social
relationships. In these cases, parties gradually develop mutual trust, not
only in the legal aspect but also in everyday sociological dimensions. In
such a relationship, each contract is, in a sense, just a superficial expression of this basic trust and the social relationship. The contract is supported by implicit expectations that cannot be expressed in words but are
based on feelings of trust developed over a long period of time. The simplistic classical idea of a contract is obviously not sufficient to explain this
type of contractual relationship.

Third, in many cases, the contract is performed well after the agreement
is reached. This creates the risk that a rapid change of circumstances may
render the contract unenforceable. Whether the contract should be performed according to the written agreement or revised to meet a changing
situation is something that should always be kept under consideration by the
parties to a contract. As the relevance of the contract to each party changes
with time and changing circumstances, the parties should try to continually
adapt their contract to meet the new situation. One party's insistence on
strict adherence to the written contract may lead to a breakdown of the contractual relationship or even to the insolvency of the other party. The success
of a contractual relationship should not be measured at the moment the
agreement is reached, but should be measured as a process of performance.

Our highly complex societies and complicated trading patterns require a
more realistic concept of contract. In particular, we should consider the social background in which contractual behaviour takes place, as its meaning
continues to change.

Avoiding Contract Law

There is a deep gap between contract law and the reality of everyday contracting behaviour. The most common example of this gap is the avoidance
of courts in cases where there is a contractual disagreement.

As early as 1963, scholars pointed out that most contractual disputes
were resolved without mobilizing legal sanctions or enforcing clauses in the
contract.[4] According to Macaulay, even when a detailed contract exists,
businesspeople usually negotiate problems as if there were no written agreement. This is done in order to preserve a good business relationship and

their reputations. Macaulay also points out that strict enforcement of a written agreement could have detrimental effects on businesses.

It may be surprising that this is not a description of the contract behaviour of people in an Asian society. It is a description of Americans (the data were collected in a rural Wisconsin town), who are usually regarded as highly litigious. If this kind of behaviour can be found even in the United States, we need to reveal and analyze the factors that can lead contracting parties to resolve contractual disputes outside the legal system. It may also be useful to look at the social roles that contract law can play in our society. Otherwise, Macaulay's observation would equal a death sentence for contract law as it would be rendered useless in everyday practice. Fortunately, there are theories that can help explain why parties do not always rely on the legal system to settle contract disputes. These theories take account of the sociological and realistic aspects of contract behaviour.

The Transformation of Contract Theory with Sociological Insight

A Theory of Relational Contract
Taking account of the reality of everyday contract behaviour, Macneil formulates a theory of contract based on a sociological point of view. He sees a contract as a projection of the contracting parties' goal to realize a specific exchange in the future. If a contract is merely a projection of some future exchange, a promise or a clear mutual agreement has no essential place in a contract. In Macneil's view, a contract is based on more than just a promise between parties; it is based on expectations that are buried in social relationships, like those found in business communities, organizational structures, franchise systems, and so on. Macneil calls this type of contract a *relational contract.*[5]

Of course, some types of contract fall into the relational contract category, whereas others fit into the classical contract model – *i.e.,* temporally isolated contracts. Most contracts, however, including a typical one-time contract like purchasing gas, inevitably contain elements of a relational contract.

The Organizational Influence on Contracts
I would like to mention one more theoretical challenge to the common understanding of contract. Rakoff argues that standard-form contracts do more than simply stabilize contractual relations with other parties to the contract. Standard-form contracts also establish efficiency and stability

within the organization using the standard-form contract. This is done by reducing communication costs in the organization and by imposing the ideas contained in the contract on all subordinate parties without explanation or without confirming the decision-making power structure of the organization.[6]

Although Rakoff's intention as a critical legal scholar is to deny the legal validity of the standard-form contract and to criticize domination by private companies, this is not relevant to the point under discussion. We can still obtain useful insights from his argument that a contract is not a dyadic action but is situated in the context of both parties' organizational and sociological circumstances.

Following his line of thought, we can construct the following hypothesis: the more complicated the power structure of an organization, the more the standard-form contract serves to preserve stability and efficiency within that organization. This is because if many actors within an organization participate in the formation of a contract, many aspects related to the internal power relationships within the organization will also be considered in the contract.

The Implications for Comparative Studies of Contract Behaviour
The theoretical challenges discussed above come from Western legal scholarship. The concept of a relational contract is not new to Japanese legal scholarship, however, because Japanese courts explicitly and implicitly consider the relational aspects of contracts. Moreover, even if the American business behaviour of avoiding the legal system to solve contractual disputes appears similar to the Japanese or Thai attitude of avoiding the legal system, there must be an essential difference in the deep structure that produces this superficially similar behaviour and attitude.

In my view, the aforementioned challenges to contract theory also give us a chance to think about cultural differences in behaviour and in the concept of contract. This is because if contract theory seriously considers the organizational background of parties and the sociological dimensions of trust and social relations, inevitably we have to scrutinize the structure of cultural ideas and the formation of social organization in each society.

I believe we can construct a theoretical framework to understand Japanese and Thai contract behaviour by analyzing their respective ideas and beliefs related to contracts. This will lead to empirical studies, the results of which will in turn contribute to the understanding of the nature of contracts.

First, we have to think about the concept of contract in the context of the social relationship between the contracting parties. Such social relationships have many different dimensions. For example, there are economic, sociological, and emotional dimensions. The meaning of contract for each party is deeply rooted in these non-legal dimensions. These dimensions of social relationships are based on society's social structure and on its cultural organization. If legal scholarship and the courts ignore these non-legal dimensions of contracts, their decisions and proposals cannot effectively manage real problems in the everyday practice of contracts, and contractual parties will continue to avoid the courts when solving their contractual disputes. When considering contracts between Thai and Japanese companies, it is therefore important to analyze the Thai-Chinese family networks and the Japanese concept of harmonious social organization.

Second, each party's organizational characteristics are important. In a business community, a party to a contract is often a complex social organization, such as a huge private company. In my view, the division of decision-making power in an organization is especially important in determining contract behaviour. As Rakoff points out, if decision-making power is widely distributed in an organization, the company has to prepare clear and detailed written agreements, not necessarily intending to bind the other party but to control its own inner power structure .

Third, we have to distinguish between two types of contract law avoidance. One type is where the parties avoid using the courts to resolve contractual disputes, even though the parties have a clear written agreement that has been breached. In this case, we have to consider what the social function of the written agreement is for each party. The other type is where the parties avoid making written agreements or contractual clauses altogether. Here we have to consider how each party preserves its contractual relations without a clear written agreement and how the parties keep their relationship problem-free.

Based on these theoretical considerations, I will analyze the data obtained through my field research.

The Behaviour of Japanese-Thai Companies during the Economic Crisis

An Overview of the Results of the Field Survey
This field research consists of a survey combined with follow-up interviews. I sent surveys to Japanese-Thai joint companies operating in Thailand and to exclusively Thai-owned companies that are believed to have a relationship

with Japanese companies. This was done in order to discover their perceptions of contracts and their behaviour around the time of the 1997 Asian
Financial Crisis. I sent 209 questionnaires to Japanese-Thai companies and
received 57 valid replies; 400 questionnaires went to Thai companies and
elicited 132 valid replies. This survey was done in September 1999.[7] After
receiving the replies, I conducted 15 intensive interviews with Japanese
businessmen working for Japanese-Thai companies.

Although this was just an exploratory survey and was not statistically
analyzed, I would like to present some of the results that display differences
between Thai-owned companies and Japanese-Thai-owned companies in
the perception of contracts.

General Attitudes about Contracts

Q1:   *If there were no legal sanctions for breach of contract and compliance,
       how much would your company's operation be affected?*

	Japanese	Thai
(a) Not much	19	16
(b) Substantially and detrimentally	28	112
(c) Substantially and beneficially	0	0
(d) Substantially in both directions	9	4

The most obvious difference is the proportion of respondents that chose
(a). Nearly 34 percent of the Japanese businesspeople surveyed believed
that, even if there were no system of contract law, their transactions would
continue to work without any serious difficulties. Only 12 percent of Thai
businesspeople shared this belief. This result clearly expresses the Japanese
tendency to avoid contracts and depend on other means of social control, at
least on an ideological level.

How Thais View the Attitudes of Japanese and Other Foreign Companies

Q2-1: *In your company's experience, how do Japanese companies draft con-
      tracts in comparison with foreign companies?*

	Japanese companies	Asian companies	Western companies
(a) Carefully in detail	12	47	72
(b) Loosely	98	85	7

Q2-2: In your company's experience, how do Japanese companies respond to changes in market conditions affecting performance in comparison with foreign companies? (multiple choices)

	Japanese	Asian	Western
(a) Rely more strictly on written contracts	45	62	73
(b) More flexible with regard to written contracts	52	56	26
(c) Helping the other parties in good faith even if it results in a loss to themselves	52	36	3

Q2-3: In your company's experience, how do Japanese companies draft contracts in comparison with Thai companies?

(a) Carefully in detail	0
(b) Loosely	54

According to the answers to these questions, it is clear that Thais view the Japanese to be the least legally minded and the most flexible in drafting, enforcing, and varying contracts, compared with Westerners and other Asians.

How Japanese View the Thai Attitudes

Q3-1: In your company's experience, how do Thai companies draft contracts in comparison with Japanese companies?

(a) Carefully in detail	12
(b) Loosely	31

Q3-2: In your company's experience, how do Thai companies respond to changes in market conditions affecting performance in comparison with Japanese companies?

(a) Rely more strictly on written contracts	9
(b) More flexible	36

Some Japanese view Thais as comparatively more legally minded, both in making written agreements and in enforcing or changing them, but no Thai views the Japanese as more legally minded. When describing themselves, some Japanese corporations indicated that they tend to view themselves as more flexible and not legally minded.

The Reality of the Contents of Contracts

Q4: Which of the following means of dispute resolution does your company's contract with (Japanese/Thai) companies usually include in a written agreement? (multiple answers)

	Japanese	Thai
(a) Courts	18	10
(b) Arbitration Clause	18	6
(c) Good Faith Negotiation Clause	29	29
(d) No Clause for Dispute Resolution	15	87

In spite of the Thai and Japanese perception of their attitudes towards contracts as indicated in previous questions, the reality of the content of contracts shows a different result. Thai companies usually do not have dispute resolution clauses in their contracts. On the other hand, a large percentage of Japanese companies do have clauses specifying dispute resolution methods. Is this a contradiction between perception and reality? Or is there a way of explaining this apparent contradiction? To answer these questions, we required more detailed data. Such data were obtained through interviews.

Japanese "Trust" and the Thai-Chinese Network:
The Case of a Small Electric Appliance Company

One Japanese-Thai joint company that was interviewed produces and trades in small electric appliances. The Thai partner comes from a well-known Thai-Chinese family, and there is one Japanese manager, who represents the Japanese partner. The company sells its products to small or medium-sized wholesalers and retailers, who are usually members of the Thai partner's Thai-Chinese family network. Although it is possible for buyers to change their business partners at any time, their relationships tend to be fairly long-term. They never make any documents other than invoices. The single Japanese manager takes charge of most aspects of the company's everyday operations, such as management of the workers, sales negotiation, and some negotiations concerning disputes. If any serious problems or disputes develop, however, it is usually the Thai partner who deals with them.

We can see two interesting characteristics in this business relationship. The first characteristic is the simple decision-making structure. Although it is a joint company, almost all the power to make everyday decisions is held by the Japanese manager, and the Thai partner takes a role only when it is necessary to negotiate with the Thai-Chinese buyers. The Thai-Chinese buyers are family companies. As a result, their decision-making structure is also relatively simple. This business relationship appears to conform to Rakoff's argument that parties with no need to take complicated organizational patterns of power distribution into account have little need for written contracts.

The other characteristic is the informal social ordering through Thai-Chinese family networks compared with the Japanese way of building trust. Although my data are not sufficient to examine the function and quality of Thai-Chinese networks based on mutual support and trust, I found the Japanese manager's beliefs to be very informative. He is critical of the traditional Japanese way of doing business in which wining, dining, playing golf, and enjoying karaoke with clients are virtually indispensable. Although he attends the occasional funeral or party held by a buyer's family, his efforts are concentrated on improving the quality of his company's products. He believes that the typical Japanese way of doing business does not work well in Thailand. He believes that in Thailand trust can be built up by providing quality products at a good price and by establishing a common sense friendship with buyers. In Thailand, the quality of products and the price (a rational economic dimension) and common sense friendship (a relational dimension) are considered to be indispensable factors in doing business.

In this case, a simple decision-making structure for both the joint company and its buyers, an informal social ordering through Thai-Chinese family networks, and some basic ways of building trust enable the parties to do business with minimal consideration of formal contract law.

During the Asian Financial Crisis, many of the joint company's buyers decided to delay payment or, in some instances, not to pay their debts at all. As is common practice in Japanese companies, the Japanese manager evaluated the situation and decided that most of the buyers were sincere, and he negotiated a repayment plan with them. Some of the buyers went bankrupt, however, and he had to take them to court. The key question is why he decided to take these cases to court.

There was no expectation of resolving the problems or of being repaid because the bankrupt buyers had no resources to make payments. The reason the Japanese manager took the cases to court was simply to satisfy the Japanese parent company. It was necessary to get a court to declare the debtors bankrupt in order to allow the parent company to write off the losses.

In my view, this is the most common reason that Japanese companies take cases to court. For them, the courts are not a forum for resolving their disputes. Rather, they are a means of obtaining documents to pass on to their parent companies and to the tax office.

Rakoff's argument for an organizational influence on contract documents can be equally applied to dispute resolution. In the case of the Japanese-Thai joint company, the need arising from the company's own internal organizational structure is the compelling reason for pursuing debtors in court.

Helping, Fostering, and Constructing Strong Ties:
The Case of the Motor Industry

During the Asian Financial Crisis, the reaction of the motor industry to the problems of parts suppliers was an excellent example of the Japanese attitude towards contractual relations. Most parts suppliers were faced with financial difficulties and some went bankrupt. Toyota and other Japanese car companies got together and discussed ways in which they could help their suppliers. They ultimately decided to buy parts at twice the ordinary price from all suppliers, and most suppliers were able to survive the crisis.

Was this behaviour reasonable from an economic perspective? Viewed in terms of short-term profit, it was absolutely unreasonable behaviour. The motor industry cannot continue to grow without reliable parts suppliers, however. The Japanese motor industry in Thailand is now trying to shift from production of motor vehicles sold exclusively in Thailand to production for export to Oceania. They need suppliers that can meet international standards of quality. It is therefore advantageous, from a long-term point of view, for Japanese car companies to help and foster their suppliers and establish strong family-like ties. I should add that the majority of suppliers in Thailand are Japanese-Thai joint companies.

Even if it was economically reasonable in the long run, the reaction of the car companies to the Asian Financial Crisis was unusual. Japanese companies typically believe in maintaining good relations while simultaneously making a profit. In this case, the written contract was not important. This shows that even a large company such as Toyota does not always require adherence to written agreements. Maintaining good relations is often considered to be much more important than the obligations of a written contract. After all, the contract law system can protect only short-term profits, and insisting on strict adherence to contracts can often destroy relationships, and therefore long-term profits.

From a Japanese point of view, avoiding contract law and the courts can be a reasonable way to preserve good relationships and pursue long-term profits. The expectation that both parties will cooperate to maintain trust is the most essential part of their social relationship.

Rethinking the Role of Contract Law and the Courts: Some Implications

The Circular Construction of Contract Law and Social Dimensions of Contract

In spite of my analysis so far, it is not fair to say that contract law plays no role in the world of Japanese business. Often the legal system cannot directly control social behaviour in the way it intends to. This is because social behaviour is affected by many social and ideological dimensions, not just the legal system. The legal system has both fundamental and indirect roles in shaping social behaviour, however. It provides a base on which other social dimensions are formed.

For example, let us consider the concept of the "equally bound guarantor." This is a scheme where the guarantor has to take over exactly the same responsibility as the original debtor. In Japan, most owners of family companies accept this responsibility on behalf of their company. If the company goes bankrupt, the owner has to cover the losses with his private assets. This scheme forces owners to be very responsible in the way they run their businesses, and it forces them to construct their contractual relations on a basis of personal trust. This is reflected in the Japanese car industry's behaviour of helping, fostering, and building up strong ties with parts suppliers in Thailand in response to the Asian Financial Crisis. In this way, the legal system constitutes a base on which social dimensions of behaviour are formed.

We must remember, however, that other dimensions of social organization shape the legal system itself. The "equally bound guarantor" scheme itself is based on Japanese ideology and the nature of social relationships. In this sense, the relationship between the legal system and other dimensions of social organization has a reflective nature. In trying to understand this point, it is useful to ask to what extent a specified legal scheme influences and constructs a base for everyday social behaviours.[8]

When discussing the function of contract law or its usefulness in a society, we should not focus on its direct effects. We should instead focus on both its indirect and fundamental effects on social dimensions around which contract behaviour takes place. Even if people avoid using contract law in everyday practices, it remains alive.

What Should Courts Do?

Courts should consider the ways in which contracts are used in the real world. If courts continue to use the traditional method of making decisions by applying legal rules to the clauses of a contract, contracting parties will, in most cases, continue to avoid using courts to resolve contractual disputes. Courts often ignore the important social dimensions of disputes. Because of this, court decisions may appear vague, confusing, or even meaningless to parties who are not legally trained (even though the decision may seem transparent and clear to lawyers). A transparent social order cannot be attained by the formalistic application of legal rules. It can be obtained only by considering the social dimensions of contracts and making court decisions understandable to average people. Decisions should be transparent not only to lawyers and judges but also to parties who are engaged in everyday socio-legal practices.

One way to accomplish this objective is to ensure that judges receive information on customs and the nature of relationships in the business community and adjust their decisions accordingly. Obtaining information of this type is very difficult, however, for judges who do not have business experience.

Another way to satisfy this need is to emphasize the process of negotiation even in the courts. In this model, parties bring the social dimensions of disputes to the court, where mediation is offered before normal litigation takes place. This flexible approach can have positive effects.[9]

Whatever devices we invent in the litigation process, the most important thing to remember is that contracts consist of many different social dimensions, and it is necessary for the courts to scrutinize all of them in order to be able to make decisions that are acceptable and useful for the parties to the contract.

NOTES

1 De Certeau points out how local people implicitly reshape an imposed alien system into a different one. See Michel de Certeau, *The Practices of Everyday Life* (Berkeley: University of California Press, 1984).
2 Some early works in legal anthropology made this assumption, *e.g.*, Laura Nader and Duane Metzger, "Conflict Resolution in Two Mexican Communities" (1963) 65 American Anthropologist 584.
3 In Japan, tenants have until recently been given strong protection from eviction by landlords. Landlords must have a just reason to terminate the lease or reject renewal of the contract even at the end of its period, and the just reason has been strictly interpreted in favour of tenants by the courts. This tendency may reflect both the social situation in which there was a shortage of housing after the Second World War, and cultural factors such as weak property rights consciousness.
4 Stewart Macaulay, "Non-Contractual Relations in Business: A Preliminary Study" (1963) 28 American Sociological Review 55.
5 Ian Macneil, "The Many Features of Contracts" (1974) 47 Southern California Law Review 691; Ian Macneil, "Relational Contract: What We Do and Do Not Know" (1985) Wisconsin Law Review 483.
6 Todd Rakoff, "Contract of Adhesion: An Essay in Reconstruction" (1983) 96 Harvard Law Review 1173.
7 Targets for this survey were picked from the companies listed on the Member List of the Japanese Chamber of Commerce.
8 The circular and reflective relationship between law and everyday practice is examined theoretically by critical legal studies and interpretive approach scholars. See, *e.g.*, David Kairys, ed., *The Politics of Law: A Progressive Critique* (New York: Basic Books, 1998), and Austin Sarat and Thomas R. Kearns, eds., *Law in Everyday Life* (Ann Arbor: University of Michigan Press, 1993).
9 The Ontario Mandatory Mediation Program is an example.

NAFTA, Labour Mobility, and Dispute Resolution within a North American Context

KATHRINE RICHARDSON

Signed in 1994, the *North American Free Trade Agreement*[1] (NAFTA) opened the borders between Canada, Mexico, and the United States for a variety of goods, services, investment, government procurement, technical trade, intellectual property, competition policy, and, finally, labour mobility. NAFTA is widely known for liberalizing trade in many of the goods and services that flow within the borders of North America. What is not nearly as well known, however, is that Chapter 16 of NAFTA liberalized the mobility of businesspeople. Chapter 16 deals specifically with the temporary entry of business visitors, investors and traders, intracompany transferees, and professionals. This essay will focus only on the movement of professionals seeking "Treaty NAFTA" (TN) status under Chapter 16. (Canadians, for the most part, are visa exempt when seeking entry into the US.) Despite Chapter 16's low profile, its mobility provisions have been a success and have facilitated the movement of North American professionals back and forth across the continent's borders. In fact, over the past fourteen years, approximately 120,000 Canadians have been admitted into the US as professionals under NAFTA. Since 2005, the number of TN statuses issued to Canadians has been steadily rising (see Figure 1).

NAFTA's labour mobility provisions under the TN category are designed to allow the freer movement of certain categories of professionals without the bureaucratic problems of the H-1B visa, the most common visa issued to foreign professionals working in the US. The purpose of the TN category is

FIGURE 1

Professional worker visas (Treaty NAFTA, or TN, status) issued to Canadians from 1994 to 2008

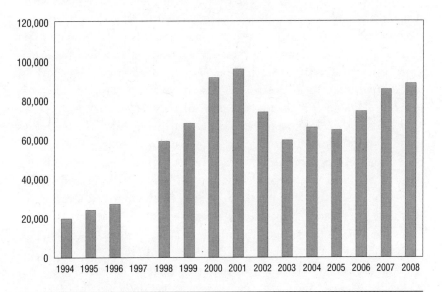

Note: There is no data for 1997.
Source: US Immigration and Naturalization Service and Department of Homeland Security *Yearbook of Immigration Statistics,* various years.

to help create a more fluid North American border for working profession-als. In fact, the category now accommodates sixty-five specific classes of professions, most of which require an undergraduate degree. It offers Can-adian professionals who wish to work in the US four advantages over the H-1B visa. First, the applicant need not file a non-immigration petition with a Department of Homeland Security (DHS) Service Center before entering the US. He or she can present all materials and documentation at the port of entry or preflight inspection station. Second, Canadian TN applicants are not required to obtain approval of a labour condition application from the US Department of Labor, which is mandatory for the H-1B visa. Third, un-like the H-1B visa, the TN status does not impose a maximum period of stay of six years, and TN status may be held indefinitely. Fourth, there is no limit to the number of Canadian nationals who may be admitted into the US in any one year. Currently, the H-1B category imposes a limit of 65,000 new admissions for fiscal year 2010, which began on 1 October 2009.[2] Despite all the perceived gains associated with the TN category, however, the H-1B visa has not been phased out because it is still one of the few temporary US work visas available to foreign nationals who are neither Canadian nor Mexican.

Although the TN category has been a tremendous plus for the North American business community and the mobile North American professional, four professions listed under NAFTA – software engineers, computer systems analysts, management consultants, and scientific technicians – face more obstacles than the other sixty-one listed professions. The way NAFTA was crafted, the rather esoteric job descriptions and nature of the work these professions do, the lack of a professional/institutional organization associated with these four professional categories, and the variety of ways that frontline immigration officials understand and interpret NAFTA at each Canada-US port of entry can lead to a host of problems for firms trying to hire these types of professionals under NAFTA.[3] In fact, the rigid reading of the TN category by DHS officers at ports of entry appears to have become the most significant hazard involved in applying for TN status. In effect, DHS inspecting officers have an unfettered right to deny or approve TN status applications at US ports of entry. As a result, the benefit associated with the TN category – namely, port-of-entry adjudication, which was lauded for its presumed speed, efficiency, and elimination of months of waiting for visa approval – is now becoming its greatest obstacle. Thus, Chapter 16 is an imperfect mechanism for increasing the mobility of North American professionals, and its actual implementation may not necessarily reflect the spirit of facilitation that surrounded its drafting in the early 1990s.

Chapter 16 of NAFTA and Dispute Settlement Mechanisms

Despite the challenges associated with Chapter 16, such as the ones mentioned above, no formal complaint or lawsuit involving Chapter 16 has been settled using NAFTA's formal dispute settlement mechanism found in Chapter 20.[4] Although NAFTA has a highly sophisticated dispute settlement mechanism (Chapters 19 and 20[5]), under which disputes may be argued and settled under NAFTA or World Trade Organization (WTO) provisions, its legitimacy has recently been called into question. This is especially true after the 2006 Canada-US *Softwood Lumber Agreement,* which rules out resorting to Chapter 20 dispute settlement procedures.[6] Nevertheless, within the first decade of NAFTA, the formal dispute resolution mechanism of an arbitral panel (Chapter 20) ruled on Canada's high tariffs on US dairy products. The five-member panel, which included two Americans, all ruled in favour of Canada, concluding that the NAFTA parties intended to exempt from the general obligation under NAFTA to eliminate tariffs Canada's "domestic supply management regime" for certain agricultural products.[7] The same panel also found in favour of Mexico in its dispute with the US over the importation of corn brooms, although it took over a year for the US to comply with this ruling.[8] Thus, NAFTA's dispute resolution mechanism has been shown to work in other circumstances. This, then, begs the question of why it has rarely been used for discrepancies between regimes governing professional labour mobility using the TN status under Chapter 16. The following section will introduce the five key research questions that this essay addresses. All the questions explore why the formal dispute resolution mechanism is avoided in cases involving Chapter 16.

The Research Questions

As mentioned earlier, there have been a number of problems with the implementation of Chapter 16. Despite the option to use the formal dispute settlement procedures found in Chapter 20, to date almost all problems arising under Chapter 16 have been dealt with informally or through "soft dispute resolution." *The key here is that not all of NAFTA's disputes are formal.* In fact, the actual NAFTA document was designed so that there are intergovernmental advisory committees and working groups dedicated to most of the NAFTA chapters. These groups deal with discrepancies and issues so that they do not become large problems. Thus, despite the strong rules surrounding the dispute settlement mechanisms described in Chapters 19 and 20, NAFTA also developed softer "rules" that relied much more heavily on the "norms" of all affected parties. This was done so that the formal rules of dispute settlement could be avoided.

The "rules" and "norms" surrounding these seemingly effective soft dispute resolution procedures provide the background for the first research question: (1) Why are these "soft" dynamics so successful for Chapter 16? The dynamics of rules and norms will also be applied to other parameters associated with "soft dispute resolution" regarding Chapter 16. Thus, the second and third research questions are: (2) How are norms and rules applied to the mechanism and professional culture of the Temporary Entry Working Group (TEWG) dedicated to Chapter 16 of NAFTA? and (3) What is the TEWG's relationship to the actual North American ports of entry where TN status applications are adjudicated? The last two questions will examine the four professions that have difficulties with the TN status: (4) What is the organizational capacity of each of the four professions? and (5) What is the organizational capacity of the industries and firms associated with each of these four professions? All five questions will be analyzed in terms of their contributions towards soft dispute resolution.

These five questions create a very interesting framework for trying to understand trade/labour mobility disputes in a North American context. From a broad Canadian and US perspective, both countries have similar overall cultural norms regarding rules and laws. This may be attributed to British common law, which influenced the legal structures of both countries, and the fact that the US and Canada borrow many laws and policies from each other. For example, much of Chapter 16 was derived directly from the Canada-US *Free Trade Agreement* signed in 1989, which had its origins in US domestic law.[9] Despite the broad similarities of norms and values reflected in laws and policies, however, there is significant variability in the interpretation and understanding of these rules when viewed through the lens of local norms. For the purposes of this study, a solid example of this may be seen in the variability between each Canada-US port of entry in the interpretation of NAFTA Chapter 16 applications. This will be explored at length later in the essay. The focus now turns to the theoretical basis for assessing and understanding the ideas and cultural influences behind norms and rules.

Theoretical Background

Finnemore and Sikkink discuss the relationship between rules and norms in the context of how certain norms at the bureaucratic level influence international politics.[10] Their study spends considerable time defining what norms are, the relationship between domestic and international norms, and whether norms have stability. Although their research is aimed at examining dynamic international issues, such as women's suffrage and the banning of land mines, the authors' topic areas and concepts may be applied to the detailed implementation of a regional trade agreement such as NAFTA. They stress that norms involve a prescriptive (or evaluative) quality of "oughtness" that set norms apart from other kinds of rules.[11] They go on to stress that there are no "bad norms" from the perspective of those promoting the norms. For example, in the eighteenth century, slaveholders and non-slaveholders believed that slavery was an appropriate practice. Without this belief, the institution of slavery would not have been possible.[12] Although norms may be difficult to document empirically, they promote shared moral assessment among participating actors and leave extensive trails of evidence of their influence. In addition, norms are usually found naturally at

FIGURE 2

System of communication and influence that was envisioned for all parties affected by Chapter 16 of NAFTA

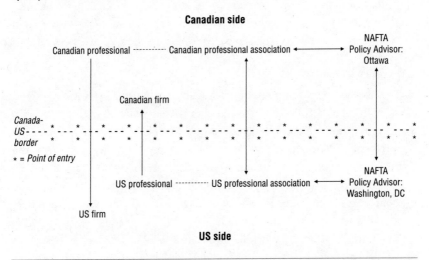

the community or regional level (in this case, the Canadian and US immigration authorities, North American firms and industries using Chapter 16, and domestic professions listed under NAFTA) but not at the international level. Norms also vary between countries in their strength and influence.

The foregoing information about what norms are and where they might be found provides a solid framework for explaining the variability in how NAFTA is interpreted by Canadian and US border officials and the many US ports of entry. Although the actual "rules" of NAFTA have been constructed and approved by each signatory country, there is considerable leeway in the interpretation and implementation of NAFTA's guidelines.[13] How its front-line officials understand and interpret NAFTA applications is up to each country. Thus, domestic norms set the tone for the actual interpretation of NAFTA applications. When NAFTA was created, there was a general idea that North American professions listed under Chapter 16 would meet and help to "harmonize" their needs and standards (usually through agreed-upon norms).[14] NAFTA's drafters (as directed under Chapter 12, which deals with services) envisioned that these professional associations would contribute to the harmonization of a seemingly "chaotic web-like" system of minimum coordination between all signatory regime parties and affected private parties[15] (see Figure 2).

As mentioned earlier, this essay will explore whether or not this strategy was successful, especially for software engineers, computer systems analysts, management consultants, and scientific technicians. The next section will review the methodology used to explore the five research questions.

Methodology

In-depth, quasi-structured interviews regarding Chapter 16 were conducted between 2004 and 2006 with a policy specialist associated with Citizenship and Immigration Canada (CIC) and a policy specialist associated with the Department of Homeland Security (DHS). Two policy specialists with the Canadian Department of Foreign Affairs and International Trade (DFAIT) were also interviewed during this period. The following paragraphs provide the actual questions used and the reasoning behind the content of the questions posed to the policy specialists.

The Temporary Entry Working Group (TEWG) of Chapter 16 is seen as pivotal to the soft dispute resolution mechanism that deals with disputes between parties as they arise. Although the TEWG does not always have a direct impact, the US and Canadian policy advisors who make up the TEWG are considered the main officials who handle the day-to-day issues of Chapter 16 in addition to representing their respective governments' interests at an annual meeting mandated by Chapter 16.[16] Thus, it was important for this study to gain a greater understanding of the actual TEWG and its professional and cultural history, and to comprehend why and how this working group came into being. It was also important to understand the culture within the group and the key factors that enable such an important working group to operate continually at such an informal level. Understanding the professional and personal backgrounds of the people who make up the TEWG helped shed light on the unique character of the group.

The following questions were put to the four policy specialists from the CIC, DFAIT, and DHS:

1 How did this negotiating and decision-making body come into being?
2 Why are the primary representatives of the working group from the policy realm of federal immigration departments rather than from international trade departments?
3 Why is there so much informality over conflict resolution between all parties involved?

4 How would one describe the levels of trust between the representatives of NAFTA signatory countries?
5 Does Mexico have the same level of familiarity and comfort with the US as Canada is perceived to have?
6 What about the professional and educational backgrounds of the members of the working group?

Overall, the primary purpose of Chapter 16 is to permit professional labour mobility so that North American firms may be more competitive, and to reflect national interests within the North American economic and political context. Thus, it is essential for the working group to gain insights from many private business interests into how best to create a trade agreement with a business and professional skills provision that can best serve North American business interests as well as professional labour interests (see Figure 2). In addition, in almost all democratic processes, there is advice, directive, and influence from the many different constituencies and interests that make up a democracy. The following questions help reveal which institutions are most influential in Chapter 16 development, and why. These additional questions were also posed to the three Canadian policy specialists and one US policy specialist:

1 Who (which institutions) were the most influential when NAFTA was originally drafted?
2 Who (which institutions) are most influential as NAFTA is updated (e.g., Canadian Parliament, US Congress, Fortune 500 companies, small high-tech firms, CIC, DHS, American Immigration Lawyers Association, and so on)? Why? How?
3 Who (which institutions) are most influential if a conflict arises under Chapter 16 of NAFTA? Why? How?
4 Who (which institutions) are the least influential in the development of Chapter 16 of NAFTA? Why? How?

The experiences of frontline immigration officials at ports of entry between Seattle and Vancouver, and those of Seattle- and Vancouver-based firms that use the NAFTA status, are drawn from the author's unpublished dissertation, *Sieve or Shield: The Canada-US Border and Labour Mobility under NAFTA and Post 9/11*,[17] and will be applied to this study's findings. From February 2003 through June 2006, interviews were conducted with Canadian and US port-of-entry immigration officials in the new Customs and Border Protection Service (CBPS) under the Department of Homeland Security and the new Canadian Border Services Agency (CBSA). High-tech firms and immigration lawyers located in Seattle and Vancouver were interviewed regarding their experiences with moving high-tech professionals across the Canada-US border under NAFTA.

Research Findings

The interviews revealed some very interesting facts and realities about the dispute resolution mechanism tied to Chapter 16 and why it will most likely never be used to resolve Chapter 16 disputes. This section will provide some answers to the five research questions described above, with particular emphasis on how norms and rules affect these findings.

The Many Avenues for Resolving Chapter 16 Disputes

Although NAFTA has two chapters (Chapters 19 and 20) dedicated entirely to formal dispute settlement, most disputes that fall under NAFTA are never handled formally. As mentioned earlier, NAFTA was designed with intergovernmental advisory committees and working groups that deal with discrepancies and issues on a routine basis so that they do not become larger problems.[18]

From an administrative perspective, Article 1606 covers the dispute settlement mechanism of Chapter 16 and reads as follows:

1. A Party may not initiate proceedings under Article 2007 (Commission Good Offices, Conciliation and Mediation) regarding a refusal to grant temporary entry under this Chapter or a particular case arising under Article 1602 (1) unless (a) the matter involves a pattern of practice; and (b) the business person has exhausted the available administrative remedies regarding the particular matter.

2. The remedies referred to in paragraph (1)(b) shall be deemed to be exhausted if a final determination in the matter has not been issued by the competent authority within one year of the institution of an administrative proceeding, and the failure to issue a determination is not attributable to delay caused by the business person.

The formal rules of Chapter 16 almost create a catch-22 for any aggrieved party wanting to seek formal dispute resolution through Chapter 20. For example, the term "pattern of practice" in Article 1606 means that one or two of the parties must be able to demonstrate that a certain unfair trade practice is occurring at one or more ports of entry when the parties of one country try to enter the country of another party but are not allowed to do so despite the fact that the parties of the first country are following seemingly correct NAFTA guidelines. This is very difficult to prove for firms trying to move new professional employees across the border through TN status, since many of the firms that have difficulties are smaller and are associated with newer industries that are not organized politically, such as information technologies and biotechnologies. In addition, the aggrieved NAFTA applicant, the applicant's firm, or the attorney representing the applicant or the applicant's firm has many different formal avenues for channelling a complaint regarding Chapter 16, and must have exhausted all these channels before being able to seek formal dispute resolution according to Chapter 20.[19]

These formal avenues include: (1) taking the matter up with a supervisor and/or port director at the port of entry where a seemingly unfair ruling on a NAFTA application took place; (2) taking the matter up with the country's regional headquarters (*e.g.*, DHS in Seattle and the CBSA in Vancouver); (3) taking the matter up with the regime's headquarters in Ottawa, Washington, DC, or Mexico City, which usually routes the matter to the TEWG; or (4) taking the matter directly to the departmental minister or commissioner responsible for the implementation and management of Chapter 16 of NAFTA.

Article 1606 mandates that an aggrieved party exhaust all these formal avenues. If the aggrieved party cannot gain entry into another NAFTA country's space within a year, the aggrieved party must file the formal complaint within the same year. If a resolution cannot be found through the four administrative processes, the aggrieved party would have to hire a trade attorney rather than an immigration attorney to represent it, but trade attorneys are very difficult to find.[20] Because the various administrative channels must be sought and exhausted within a year's time, and because a formal complaint needs to be filed by a trade attorney within the same year that all the other administrative channels are exhausted, it seems impossible to get access to the "hard" administrative process found in Chapter 20. Thus, the administrative rules of NAFTA (perhaps inadvertently) direct all disputes regarding Chapter 16 towards softer informal mechanisms, which are subject to very interesting norms. These more informal dispute mechanisms and their norms will be explored in the next three sections.

The Structure and Culture of the Temporary Entry Working Group
This section describes the make-up, mandate, mechanisms, and professional culture of the Temporary Entry Working Group dedicated to Chapter 16,
and the TEWG's relationship to the North American ports of entry where
NAFTA applications are adjudicated. It also attempts to answer the second
and third research questions: "How are norms and rules applied to the
mechanism and professional culture of the TEWG dedicated to Chapter 16
of NAFTA?" and "What is the TEWG's relationship to the actual North
American ports of entry where TN status applications are adjudicated?"

The TEWG has three co-chairs, one from each NAFTA country. The
Canadian co-chair is the Director of Economic and Policy and Programs
Division, Citizenship and Immigration Canada.[21] Officials from other government departments, such as International Trade Canada and Human Resources and Skills Development Canada, play supporting roles. The Mexican
co-chair is the Coordinator for International and Inter-Institutional Relations, National Migration Institute (Instituto Nacional de Migracion, or
INM). Other officials from the INM and the Foreign Relations, Economy,
and Public Education secretariats and ministries play supporting roles. The
US co-chair is the Special Policy Advisor, Border and Transportation Security Policy, International Affairs, Department of Homeland Security, and
other officials come from the DHS, the Office of the United States Trade
Representative, and the Departments of Labor and Commerce.

The TEWG is mandated by NAFTA Article 1605 to meet once a year,
usually in the fall. The three governments take turns hosting the meeting,
which discusses issues pertaining to the implementation, administration,
and modification of Chapter 16.[22] Any outcomes from the annual meeting
are documented in "interpretive notes." If immigration officers in the field
(*e.g.*, at ports of entry) need to be informed about a TEWG decision or policy
change, they are sent specific administrative instructions, and immigration
manuals are updated. TEWG decisions sometimes do not result in policy
changes, however, especially immediate ones. In fact, some TEWG decisions are actually "proposals" or "recommendations" that must be sent to
the Free Trade Commission (FTC) for approval. (See Figure 3 for a diagram
of the chain of command regarding changes to NAFTA.) Even after FTC
approval, other ratification or approval processes may be required (*e.g.*, by
the US Congress) before a change in NAFTA becomes official. There is also
tension between obligations under Chapter 16 and each party's general provisions regarding temporary entry, where rules and norms equally influence
the nature of the dialogue and outcomes.

FIGURE 3

Chain of command regarding changes to NAFTA from a Canadian perspective

Trade Minister or Free Trade Commissioner
↓
Trade Deputy Minister
↓
Assistant Deputy Minister for International Trade
↓
NAFTA Coordinator/Director General
↓
Committees – Subcommittees – Working groups
↓
NAFTA (22 chapters and two side arguments)

Unlike the European Commission, which issues directives to its members and ensures that all member countries implement the European Union's directives and policies uniformly, NAFTA only sets out obligations for each signatory country. It is up to each country to interpret these obligations and mandates without an overseeing body such as the European Commission.[23] The general obligations of Article 1602 of NAFTA are so broad that there is much room for interpretation by the parties involved with Chapter 16 (see Figure 1). This is why norms have such an impact on this trade agreement.

Section 2 of Article 1602 states:

1. The Parties shall endeavor to develop and adopt common criteria, definitions and interpretations for the implementation of this Chapter.

This is a very broad directive that provides little guidance for the process of policy development and implementation. In fact, it is up to representatives (usually the TEWG) of each NAFTA country to work together and "develop and adopt common criteria, definitions, and interpretations for the implementation of this Chapter." At the same time, the parties must also ensure that these NAFTA interpretations do not conflict with domestic policies.[24] Each signatory country has very different interests and priorities concerning the mobility of international business professionals and executives, and this is reflected in the process of developing interpretations of NAFTA.

For example, the key Canadian senior policy advisor for Chapter 16 has a much broader mandate than his or her US counterpart when it comes to allowing foreign professionals into Canada (especially Americans). This may be attributed to Canada's relatively permissive stance towards immigration, which includes giving foreign professionals the right to long-term work and eventual immigration into Canada.[25] On the other hand, the key US senior policy advisor is hemmed in by many checks and balances if any portion of Chapter 16 is to be modified.[26] For example, the US International Trade Commission must notify the Congress if any formal changes to Chapter 16 are being considered. These proposed changes must then be placed in the Federal Register and be subject to public comment for a certain period (usually sixty days). Various congressional committees must also be notified if modifications to Chapter 16 are proposed. The final step on the US side is actual ratification of these formal changes by the Senate.

The Mexican experience with Chapter 16 has been characterized by trepidation. A key reason for Mexico's reluctance to discuss further development of Chapter 16 is that Mexico is nowhere near US and Canadian levels of economic development, especially when it comes to exporting professional labour. Thus, when something is negotiated, the Mexicans never know whether it will help or hinder their position in the future. Similar to the US, Mexican representatives must seek approval from the Mexican Senate when new professional categories are added to Chapter 16, and the Mexican Senate does not move quickly on issues having to do with NAFTA.[27] One possible reason for this is that Mexico believes that the agricultural component of NAFTA favours the US, and one way that the Mexicans can retaliate indirectly is by slowing down other components of NAFTA's development, such as Chapter 16. For example, between the US's checks and balances and Mexico's seemingly deliberate slowness, the formal process of adding two additional professional categories ("actuary" and "plant pathologist") took over seven years.[28] Thus, the formal rules and processes found within the domestic realm of both the US and Mexico compensate for the lack of clear rules and directives in Section 2 of Article 1602 regarding the formal process of implementation and continued development of Chapter 16. These domestic precautions have, in some ways, encouraged professionals who work on NAFTA to use other available avenues if matters need to be dealt with quickly.

For negotiating Chapter 16, such avenues include direct discussions and negotiations within the TEWG. The TEWG meets formally each year to discuss a range of issues regarding Chapter 16, and problems that arise may be discussed at this time. Alternatively, the matter may be discussed informally by e-mail between the members of the TEWG, and the problem may be resolved without being made a formal meeting item. The ability to discuss matters – such as consistent port-of-entry adjudications, types of professions to be considered under NAFTA, or general statistical records – so informally rests heavily on the policy advisors' sense of professional trust and familiarity with one another. In addition, both Canadian and American policy advisors have a certain level of comfort with NAFTA, know its limitations, and appear to be comfortable with its lack of solid rules of process. It is here that the norms of the TEWG come into play. At the time the interviews were conducted in 2005, both policy advisors had represented their respective governments on Chapter 16 for over five years and were comfortable enough with each other that many matters could be resolved informally through e-mail. This enabled them to proceed through their annual formal meeting with all decisions based on consensus.

The Mexican representative on the TEWG is seen as somewhat new, however, having been on the TEWG for approximately only three years when the interviews were conducted. As mentioned earlier, many of the issues involving Chapter 16 do not really apply to Mexico's situation. In fact, Mexico has repeatedly wanted to add paraprofessionals to NAFTA's list rather than building the existing list of professionals.[29] In addition, the Mexican representative frequently wants to discuss refugees, statistics, and low-skilled workers, which do not fit under the umbrella of NAFTA. The US representative frequently has to have one-on-one in-depth discussions with the Mexican representative about matters related to security along the US-Mexico border, which detract from matters that deal directly with Chapter 16 of NAFTA. Such matters are bilateral issues between the US and Mexico rather than trilateral issues involving Canada.[30] Thus, much of the TEWG's business does not necessarily reflect similar levels of economic development or norms. This "awkwardness" was anticipated during the inception of NAFTA in the early 1990s, however, and is considered an example of growing pains within the larger trade document.[31]

In short, the Canadian and US policy advisors have a very strong and committed professional relationship and have resolved many concerns and discrepancies over Chapter 16 either informally through general e-mails or at the TEWG's annual meeting, which usually results in a memorandum of understanding (MOU) that is then disseminated to all ports of entry that adjudicate TN status applications. Despite their shared norms, however, the actual interpretation of these MOUs and of the NAFTA document itself varies considerably between Canada and the US and among US ports of entry, as we shall see next.

NAFTA TN Status Temporary Entry Adjudications at Ports of Entry
NAFTA sets up provisions and it is the responsibility of each country to interpret them. This means that three different national systems interpret and adjudicate NAFTA, unlike the case of EU provisions on labour mobility and border security, where each signatory country must follow the same system of interpretation and adjudication designed by the EU. Despite differences in the domestic culture of each country, the TEWG has a strong cultural norm of professional understanding and communication, especially between Canada and the US, resulting in the resolution of many problems by e-mail or a formal memorandum of understanding (MOU). In contrast to these apparently similar norms within the TEWG, the actual culture and norms at the different ports of entry vary considerably. This can result in varying interpretations of the NAFTA document and of MOUs. This section will examine this phenomenon in greater detail and continue to explore the third research question: What is the TEWG's relationship to the actual North American ports of entry where TN status applications are adjudicated?

TN Status Adjudications
The actual TN status adjudications between US ports of entry are somewhat erratic, especially with NAFTA professions that do not have official licensing obligations or where the degree and the job title are not a direct match.[32] Thus, the professional jobs of management consultants, computer engineers, computer analysts, and scientific technicians listed under NAFTA sometimes run into controversy at US ports of entry. This pattern of behaviour has led to "port shopping," where an attorney advises his or her client regarding which ports of entry to use or avoid based on the "port culture" – the way the port of entry interprets NAFTA. Historically, this port culture has been based on each port director's attitude towards NAFTA, and whether the port director interprets NAFTA in a "restrictive" or "facilitative" manner.[33] Thus, despite the direct rules of NAFTA, the actual interpretations at ports of entry are subject to local norms of attitude and understanding of the port directors.

Canadian ports of entry are not susceptible to port shopping for various reasons. First, Canada has a comparatively "facilitative" spirit towards NAFTA and the entry of foreign professionals and executives into its regime; it does not see the entry of foreign professionals as a threat to the jobs of Canadians.[34] There is also a much clearer and more open chain of communication and feedback between ports of entry and headquarters than in the US system. In fact, Canadian port-of-entry immigration officers have always had ongoing training regarding NAFTA, which is something that is just being implemented in the US.

Modes of Communication
The modes of communication between ports of entry and headquarters vary considerably between the US and Canada. The US experience was seen as very "top down" by interviewees: directives would be sent from headquarters, but there was very little encouragement for frontline officers who adjudicate TN status applications to relay information back to headquarters. Communication within actual ports of entry was considered very strong, with on-the-job training and, at the beginning of NAFTA implementation, the placement of officers at key urban US ports of entry who provided professional advice to staff on NAFTA. By 1999, however, these NAFTA officers had ceased to play a key role at ports of entry, and information regarding NAFTA policies and updates apparently became more inconsistent between different ports of entry, which also contributed to port shopping.[35] Since the creation of the Department of Homeland Security in November 2002, there has been a more deliberate effort to disseminate and correctly implement policy updates and MOUs originating from headquarters. Even before the Immigration and Naturalization Service (INS) was absorbed by the DHS in March 2003, it was making deliberate and conscious efforts to rein in ports of entry and have them follow directives and instructions from headquarters in Washington, DC. These efforts were clearly demonstrated in a one-page memorandum from former INS Commissioner James Ziglar to all regional and district directors, entitled "Zero Tolerance Policy":[36]

> Effective immediately, I am implementing a zero tolerance policy with regards to INS employees who fail to abide by Headquarters-issued policy and field instructions. I would like to make it clear that disregarding field guidance or other INS policy will not be tolerated. The days of looking the other way are over ... It is also imperative that each employee review and understand issued field guidance. Each supervisor is to ensure that each employee has not only read the field guidance, but that they are also implementing the guidance. Individuals who fail to abide by issued field guidance or other INS policy will be disciplined appropriately.

The memo was eventually rescinded, apparently because of its strong tone, but it showed clear awareness of the problem of disregard for policy and formal training manuals in the field. Subsequent efforts to better educate US immigration field personnel have had mixed results. A year and a half later, in October 2003, a well-regarded US immigration attorney in Seattle who was interviewed by the author reported that there was still considerable variability between US ports of entry, even under the auspices of the new Department of Homeland Security.[37] This will be explored in greater detail below, in the subsections "Training and Education" and "Powers of Port-of-Entry Officers and the General Public's Impressions of Them."

The Canadian experience may be described as an iterative and deliberate one with regard to the adjudications of TN status applications at ports of entry. If an issue arose at a port of entry, there was a set chain of communication to be followed, from the port of entry to its regional office, and thence to Citizenship and Immigration Canada and Canadian Border Services Agency headquarters, where the issue was discussed and a determination was usually made in the form of a memo. The memo was then sent back to all regional offices and ports of entry in order to update frontline officers on how an issue should be handled. Perhaps most impressive is the fact that frontline Canadian immigration officers knew that this system was in place and were very comfortable using it and explaining it to the author in detail.[38]

Training and Education

Before being absorbed by the US Department of Homeland Security in March 2003, the former Immigration and Naturalization Service placed more emphasis on on-the-job training and formal training of selected Free Trade Officers at ports of entry rather than the entire staff. Thus, frontline immigration officers received a limited amount of formal training on the interpretation of NAFTA applications and relied on the expertise of the Free Trade Officers in addition to other more senior port-of-entry immigration officers. Port-of-entry immigration officers also had the American *NAFTA Handbook,* the NAFTA document itself, and the State Department website as points of reference when interpreting NAFTA applications. From the time that the INS was absorbed by the DHS in March 2003, there has been a very different approach to training and education. Now, all DHS personnel are in a constant state of formal training, with mandatory requirements and topic areas that must be completed by certain dates.[39] With this new approach, all port-of-entry officers are much more likely to have been given the same information regarding NAFTA interpretation. This may contribute to a decrease in port shopping over time, but this remains to be seen.

Historically, many port-of-entry officers spent some time in the US military before joining the INS.[40] In some way, this prior work experience may contribute to the "paramilitary" culture still encountered by many people seeking entry into the US. Since the inception of the DHS, however, there has been an effort to draw more broadly from the local community in an attempt to hire officers with very diverse backgrounds who can speak languages other than English and Spanish, and who have experience with and insights into other cultures that the more traditional DHS officer does not have. The US Customs and Border Protection Area Port Director, Vancouver International Airport, stated in our interview:[41]

> We [the US government] are an equal opportunity employer. Positions within the [DHS] Customs and Border Protection Service are open to men and women ... [In order to qualify], a person must be able to carry a firearm and meet the physical endurance tests. We look forward to having a diverse staff not only adding women to the staff, but also representatives of the community. It is very helpful in this job for people who can speak different languages. We are very diverse and proud of that. All federal services have a component for military preference. I am a veteran. I do get extra points for being a veteran. However, one must meet the qualifying criteria before the veteran points are applied ... The airlines hire professional translators. However, [due to our diversity] we are able to use our own employees [as translators]. For example, the young lady that we walked past on our way to my office was born in Thailand, so she speaks Cambodian and Thai, so there are definite benefits to having a staff that speak many languages. For example, our staff can monitor what is being said between the translator working for the airline and the passenger being questioned. They can monitor the questions being asked and the answers being said. We found in L.A. that the [airline] translators were changing the people's answers, or telling the people, "I'm going to say that you said this." Not knowing that our employees spoke the language. You should see their faces when they find out that we can understand what they are saying!

Training and formal education are also key to how Canadian port-of-entry officers understood and adjudicated NAFTA applications. Canadian officers have sixteen hours of mandatory training annually, and interoffice memos keep them updated on Chapter 16 and related matters. They can also refer to a Canadian version of the *NAFTA Handbook* and to the NAFTA document itself. Most port-of-entry officers have at least some post-secondary education, and many have four-year university degrees. Unlike in the US, there is no strong connection to the Canadian military in the form of a hiring preference.[42] Citizenship and Immigration Canada has long had a commitment to hiring a diverse and representative staff who can speak a wide variety of languages and who have considerable experience with other cultures. This is something that the DHS is just beginning to do.

Thus, Canada and the US have followed different approaches when it comes to training their port-of-entry officers on the specifics of NAFTA. The Canadian side has tended to rely on a more rules-based approach to education, with a mandated systematic approach going from headquarters to each port of entry and thence to each port-of-entry officer. Historically, the US side has relied more on a rules and norms approach, with only a select few Free Trade Officers being formally trained on NAFTA (rules approach) and then conducting on-the-job training for regular port-of-entry officers (norms approach). Since the inception of the DHS, however, the US system of training has become more similar to the Canadian (strong rules approach), with a more formal and mandated approach to training, directives coming straight from headquarters, and all port-of-entry officers being trained by a certain date. In addition, the DHS's current emphasis on diversity in hiring is one that has characterized the Canadian approach for many years.

Powers of Port-of-Entry Officers and the General Public's Impressions of Them

The powers of US port-of-entry immigration officers have expanded considerably in the past ten years. Beginning in 1996 under the *Illegal Immigration Reform and Immigrant Responsibility Act* (IIRIRA),[43] the rights of non-citizens and non-permanent residents living in the US have eroded considerably. For example, under the IIRIRA, they no longer have access to many of the due process rights under the US *Bill of Rights*.[44] In fact, persons belonging to these two groups may be subject to expedited removal proceedings (including being barred from entering the US for up to five years) if their intent of entry is deemed fraudulent by the port-of-entry officer.[45] Zisman summarizes some of the IIRIRA's key features directed at managing the Canada-US border:[46]

The powers to search are unbound by warrant when a person is seeking admission into the United States. The power to arrest is based on the inspector's "reason to believe that the alien so arrested is in the United States in violation of any such law" ... and can also do so within a reasonable distance from "any external boundary of the United States ... and within a distance of twenty five miles from any such external boundary to have access to private lands."

In addition, since August 2003, US immigration attorneys have been barred from accompanying their clients to ports of entry unless the person seeking entry is the subject of a criminal investigation.[47] Even though US law had technically not allowed attorneys to accompany their clients to ports of entry, the usual practice had been to allow a person's attorney access to the port of entry at the time the person sought entry into the US under NAFTA. Thus, after the terrorist attacks of 11 September 2001, US ports of entry have taken a much stronger approach towards upholding new laws and rules, which are seen as stricter in many instances. Finally, the *USA PATRIOT Act*[48] passed in 2001 applies not only to foreigners but also to US citizens.

Thus, port-of-entry DHS officers have enormous power over persons seeking entry, and also over all people and property within a twenty-five mile zone from the Canada-US border. These measures may be considered somewhat draconian, and at the time of writing of this essay in 2006, there are efforts to create greater checks and balances within the DHS at the ports of entry, and to reinstate more individual rights of persons in response to the *USA PATRIOT Act*. In an era when DHS officers are gaining more rights and powers, they are also mandated to complete "professionalism training." This includes approximately eight hours of instruction on how to conduct oneself even in the most difficult of situations. In addition to the "constant state of training" of DHS officers, "professionalism training" was mandated directly by former DHS Secretary Tom Ridge. This mandate was developed in response to officers' alleged meanspiritedness and attitude of general disrespect towards members of the general public who sought entry into the US.[49] Despite this effort to instill a sense of professionalism in all DHS employees, the department's reputation of being disrespectful and aggressive towards people seeking entry into the US will take considerable time to change. Somewhere between stricter laws and mandates (rules) and professionalism training (prescribed norms) rests the attitudes and aptitudes for adjudicating and administering TN status applications. Historically, US port-of-entry officials have been seen as somewhat restrictive when it comes to adjudicating such applications, but more education, clearer directives from headquarters, and professionalism training may help inculcate into them a new, more progressive attitude towards NAFTA.

The Canadian experience regarding powers and the public's impressions of port-of-entry officers is nowhere near as dramatic or as turbulent as that of the US. Canadian port-of-entry officers have always had many powers and rights over persons seeking entry into Canada, but the *Canadian Charter of Rights and Freedoms*[50] applies to all people at ports of entry regardless of their citizenship. This gives non-Canadian citizens certain due process rights, but Canadian port-of-entry officers have had the right of expedited removal before the US granted this right to its officers in the IIRIRA. In addition, Canadian officers are much less tolerant of non-Canadian citizens who have committed legal offences. For example, the Canadian government has no tolerance for non-citizens who have been convicted of driving a car under the influence of alcohol, assaulting another person, or other legal violations, which are deemed permissible under US law for foreigners seeking entry into that country. Thus, the seemingly permissive and non-aggressive Canadian officers have actually had in place much stricter laws and less tolerance of foreigners longer than their American counterparts. Before starting work in the field, however, all CIC and CBSA officers must sign a code of conduct stating that they will be professional and treat everyone with dignity and respect no matter what the situation.[51] This measure has been in effect for the past twenty years and is something that the US is only just beginning to emulate with its professionalism training.

The foregoing should help dispel some of the myths surrounding the laws (rules) and cultures (norms) at US and Canadian ports of entry. Overall, the US is becoming more like Canada in its tougher stance towards foreigners who may be deemed inadmissible. (It is interesting to note that it was not until 1982, when the *Charter* was ratified, that all people on Canadian soil were ensured certain rights that the state must respect; in contrast, beginning with the Bill of Rights in 1789 through the 1960s, with the US Supreme Court expanding the protection of individuals accused of criminal acts, especially in the areas of confessions (*Miranda v. Arizona*), search and seizure (*Mapp v. Ohio*), and the right to an attorney (*Gideon v. Wainwright*),[52] all people on American soil are ensured individual civil liberties that the state must respect. The Americans are also only just beginning to recognize the importance of incorporating professionalism into port-of-entry culture, whereas this concept has been a pillar of Canadian officer training for over twenty years.[53] In summary, the US and Canada are converging in many laws/rules and cultural norms surrounding management and communication at ports of entry. Table 1 summarizes many of the differences and similarities between Canada and the US in this regard.

TABLE 1

Comparison between Canadian and American characteristics with regard to attributes that contribute to different norms

Attribute	Canadian	American
NAFTA adjudication	Seemingly consistent from port to port	• Varies from port to port (based on "port culture")
Mode of communication of problems/issues	Iterative and deliberate	• Top-down and seemingly inconsistent; more deliberate post 9/11
Training	Mandatory 16 hours annually	• 8 hours in academy on on-the-job training • "Constant" state of training post 9/11
Education	Majority have 4 years of college or more	• Majority have 2 years of college or less • Military hiring preference • More culturally diverse and educated post 9/11
Powers of frontline immigration officers	Wide range of right on behalf of the sovereign, more so than American officers	• Wide range of rights but less than Canadian officers • Individuals (citizens and foreigners) also have rights • Creation of Department of Homeland Security with heavy and deliberate "security" focus post 9/11 • Foreigners have fewer rights since 1996 under the IIRIRA.
General impression of immigration officers	Perceived as "facilitative" towards NAFTA	• Perceived as "militaristic" and "restrictive" towards NAFTA and disrespectful towards TN status applicants

To answer the last two research questions, we turn now to the question of how firms and professionals that use the TN status negotiate their needs within the complex NAFTA web (Figure 2), and how both groups fit into this web of interactions across the Canada-US border.

Impacts and Influences on Stakeholders

When NAFTA was drafted in the early 1990s, it was understood that the various professions and their associations would help mould the agreement (as described in Article 1210).[54] For professions that had viable and active associations or licensing requirements, this has worked reasonably well, with regard to both being placed on or taken off the list.[55] This system has not worked as effectively for professions that are not licensed or that do not have active national associations that can represent their concerns. This section will explore the last two research questions: "What is the organizational capacity of each of the four professions that have difficulties with the Treaty NAFTA status?" and "What is the organizational capacity of the industries and firms associated with each of these four professions?"

The inability to form coherent and credible professional associations is a major reason that software engineers, computer systems analysts, management consultants, and scientific technicians all have so many challenges when negotiating their way through US ports of entry. Besides not being licensed, all of these professions, except for management consultants, are new professions that have been in existence for approximately only thirty years. The combination of not being licensed, not having a strong national professional association, and the general newness of the type of work compounds the problem of not being able to effectively explain to the TEWG, which has considerable powers under Chapter 16, the type of work that these professionals do. In addition, the lack of tangible licences or certifications makes it extremely difficult for these four types of professionals at the actual ports of entry, where officers favour official documentation in the form of degrees, licences, certifications, and so forth. The lack of institutional clout places these people in a difficult position, since there are few organizational channels for negotiating within the NAFTA web (see Figure 4). In fact, the firms hiring such professionals must perform most of the lobbying and communications on their behalf, which was not envisioned in the original NAFTA web.

By default, North American firms are responsible for mediation and negotiation when it comes to addressing difficult entries under NAFTA and dealing with the TEWG.[56] This places an incredible burden on these firms for various reasons. First, many firms that hire people in these newer professions are fledgling firms in the high-tech or biotechnology industries. These firms do not have the staff or the political acumen, usually executed through lobbying efforts, to articulate their problems to the TEWG and to politicians. Larger firms that have these same problems with NAFTA at ports of entry have vast resources that include experienced human resources personnel, access to in-house and specialized immigration attorneys, and their own lobbyists. The power differential between these small and large firms has resulted, to some degree, in port-of-entry officers' being much more familiar with the larger firms. As a result, they are usually more comfortable issuing TN statuses to applicants associated with larger firms rather than smaller firms.[57]

This has placed smaller North American firms in a difficult position with regard to NAFTA. Smaller high-tech and biotech firms often, as a matter of survival, must be able to hire and move employees around North America and throughout the world upon firm inception.[58] This is a tall order for new firms, especially those that are rich in ideas but poor in financial resources. This predicament has forced many small firms to initially forgo hiring attorneys who could provide professional expertise regarding the preparation of TN status applications. Since 2001, however, many smaller firms have had to hire immigration attorneys to help with the preparation of such applications, since the climate at ports of entry is much more restrictive than prior to 9/11. Although originally not envisioned in the Chapter 16 "grass-roots" web (see Figure 2), attorneys are playing a greater and greater role in moulding and refining the details of Chapter 16 for both small and large firms. The drafters of NAFTA envisioned the attainment of some sort of "harmonization" in the implementation of NAFTA,[59] but did not anticipate that immigration lawyers would play such a central role in this harmonization. (See Figure 4 for a more accurate representation of the current weblike structure for Chapter 16.) By default, immigration attorneys are providing the political input that was envisioned for professional associations and firms. From a policy development perspective, however, the persons interviewed for this study stressed that some of these immigration attorneys have not been able to offer the innovative ideas and vision required to guide the continued development of Chapter 16 of NAFTA.[60]

Conclusion

Despite variations between different US ports of entry and between the characteristics of Canadian and American personnel at such ports, disputes

FIGURE 4

The real-world system of communication and influence under Chapter 16 of NAFTA

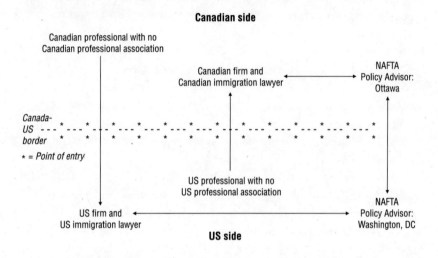

related to Chapter 16 have been settled over the past fourteen years without recourse to NAFTA's formal dispute settlement mechanisms (found in Chapter 20). This may be attributed in large part to the structural difficulties of actually meeting the requirements for Chapter 20, the well thought out structure of the Temporary Entry Working Group, the fact that the TEWG's members appear dedicated to making Chapter 16 a smooth-running component of NAFTA in an effort to avoid formal controversy, and the fact that much of the TEWG operates under similar norms. On the other hand, the ports of entry (especially in the US) do not have the same norms. They need rules to follow, otherwise they resort to local norms, which historically have varied considerably from port to port. Since 9/11, however, the US has been following the Canadian example of mandatory and constant training in addition to the devolution of powers and authority to port directors and port-of-entry officers. Many of these powers used to be held by district directors. Ideally, the mandates regarding education will act as a counterweight to the increasing powers that DHS port-of-entry officers have over both foreigners and citizens who are seeking entry into the US. Strong state powers coupled with mandated constant education has worked well for Canadian port-of-entry officers, who maintain the security of Canada's borders yet are seldom seen as intimidating or aggressive.

Another factor that accounts for the non-use of formal dispute resolution in connection with Chapter 16 is the lack of organization among smaller high-tech firms, both politically and legally. Also, many of the professionals listed under Chapter 16 of NAFTA are not officially licensed in North America, despite directives found in Chapter 12, and so do not have an organizational body to articulate their complaints and recommendations for improvement. By default, immigration lawyers are filling this void, which was not intended in the original structure of NAFTA. Figure 4 provides a more realistic depiction of the realities of Chapter 16, especially for smaller high-tech and biotech firms that must operate in the global economy right from the start. Such firms do not have the financial resources or professional expertise to negotiate the complexities of international borders or to lobby the policy officials who develop and guide much of Chapter 16's continued development.

A major challenge for these firms and for their nascent industrial associations is to develop connections and relationships with these key policy officials, as well as to become familiar with local ports of entry and the officers who staff them. These direct relationships between the firms and policy makers and adjudicators will help alleviate the burden of immigration lawyers who are constantly acting as go-betweens.

NOTES

1 *North American Free Trade Agreement between the Government of Canada, the Government of Mexico and the Government of the United States,* 17 December 1992, Can. T.S. 1994 No. 2, 32 I.L.M. 289 (entered into force 1 January 1994) [NAFTA].
2 Besides the main cap of 65,000 H-1B visas, an additional 20,000 H-1B visas are available to only those foreign nationals who have obtained an advanced degree from a US university or other US academic institution. US universities, university-affiliated nonprofits, and nonprofit or governmental research organizations are exempt from these H-1B caps. These employers must file H-1B petitions, but their petitions can be filed at any time.
3 Although art. 1210 of NAFTA governs licensing and certification of service providers, under Chapter 12 (governing trade in services), these four professions listed under Chapter 16 do not have professional licences or certifications and are not governed by professional bodies or associations. See J. Vázquez-Azpiri, "Through the Eye of a Needle: Canadian Information Technology Professionals and the TN Category of the NAFTA" (2000) 77 Interpreter Releases 805.
4 Interview with James Vázquez-Azpiri, Attorney at Law, Cooley Goodward LLP, San Francisco (21 October 2003). It should be noted that Canada and Mexico lodged a complaint under Chapter 20 when the US restricted entry of Canadian and Mexican persons who traffic in Cuban confiscated goods under the 1996 *Cuban Liberty and*

Democratic Solidarity (Libertad) Act of 1996 (*Helms-Burton Act*), Pub. L. No. 104-114, [1996] 110 Stat. 785. The US maintained that such restraints are exempt as national security measures, whereas Canada and Mexico argued that they directly contravened the temporary entry rights enshrined in Chapter 16. The complaint never went to arbitration, only because then President Clinton suspended application of the *Helms-Burton Act* in pursuit of an intergovernmental agreement on trade with Cuba. See Ralph H. Folsom, *NAFTA in a Nutshell* (St. Paul, MN: West Group, 1999). Canada and Mexico eventually did not challenge *Helms-Burton* within the framework of NAFTA. See Kristopher Moore, "Cuba in the Wake of NAFTA" (2004) 8 Revista Mexicana de Estudios Canadianses 145 at 151, online: Redalyc <http://redalyc.uaemex.mx/src/inicio/ArtPdfRed.jsp?iCve=73900808>.

5 Chapter 19 deals primarily with anti-dumping and countervailing duties. Chapter 20 creates general dispute settlement procedures and is seen as an alternative to the *General Agreement on Tariffs and Trade* (GATT).

6 Stephen Clarkson, *Does North America Exist? Governing the Continent after NAFTA and 9/11* (Toronto: University of Toronto Press, 2008).

7 D. Lopez, "Dispute Resolution under NAFTA: Lessons from the Early Experience" (1997) 21 Texas International Law Journal 166.

8 David A. Gantz, "The United States and NAFTA Dispute Settlement: Ambivalence, Frustration and Occasional Defiance" in Cesare Romano, ed., *The Sword and the Scales: The United States and International Courts and Tribunals*, Arizona Legal Studies Discussion Paper No. 06-26 (2009) 356, online: Social Science Research Network <http://ssrn.com/abstract=918542>.

9 Paul Henry (Trade Policy Advisor, Economic Policy and Programs Division, Citizenship and Immigration Canada), "The Two Way Influence of National Policy Measures and International Trade Agreements" (Paper presented at the Migration and International Trade Investment: North American Experience and Policy Development, International Metropolis Conference, Vienna, 15-19 September 2003).

10 Martha Finnemore and Kathryn Sikkink, "International Norm Dynamics and Political Change" (2005) 52 International Organization 887.

11 *Ibid.* at 891.

12 *Ibid.*

13 It is unlike the EU model, which puts national governments in a vertical relationship with an international body but in a horizontal relationship with each of the other signatory regimes. See J.S. McKennirey, "Labour in the International Economy" (1996) 22 Canada–United States Law Journal 183 at 191.

14 Noemi Gal-Or, "Labour Mobility under NAFTA: Regulatory Policy Spearheading the Social Supplement to the International Trade Regime" (1998) 15 Arizona Journal of International and Comparative Law 374; James McIlory, "NAFTA Cross-Border Provision of Services" (1996) 22 Canada–United States Law Journal 203 at 204.

15 Gal-Or, *ibid.* at 412.

16 Article 1605, NAFTA, *supra* note 1 at 605.

17 Kathrine Richardson, *Sieve or Shield: The Canada-US Border and Labour Mobility under NAFTA and Post 9/11* (PhD dissertation, Department of Geography, University of British Columbia, 2006) [unpublished].

18 Folsom, *supra* note 4.
19 Interview with Policy Specialist C-1, Citizenship and Immigration Canada (19-21 October 2004).
20 *Ibid.*
21 The information provided in this paragraph is based on an e-mail conversation and interview with Policy Specialist C-1, Citizenship and Immigration Canada (11 June 2004).
22 It also discusses possible measures to increase facilitated liberal temporary entry of businesspeople.
23 Chapter 16 of NAFTA, *supra* note 1.
24 *Ibid.*
25 K. Richardson, R. Florida, and K. Stolarick, "Locating for Potential: An Empirical Study of Company X's Development Centre in Vancouver, British Columbia" (Paper presented at the twelfth Uddevalla Symposium, Bari, Italy, 13 June 2009); J. Biles, E. Tolley, and H. Ibrahim, "Does Canada Have a Multicultural Future?" (2005) 4 Canadian Diversity 23.
26 NAFTA, *supra* note 1.
27 Interview with Policy Specialist US-1, Department of Homeland Security (22 January 2005).
28 Formal talks on adding these two professions to NAFTA's listing of sixty-three professional categories began in 1998. The professions were not formally adopted under NAFTA until July 2004.
29 Policy Specialist US-1, *supra* note 27.
30 Policy Specialist C-1, *supra* note 19.
31 McKennirey, *supra* note 13.
32 Vázquez-Azpiri, *supra* note 3.
33 Richardson, *supra* note 17.
34 *Ibid.;* Gal-Or, *supra* note 14.
35 G. Boos and R. Pauw, "Reasserting the Right to Representation in Immigration Matters Arising at Ports of Entry" (2004) 9 Bender's Immigration Bulletin 385.
36 Internal Memorandum from James Ziglar, former Immigration and Naturalization Service Commissioner, to all US INS Regional [and] District Directors, "Zero Tolerance Policy" (March 2002).
37 Richardson, *supra* note 17.
38 *Ibid.*
39 *Ibid.*
40 *Ibid.*
41 Interview with US DHS Customs and Border Protection Area Port Director, Vancouver International Airport (28 October 2004).
42 Richardson, *supra* note 17.
43 *Illegal Immigration Reform and Immigrant Responsibility Act of 1996,* Pub. L. No. 104-208, Div. C, [1996] 110 Stat. 3009-546 [IIRIRA].
44 See R. Zisman, "The 4th Amendment and Your Laptop" (Paper presented at the American Immigration Lawyers Association Continuing Legal Education Conference, Montreal, 7 September 2007), for a discussion of the "international border

exception" and the Fourth Amendment to the US Constitution (protection of all persons under US jurisdiction from arbitrary searches and seizures). Specifically, Zisman argues that the international border exception does not exclude a "reason-ableness" standard for non-routine searches at international ports of entry. There must be a demonstrated reasonable suspicion of illegal activity to warrant a non-routine search of any persons at US ports of entry. This is in contrast to a routine search, which is considered reasonable by its very nature since it occurs at the inter-national border and involves only limited intrusion. Zisman continues by noting that the search standard for "routine" searches is based on the established legal principle that a person's expectation of privacy is diminished at a border because he or she is on notice that a search may be conducted.

45 E. Yost, "Recent Developments in US Immigration Laws Affecting Entry of Can-adians into the United States" (2003) 29 Canada–United States Law Journal 105.

46 *US Immigration and Nationality Act of 1952,* Pub. L. No. 82-414, [1952] 66 Stat. 242, section 287 (Reflecting Amendments by IIRIRA, *supra* note 43), quoted in R. Zis-man, "The US Admission and Inspection Process in a Nutshell," presented on behalf of Preshaw and Zisman to the Pacific Corridor Enterprise Council in conjunction with the British Columbia Institute for Studies in International Trade (13 May 2004).

47 Letter from Michael P. D'Ambrosio, Director, Field Operations, US Customs and Border Protection, Department of Homeland Security, Buffalo, NY, to Mr. Mark Kenmore, American Immigration Lawyers Association (AILA) Chapter Chair, Buf-falo, NY (28 August 2003). The reasoning behind this decision is that a port-of-entry application for admission into the US is a civil matter. Thus, there is no right to have counsel present. At their discretion, however, US Customs and Border Protection port-of-entry officers may or may not permit an attorney to accompany an applicant who is seeking admission into the US, and to articulate facts or laws on behalf of the foreigner. See American Immigration Lawyers, "Access to Counsel," Issue paper, American Immigration Lawyers Association, Washington, DC, 20 July 2006.

48 *Uniting and Strengthening America by Providing Appropriate Tools Required to Intercept and Obstruct Terrorism Act of 2001,* Pub. L. No. 107-56, [2001] 115 Stat. 272 [*USA PATRIOT Act*].

49 Richardson, *supra* note 17.

50 *Canadian Charter of Rights and Freedoms,* Part I of the *Constitution Act, 1982,* being Schedule B to the *Canada Act 1982* (U.K.), 1982, c. 11 [*Charter*].

51 Policy Specialist C-1, *supra* note 19.

52 *Miranda v. Arizona,* 384 U.S. 436 (1966); *Mapp v. Ohio,* 367 U.S. 643 (1961); *Gideon v. Wainwright,* 372 U.S. 335 (1963).

53 *Ibid.*

54 Gal-Or, *supra* note 14 at 378.

55 For example, North American journalists asked to be removed from the NAFTA list because most journalists did not have a four-year university degree, which was a requirement for this profession under NAFTA. Actuaries, on the other hand, worked together through their Canadian and American associations before approaching the TEWG in 1998 with a proposal to be placed on the NAFTA list. Interview with Terry Preshaw, Preshaw and Zisman, Everett, WA (20 January 2004).

56 Policy Specialist C-1, *supra* note 19.

57 Richardson, *supra* note 17.

58 *Ibid.;* Anna Lee Saxenian, "Brain Circulation: How High-Skilled Immigration Makes Everyone Better Off" (2002) 20 The Brookings Review 28.

59 Gal-Or, *supra* note 14.

60 Richardson, *supra* note 17.

The TRIPS Agreement and New Developments in Intellectual Property Law in China

LIAO ZHIGANG

One outcome of the eight-year Uruguay Round of multilateral trade negotiations under the *General Agreement on Tariffs and Trade*[1] (GATT) was the *Agreement on Trade-Related Aspects of Intellectual Property Rights*[2] (the TRIPS Agreement), which is the most far-reaching and comprehensive legal regime ever concluded at the multilateral level in the area of intellectual property rights (IPR). It supplements and modifies the "elderly" conventions governing IPR, the most important of which (the *Paris Convention for the Protection of Industrial Property*[3] and the *Berne Convention for the Protection of Literary and Artistic Works*[4]) were first elaborated at the end of the nineteenth century. Certainly, these conventions were periodically revised (six major revisions in the case of both *Berne* and *Paris*) in order to promote, in a gradual and incremental manner, a quasi-uniform international regulation of industrial property and copyright. Compared with the results of those revision exercises, however, the TRIPS Agreement constitutes a major qualitative leap. It radically modifies not only the context in which IPR is considered internationally but also its substantive content and the methods for its enforcement and dispute settlement. The TRIPS Agreement surpasses all prior international conventions not only in the breadth of intellectual property rights covered but also in the acquisition, maintenance, and scope of protection, as well as the requirement of adequate and expeditious enforcement. Thus, unlike former international conventions, it does not merely state the rights and minimum standards that Members must acknowledge, namely, the subject matter to be protected, the rights to be conferred and permissible exceptions to those rights, and the minimum duration of protection. It also defines in great detail the national civil, administrative and criminal procedures, provisional measures, and special requirements related to border measures that Members should make available to enable rights holders to enforce their intellectual property rights. For example, Article 41 of the Agreement sets out general standards to be met by a Member's enforcement procedures. They must be available under a Member's law so as to permit effective action against any act of infringement of intellectual property rights covered by the Agreement, including expeditious remedies to prevent infringements. The procedures are to be applied in such a way as to avoid the creation of barriers to legitimate trade and to provide safeguards against their abuse. The TRIPS Agreement has also strengthened IPR in the following additional areas: stronger protection of trademarks; greater protection for industrial designs; establishment of the rules on compulsory licensing necessary for developing countries; extension to a worldwide level of semiconductor protection; and setting up of a Council for Trade-Related Aspects of Intellectual Property Rights to monitor the smooth running of the Agreement.

The TRIPS Agreement requires that the substantive obligations of the main conventions of the World Intellectual Property Organization (WIPO) must be complied with. With the exception of the provisions of the *Berne Convention* on moral rights, all the main substantive provisions of these conventions are incorporated by reference and thus become obligations under the TRIPS Agreement between World Trade Organization (WTO) members. Article 2 of the TRIPS Agreement, entitled "Intellectual Property Conventions," establishes the basic link between the TRIPS Agreement and the IPR conventions. It reads as follows:

1. In respect of Parts II, III and IV of this Agreement, Members shall comply with Articles 1 through 12 and 19 of the Paris Convention (1967).
2. Nothing in Parts I to IV of this Agreement shall derogate from existing obligations that Members may have to each other under the Paris Convention, the Berne Convention, the Rome Convention[5] and the Treaty on Intellectual Property in Respect of Integrated Circuits.

What is unusual about the TRIPS Agreement is that not only one but several multilateral conventions are modified by it. Obviously, a basic objective of the proponents of the TRIPS Agreement was to avoid the time-consuming amendment procedures of individual IPR conventions, and to work instead towards a comprehensive new agreement that would supplement and modify existing conventions.

In each of the main areas of intellectual property covered by the TRIPS Agreement, the Agreement sets out the minimum standards of protection to be provided by each Member. Each of the main elements of protection is defined: the subject matter to be protected, the rights to be conferred and permissible exceptions to those rights, and the minimum duration of protection. The Agreement sets these standards by requiring, first, as I have already mentioned, that the substantive obligations of the main conventions of WIPO are incorporated by reference and thus become obligations under the TRIPS Agreement between WTO members. The relevant provisions are to be found in Articles 2(1) and 9(1) of the TRIPS Agreement. Second, the TRIPS Agreement adds a substantial number of additional obligations on matters where the pre-existing conventions are silent or were seen as being inadequate. The TRIPS Agreement is thus sometimes referred to as a "Berne and Paris–plus Agreement."

The second main set of provisions deals with domestic procedures and remedies for the enforcement of intellectual property rights. The first one is contained in Part II of the Agreement, which specifies the standards concerning the availability, scope, and use of IPR. The Agreement lays down certain general principles applicable to all IPR enforcement procedures. In addition, it contains provisions on civil and administrative procedures and remedies, provisional measures, special requirements related to border measures, and criminal procedures. These provisions specify, in a certain amount of detail, the procedures and remedies that must be available so that rights holders can effectively enforce their rights.

It is worth mentioning the North-South asymmetries in the formation and implementation of the TRIPS Agreement. As Correa points out, developing countries have been forced to agree to TRIPS. Many developing countries have had or have to change their IPR regimes quite radically to fulfill the TRIPS Agreement's requirements. A United Nations report suggests that negative short- to medium-term effects may occur, such as increased product prices and more difficult access to technologies.[6] Nevertheless, the authors believe in long-term benefits, such as the protection of domestic inventions and the augmentation of innovative spirit. Governments in developing countries have had and have to find a balance between the need to protect intellectual property and the requirement to diffuse certain technologies in order to increase welfare.[7] Moreover, domestic output of developing countries and employment of producers of counterfeit goods will decrease. Employment, wages, and tax receipts will shrink and governments of these countries will have to invest largely in administrative resources to enforce changed legislation.[8] Developing countries are concerned that a strengthened, worldwide IPR system may lead to anticompetitive tendencies, with negative effects on welfare in these countries. Transnational corporations may abuse their monopoly power gained through their intellectual property, or the transfer of technology may be restricted.[9]

Overview

At a general level, there may be some disparities between the multilateral trade agreements concluded within the framework of the Uruguay Round, including the TRIPS Agreement, and the implementing legislation of Members. How such discrepancies may be overcome or reconciled within each member state will depend on the legal status of treaties in each state's constitutional system.

Many countries, including China, are affected by the TRIPS Agreement. Perhaps no other trade-related issue has received so much attention in recent years in connection with China's WTO application. This is because of China's attitude towards IPR and lack of enforcement within China's borders. China has made great efforts and has achieved some progress in the protection of IPR, however. Since 1979, it has incrementally established a legal system for IPR protection, promulgating, for example, the *Trademark Law*, the *Patent Law*, the *Copyright Law*, the *Law against Unfair Competition*, and so on. China has also revised some of the acts and regulations in accordance with its domestic changes and newly signed international treaties. There is an enforcement system (both judicial and administrative) for IPR protection, and numerous domestic and foreign disputes have been settled successfully. Finally, Chinese scholars have been active in academic studies and discussions of IPR protection, and Chinese society has become increasingly aware of IPR.

Applications for patents and registration of trademarks continue to grow year by year. Meanwhile, patent examination and grants have been speeded up, and more effective measures have been adopted to stop copyright infringement and piracy. Customs officials' efforts in protecting IPR have guaranteed the smooth growth of foreign trade. Public security authorities and the cultural affairs administration have tightened control of the audiovisual market by cracking down on illegal and criminal activities, such as copyright infringement, piracy, and illegal publications. The protection of new varieties of plants was formally initiated. At the same time, China has strengthened cooperation in the field of intellectual property rights with international organizations and countries throughout the world.

According to the *General Principles of the Civil Law of the People's Republic of China*, from the moment China signs an international treaty, the treaty is automatically part of Chinese domestic law, except those provisions about which China has declared reservation beforehand.[10] Thus, unlike in the Anglo-American legal system, it is not necessary for China's legislative body to publish any act approving the treaty as domestic law.

Some problems still exist, however, and we will discuss some of them in detail later. The improvement of the legal system and the radical economic changes in China have made the concept of "private rights" associated with IPR no longer alien to Chinese government officials or ordinary people. After fifteen years of delay, China has at last achieved its formal integration into the global trading system by becoming a member of the WTO. Because it promises to fulfill all the obligations of the TRIPS Agreement without any transitional arrangements, it is urgent for China to adapt its legislation and improve the enforcement of IPR protection.

The Chinese Patent Law and Its Revision

The *Patent Law of the People's Republic of China* was adopted by the National People's Congress in March 1984[11] and first amended in September 1992. The *Decision Regarding the Revision of the Patent Law of the People's Republic of China* was adopted at the Seventeenth Session of the Standing Committee of the Ninth National People's Congress on 25 August 2000. It was amended again on 27 December 2008. The new *Patent Law* raises the standards of patent protection, simplifying the procedure for examination and approval of patents and readjusting some relevant provisions in accordance with the requirements of the TRIPS Agreement. The revision of the Implementing Regulations of the new *Patent Law* was approved and promulgated by the State Council on 15 June 2001. Both the *Law* and its Implementing Regulations came into effect on 1 July 2001. The Regulations were amended again on 9 January 2010. The major amendments are summarized below.

New Provision Governing Offering for Sale

According to the TRIPS Agreement, the patent owner shall have the exclusive rights to prevent third parties not having the owner's consent from the act of offering to sell a patented product or the product obtained directly by a patented process.[12] With this provision, the owner can prevent potential patent violators from keeping the infringing product in a storehouse, promoting sales, or making preparations. This is a very important weapon that enables the owner of a patent to prevent an imminent infringement or the disposal of the infringing goods outside the channels of commerce. In order to enhance the protection afforded by the *Patent Law* and make it correspond to the requirements of the TRIPS Agreement, the provision has been added to the revised *Patent Law*.

Improved Procedures for Application, Examination, and Approval
"Procedures concerning the enforcement of intellectual property rights shall be fair and equitable. They shall not be unnecessarily complicated or costly, or entail unreasonable time-limits or unwarranted delays."[13] This is one of the general obligations of intellectual property rights enforcement in the TRIPS Agreement, and the starting point of Chinese intellectual property legislation as well. Many changes have been made to the new *Patent Law* to optimize procedures, conserve resources, and reduce lawsuit formalities.

- China became a Contracting Party of the *Patent Cooperation Treaty*[14] (PCT) on 1 January 1994. The Chinese State Intellectual Property Office is a Receiving Office, International Searching Authority, and International Preliminary Examining Authority under the PCT. In order to facilitate patent applications through the PCT, protect legitimate interests, and emphasize the international obligations of the patent administration, Article 20 of the new Chinese *Patent Law* clarifies the legislative authority for international application under the PCT and regulates some relevant issues in principle.
- In 1992, the opposition procedure, which could be initiated before the grant of a patent, was replaced by a revocation procedure, which could be initiated after a patent had been granted. It was hoped that the revocation procedure would encourage the public to report apparent errors in the grant of rights so that the patent administration could correct its own mistakes in a timely manner. The revocation procedure overlapped the invalidation procedure, however, thereby prolonging the process. Furthermore, there were many cases in which infringers used the revocation procedure maliciously, and patent holders could not protect their own legitimate interests through an invalidation procedure. The new *Patent Law* cancelled the revocation procedure.

- Article 32 of the TRIPS Agreement stipulates that "an opportunity for judicial review of any decision to revoke or forfeit a patent shall be available." Due to a shortage of human resources in the past, the *Patent Law* of 1984 and 1992 provided an opportunity for judicial review for a patent of invention only; the decisions of the Patent Re-examination Board to reconfirm or forfeit patents of utility model or industrial design were final. According to the new *Patent Law*, decisions on the reconfirmation and invalidation of all patents may be reviewed by the courts.
- In the spirit of the organizational reform, administrative bodies, at least in principle, should not interfere in the exercise of parties' civil rights. For this purpose, some amendments have been made to the *Patent Law*. First, a contract for assigning a patent or the right to apply for a patent became effective from the date of registration by the patent administration under the State Council, and an announcement was no longer a necessary condition for such a contract to be valid. Second, the provision that international application by Chinese entities or individuals must have the consent of the departments concerned under the State Council was deleted, meaning that Chinese entities and individuals may apply for foreign patents without the approval of the national patent administration. There is one exception: with regard to inventions that involve national security or major interests and that need to be kept confidential, the relevant provisions of the *Patent Law* must be complied with.

New Provisional Measures before the Institution of an Action
Article 41(1) of the TRIPS Agreement requires that Members "ensure that enforcement procedures ... are available under their law so as to permit effective action against any act of infringement of intellectual property rights ... including expeditious remedies to prevent infringements." Article 50(1) of the Agreement stipulates that "the judicial authorities shall have the authority to order prompt and effective provisional measures: (a) to prevent an infringement of any intellectual property right from occurring ... [and] (b) to preserve relevant evidence in regard to the alleged infringement." To conform to the TRIPS Agreement, Article 61 of the revised *Patent Law* provides that "the patent holder and interested persons may apply for a preliminary injunction or attachment from a court before bringing a lawsuit, if they could reasonably prove that some people are infringing or will infringe the patent, and any delay of measures is likely to cause irreparable harm to their legitimate interests." This amendment is considered a development of Anton Piller orders and the injunction system.[15]

Limitations and Exceptions

Article 30 of the TRIPS Agreement provides that limitations or exceptions to the exclusive rights conferred by a patent cannot "unreasonably conflict with a normal exploitation of the patent" and cannot "unreasonably prejudice the legitimate interests of the patent owner, taking account of the legitimate interests of third parties." According to the former Chinese *Patent Law*, it was not an infringement of a patent to use or sell the infringing products without knowing the truth; the infringers would not bear any civil responsibility. This provision conflicted with the TRIPS Agreement and common international practices, and severely damaged the legitimate interests of patent holders. The new *Patent Law* stipulates that the acts of bona fide third parties involving the use, offering for sale, or sale of a product that violates a patent are infringements of the patent rights. Infringers may not bear civil liability if they can prove that they obtained the products from legitimate channels of distribution, but they must desist from the infringement.

In addition, in the Chinese patent system, there are three kinds of compulsory licences: compulsory licence with reasonable conditions, compulsory licence for the sake of public interests, and compulsory licence of dependent patents. For the compulsory license of dependent patents, the new *Patent Law* prescribes that the invention or utility model claimed in the second patent shall involve an important technical advance of considerable economic significance in relation to the invention or utility model claimed in the first patent. It is more transparent and easier to operate than the provision in the former *Law*, and this brings the *Patent Law* in line with the TRIPS Agreement. Some other provisions, such as the scope and duration of a compulsory licence, were moved from the Implementing Regulations of 1992 into the *Patent Law*.

A New Method of Calculating Damages for Infringement

In order to maintain justice and to ensure the patent holder adequate damages to compensate for any injury suffered because of an infringement, the *Patent Law* specifies that the amount of damages for a patent infringement shall be calculated according to the actual loss suffered by the rights holder or the unjust profits of the infringer due to the infringement. If it is difficult to measure such actual losses or unjust profits, the amount of damages may be determined by consulting the appropriate multiple of the patent royalties. The last part of this provision was added in 2000. According to Article 21 of *Several Provisions of the Supreme People's Court on the Adjudication of*

Cases over Patent Disputes (a judicial interpretation adopted by the Supreme People's Court on 19 June 2001), "when the losses of the patent holder or the profits of the patent infringer are difficult to determine, the People's Court may, where the patent royalties can be referred to, determine damages on the basis of the category of patent involved; the nature and facts of the infringement; the amount of the said patent royalties; and the nature, extent, and duration of the patent licence, with reference to one to three times the royalties." Where there are no patent royalties to be referred to or the royalties are obviously unreasonable, the People's Court may, in light of certain factors, such as the category of patent involved, the nature and facts of the infringement, and so on, decide on an amount of damages between 5,000 and 300,000 Yuan RMB in general, but not exceeding 500,000 Yuan RMB at most. In practice, the court always considers ordering the infringer to pay the rights holder reasonable expenses, as stipulated in Article 22 of the abovementioned court provisions.

Improved System of Utility Model Patent and Industrial Design Patent

The *Patent Law* clarifies the patentability of industrial design in such a way that any independently created design for which patent right may be granted must not be identical with and similar to (formerly "or similar to") known designs, namely, any design that, before the date of filing, has been publicly disclosed in publications in China or abroad or has been publicly used in China; it must also not conflict with prior legitimate rights obtained by other people.

In order to prevent rights holders of utility model patents from misusing their rights and frustrating others in their production and operation activities, Article 57 of the *Patent Law* stipulates that, if a utility model is involved in a controversy over patent infringement, the court or patent administration may request the patent owner to furnish them with a patent search report made by the national patent administration under the State Council. The Chinese State Intellectual Property Office is preparing a third revision of the patent law to improve the examination mechanism for utility model and design patent applications, in an effort to weed out such "junk patents" before they are issued and to discourage people from submitting such applications.

The *Patent Law* states that the rights concerning utility models and industrial designs become operative from the date of public notice, as in the case of the invention patent.

Stronger Administrative Enforcement of Patents

To clarify the functions of local patent offices and strengthen administration and law enforcement, Article 3 of the *Patent Law* clearly indicates that the patent administrative organ under the State Council is responsible for the administration of patents nationwide, while the patent offices of provinces, autonomous regions, and municipalities directly under the central government are responsible for managing patent affairs in their own administrative areas.

The *Patent Law* clarifies that patent administrations are empowered to determine when an infringement has occurred and order the doer to stop the infringement, and even apply to the courts for enforcement if necessary. Patent administrations also deal with disputes concerning the amount of damages, using mediation upon the request of the parties.

The *Patent Law* authorizes patent administrations to investigate and deal with cases of patent counterfeiting, or the passing off of the patent of another person as one's own, to order correction and public notice, to confiscate illegal gains, and to impose a fine of no more than three times the amount of the illegal gains or a fine below the prescribed amount of 50,000 Yuan RMB.

The *Patent Law* also emphasizes that patent administration staff must be diligent, honest, pragmatic, and efficient. They should also handle all applications and requests relating to patents objectively, impartially, accurately, and promptly.

Promotion of Technical Innovation

To promote the development of high technology, facilitate industrialization, and incorporate patents into the system of technical innovation, the wording of one of the purposes of the *Patent Law* was changed from "to promote the development of science and technology" to "to promote scientific and technological advancement and innovation." The provision concerning the holding of patent rights by entities of public ownership was deleted. The definition of in-service invention-creation was made more reasonable, making it clear that in-service inventors or creators will receive remuneration and be rewarded. Further, the new law provides that "for an invention-creation made by using the materials and technical means of the entity, and where the entity and the inventor or creator had entered into an agreement under which there were provisions on who has the right to apply for a patent and to whom the patent right belongs, the provisions of the agreement shall prevail."

Remaining Problems
Despite these improvements, there are still some problems with the new
Patent Law. For example, there is no provision governing acts of indirect
infringement (or indirect use of invention-creation, namely, supplying or
offering to supply a person with means relating to the essential element of
the invention-creation, for the purpose of putting it into effect). This is different from the patent laws of many other countries, and it has caused in-
convenience for the courts. In addition, the criteria for determining
infringement need to be further improved; a provision regarding the preservation of evidence needs to be added; there is a literal difference between
Article 5 of Chinese *Patent Law* and Article 27 of the TRIPS Agreement,
which cover non-patentable inventions that may be prohibited by domestic
law; the compulsory dissemination and exploitation of some invention patents in Article 14 partially conflicts with the TRIPS Agreement; the protection of utility models is not effective enough; and the examination system
and grant procedures for patents are not very efficient.

Amendments to the Chinese Trademark Law
The Trademark Law of the People's Republic of China was adopted in 1982
and amended in 1993. To make it more compatible with the requirements of
the TRIPS Agreement, to stop various trademark infringements, and to
standardize market activities, the National People's Congress Standing
Committee revised the law for a second time on 27 October 2001. The new
Trademark Law entered into force on 1 December that same year. The
Trademark Law 1993 consisted of eight chapters and forty-three articles,
whereas the current law consists of eight chapters and sixty-four articles.
The major amendments are summarized below.

New Subject Matter That Can Be Protected
Article 15 of the TRIPS Agreement states: "Any sign, or any combination of
signs, capable of distinguishing the goods or services of one undertaking
from those of other undertakings, shall be capable of constituting a trademark. Such signs, in particular words including personal names, letters,
numerals, figurative elements and combinations of colours as well as any
combination of such signs, shall be eligible for registration as trademarks."
According to Article 6 of the *Paris Convention*, "in determining whether a
mark is eligible for protection, all the factual circumstances must be taken
into consideration, particularly the length of time the mark has been in
use." The Chinese *Trademark Law* was revised in accordance with these

provisions.[16] In addition, collective marks, certification marks, geographical indications, and three-dimensional marks can be protected, and are defined in specific terms for the first time.[17] In earlier versions of the law, China had no provisions governing the registrability of trademarks with "secondary meanings," although, in practice, some such trademarks, such as Wuliangye, Mao Tai, Liang Mianzhen, Caoshanhu, Lengsuanling, and so on, were registered by the Chinese Trademark Office. Article 11 of the current law states explicitly that such trademarks are registrable.

Elimination of Unreasonable Limitations Placed on Trademark Owners

Several unnecessary limitations placed on trademark applicants and owners made it very difficult to protect some people's civil rights and to settle disputes fairly. Formerly, only enterprises, institutions, or individual producers and traders, but not every individual, intending to acquire the exclusive rights to use a trademark or service had to file an application for registration of the trademark or service mark. The Preamble of the TRIPS Agreement stresses that "Members ... *Recogniz*[e] that intellectual property rights are private rights." Nobody can deprive a natural person of his or her private rights, so these limitations were removed in accordance with international custom. Any natural person, legal entity, or organization can be an applicant or rights owner of a trademark. Furthermore, conditional coexistence of some relevant rights belonging to different people on a trademark is now permissible.[18]

Clarification of the Scope of Protection

Three items in Article 52 (formerly Article 38) concerning acts that infringe registered trademarks were revised. For instance, using signs identical with or resembling a registered trademark on identical or similar goods or services without the permission of the trademark registrant (formerly the trademark owner) is prohibited if such an act would likely result in confusion or deception. This set a general standard for determining an infringement of a registered trademark. In addition, marketing goods bearing a replaced trademark infringes the exclusive rights of the registered trademark (unless the registered owner grants permission).

Simplified and Improved Procedures for Maintaining Trademarks

The ignorance of Chinese enterprises concerning trademark rights has led to some renowned domestic trademarks' being registered in overseas markets by foreign companies. In 1998, a trademark infringement shocked the

Chinese business community and caused great controversy. A foreign trading company in Shenzhen rushed to register more than 200 popular domestic trademarks from 1995 to 1998, intending to seek exorbitant profits from the transfer of these trademarks to the enterprises that actually used them.[19] Such misconduct not only jeopardized the interests of the original trademark users but also infringed upon the interests of consumers. Any registrations that are clearly malicious, as in the case of the company in Shenzhen, should be severely punished. The revised law clearly defines various trademark violations to ensure strict enforcement. It includes provisions regarding the timely revocation of improperly registered trademarks in order to minimize damage to the injured parties. China adopted the "first-to-file principle" in trademark registration, but the Trademark Office also takes into account prior use of a trademark when it examines an application. An application for registration of a trademark must not prejudice any existing prior rights of other people, such as protectable trade names, industrial designs, copyrights, rights of names, geographical indications, rights to portraits, rights of merchandising, and rights of prior use. Also, an applicant cannot use unfair means to pre-emptively register a trademark connected to other people. This is considered one of the conditions for the registration and use of a trademark.

In keeping with Article 41(4) of the TRIPS Agreement, administrative decisions made by the Trademark Review and Adjudication Board are no longer final. Any interested party dissatisfied with a decision of the board may, within thirty days from the date of receipt of the notice, institute legal proceedings in the People's Court.[20] Specifically, the *Trademark Law* provides an opportunity for judicial review of any administrative decision to reconfirm, revoke, or forfeit a trademark registration.

Explicit and complete provisions are set forth in the *Trademark Law* with respect to the right of priority and of the provisional protection of trademarks used in exhibitions.[21] The *Trademark Law* added provisions governing the priority for application: applicants may request a period of priority not longer than six months from the date of first filing in a foreign country or first use at an international exhibition sponsored or recognized by the Chinese Government.

Strengthened Judicial and Administrative Protection of Trademarks
With regard to trademark protection, as with patents and copyright, China has formed a unique "dual-track system" featuring the cooperation of judicial and administrative bodies. This has proven in practice to be an effective

system of law enforcement. Also, administrative authorities for industry and commerce at all levels have become a major force in trademark law enforcement. Major changes in the *Trademark Law* include the following:

- In order to strengthen the administration of trademarks, the administrative sanction for acts of trademark infringement has been intensified. Once an act of trademark infringement is demonstrated, the Administration for Industry and Commerce (AIC) may order the cessation of the infringing act, confiscate and destroy infringing goods or relevant tools, or impose a fine. Any infringement that is serious enough to constitute a crime should be handled by judicial bodies.[22]
- Under Article 38 of the former *Trademark Law*, an infringement of trademark occurred only if a person knowingly sold commodities carrying infringing trademarks. In practice, it was difficult to determine whether a person was aware that his or her goods infringed a trademark. The revised *Trademark Law* stipulates that all acts involving the sale of commodities carrying infringing trademarks, whether done knowingly or not, are infringing acts. Infringers may not be held liable, however, if they can prove that they acquired the infringing goods from a lawful source.
- Provisional measures that can be taken before the institution of an action were added to the *Trademark Law*. The trademark owner or an interested person may apply for a preliminary injunction or attachment from a court before bringing a lawsuit. To be granted a preliminary injunction, the plaintiff must reasonably prove that some person or group is infringing or will infringe a registered trademark, and that any delay of measures is likely to cause irreparable harm to the plaintiff's legitimate interests.
- The new *Trademark Law* clearly indicates that damages awarded to a plaintiff for trademark infringement will include the actual losses or unjust profits, and reasonable expenses incurred by the plaintiff while trying to stop the infringing acts (such as attorney's fees, appraisal fees, and fees for investigation and taking of evidence, etc.). If it is difficult to measure the actual losses or the unjust profits, the amount of damages may be determined by referring to the statutory standard (*i.e.*, not exceeding 500,000 Yuan RMB) and the circumstances of the infringing act.

When investigating and handling suspected infringement of a registered trademark, the administrative authority for industry and commerce at or above the county level may exercise the following functions and authorities:

- Making contact with the interested parties and investigating the events connected with the alleged infringement of the exclusive right to use the trademark.
- Reading and making copies of the contract, receipts, account books, and other relevant materials of the interested parties that relate to the infringement.
- Inspecting the site where the alleged infringement of the exclusive right to use the trademark took place.
- Inspecting any articles relevant to the infringement. Any articles that have been used to infringe another person's exclusive right to use a trademark may be sealed or seized.

  When the administrative authority for industry and commerce exercises the preceding functions and authorities, the interested parties must cooperate and help, and must not refuse to do so or stand in the way.

- In order to stop an infringing act, the revised law allows any trademark registrant or interested party to file an application with the People's Court for preservation of evidence before instituting legal proceedings in the People's Court. This is allowed where the evidence may be destroyed or lost or may be difficult to obtain in the future.

Increased Protection for Well-Known Trademarks

Extended rights for well-known trademarks are provided for in Articles 16(2) and 16(3) of the TRIPS Agreement. This protection is intended to prevent third parties from taking commercial advantage of the very valuable goodwill associated with well-known trademarks. The protection of well-known trademarks is now explicitly provided for in China's *Trademark Law*. Any application to register a sign identical with or similar to a well-known trademark will be rejected, and any sign that would likely cause confusion because it copies, imitates, or translates a well-known trademark will be prohibited from registration and use. The protection is extended to services and goods that are not similar, provided that confusion or damage to the trademark owner may result. For the owner of a well-known trademark, a request for the revocation of a malicious registration is not limited to the ordinary five-year period. In addition, registration will not be considered a precondition of protection for a well-known trademark in China. In determining whether a trademark is well known, knowledge of the trademark in the sector of society in which it is relevant will be specifically taken into account.

The Trademark Law and Its Implementing Regulations

The *Trademark Law* was enacted several years ago. When it was first en-acted, many of its provisions were simply statements of principles and were therefore difficult to apply. Empowered by the National People's Congress, the State Council revised the Implementing Regulations three times. Some provisions in the revised regulations did not have corresponding legislative authority from the *Trademark Law,* however. For example, there is no provi-sion in the *Law* governing the procedure of administrative review, but the Implementing Regulations say that it is necessary for an administrative case to apply for administrative review before bringing an action to the court. Such contradictions cause problems in practice and must be rectified. Some of the problems have now been resolved.

Recommended Changes to the Trademark Law

The following changes to the *Trademark Law* are recommended to further streamline the law and bring it into closer alignment with international practice:

- Medicine, veterinary products, and tobacco must have a registered trade-mark, otherwise the commodities cannot be sold in the market. This pro-vision has hindered the development of some enterprises. In the rest of the world, a system of compulsory registration is quite rare, so it would be good to eliminate it from the *Trademark Law.*
- In order to strengthen enforcement, measures related to importation should be added to the *Trademark Law.* If the holder of a registered trademark has valid grounds for suspecting that counterfeit trademark goods may be imported, the trademark holder should be able to lodge an application for the suspension of the release of the goods into free circulation. The competent authorities should have the power to order such goods to be disposed of outside the channels of commerce or to be destroyed.
- The three-month opposition period before registration under the *Trade-mark Law* has proved to be practically useless. To simplify the formalities and speed up the process of a trademark registration, it is necessary to move the opposition procedure to right after the registration.
- According to some scholars, defensive trademarks and associate trade-marks should also be protected by the Chinese *Trademark Law.*
- Article 48(1) of the TRIPS Agreement states: "The judicial authorities shall have the authority to order a party at whose request measures were

taken and who has abused enforcement procedures to provide to a party wrongfully enjoined or restrained adequate compensation for the injury suffered because of such abuse. The judicial authorities shall also have the authority to order the applicant to pay the defendant expenses, which may include appropriate attorney's fees." Article 50(7) states: "Where the provisional measures are revoked or where they lapse due to any act or omission by the applicant, or where it is subsequently found that there has been no infringement or threat of infringement of an intellectual property right, the judicial authorities shall have the authority to order the applicant, upon request of the defendant, to provide the defendant appropriate compensation for an injury caused by these measures." The *Trademark Law* should add provisions governing these matters.

Amendments to the Chinese Copyright Law

The *Copyright Law of the People's Republic of China* was enacted in September 1990. In some ways, it is reflective of a traditional planned economy and conflicts with the principles of a market economy. Because the arrival of a knowledge-based economy and new technologies has created changes in the realm of copyright, copyright law may be one of the most problematic areas affected by China's entry into the WTO.

The National People's Congress Standing Committee revised the *Copyright Law* on 27 October 2001, and again on 26 February 2010. The major changes are summarized below.

Protection for Citizens versus Protection Given to Foreigners

Under the former copyright regime, foreign citizens of members or parties to various international conventions enjoyed a higher level of copyright protection than Chinese citizens. For example, Article 16 of the *International Copyright Treaties Implementing Rules of the People's Republic of China* adopted in September 1992 by the State Council stipulates that, in the case of public performance, recording, and broadcasting of foreign works, prior permission of the copyright owner and the collective copyright management agencies is required. According to the *Copyright Law,* however, similar exploitation of published Chinese works does not require permission from the copyright owner, unless the owner has declared that such exploitation is not allowed. There were also some disparities between the *Copyright Law* and the *Regulations on Computer Software Protection.* For example, the *Regulations* stipulated that registration of software is the prerequisite for requesting an administrative handling or legal proceeding in a rights dispute, and the term of protection for software was only twenty-five years. In the *International Copyright Treaties Implementing Rules,* however, foreign computer programs are protected as literary works, may not be subject to registration, and enjoy a term of protection of fifty years. The requirement of registration for Chinese computer programs was set aside by a circular from the Supreme People's Court in 1993, and the *Regulations on Computer Software Protection* were revised accordingly on 20 December 2001.

Another example involves rental rights, which the *United Nations Conference on Trade and Development (UNCTAD)* and the *International Centre for Trade and Sustainable Development (ICTSD)* describe as follows:

> A rental right, in general, is a subset of the right of distribution that is more commonly recognized in a variety of different forms in domestic and international agreements. Broadly speaking, the distribution right encompasses rental, lending and resale rights. Under a rental right, the copyright holder may collect royalties from third parties engaged in the commercial rental of their copyrighted works. TRIPS establishes a rental right in respect of computer programs and cinematographic works. Under the terms of the Agreement, owners of these two categories of works must be granted the right to "authorize or prohibit the commercial rental to the public of originals or copies of their copyright works." With respect to cinematographic works, a Member may choose not to grant a rental right unless commercial rental has led to widespread copying such that the exclusive right of the owner to reproduce the work is materially impaired. The rental right is also not applicable to objects that contain computer programs, where the program is not itself the essential object of the rental.[23]

Formerly, laws governing rental rights were unfair to Chinese nationals, but some rental rights have now been improved.

New Subject Matter That Can Be Protected

The revised *Copyright Law* provides protection for databases. A database created by the compilation of data that does not constitute works and has originality in the selection and arrangements of the contents is protected as a work of compilation.[24]

The TRIPS Agreement requires that compilations of data or other materials should be protected because the selection or arrangement of their contents constitutes an intellectual creation and should be protected as such.[25] In the former Chinese system, a compilation was the creation of a work by assembly of a number of selected pre-existing works; compilations of data and other materials not protectable under the *Copyright Law* were excluded. According to the *International Copyright Treaties Implementing Rules,* however, a foreign database may be protected as a compilation. With the development of electronic databases, database operators have begun to worry about the legal protection of their intellectual products. *Beijing Sunshine Data Co. v. Shanghai Bacai Data and Information Co.*[26] was the first case in China concerning intellectual property protection of an electronic database and an electronic network transmission. The lower court could not invoke any provision from the *Copyright Law,* but the court of second instance, the Beijing High People's Court, clarified that an electronic database was a subject matter of China's intellectual property laws. Before this case, a database was not a legal concept formally accepted by China's intellectual property laws.

Expanded Economic Rights of Copyright Holders

Under the former *Copyright Law,* copyright holders enjoyed a higher level of moral rights, such as the right of publication, right of paternity, right of modification, and right of integrity, which were perpetual and independent from economic rights. The protection of economic rights was comparatively low. Several changes were made when the law was revised.

Rights of public performance and broadcasting were expanded. Such rights include not only live performances and direct broadcasting but also mechanical performance and broadcasting through machines and other technological means. Performers are to receive remuneration for their performances.

Rental rights and rights of information distribution on networks were incorporated. With respect to computer programs and cinematographic works, the TRIPS Agreement requires that Members provide authors and their successors in title the right to authorize or prohibit temporarily commercial rental of originals or copies of their copyright works, including cinematographic works, works created by means similar to that for producing cinematographic works, and computer software.[27] In the past, rights holders in China had the rights of distribution, which included providing a certain number of copies of a work to the public through selling, renting, or other means, insofar as the said number of copies satisfied the reasonable needs of the public. It appears *prima facie* that this provision of the original *Copyright Law* met the requirements of the TRIPS Agreement and even surpassed the requirement, but it was actually injurious and unfair to rights holders because it was very difficult for them to exercise the rights. The *International Copyright Treaties Implementing Rules* give copyright owners of foreign works the right to authorize or prohibit rental of copies of their work after the authorized sale of such copies. The scope of protection is too wide, and the level of protection is too high. None of the abovementioned provisions, both in the *Copyright Law* and in the *International Copyright Treaties Implementing Rules*, referred to the rental of original works. It is necessary to list the rental rights separately and to clarify the scope of their protection in the *Law*.

The rights of information distribution on networks refers to the right to authorize or prohibit the dissemination of copyright works in a manner that allows members of the public to access these works from a place and at a time individually chosen by them.[28] This is also a requirement of the TRIPS Agreement, the *WIPO Copyright Treaty*,[29] and the *WIPO Performances and Phonograms Treaty*.[30]

Deletion or Revision of Some Unreasonable Limitations and Exceptions
Several unreasonable rules relating to statutory licences in the former *Copyright Law* conflicted with the standards of the *Berne Convention*, the TRIPS Agreement, and the laws of most foreign countries, and had negative effects in practice. Several changes were made when the law was revised.

The scope of statutory licences was adjusted. Two types of statutory licences were added, one for broadcasting stations and TV stations to produce and broadcast programs based on published works, and the other for textbook compilation units to compile and publish textbooks for nine-year compulsory education and for the national education plan. Such exploitation may not require permission from the copyright owners but requires that remuneration be paid. Also, the legitimate interests of the owners should not be prejudiced.

Unreasonable limitations were deleted or revised. Articles 22(3), 22(4), 22(9), 22(11), 35, 37, 40, and 43 were revised according to the requirements of the *Berne Convention*. When newspapers and periodicals reprint published works or when performers conduct commercial performances based on published works, arrangements can be made through a blanket licence with the collective copyright management agencies. When using background music, businesses must obtain permission from the music copyright holder and pay for the use of the music. According to the media, many hotels have paid hundreds of thousands of Yuan RMB to copyright holders to use their works as background music.[31]

Stronger Judicial and Administrative Enforcement
Copyright administrations now have greater powers to order infringers to stop infringing acts, to confiscate or destroy the infringing copies, to impose fines, to seize materials, to seize tools and equipment used to make copies, and so on.[32]

Provisional Measures before the Institution of an Action
The copyright owner or an interested person may apply for a preliminary injunction or attachment from a court before bringing a lawsuit. This can be done if they can reasonably prove that a person or group is infringing or will infringe their copyright, and that any delay in implementing measures is likely to cause irreparable harm to their legitimate interests.

Furthermore, before instituting legal proceedings, a copyright holder or interested party may file an application with the People's Court for preservation of evidence. This can be done when evidence may be destroyed or lost or may be difficult to obtain in the future.

Statutory Damages
The amount of statutory damages is regulated. If it is difficult to measure the actual loss or the unjust profit caused by the infringement, the amount of damages may be determined reasonably by referring to the statutory standard (not exceeding 500,000 Yuan RMB) and factors such as the social impact of the infringing acts, the means, circumstances, duration, and range of the infringement, and so on. Reasonable expenses necessary for stopping the infringing acts are also taken into account.[33]

The Legal Status of Collective Copyright Management Agencies
The legal status of collective copyright management agencies has been clarified.[34] These bodies are necessary for authors to exercise their copyrights. China set up a copyright information management organization named China Musical Works Copyright Association in 1992. It suffered considerable hardship because such a body was not stipulated in the *Copyright Law*.

Miscellaneous Provisions
The revised *Copyright Law* explicitly indicates that economic rights are transferable. The former *Law* was not clear on this point, and two opinions formed about whether a copyright could be transferred. Now it is stipulated that a copyright can be transferred either in whole or in part. The main clauses of copyright assignment contracts are also further regulated.

A provision regarding the legal liabilities of publishers, producers, distributors, and renters of reproductions of works was added to the *Copyright Law*. Where such parties cannot prove that their reproductions have legitimate sources, they can be held legally liable.[35]

China has never stopped working on new laws and regulations for protection of intellectual property rights. For example, *Judicial Interpretations by the Supreme People's Court and the Supreme People's Procuratorate on Several Issues of Concrete Application of Laws in Handling Criminal Cases of Infringing Intellectual Property*[36] went into effect on 22 December 2004, while the *Regulations for the Collective Administration of Copyright* became effective on 1 March 2005 and the *Regulations on the Protection of Right of Communication through Information Network* on 1 July 2006.

The Chinese National People's Congress approved a number of amendments to the *Patent Law of the People's Republic of China* on 27 December 2008, resulting in the third revision of the *Law*. The revisions dealt with changes to patent application filing, criteria for granting patents, protection of patent rights, compulsory licensing, and so on. The latest revised *Law* went into effect on 1 October 2009.

The Decision Regarding the Revision of the Copyright Law of the People's Republic of China was adopted at the Thirteenth Session of the Standing Committee of the Eleventh National People's Congress on 26 February 2010. The third revision of Trademark Law of the People's Republic of China is in progress, and the draft has been submitted to the Legislative Affairs Office of the State Council for review. The *Regulations on Customs Protection of Intellectual Property Rights* was amended by the State Council on 17 March 2010, and went into effect on 1 April 2010.

Conclusion

At a general level, there may be some disparities between the multilateral trade agreements concluded within the framework of the Uruguay Round, including the TRIPS Agreement, and the implementing legislation of Members. Many countries, including China, are trying to fulfill their obligations under the TRIPS Agreement. In fact, China has made great efforts and achieved some progress in the protection of IPR, although some problems still exist.

The year 2009 was a key year for the fulfillment of the National Intellectual Property Protection Strategy. With economic construction as the core task, the Chinese government has had some preliminary successes in its efforts to weather the worldwide financial crisis and implement the strategy. Specifically:

- Progress has been made in further rationalizing the intellectual property protection legal regime.
- Different procedural breakthroughs have paved the way for professionalizing the process of intellectual property examination and registration.
- Cooperation among related sectors has facilitated the administrative enforcement of intellectual property rights.
- Judicial enforcement has become the main channel for intellectual property protection.

Furthermore, the fair and efficient adjudication of intellectual property cases according to law has made the judicial system a leading force in intellectual property protection. Judicial protection has served the needs of socioeconomic development while helping to fulfill the National Intellectual Property Protection Strategy. Enhanced judicial supervision and guidance has led to greater consistency in adjudication practices and decision making, and capacity-building initiatives directed towards intellectual property judges have improved judicial competence and quality.

NOTES

1 *General Agreement on Tariffs and Trade,* 30 October 1947, 55 U.N.T.S. 187, Can. T.S. 1947 No. 27 (entered into force 1 January 1948) [GATT].
2 *Agreement on Trade-Related Aspects of Intellectual Property Rights,* 15 April 1994, *Marrakesh Agreement Establishing the World Trade Organization,* Annex 1C, 1869 U.N.T.S. 299, 33 I.L.M. 1197 [TRIPS Agreement].
3 *Paris Convention for the Protection of Industrial Property,* as last revised at the Stockholm Revision Conference, 14 July 1967, 21 U.S.T. 1583, 828 U.N.T.S. 305 (entered into force 26 April 1970) [*Paris Convention*].
4 *Berne Convention for the Protection of Literary and Artistic Works,* 9 September 1886, as revised at Paris on 24 July 1971 and amended in 1979, S. Treaty Doc. No. 99-27 [*Berne Convention*].
5 *International Convention for the Protection of Performers, Producers of Phonograms and Broadcasting Organizations,* 26 October 1961, 496 U.N.T.S. 43.
6 Carlos M. Correa, *Intellectual Rights, the WTO and Developing Countries: The Trips Agreement and Policy Options* (London: Third World Network, 2000) at 3.
7 UNCTAD Secretariat, *The TRIPS Agreement and Developing Countries* (Geneva: United Nations Conference on Trade and Development, 1997) at 7.
8 *Ibid.* at 16.

9 Sophie Messner, *Implications of the TRIPS Agreement under the GATT for Developing Countries* (PhD dissertation, Wirtschafsuniversitat, Wien, 1997) at 58.

10 *General Principles of the Civil Law of the People's Republic of China* [C. civ.] art. 142 (P.R.C.).

11 *Patent Law of the People's Republic of China* (as adopted at the Fourth Session of the Standing Committee of the Sixth National People's Congress on 12 March 1984) [*Patent Law*].

12 TRIPS Agreement, *supra* note 2, art. 28(1).

13 *Ibid.*, art. 41.

14 *Patent Cooperation Treaty*, 19 June 1970, 28 U.S.T. 7645, 1160 U.N.T.S. 231, 9 I.L.M. 978.

15 An Anton Piller order is a court order permitting a person to enter and search another person's premises and seize evidence for use in a court case, particularly one that involves copyright, trademark, or patent infringement, in order to prevent the destruction of such evidence. It is named after the plaintiff in the English case *Anton Piller KG Manufacturing Processes Ltd.* [1976] Ch 55 (C.A.).

16 *Trademark Law of the People's Republic of China* (as adopted at the 24th Session of the Standing Committee of the Ninth National People's Congress on 27 October 2001) [*Trademark Law*] arts. 8 and 11.

17 *Ibid.*, arts. 3 and 16.

18 *Ibid.*, art. 5.

19 Nie Wei, "Trademark Pre-emptive Registration Encountered 'Red Light,'" *Economic Daily*, 5 July 1998 (the second printing plate).

20 *Trademark Law*, *supra* note 16, arts. 32, 33, 43, and 49.

21 *Ibid.*, arts. 24 and 25.

22 *Ibid.*, arts. 53 and 54.

23 UNCTAD-ICTSD, *Resource Book on TRIPS and Development* (New York: Cambridge University Press, 2005), 171, online: IPRsonline <http://www.iprsonline.org/unctadictsd/ResourceBookIndex.htm>.

24 *Copyright Law of the People's Republic of China* (as adopted at the Fifteenth Session of the Standing Committee of the Seventh National People's Congress on 7 September 1990, and revised in accordance with the Decision on the Amendment of the Copyright Law of the People's Republic of China adopted at the Twenty-Fourth Session of the Standing Committee of the Ninth National People's Congress on 27 October 2001, and again on 26 February 2010) [*Copyright Law*].

25 TRIPS Agreement, *supra* note 2, art. 10(2).

26 *Beijing Sunshine Data Co. v. Shanghai Bacai Data and Information Co.*, 1997, Beijing High People's Court (Gao Zhi Zhong Zi No. 66).

27 TRIPS Agreement, *supra* note 2, art. 11.

28 *Copyright Law*, *supra* note 24, art. 10.

29 *WIPO Copyright Treaty*, 20 December 1996, S. Treaty Doc. No. 105-17, 36 I.L.M. 65.

30 *WIPO Performances and Phonograms Treaty*, 20 December 1996, S. Treaty Doc. No. 105-17, 36 I.L.M. 76.

31 *E.g.*, "Yin zhu xie: dai shou bei jing yin yue ban quan fei fu he fa lu gui ding" [It is legal to take in the royalty for the background music], online: Baidu <http://hi.baidu.com/

seafeng3/blog/item/e464caf38d348757342acc44.html>; "Bo fang bei jing yin yue ye de fu fei?" [Should playing background music pay for the royalty?], online: *People's Daily* <http://www.people.com.cn/GB/guandian/183/6103/6104/20030520/996449. html>.

32 *Copyright Law, supra* note 24, art. 48.
33 *Ibid.,* art. 49.
34 *Ibid.,* art. 8.
35 *Ibid.,* art. 53.
36 Adopted at the 1331st Session of the Judicial Committee on the Supreme People's Court on 2 November 2004 and the 28th Session of the Tenth Procuratorial Committee of the Supreme People's Procuratorate on 11 November 2004 and to be effective as of 22 December 2004.

Competition Policy, Capacity Building, and Selective Adaptation
Tentative Lessons from Japan's Experience with Anti-Cartel Policies

RICHARD SCHWINDT AND DEVIN McDANIELS

Over the past twenty years, there has been a remarkable increase in the number of jurisdictions that have implemented comprehensive competition policies.[1]

> The enactment of competition legislation has become a global phenomenon. Competition law has, in effect, become the latest fashion. To be someone, it appears, everyone – including the members of the APEC community – must have a competition statute. For some (particularly the countries of Central and Southeastern Europe as well as the Baltic states) the explanation lies in more than pure fad. To be someone means to be a member of the European "club" and true to the tradition of elite clubs everywhere, proper dress – in this case competition legislation acceptable to those who run the club – is one of the prerequisites of membership.[2]

There are a number of factors, besides faddishness, that explain this recent proliferation of competition policy regimes. Developing countries with emerging market economies recognize the benefits that such policies can provide for the development process. Countries in transition from centrally planned to market economies see a role for competition policy, both as a mechanism to encourage the operation of efficient markets and as an antidote to entrenched, recently privatized dominant firms in specific industries. There has been encouragement, sometimes pressure, from trading partners and trade organizations for the adoption of rules that will curb anti-competitive structures and behaviour that impair international trade. Accession to free trade groups, such as the European Union (EU), has required establishment of a competition policy. As a result, a good number of jurisdictions with little competition policy experience and quite different motivations are striving, some struggling, to implement such policies. In response, jurisdictions with mature competition policy regimes have assisted in capacity building, both individually and collectively.

The development of competition policy is largely based on North American and, more recently, Western European experiences. United States antitrust policy, with a century of development, is clearly mature and, in the view of most commentators, comprehensive and largely consistent with modern economic thought. Despite this recognition, those in the business of helping to build the capacity to implement competition policy do not recommend that their clients simply adopt the American rules.[3]

It stands to reason that competition policy systems will be influenced by the economic, institutional, legal, and cultural settings of the adopting jurisdiction. The question is how the system will be influenced. It is important that "solutions to competition issues" achieve the overarching goal of competition policy – the effective operation of markets. Capacity builders do not have a clearcut understanding of how the mix of economic, legal, institutional, and cultural influences impinges on the implementation of an effective system. Indeed, they spend considerable effort trying to determine the best building tools as they choose between assistance in drafting rules, training the judiciary, training competition agency officers, and seconding their own experienced staff to work with newly established agencies.[4] If there were a way to predict how specific policies would be adapted to local conditions, and which local conditions would be amenable or inimical to effective policy implementation, the job of capacity building would be a lot easier.

A potential tool to assist in this regard is Potter's *selective adaptation model*.[5] The model identifies the role of local conditions in the adaptation of foreign rules. It has been successfully applied to China's adaptation of property law, administrative law, and corporate governance rules. The question we address is whether and how it can be applied to the adaptation of competition policy.

This essay reflects our first steps towards an answer. It involves an *ex post* descriptive analysis of the initiation and first fifty years of enforcement of anti-cartel and merger control rules in Japan. The analysis is conducted from the perspective of the selective adaptation model. We readily admit that we rely largely on secondary sources (and there is an extensive, indeed voluminous, literature) and acknowledge we are neither Japanologists nor legal scholars. Nonetheless, we think the exercise will be worthwhile if it provides some insights into how competition rules will likely be adapted in developing and transitional economies, and what the sponsors of capacity building should emphasize in the pursuit of successful policy implementation. The former Secretary General of the Japanese competition policy authority, the Japan Fair Trade Commission, acknowledges that Japan's mixed experience with competition policy can provide lessons for capacity builders:

> Therefore, unfortunately, it must be said that Japan had experienced too late as well as too small steps taken in the field of competition law.
>
> However, this might mean that Japan can offer valuable lessons to many countries in the world that are going to start serious enforcement efforts of their competition laws from now on. After 1990, many countries had adopted competition laws, but it seems to be very difficult for the enforcement agency of competition laws to establish itself in such a short period of around 10 years in view of the experiences of our country.[6]

The purpose of this research is to identify those lessons. We begin by describing the selective adaptation model. Next, we identify the core areas of competition policy and the basic elements of implementation (the rules, enforcement, and outcomes). We then explore Japan's experience with two of the core elements of competition policy (cartel and merger control) through the lens of selective adaptation.

Selective Adaptation

The basic premise of the selective adaptation model is straightforward. When a jurisdiction adopts an alien set of rules, it will not do so holus-bolus. The rules, and more importantly the implementation of the rules, will be adapted to local conditions. More challenging is identifying and measuring the forces that influence the direction and extent of the adaptation. Why is it that one jurisdiction can take a set of rules off the shelf, clone the implementation procedures of established regimes, and achieve the desired policy goals, whereas, in other cases, adaptation is extensive and painfully slow, and, in some cases, results in policy with unforeseen and undesirable consequences?

The selective adaptation model sets out a number of factors that will condition the establishment and implementation of foreign norms as reflected in rules, structures, processes, and practices.[7] It starts by asking how much room the local jurisdiction has to adapt or modify the foreign norms. Then, given binding constraints, what factors influence the level and direction of adaptation?

The room for adaptation depends first on the power relationship between the source of the foreign norms and the local jurisdiction.[8] At one extreme, there might be no power issue at all. For example, a local jurisdiction in transition from a centrally planned to a market economy might completely voluntarily adopt a Western-style competition policy with little modification to facilitate the transition, even though the policy is "foreign." At the other extreme, a foreign jurisdiction might be in a position to force its norms on the local environment, as in the case of military occupation. The power of the source of the foreign norms can come through the carrot or the stick. The promise of sought-after membership in a customs union can provide a powerful enticement to voluntarily adopt foreign regulatory norms;[9] the threat of trade sanctions can provide an equally powerful incentive.

Once the binding constraints are set, the degree and direction of adaptation depends upon perception, legitimacy, and complementarity. Local perceptions of the purpose (both declared and undeclared), content, and effects of foreign rules and regulatory norms impinge upon their implementation in the local context. If foreign and local perceptions are parallel, modification of the foreign norms will, everything else being equal, be more moderate. Legitimacy involves the extent to which the members of the local jurisdiction agree with the purpose and projected results of the foreign rules. Complementarity can be viewed as the extent to which foreign and local regulatory norms can be combined to achieve a desired outcome. In other words, if the foreign rule assists in achievement of a local priority, it is more likely to be accepted. Conversely, if the foreign rule is seen to hinder achievement of the local priority, it is more likely to be resisted (or adapted to the point of non-recognizability).[10]

Competition Policy

Before applying the selective adaptation model to the Japanese experience with competition policy, it is necessary to identify the specific policies that are to be considered and the elements (such as rules, enforcement, and outcomes) that will be emphasized.

Core Areas of Competition Policy

There is no universal agreement on what precisely comprises competition policy. Some would include a broad set of policies that influence industrial structure, conduct, and performance, including direct regulation (and deregulation), privatization policies, foreign investment policies, and antitrust policies. Others point to antitrust policies alone. To make the analysis tractable, we will focus on two of the three core areas of antitrust policy: horizontal agreements and mergers.[11]

Horizontal agreements are arrangements between direct competitors that constrain independent behaviour. They include joint ventures, specialization agreements, joint research and development projects, joint advertising campaigns (or agreements to restrict advertising), some trade association activities (such as agreements to adhere to common standards or common terminology), purchasing groups, bid rigging, and outright cartelization intended to restrict supply and raise price. Almost without exception, jurisdictions with mature competition policy regimes have strong and well-enforced rules prohibiting naked cartelization, bid rigging, price fixing, and market sharing. This is so for two reasons. First, there is near universal agreement among economists that naked cartels, on balance, result in inefficient outcomes.[12] Second, the remedy for an offensive horizontal agreement is obvious – the parties must stop the offensive behaviour. This combination of agreement over the deleterious effects of the behaviour and an obvious, operational remedy has led to the control of cartels as a primary concern of both established and emerging competition policy regimes.

Horizontal mergers involve the amalgamation of competing businesses. By definition, the removal of a competitor from the market reduces competition, but the end result might well be no impact on equilibrium prices or quantities. On the other hand, some mergers can create or substantially increase market power and are likely to have harmful effects on prices and quantities. Compared with cartelization, there is much less consensus among economists on the impacts on social welfare resulting from horizontal mergers between significant market participants. Nonetheless, in many mature competition policy jurisdictions, merger rules are well developed and are actively enforced. This has much to do, once again, with the existence of an obvious, operational remedy. Parties to a proposed merger can simply be prohibited from proceeding. It is well recognized that anticompetitive, extant market structures are often very difficult to correct. High levels of concentration can lead to interdependence and a dampening of competition, but if market shares have been honestly won, it is difficult to alter the market structure. Dismemberment is strong medicine and is rarely prescribed, but it is relatively easy for public policy to stop the accretion of market share through horizontal mergers.

Elements of Policy

In attempting to operationalize the application of the selective adaptation model to the implementation of these areas of competition policy, we will focus on two elements, the rules and the enforcement.

Adaptation can begin with the actual drafting of the rules. For example, a current area of concern among competition policy practitioners, particularly in Canada, is the role of an efficiency defence in merger cases. On the surface, the issue is fairly simple. Should an anti-competitive merger be allowed if it generates substantial efficiencies? And, if such a defence exists, how is the trade-off to be measured? Societal norms come into play in answering these questions. In a jurisdiction that puts great faith in the ability of markets to achieve efficiency without resort to anti-competitive mergers, the rules might not allow for an efficiency defence. Where such a defence is allowed, the rules might stipulate how the trade-off is to be measured (for example, is it to be total social surplus, consumer surplus, or some hybrid?). Again, norms will play a role. The United States adheres to a "price test." If an anti-competitive merger results in cost savings so great that the post-merger price is expected to fall, the merger may be allowed. Here the norm emphasizes consumer well-being at the expense of the producer. Currently, Canadian jurisprudence is struggling with this trade-off as the legislation explicitly allows for an efficiency defence but does not provide much guidance on how it is to be measured.

Regardless of the rules that are legislated, the efficacy of the policy will depend upon its enforcement, which is obviously susceptible to adaptation. The composition, role, resources, and attitudes of the enforcement body will directly influence the way in which the rules are implemented.

The Japanese Experience

We turn now to a descriptive analysis of Japan's implementation of competition policy. The story begins with a very brief sketch of the historical context.

Background

The business history of Japan leading up to the 1947 introduction of competition policy by the American occupying forces has been extensively documented elsewhere,[13] but some key parts are relevant to our analysis. The legacy of government-led industrialization in Japan beginning in the Meiji period is important. Dating back to the Tokugawa Shogunate, Japanese industry was regarded as an instrument of national policy, and so was developed and directed by political elites.[14] The 1868 Meiji Restoration of imperial rule and the associated impetus for development was conducive to government intervention in and guidance of the economy,[15] and government-led development through active investment in and control of the economy persisted through the turn of the century.[16] The Meiji government actively promoted specific large-scale sectors, starting with defence-related industries such as munitions and shipbuilding, and turning later to consumer goods industries. Policies included creation of state enterprises and encouragement of technology transfers from the West to equip those enterprises. In the 1880s, government ministries fostered the growth of trade associations in small- and medium-scale industries to facilitate the Meiji developmental agenda. Through these trade associations, government ministries sometimes administered horizontal agreements in specific industries (paper manufacturing and cotton spinning are examples) to avoid excessive competition and declining product quality, which were thought to be inevitable in the absence of cartels.[17] Eventually, the state of public finances led to privatization of these large state-developed enterprises. The public assets were sold to private interests, and ended up being concentrated in the hands of "preferred" business groupings, which eventually became the *zaibatsu*.[18]

In the 1920s, cartelization policies were championed by government ministries to prevent excessive competition among the *zaibatsu* combines that had come to dominate the Japanese economy.[19] From the government's perspective, cartels prevented destructive competition and served as a mechanism for guiding the economy.[20] Given these perceived benefits, cartels were encouraged and enforced through trade associations, beginning with export industries in 1925.[21] Legislation termed the *Export Society Law* and the *Major Export Commodities Industrial Association Law* legalized horizontal agreements among export sectors and gave government ministries the ability to force firms to join export cartels.[22] With the Great Depression and subsequent militarization of Japan came more extensive cartelization of the economy. During the 1930s, garden-variety cartel agreements appeared in sectors such as wholesaling, coal mining, cement, and textiles.[23] These arrangements restricted production, fixed prices, and allocated markets, and were often enforced by government ministries.[24] Leading up to the Second World War, trade associations in strategic industries were transformed into wartime control associations (*toseikai*), under direct bureaucratic control, while trade associations in other sectors operated as independent cartels with government support.[25]

Norms and practices influencing merger policy also emerged during the prewar period. As noted earlier, government-directed development and the eventual divestiture of assets to privileged families led to the formation of the *zaibatsu*.[26] These business groupings exerted control over their subsidiaries though a variety of measures, including shareholding through holding companies, interlocking directorates, centralized buying and selling, written agreements, and ownership of financial institutions.[27] These "control techniques" laid the groundwork for the postwar structure of the economy. In particular, the main bank system, in which business groups (*zaibatsu* and later *keiretsu*) were associated with a particular bank, grew out of these *zaibatsu* control techniques and would later have a significant effect on merger policy. The practice of cross-shareholding (between business group-linked firms as well as between firms and their main banks) was an essential aspect of this control system, and also became ingrained in Japanese economic practice during this period.

In the interwar years, the 1938 *National General Mobilization Law* gave the government authority to force mergers in strategic industries.[28] In 1941, the *Major Industries Association Ordinance* gave industry control associations the ability to compel horizontal mergers between small and medium firms.[29] These laws were designed with wartime command of the economy in mind, and resulted in increased concentration and decreased competition in the immediate postwar Japanese economy. More significantly, they established the principle that mergers, like horizontal agreements, were subject to bureaucratic guidance and permission.

At the end of the Second World War, Japan was placed under an American-led occupation (termed the "Supreme Command of Allied Powers," or SCAP). The United States believed that the restructuring of Japan's economy to attain "economic democratization" was a necessary step towards avoiding future conflict, and three primary policies were implemented to achieve this end. First, the *zaibatsu* were dissolved in order to deconcentrate economic power. Second, Japan was directed to draft and implement antitrust legislation. In 1947, the *Law Concerning the Prohibition of Private Monopoly and the Maintenance of Fair Trade* (popularly known as the *Antimonopoly Law*, or AML) was passed, and a new body, the Japan Fair Trade Commission (JFTC) was created to enforce this law.[30] Third, the harmful conduct of trade associations was to be halted. In 1946, SCAP began dissolving the wartime control associations as part of this economic democratization, but the process was never fully completed for fear of serious economic destabilization.[31] In order to deal with potential anti-competitive behaviour on the part of trade associations, the *Trade Association Law* was passed in 1947, prohibiting all significant functions of these organizations. These new laws were not well received by government ministries (particularly the Ministry of Commerce and Industry, which later became the Ministry of International Trade and Industry [MITI] and, more recently, the Ministry of Economy, Trade and Industry [METI]) or by businessmen accustomed to the prewar government guidance and cartelization, as the AML and *Trade Association Law* severely limited their ability to continue these practices.[32]

Although prewar Japan was characterized by a plethora of horizontal agreements, many mandated by government, it is important to note that industries were not particularly highly concentrated in an industrial organization sense during this period. Although aggregate concentration was high in that a handful of *zaibatsu* controlled a large share of industrial assets, the *zaibatsu* were generally conglomerates; they did not focus on single industries and markets. Seller concentration in individual markets, which is a basis for the market power concerns of competition policy, was not significantly greater than that found in the United States in the 1950s. Based on data from the early and mid-1950s, Bain[33] found that top-level seller concentration in Japan was about the same as, or slightly greater than, in the United States. A decade later, Caves and Uekusa[34] came to much the same conclusion using a broader sample of industries and a later time period. The point here is that in the early postwar period, Japan's industrial structure, in terms of concentration measures, was no less "competitive" than that of the United States. Industry conduct certainly differed, but structure did not. It follows that a productive competition policy would focus on anti-competitive conduct and, when necessary, implement conduct-oriented remedies.

In the discussion that follows, we will refer to two key economic indicators: the annual rate of growth of real gross domestic product (GDP), and annual percent changes in price levels. These are shown in Figure 1. The period 1953-73 were boom years, with annual GDP growth averaging 10 percent. Growth dropped with the first oil shock in the early 1970s, and then maintained a healthy average of 4 percent until the end of the 1980s. The 1990s and the first years of the new century were marked by economic stagnation. Inflation was very modest in the 1953-72 period, spiked with the oil

FIGURE 1

Year-to-year changes in consumer prices and real GDP in Japan, 1953-2004

Source: Derived from a search of International Monetary Fund Databases electronic data files, series 158/64.x, 158/99B.C., 158/99BVR, Simon Fraser University Library (November 2005).

shock, and then fell back to its pre-shock level. The 1991-2004 period saw very low inflation, and in some years actual deflation.

The Regulatory Norms

A thorough description of a society's norms is a daunting task, and one best left to initiates. Here we identify what most commentators believe to be the basic norms underlying a jurisdiction's views on competition policy. In the case at hand, American rules were imported into Japan, so the norms in these two jurisdictions need to be reviewed.

Most, if not all, US undergraduate textbooks dealing with antitrust economics include a discussion of the political, social, cultural, legal, and economic underpinnings of that country's competition policy. There is usually reference to the importance of liberal individualism (whether couched in those terms or not), emphasis on the concepts of freedom of opportunity and freedom of choice, and acknowledgement of Americans' abiding mistrust of the concentration of power, whether in public or private hands. The

American historian Richard Hofstadter claimed that the goals of US antitrust policy were of three kinds:

> The first were economic; the classical model of competition confirmed the belief that the maximum of economic efficiency would be produced by competition ... The second class of goals was political; the antitrust principle was intended to block private accumulation of power and protect democratic government. The third was social and moral; the competitive process was believed to be a kind of disciplinary machinery of the development of character, and the competitiveness of the people – the fundamental stimulus to national morale – was believed to need protection.[35]

This is not to say that the norms underlying antitrust policy have been completely consistent over the past century. When markets falter, faith in individual efforts and fear of big government and big business can diminish. Nonetheless, while enthusiasm for antitrust enforcement might wax and wane, depending upon the economic and political mood of the country, the antitrust laws have remained in place, and "throughout the 20th century, America's antitrust laws have coexisted uneasily with policies that favor extensive government intervention in the economy through planning, ownership, or sweeping controls over prices and entry."[36]

Ignoring for a moment the support for antitrust policy on economic efficiency grounds, the core values or norms that underlie Americans' commitment to antitrust policy are a dedication to the protection and enhancement of individual freedom and a concomitant distrust of concentrated economic power. According to Hadley, this runs counter to core Japanese norms: "The Japanese tradition puts emphasis on the group, and further lacks the notion that power is likely to be abused. In our Western individualistic tradition we worry about power and suspect the motives of businessmen gathering together to discuss prices, output, etc."[37]

There seems to be some (but not complete) consensus that there was a significant difference between these two countries in terms of regulatory norms – individualism versus group orientation, and statism versus anti-statism.[38] Clearly, there are other important societal norms but this subset, which we are calling regulatory norms, are particularly important with respect to competition policy. In turn, these regulatory norms are instantiated in observable rules and the processes and practices of enforcement and adjudication institutions.

Conformity with regulatory norms leads to certain types of behaviour. For example, a group orientation leads to an emphasis on social harmony and consensus. This emphasis in turn leads to an aversion to competition and a lack of faith in market mechanisms because these forces could upset the maintenance of harmony within the group.[39] Combine this with a statist propensity and the result is a set of norms that is consistent with state intervention in the economy, and a lack of interest in pro-competition policies. And so it was in Japan.

As noted in our brief historical sketch, Japan's rapid industrialization after the Meiji Restoration owed much to state intervention. The overall policy was an obvious success and understandably legitimized government intervention in the economy.

First argues that Japan's history of economic development led to what he calls a bureaucratic regulatory culture,[40] which he defines as follows: "A bureaucratic regulatory culture is focused on how the economy should be structured and run. Its core concern is economic welfare and it works by guidance. This type of regulation is group-oriented, theory-based, and forward-looking. The decision-making model is consensual, and rigorous justification for particular decisions is not only unnecessary but may be unwise."[41]

Within this normative framework, cartels and trade associations played a valuable role, in that they enabled the government to guide the economy towards particular industrial policy goals, to gather information about industries, and to communicate with industries.[42] Information exchange facilitated by trade associations is particularly useful, and was fostered by the government within this regulatory culture.[43] Mergers and acquisitions were also important in this kind of a regulatory regime; control of mergers enabled the bureaucracy to shape the economic structure as it saw fit.

First draws a distinction between the regulatory cultures that characterized the conception and implementation of antitrust in the United States and in Japan. US competition policy operates within a framework of legalistic regulation intended to protect victims from improper business conduct. In Japan, however, "antitrust ... was placed in a very different regulatory culture, one which viewed antitrust (and economic law) as a tool of government that bureaucrats might use to guide and manage the economy."[44] Iyori has the same view, namely, that "the [anti-monopoly] law in Japan is, by contrast [to the law in the West], considered primarily an instrument of government control, especially bureaucratic control."[45] Along these same lines, Ramseyer argues that this "perception of harmony is crucial for it plays a central part in legitimating bureaucratic rule in Japan."[46]

Application: Cartels

For convenience, we have divided the evolution of cartel policy into a number of periods. Each is marked by a change in the environment that impacted the adaptation process.

Adoption: 1947-52

The power relationship between foreign and local regulatory norms during the postwar occupation of Japan is clear. By all accounts, Japan's *Antimonopoly Law* was drafted and passed under pressure from American authorities. "The record of drafting the AML reveals an authority imbalance between the two sides. The US side set the broad policy direction for the legislation, a policy direction that Japan, under occupation, had little choice but to follow."[47] In the years immediately following the imposition of the AML, the presence of the Occupation forces maintained similar power relations between the two parties.

Under these circumstances, there was not a lot of room for the Japanese negotiators to selectively adapt the rules dictated by the victors. The US terms were adopted regardless of whether the underlying norms fit with Japanese views in terms of perception, legitimacy, and complementarity.

There is some question concerning Japanese perceptions of the purpose and goals of the AML. First contends that "negotiators from Japan's government understood perfectly well what the legislation was about."[48] Caves and Uekusa argue that the AML "employed novel terms such as 'public interest,' 'substantial,' and 'competition' that conveyed no clear meaning to the Japanese public who would have to comply with it."[49] Hideaki Kobayashi (1997), a high-ranking official in the JFTC, states that "the competition law, when it was introduced 50 years ago, was something totally unknown to political leaders, government officials, and the general public in Japan."[50] Rather than the policy's simply being "unknown," some Japanese apparently believed that there were sinister motivations behind it, seeing the AML as a foreign method of keeping Japan weak and subordinated to the US. "There are many who profess, and in all honesty believe that the Antimonopoly Law, [along with the Labour Standards Law,] was forced by the victors on the defeated nation for the covert purpose of keeping down her economy in a weak condition."[51]

In any case, given the statist views held by Japanese policy-making elites, it was not surprising that policies to facilitate unregulated, competitive markets were not embraced (rejection was not on the table). What were the preferred policies, however? In his analysis of the original intent of the

AML, First emphasizes the role of the Special Survey Committee (SSC), a group of economists and technical experts that was formed just before cessation of hostilities to plan for postwar reconstruction.[52] The SSC report was published in March 1946 and was wide- ranging.[53] It provides valuable insights into the Japanese position on issues relevant to competition policy generally and horizontal agreements specifically. The recommendations of the report were not directly implemented, but they did provide a conceptual basis for economic planning over the next decades.[54] The career of the report's initiator, Saburo Okita, reflects that influence.[55]

The SSC's proposals for revamping the organization of Japanese industry merit review.

Reorganization of the Industrial Setup. The industrial setup was as firmly connected to the State structure as was the financial setup. In order to democratize the industrial setup it will be therefore necessary to get rid of the past feudalistic and militaristic capitalist system by relieving the industries of State power once and for all. This will make it difficult in principle for big business to make an appearance in Japan in the future. On the other hand, in order that technological levels be elevated and the rationalization of business management be accomplished it is desirable that big business management be accomplished and that big business enterprises grow. Such basic industries as railways, communication, electric power generation, steelmaking, coal mining, and fertilizer manufacture absolutely need large-scale operations. In a country like Japan, where domestic markets are small and the raw materials base is weak, free competition in these basic industries would not necessarily result in their growth, and the need will arise to nationalize these industries or give them a public character. Nationalization however, will have to be accomplished by measures designed to wipe out the bureaucratic inefficiency of the past.

At the same time, those basic industries which serve domestic non-governmental or export demand and do not necessarily require a large scale operation need to be encouraged to compete as freely and fairly as possible. Export industries especially would need a system that is so flexible as to allow them to undertake dynamic production in accordance with changing world market conditions.

It will be necessary, in this context, that the Toseikai (Control Associations), which was founded during the war, should be reorganized into an autonomous association and given the character of an organ representing the collective will of business entrepreneurs. At the same time a system

should be established in which public control will be exercised over industries so that the interest of consumers can be protected.[56]

Basic industries that produced public goods or verged on natural monopoly should be nationalized or "given a public character," which presum-
ably meant they should be subjected to direct regulation. Basic industries
with limited-scale economies that produced for domestic private sector demand or export markets should compete without government ownership or
direct regulation. The wartime cartels (*toseikai*) that were mandated and
effectively controlled by the government should be resurrected as private
organizations, operating without government interference, although consumer interests were to be protected. Ultimately this did not happen, thanks
to the implementation of the AML.[57]

The proposals for smaller, non-basic industries also called for cooperation between competitors:

> Smaller enterprises posed serious economic and social problems in the
> past. We should not, in eager pursuit of ease in the immediate future, allow
> them to present such problems again in a more serious form in the modern
> age ... It must not be forgotten, however, that more essential measures are
> to improve the quality of these enterprises by introducing technical ration-
> alization and economic organization into them. The following are the prin-
> cipal measures that should be taken ...
>
> 2. *Promotion of Cooperation among Smaller Enterprises.* Industrial as-
> sociations need to expand their past function of purchasing raw materials
> and selling products jointly to include technological interchanges, joint use
> of productive equipment, and improvement of working conditions. Smaller
> firms may be enabled in this way to benefit substantially from the advan-
> tages of large-scale business management. It is also quite desirable that
> smaller enterprises thus collectivized rationally would compete with other
> collectivized regional groups of smaller firms and collectively improve their
> technological level and efficiency.[58]

In short, horizontal agreements among competitors were viewed by the
Japanese as legitimate and complementary to programs for postwar
construction.

The dominant position of the occupiers in the power relationship was
clearly reflected in the original wording of those sections of the AML that
dealt with cartels. Simply, Article 4 of the law prohibited cartels *per se*. As

such, any "agreements among enterprises in a competitive relationship as regards price, territory of activities, quantity of production, and other terms of business" were prohibited unless the impact on competition of the agreement was "negligible."[59] The inclusion of the outright *per se* prohibition of cartels was at the firm insistence of American negotiators, to the dismay of Japanese negotiators of the AML. In the final stages of drafting, the Japanese representatives requested (to no avail) that the wording of Article 4 be changed so that cartels would be prohibited only if they "substantially restrained competition ... contrary to the public interest."[60]

Despite this *per se* prohibition, another potential source of horizontal agreements remained: trade associations. As discussed above, in 1946 SCAP dissolved the wartime control associations due to their role in cartelization of the Japanese economy. Nevertheless, many of these dissolved associations reappeared within a few years as trade associations under different names, while maintaining very similar functions and personnel. Although the trade associations were private sector institutions, the bureaucracy continued to wield significant influence and employed the associations in their efforts to control and direct the economy.[61] The inability of the Occupation authorities to prevent the re-emergence of previously dissolved associations resulted in the passage of the *Trade Association Law* (1947) to complement the AML and specifically deal with antitrust violations by trade associations.[62] Price fixing by associations was made *per se* illegal, and they were prohibited from engaging in a broad range of activities that could assist interfirm cooperation.[63] Furthermore, any undue influence wielded by bureaucrats over trade associations was considered a violation.[64] Here the Japanese (government and business) adaptation to the original order to dissolve the *toseikai*, through public reformation of trade associations, was thwarted by supplementary legislation from the Occupation authorities.

The Japan Fair Trade Commission, a new quasi-judicial agency, was created to enforce the AML. In First's view, the most "critical point of contention" between the Americans and the Japanese was how independent the agency would be and to which government official it would report.[65] Ultimately, the JFTC nominally was given a good deal of independence and, at the recommendation of the Americans, was made accountable to the prime minister. The JFTC was not given cabinet rank and this, according to Fry, put it in a subservient position relative to other ministries responsible for economic regulation, specifically MITI and the Ministry of Finance.[66] This relationship became quite important during the 1952-72 period.

In effect, the JFTC was given exclusive jurisdiction over enforcement of the AML. Miwa and Ramseyer, First and Shiraishi, and Beeman are of the view that this "monopoly over antimonopoly services" impaired enforcement from the outset.[67] "The point of departure for any discussion of the JFTC's role must be the fact that the Commission essentially maintains a monopoly on antimonopoly services in Japan ... One Japanese scholar has labeled the JFTC's commanding position over antitrust enforcement the 'original sin.'"[68]

According to First, Japanese negotiators of the AML knowingly sought to hobble private enforcement by requiring victims of anticompetitive acts to channel complaints through the JFTC.[69] Only after the agency makes a decision can the aggrieved party file a damage suit. Also, unlike in the United States, there was no provision for triple damages. These disincentives, combined with other more general constraints on litigation, led Ramseyer to conclude that "the institutional barriers to litigation in Japan have, it appears, all but eliminated private antitrust damage suits."[70]

First concludes his review of the original intent of the AML by arguing that the enforcement mechanism was intended to keep competition policy a component of bureaucratic economic regulation: "Japan fought hard to keep antitrust enforcement within the control of the bureaucracy by narrowing the private right of action and resisting all efforts to provide the antitrust enforcement agency with a legal staff that could independently seek relief in court. Antitrust enforcement would be a component of bureaucratic economic regulation rather than a part of a legal system which could be utilized by those harmed by anticompetitive conduct."[71]

In sum, the power relationship during the drafting of the AML obliged Japan to enact anti-cartel legislation that was not reflective of Japanese regulatory norms. On the other hand, the mechanics of enforcement, specifically the role of the JFTC, were consistent with those norms.

Adaptation: 1952 to the Present

Given the short time period in which the AML was crafted, and the dominant power of the Occupation authorities, the initial period of implementation of competition policy in Japan might be better described as adoption rather than adaptation. When the Occupation ended in 1952, the previously binding power constraints weakened and adaptation became possible. The following half-century can be divided into three periods: (1) the so-called Dark Ages of Japanese antitrust from 1952 to 1972, when competition policy

was brought into line with the local regulatory norms; (2) a period of resuscitation from 1972 up to the late 1980s, when local norms slowly came
into greater alignment with foreign norms; and (3) the period from the
early 1990s to the present, when altered power relationships combined with
a failure by the bureaucratic regulatory regime to maintain economic performance led to a more profound acceptance of the principles and practices
of American antitrust policy.

What follows is descriptive analysis in broad-brush strokes. We do not
provide a complete review of the voluminous literature dealing with the
evolution of Japanese competition policy. The purpose is simply to see
whether the selective adaptation model can help explain that evolution.

The "Dark Ages": 1952-72.   The later years of the American Occupation
marked a "reverse course" in US policy. With the onset of the Korean War,
the US had a strong strategic interest in a robust Japanese economy, an
economy that was struggling with reconstruction. "Democratization" of
the economy took a backseat to recovery, and American interest in the enforcement of the AML and industrial restructuring waned.[72] Also in 1952,
the formal conclusion of the Occupation produced a fundamental change in
the power relationship between Japan and the United States.

These changes in the power dynamics empowered Japanese elites to express local regulatory norms. "No sooner had the Antimonopoly Law been
enacted than agitation began for its amendment."[73] Of particular importance to government and business leaders was reform of the cartel provisions, which they perceived as a detriment to rebuilding efforts and
achievement of higher growth rates.[74] The *Trade Association Law* was also a
major point of contention, as it essentially eliminated all significant functions of trade associations and viewed all scales of organization as synonym-
ous (two or more businessmen gathering together were treated the same
way as an industry association with 500 members), creating widespread opposition.[75] The absence of any significant political will to enforce the AML
against cartels, combined with pressure from the business lobby and government ministries to relax the cartel provision, led to amendment of the
AML in 1953.[76] The *per se* prohibition of cartels was removed from the law,
and "cartels were now prohibited only if they caused substantial restraint of
competition in a particular field of trade." Importantly, the amendment allowed for rationalization (Article 24[4]) and recession cartels (Article
24[3]), provided they were sanctioned by the JFTC. "This aspect of the

amendment signified a change in policy towards cartels in the sense that under this amendment there were 'good cartels' and 'bad cartels,' whereas in the original AML all cartels were regarded as basically bad."[77] The *Trade Association Law* was also repealed in the 1953 amendment.[78] Rules governing trade associations were amalgamated into Section 8 of the amended AML. This modified legislation was severely weakened, in that it removed all specific prohibitions on trade association activities (particularly relating to information gathering and sharing), replacing them with broad provisions,[79] "leading to a revival of cooperation within trade associations."[80]

The amendment did not satisfy the pro-cartel forces. Government bureaucrats (especially MITI personnel) and businessmen wanted to be able to establish and enforce cartels of their own accord, independent of the JFTC and above the application of the AML.[81] Their lobbying efforts were rewarded with the passage of laws granting AML exemptions to government-encouraged cartels (to restrict production, fix prices, and allocate markets) for exporters and small and medium enterprises. These were the *Export-Import Transactions Law* and the *Medium and Small Enterprise Stabilization Law*.[82] Additional laws exempting cartels, usually targeted at specific industries, were passed at the recommendation of MITI throughout the 1950s and 1960s. Industries affected included coal mining, fisheries, and distilling, to name a few.[83]

Another sort of cartel exemption emerged in the early 1950s, the "administrative guidance" cartel.[84] A government ministry (typically MITI) would recommend cartel measures (typically production cutbacks) through informal guidance offered to an industry association in response to perceived problems in that industry. Relevant government ministries negotiated with a particular industry to cut back production in the face of recession, creating a *de facto* output cartel.[85] The justification for the output recommendations was that quotas were determined by MITI, when, in fact, quotas were often the product of prior negotiation among the firms within their industry associations.[86] Beginning in 1952 with the Glorious Boren cotton-spinning output cartel,[87] similar arrangements proliferated in trade associations throughout the Japanese economy.[88]

> MITI's active encouragement of cartels through trade associations as a countermeasure to recession signaled to industries that cartels were not only permissible but desirable ... Companies learned that the default reaction to an economic problem was to talk to the other companies in the

TABLE 1

Explicit exemptions of cartels from Japan's Antimonopoly Law, 1954-73

	1954	1957	1960	1963	1966	1969	1973
Recession and rationalization cartels (AML Sections 24-3 and 24-4)	0	7	13	12	30	12	12
Laws exempting cartels among small and medium enterprises[a]	77	289	542	888	989	866	911
Other special cartel exemption laws	2	15	40	51	60	76	56
Total	79	312	595	951	1,079	954	979

Notes: Data refer to the number of cartels in effect on 31 March of the years shown.

a This category includes four laws legalizing cartels in industries dominated by small and medium enterprises: the *Medium and Small Enterprise Stabilization Law,* the *Law Concerning the Organization of Small and Medium Enterprises,* the *Export-Import Law,* and the *Law Concerning the Appropriate Conduct of Business Relating to Environmental Hygiene.*

Source: Data are adapted from Franz Waldenberger, "The Changing Role of Competition Policy in Japan" in Sarah Metzger-Court and Werner Pascha, eds., *Japan's Socio-Economic Evolution: Continuity and Change* (Sandgate, Folkestone, Kent, UK: Japan Library, 1996) at 198, 208.

industry ... Over time, the repeated negotiations among firms resulted in an increasing propensity to cooperate in many industries. The "cartel-mindedness" of the Japanese zaikai (business circles), which SCAP had tried to expunge, was revived.[89]

The resultant cartels were exempt from the AML on a quasi-legal basis in that they were an administrative measure of government. For the time being, the JFTC did not take action against these cartels.[90]

Table 1 shows the proliferation of cartels that were explicitly exempted from the AML. Waldenberger estimates that there were relatively fewer implicitly exempted administrative cartels during this period.

The reasoning behind these explicit and implicit exemptions was usually the suppression of "excessive competition."[91] Interestingly, these exempted cartels were not present in the highly productive and highly competitive sectors of the economy, but rather were concentrated in low-productivity sectors characterized by small and medium enterprises.[92] As shown in Table 1, the overwhelming majority of legal cartels fell under the small- and medium-sized enterprises exemption. The granting of exemptions in these sectors is reflective of the adaptation process. Without horizontal agreements, there would have been serious structural adjustments in these low-productivity industries, and this would have led to the "destruction of societal harmony and stability."[93]

When Iyori and Uesugi called the 1952-73 period the "Dark Ages" of antitrust in Japan, they aptly summarized enforcement of cartel provisions (or the lack thereof) during this time. By the early 1950s, the JFTC was forced to change its approach to enforcement against cartel violations, which had been relatively active under the guidance and support of American Occupation authorities.[94] Following the end of the Occupation, limited enforcement and the avoidance of legal action against violations became the modus operandi of the JFTC,[95] which launched only forty-eight formal actions against cartels between 1953 and 1972.[96] These actions generally involved a recommendation decree by the JFTC to the offending parties to correct anti-competitive behaviour. No criminal action was taken against cartels during this period. As a result, there was little deterrence of cartels that did not qualify for one of the many exemptions. There was no real penalty, monetary or otherwise.[97]

It is clear that cartel policy was extensively adapted by the Japanese during this early period and brought into line with the bureaucratic regulatory norm. In effect, the anti-cartel provisions were weakened, if not gutted, by removal of the *per se* prohibition, the revival of trade associations, the establishment of explicit and implicit exceptions to the general prohibition, limited enforcement, and weak remedies.

Resuscitation: 1972-89.   In the early 1970s, several forces combined to alter the state of selective adaptation of anti-cartel rules in Japan. Inflation stemming from the 1973 oil shock became a serious public concern and economic growth faltered (see Figure 1). The widespread cartelization of the economy was seen as part of the problem,[98] delegitimizing the local regulatory norms that had promoted horizontal agreements to begin with.

Local regulatory norms faced serious challenges in the political and economic context of high inflation in the 1970s. JFTC enforcement actions against cartels in 1973 reached record highs, but it was apparent that this was having little effect on deterring further violations.[99] In an effort to assert its ability to combat (and deter) these violations, the JFTC launched a criminal action against an oil industry cartel in 1974. This was a suitable target, given the public outcry against cartelization and the inflation related to the

oil price shock.[100] This case marked the first criminal action against cartelization in the history of the AML. Several oil companies were accused of
price-fixing and production limitation arrangements. The companies plead-
ed innocence, claiming that they were following the administrative guidance of MITI in the context of the oil crisis. The companies had a case as
MITI had offered guidance relating to output limitation,[101] but it was clear
that they had gone beyond those recommendations in their arrangements.[102]
Since they were at least partly following the administrative guidance of
MITI, the sentences imposed on the colluding executives were suspended,
as there was some doubt about whether they knew they were breaking the
law. As Sanekata and Wilks put it, "the JFTC won on enforcement but lost
on enforcement."[103] The decision of the Supreme Court of Japan in this case
did not take a definitive stance as to whether administrative guidance cartels
were legal. In essence, the Court ruled that "an agreement to restrain competition could be justified, even without exempting laws, if it was based on
a directive or entrustment of the government."[104]

Although the decision did create a potential precedent for exemptions
under administrative guidance, legislation soon aligned with the public's
growing hostility towards cartelization. In the wake of the oil cartel case, the
AML was amended in 1977 to allow for administrative surcharges against
firms involved in cartel violations. The surcharges were set at 2 percent of
sales for the period of cartelization, although small and medium enterprises
were subject to only half this rate.[105] In addition, the JFTC worked to reduce
the number of explicitly exempt cartels throughout the economy (see Table
2). "In the span of five short years between 1973 and 1977, the JFTC had
registered record numbers of formal measures against AML violations, including the use of criminal accusations; successfully undertaken an initiative that nearly halved the total number of legal cartels ... The basis for the
JFTC's successes is inseparable from the turbulent political and economic
environment in which change took place."[106]

In this new policy environment, the JFTC enacted "Guidelines Concerning the Activities of Trade Associations under the Antimonopoly Law" in
1979.[107] These guidelines clarified the JFTC's interpretation of Section 8 of
the AML and indicated what activities the JFTC would view as likely violations. Price-related violations cited by the guidelines include establishment
of a minimum sales price, a standard price, a common pricing formula, and
limits on rebates.[108] Violations are also articulated for quantity-related and
various other general acts. The guidelines also clarified available exemptions,

TABLE 2

Explicit exemptions of cartels from Japan's Antimonopoly Law, 1974-92

	1954	1957	1960	1963	1966	1969	1973
Recession and rationalization cartels (AML 24-3 and 24-4)	0	2	2	4	0	4	0
Laws exempting cartels among small and medium enterprises[a]	851	487	459	444	401	265	215
Other special cartel exemption laws	57	39	30	23	25	9	6
Total	908	528	491	471	426	278	221

Notes: Data refer to the number of cartels in effect on 31 March of the years shown.

a This category includes four laws legalizing cartels in industries dominated by small and medium enterprises: the *Medium and Small Enterprise Stabilization Law*, the *Law Concerning the Organization of Small and Medium Enterprises*, the *Export-Import Law*, and the *Law Concerning the Appropriate Conduct of Business Relating to Environmental Hygiene*.

Source: Data are adapted from Franz Waldenberger, "The Changing Role of Competition Policy in Japan" in Sarah Metzger-Court and Werner Pascha, eds., *Japan's Socio-Economic Evolution: Continuity and Change* (Sandgate, Folkestone, Kent, UK: Japan Library, 1996) at 216.

and in particular set out in some detail what types of information exchange would be viewed as beneficial and what types would be viewed as facilitating illicit horizontal agreement.[109]

With time, inflationary pressures subsided and economic growth recovered, albeit not to the very high levels of the earlier period (see Figure 1). With the return to prosperity, enforcement of anti-cartel provisions decreased.[110] From 1973 to 1977, the JFTC initiated ninety-four formal actions against cartels, compared with only thirty-two actions from 1978 to 1987.[111] Structurally depressed industries became an important policy issue in 1978, and laws were passed that year, and then reworked in 1983, to allow for extensive coordination of business activities of firms (short of overt price fixing) towards restructuring depressed industries.[112] Few horizontal agreements were exempted under these laws, but the policy imperative of aiding structurally depressed industries was an important factor in the decreased enforcement of cartel provisions.[113]

During the 1970s and 1980s, foreign regulatory norms with respect to cartels came to be selectively adapted (as opposed to being nearly rejected) in Japan. When local norms, in this case the bureaucratic regulatory regime, failed to deliver prosperity, they lost legitimacy and the public and the bureaucrats responsible for enforcement were willing to accept a policy more in line with foreign regulatory norms. With the return to prosperity, there was less enthusiasm for a strict anti-cartel policy, and local regulatory norms were once again favoured.

Enhancement: 1989 to the Present.   From the late 1980s to the present, two forces were at play to erode faith in the bureaucratic regulatory model and enhance support for a stronger competition policy. First, the Japanese "bubble economy" burst, and partial responsibility was attached to the bureaucratic regulatory regime and the "crony capitalism" it enabled. Second, the US, suffering from a substantial trade deficit with Japan and believing that its exports were impeded by restrictive practices in that country, put pressure on Japanese policy makers to more strictly enforce antitrust policy.

The bursting of the "bubble economy" in the early 1990s had a significant impact on anti-cartel policy in Japan because it affected the perceived legitimacy of the bureaucratic regulatory model. As was true in earlier periods, the model was extolled when the economy worked well and questioned during periods of poor performance. There was, however, a deeper criticism in that many now believed that the extant regulatory norms had not only failed to prevent the downturn but were partially responsible for it. Critics claimed that the network system, pejoratively called "crony capitalism," was behind a number of economic ills ranging "from complacency and uncompetitiveness rooted in inbred trade and investment practices to the protection of the corporate unfit and the spread of moral hazard due to widespread subsidies and easy bailouts."[114] Evidence also emerged that Japan's postwar recovery, and particularly its export success, were explained by high levels of domestic competition in specific industries, and not by administrative guidance. In describing the rekindled interest in competition policy in the 1990s, a JFTC official claimed that the government had come to recognize the positive relationship between competition policy and economic growth.[115] This recognition was apparently based on studies exploring the competitive advantage of Japan.[116] Perceived complementarities between competition policy and local regulatory imperatives significantly altered the state of adaptation in Japan.

During the 1980s, the relationship between the US and Japan became strained. By the mid-1970s, the US had begun to run a chronic trade deficit

FIGURE 2

US trade deficits in goods, in billions of current US dollars, 1978-95

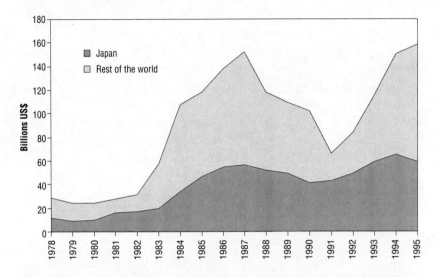

Source: Calculated by the authors using data from: Douglas A. Irwin, Table Ee551-568, "Imports, by country of origin: 1790-2001," and Table Ee533-550, "Exports, by country of destination: 1790-2001," in Susan B. Carter, Scott Sigmund Gartner, Michael R. Haines, Alan L. Olmstead, Richard Sutch, and Gavin Wright, *Historical Statistics of the United States, Earliest Times to the Present: Millennial Edition* (New York: Cambridge University Press, 2006).

in goods (between 1960 and 1975, it had, on average, experienced a modest surplus), and by the mid-1980s, the deficits had reached very high levels. A significant portion of this deficit was attributable to trade with Japan (see Figure 2). Many Americans believed that one source of the trade imbalance was the restrictive practices of Japanese firms that impeded imports from the United States. To remedy this concern, the US strongly encouraged the Japanese to strengthen the enforcement of their antitrust laws.[117]

Evidence of a changed power relationship can be found in the establishment of the Structural Impediments Initiative (SSI) in 1989-90. This marked a turning point in the enforcement of competition policy and was credited by some sources with "creating an anti-monopoly renaissance" in Japan in the 1990s.[118] These bilateral trade negotiations between Japan and the US devoted significant focus to the role of the AML and its enforcement as a means of improving the competitive environment facing American firms in

Japan. Under threat of retaliatory protectionist measures, Japan made concessions to the *gaiatsu* (foreign pressure) in some areas of concern, although there was lingering resistance regarding competition policy issues.[119] That said, the SII played an important role in accelerating ongoing changes in the Japanese public's attitude towards their regulatory regime.[120]

Responding to American demands articulated in the SII, the cartel penalties were increased (to 6 percent of sales over the period of cartelization) in a 1991 amendment of the AML.[121] In addition, the JFTC pressed to reduce the number of explicitly exempted cartels. By 1995, the number of legal cartels had declined to a "negligible level."[122] The laws permitting these legal cartels were all but repealed in the 1997 *Omnibus Act* accompanying the 1997 amendment of the AML. Enforcement action by the JFTC increased significantly from 1990 onward. The first criminal charges since the oil cartel cases of the 1970s were filed against a plastics cartel in 1991.[123] The JFTC issued new Trade Association Guidelines in 1995. They attempted to clarify what constituted acceptable "self-regulation [by a trade association]" and what would offend the AML.[124]

The strengthening of Japanese competition policy is ongoing. Further amendments to the AML were enacted in April 2005. Penalties were raised to 10 percent of sales during the period of cartelization, and to 15 percent for repeat offenders. A leniency program was introduced to encourage whistle-blowing by cartel members, an accepted method of destabilizing such arrangements. There also appears to have been an increase in private suits for damages, particularly by municipal governments that have been the victims of bid rigging.[125]

The Selective Adaptation of Anti-Cartel Policy
The selective adaptation framework helps explain the evolution of cartel policy in Japan. In the mid-1940s, when the AML was imposed on Japan, regulatory norms with respect to horizontal agreements and trade association activities diverged markedly between the source of the foreign rules (the US) and the local jurisdiction (Japan). This was reflected in perceptions of the intent and anticipated effects of the rules, the legitimacy of the rules, and views as to whether the rules were consistent with local policy goals. So great was the power imbalance between the foreign and local entities that it trumped the incompatibility of the regulatory norms and Japan reluctantly legislated a strong anti-cartel law. When the power relationship changed, the anti-cartel provisions of the AML were diluted and enforcement was largely abandoned.

A bureaucratic regulatory culture spawned bureaucratic guidance of the economy, and government bureaus actively encouraged the establishment of cartels and then used them to implement economic policy. As long as there was an apparent complementarity between bureaucratic guidance and strong, stable economic performance, government's encouragement and use of horizontal agreements among competitors was viewed as legitimate. When the economy faltered, the relationship between bureaucratic guidance and economic performance was questioned, and policy makers moved to more closely align local rules with the letter and spirit of the foreign rules that condemned anti-competitive horizontal agreements. Succinctly, Japan came to accept anti-cartel policy when policy makers came to believe that a pro-competition policy would facilitate attainment of local economic goals, namely, growth, price stability, and societal harmony. Perceptions and legitimacy followed.

Application: Mergers and Acquisitions

An analysis of Japanese merger control through the selective adaptation lens involves a more complex narrative than that of anti-cartel policy. The basis for analysis is again the recognition that Japanese economic regulatory norms value harmony in society and operate within a bureaucratic regulatory culture. With this in mind, it is important to emphasize the institutional manifestations of the norms that shaped the evolution of merger control in Japan. These include the lifetime employment system, cross-shareholding, and the main bank system.

Impediments to Merger

The pursuit of full employment has been a central goal of policy makers during the last fifty years, and is arguably part of Japan's social contract.[126] The lifetime employment system that developed in postwar Japan reflected the norm of harmony, as social stability was enhanced when the economy was near full employment.[127] The practice of lifetime employment commitments, and the strong, almost familial relationship between the management and employees of a firm created a negative perception of mergers and acquisitions (hostile or otherwise),[128] due to potential workforce rationalization that would accompany a change in ownership. This social disapproval of hostile takeovers,[129] and to a lesser extent mergers and acquisitions in general, is well noted in the literature, although it has not prevented amalgamations from occurring.

In order to deter potential acquisitions, groups of friendly firms (and their banks) developed extensive inter-corporate cross-shareholding relationships to provide a practical defence against takeover bids. Cross-shareholding was bolstered by the main bank system, whereby corporate groupings own a bank, which in turn is the principal shareholder in the group's firms. This type of arrangement provided a substitute for a legalistic corporate governance framework familiar to Western observers, and gave firms the flexibility to pursue goals beyond profit maximization. Instead, firms provided output stability and secure lifetime employment (as desired by economic bureaucrats), knowing that in case of financial difficulty, their main bank would bail them out. It can be argued that the main bank system was based on a "social presumption," namely, that the bank would support declining and failing firms and promote "survival of the weakest."[130] This normative interpretation of the institution's role is clearly in line with perceived Japanese social values of harmony and stability. Within this economic setting, shareholder rights were severely limited, firms were typically not governed with profit maximization in mind, and firms rarely went bankrupt.[131]

Seen from this local perspective, mergers and acquisitions presented either an opportunity or a threat. On the one hand, a friendly merger could help a company in trouble maintain social harmony by avoiding layoffs.[132] A merger could also reduce excessive competition in a sector, solving a problem that often arose in the eyes of economic bureaucrats. On the other hand, a hostile merger or acquisition attempt could threaten the Japanese social fabric. Layoffs resulting from restructuring under new ownership could delegitimize the main bank system (and the practice of lifetime employment), which was conceived to avoid such disruptions to the status quo. Even friendly mergers could threaten local norms, for example, by displacing an individual firm's seniority system in the process of combining with another company.[133]

As a result of local (economic regulatory and social) norms, Japanese policy makers perceived some mergers in a positive light and many others negatively. Consequently, the history of Japanese merger policy displays no tendency to encourage or discourage mergers through the selective adaptation process. Instead, a series of policies were pursued by government that attempted to control mergers and acquisitions so that their outcomes were complementary to local norms. Given the presence of a "bureaucratic regulatory culture,"[134] government bureaus promoted defences against hostile bids and avoided the troublesome prospect of profit-seeking shareholders by dampening the market for corporate control. These regulatory norms also encouraged bureaucrats to become directly involved in merger regulation, so that mergers or acquisitions perceived as beneficial (such as the rescue of a failing firm through a merger) could be achieved through informal guidance and consultations, thereby bypassing potential defence mechanisms. Hence, the selective adaptation of merger control was reflected not in the merger legislation itself but, rather, in policies designed to control behaviours associated with undesirable mergers.

The Adaptation of Merger Policy

The adaptation of merger policy can be divided into three periods: from 1947 to 1952, from 1953 to 1970, and from 1970 to the present.

From 1947 to 1952.   The legacy of wartime mergers and economic concentration contributed to the negative perception of business amalgamations on the part of the occupying Americans.[135] As a result, Article 15 of the 1947 AML forbade all mergers between potential competitors.[136] American negotiators were also able to include in the AML prohibitions on holding companies and strict limitations on stockholding by non-financial firms.[137] It was hoped that these provisions would inhibit the restoration of the prewar *zaibatsu,* a central goal of the economic reform program.[138] As with anti-cartel legislation, power relationships when the law was drafted dictated that a largely US-imposed merger policy would prevail, based on the Americans' aim of democratizing the economy.[139]

Shortly thereafter, calls for the amendment of the AML from the Japanese elite and the prospect of a conflict on the Korean peninsula resulted in a changed policy environment. At the recommendation of the US business community,[140] Occupation authorities approved slight amendments to the AML in 1949 to expedite Japan's economic recovery. Most notably, constraints on mergers and cross-shareholding by non-financial enterprises were relaxed.[141] Policy makers believed that this change in legislation would encourage foreign investment and allow the government to divest the stock that it had acquired in the *zaibatsu* dissolution efforts, thereby revitalizing the Japanese economy.[142] It was this initial amendment in 1949, however, that allowed the re-emergence of the prewar cross-shareholding and the emergence of the main bank system, as friendly firms purchased each other's stock in the equity market.[143] In contrast to non-financial firms, financial enterprises survived the Occupation dissolution program with their assets intact, and were able to hold up to 5 percent of a competitor's stock.[144] Banks in the emerging *keiretsu* groups replaced the holding companies at the core of these business groups as a next-best alternative, given the prohibition on holding companies in the AML. Ongoing efforts to rebuild shareholding alliances were accelerated by a rash of "greenmail" takeover attempts in the early 1950s, leading firms to further strengthen their shareholding defences: "Cross-shareholding arrangements in the post-war era operated as tacit mutual pacts designed to insulate the management of both sides from any market threat of hostile takeover. The purpose of most cross-shareholding is to avoid rather than confer shareholder rights, so stable shareholding relationships function as a strategy of corporate management to limit shareholder governance of the firm."[145]

Instead of firms facing shareholders' discipline, the majority of their shares were held by the main bank, which monitored firm management and provided a guarantee against failures, both managerial and financial.[146] New laws that were clearly at odds with the main bank system were passed during the late stages of the Occupation, however. In 1948, the Occupation authorities passed the *Securities Exchange Law,* and in 1950, the *Japanese Commercial Code* was revamped, both of which reflected American notions of shareholder rights. It is instructive that both laws were significantly amended or circumvented following the end of the American Occupation; indeed, *Commercial Code* reform had no effect on Japanese corporate practice for several decades following the war.[147] The American corporate governance framework conflicted with local economic and social norms due to the potential for disruptive layoffs and restructuring under a more profit-minded approach. Adaptation of this legislation to local norms enabled the main bank system to flourish. In summary, the changed power balance and resultant resurgence of local regulatory norms led to adaptation of the AML merger and stockholding policies, providing firms with the means to defend against unwanted takeovers or amalgamations.

Although this discussion has concentrated on domestic merger and acquisition policy, it is important to note an international dimension of these policies that surfaced during this period. While mergers and acquisitions among Japanese firms posed threats to social stability, similar actions from foreign sources caused even greater apprehension among the Japanese elite. Consequently, two laws were passed in the later stages of the Occupation: the *Foreign Exchange and Trade Control Law* (1949) and the *Foreign Investment Law* (1950). These laws placed all foreign investment, including acquisitions, at the discretion of the bureaucracy. If government bureaus deemed a foreign bid undesirable, it was simply barred, and for all intents and purposes, hostile bids from foreign sources were impossible.[148]

TABLE 3

Mergers in Japan by combined capital of merged entity, 1950-70

Year	Number of mergers by size of merged entity (¥ billions)				
	<0.1	0.1-1	1-10	>10	Total
1950-52	1,089	44	3	0	1,136
1953-55	919	71	17	0	1,007
1956-58	1,074	62	24	0	1,160
1959-61	1,272	140	33	3	1,448
1962-64	2,136	336	80	24	2,576
1965-67	2,386	290	69	15	2,760
1968-70	2,766	457	92	15	3,330

Note: The data show 1970 yen values.

Source: Adapted from graphical representation in Richard E. Caves and Masu Uekusa, *Industrial Organization in Japan* (Washington, DC: The Brookings Institution, 1976) at 29.

From 1953 to 1970.   For the first twenty years of the postwar period, merger and acquisition activity in Japan was rather limited, especially prior to the mid-1960s. "It seems reasonably accurate to say that in Japan, first, mergers and acquisitions involving large firms are not many; second, hostile acquisitions are infrequent; and third, at least among large firms, looser forms of combination are preferred."[149]

As Table 3 shows, the number of mergers increased steadily over the 1950-70 period, but most of these mergers were among small-scale enterprises. Acquisitions in Japan remained steady near 200 per year between 1950 and 1964. They increased sharply to 300 and then 400 per year between 1965 and 1970.[150] Compared with merger and acquisition activity in the US over a comparable period, there was far less activity in Japan.[151] "Lest one conclude that these disparities simply reflect[ed] the oversized US market for corporate control, data indicate that Japan's M&A activity is extremely low by any international measure."[152] The question is, why were there so few significant mergers and acquisitions in Japan between 1950 and 1970?

There were two principal reasons for this lack of large horizontal mergers and acquisitions: (1) the motivation for these deals was not present, and (2) their implementation was difficult. In a Western context, horizontal mergers are pursued in an effort to improve efficiency or increase market power. As will be seen, neither of these merger incentives was particularly compelling in the Japanese economy of the 1950s and 1960s.

Potential efficiency gains are often a driving force behind horizontal mergers. Following a merger, such gains are often achieved through rationalization of the two workforces into one smaller and more efficient unit. In the case of Japan, increased efficiency through rationalization was extremely difficult to achieve due to lifetime employment, rigid seniority systems, and a strong firm/employee bond.[153] If a firm hoped to increase efficiency, it would do so by internal redistribution of existing employees and resources rather than through a merger, since lifetime employment implied an increase in employees following a merger.[154] Furthermore, the necessity of adhering to existing seniority systems within firms following a merger would pose a complex puzzle that would likely result in conflict and inefficiencies. The bond between firms and their employees meant that any merger faced significant opposition from employees and management, which would harm the firm by exacerbating inefficiencies in addition to creating a negative social stigma.[155]

The pursuit of market power provided little motivation for horizontal mergers due to the prevalence of horizontal agreements in the Japanese economy over the years in question. As a result of permissive regulation, horizontal agreements provided a more expedient method of gaining market power and circumvented any potential conflicts with labour norms.

Besides a lack of motivation, it was difficult for any large merger or acquisition to come to fruition due to the prevalence of the main bank system and the complex cross-shareholding arrangements that had developed among the *keiretsu* (formerly *zaibatsu*) business groups following the war. The 1953 amendment to the AML allowed stockholding by financial institutions to increase from 5 percent to 10 percent of a firm's stock.[156] This had two important impacts on the ability of firms to merge.

First, it facilitated and legitimized the expansion of the main bank system. Banks were able to hold larger percentages of a firm's stock as stable shareholders, dampening the market for corporate control.[157] A potentially profitable merger that was not in the interest of the *keiretsu* (perhaps due to the necessity of guarding jobs or an aversion to amalgamation with entities outside the *keiretsu*) did not come to pass because the bank and other stable shareholders would simply block it. Despite the existence of the *Commercial Code*, a viable market for corporate control did not develop in Japan until at least the 1980s.[158]

Second, it increased cross-shareholding by friendly (non-bank) shareholders, further inhibiting any merger or acquisition. Part of the motivation behind this change in legislation was an increase in hostile takeover bids and greenmail in the wake of the Korean War, and Japan's associated economic slowdown.[159] Without other mechanisms of defence against unsolicited takeovers, due to underdeveloped legislation (Japanese law did not require disclosure of private shareholding interests until 1990), cross-shareholding between Japanese firms became widespread through the 1950s.[160] As a result of the 1953 amendment, cross-shareholding increased between banks and firms, and among firms, making unfriendly acquisitions even more difficult.[161]

As noted earlier, mergers and acquisitions were both an opportunity and a threat to economic bureaucrats and the policy-making elite in Japan. Consequently, the Japanese government adapted merger policy in such a way that it adhered to local norms, namely, through sponsorship of the main bank system.[162] Due to the "stable shareholders" within this corporate governance framework, firms could avoid mergers or acquisitions (even when they could be profitable) if doing so would endanger the fulfillment of labour norms.[163] The acute lack of a market for corporate control under the main bank system played a key role in protecting these norms.[164] Also, government encouragement of horizontal agreements inadvertently removed a major motivation for horizontal mergers.

Furthermore, the Japanese government provided regulatory support for cross-shareholding. A common extension of the cross-shareholding takeover defence was the offer of new shares to stable shareholders (at a discounted rate) in an attempt to thwart an unwanted suitor. Despite the fact that this práctice contradicted the *Commercial Code* and impaired shareholder rights, Supreme Court decisions confirmed its legality until the late 1980s.[165] Direct government encouragement of this practice came during the Yamaichi Crisis of 1963, when one of Japan's larger securities firms was facing insolvency due to a precipitous fall in stock prices. Japanese policy makers felt particularly vulnerable during this crisis, as recent accession to the Organisation of Economic Co-operation and Development (OECD) had meant greater openness of capital markets, increasing the potential for foreign hostile takeovers. In response, a government securities trust was set up by the Ministry of Finance to purchase shares and prevent a complete collapse of prices. The trust later proceeded to sell the shares to "group-linked companies and their banks," which enhanced cross-shareholding and curbed unfriendly acquisitions.[166] It is also important to recognize that minority and majority shareholding acquisitions were essentially unregulated.[167] The AML (Articles 9.2 and 10.1) states that stockholding must not hinder the workings of the competitive market,[168] but because the JFTC did not require any prior notification of stock purchases, it could not determine anti-competitive effects and in essence did not regulate them.[169] Stock acquisitions went largely unchallenged by the JFTC,[170] despite the potential for anti-competitive effects.[171] By not regulating these stockholding combinations, the government allowed firms to accommodate social norms within their business practices.

Japan's implementation of foreign rules governing merger policy resulted in a roundabout selective adaptation process, whereby associated rules and institutions (such as the main bank system, the structure of shareholder rights, and stockholding regulations) were modified so that mergers and acquisitions would occur only when they conformed to local norms.

In light of a lack of motivation, the existence of impediments, and antagonistic government regulatory behaviour towards mergers and acquisitions, it can be argued that Japanese firms preferred to grow internally rather than use an external growth strategy based on mergers and acquisitions.[172] If external growth was absolutely necessary, "looser combinations," such as capital integration or partial acquisitions, prevailed since these methods avoided contentious labour issues.[173]

Although large horizontal mergers were scarce, mergers were prevalent among smaller firms, as shown in Table 3. These small mergers were almost exclusively of a "rehabilitative" nature.[174] If a firm was faced with insolvency (or other problems), another firm within the same *keiretsu* would typically merge with or acquire it.[175] Often, the acquiring firm already held a large portion of the failing company's stock, meaning that an acquisition or merger was simply a deepening of a pre-existing relationship.[176] In this way, firms were able to rationalize their operations within their business groupings and ease the pain that would otherwise be felt in declining industries.[177] Since small firms were involved, the human resource constraints mentioned above[178] were more easily reconciled. Indeed, these types of purchases were welcomed by Japanese society; they were consistent with societal norms and avoided abrupt structural adjustment.[179]

In the mid-1960s, a small number of very large mergers occurred. Although the JFTC was able to prevent some early anti-competitive mergers, such as the proposed paper merger of 1968, several mergers were approved that created conditions detrimental to competition, most notably the Yawata–Fuji Steel merger of 1969.[180] Although there were some post-merger divestitures, the reformed Nippon Steel held a nearly 100 percent market share in several sectors. [181] Apparently, it was a bargain between the JFTC and MITI that allowed some of these mergers to pass: MITI would stop trying to dismantle the AML and the JFTC would take a permissive attitude towards mergers.[182] The JFTC appears to have taken this agreement to heart, as it rarely opposed large mergers or acquisitions prior to the 1990s.[183]

Most of the large mergers in Japan's history have occurred under heavy bureaucratic guidance.[184] Prior to any merger or acquisition activity, the companies involved would pay a visit to the relevant ministries, which solidified bureaucratic control over mergers and acquisitions through informal consultations and recommendations.[185] Formal decisions in these consultation cases were unusual prior to the 1990s, due to an effort to maximize bureaucratic discretion in future cases (records of informal consultations are not published either).[186] Also, government guidance aided in bypassing some of the potential obstacles to mergers mentioned above.

Foreign merger and acquisition attempts faced nearly insurmountable bureaucratic obstacles through the 1970s, as they still had to contend with the provisions contained in the *Foreign Exchange and Trade Control Law* and the *Foreign Investment Law,* both of which remained in place until the 1980s.

From 1970 to the Present. In 1971, a tender offer system was introduced. Although this was a step towards a competitive market for corporate control, hostile takeovers remained nearly impossible within this system because approvals were still at the discretion of the Ministry of Finance.[187] The regulations served as a "structural impediment" to takeovers from 1971 until 1990, when they were amended. As a result, only three tender offers were initiated during these thirty-odd years.[188] Nevertheless, the mere introduction of this system signified a first step towards a more competitive, market-oriented merger policy.

In 1977, the AML was again amended, with changes to merger policy. The permitted stockholding ratio of financial institutions was reduced from 10 percent of a firm's stock back to 5 percent, although it took over ten years to implement this change.[189] Public concern over inflation and the Oil Cartel scandal provided a policy environment conducive to pro-competitive policies, and it was hoped that this new legislation would help combat the influence of large business groupings and banks over individual enterprises and consumers as a whole.[190] At the very least, this reduction began to limit firms' defences against takeovers and remove insulation against structural adjustment, to the benefit of the competitive market.

By the 1980s, the characteristics of mergers in Japan had also begun to change. Rather than simply indicating a "company in trouble," mergers became a growth strategy for firms.[191] A study of Japanese mergers and acquisitions in the 1980s suggests that they were usually a means towards "product and market extension."[192] As the complexion of mergers changed, government policy slowly adapted. Very gradually, support for the main bank system and resistance to unsolicited takeovers waned. The reduction of stockholding ratios put a constraint on this corporate governance system, while several policy changes altered the hostile takeover norm and associated shareholding practices. In 1980, the JFTC published merger guidelines specifying market share levels (25 percent for the new entity) at which mergers would likely be challenged, in line with levels in other jurisdictions.[193] A year later, the JFTC announced another set of guidelines stipulating disclosure of private stockholding interests both yearly and following any acquisition, in order to establish whether "a joint relationship due to stockholding" existed.[194] Although this somewhat curtailed the practice of cross-shareholding because of the potential for prosecution under the AML, it was a Supreme Court decision condemning the issue of discounted shares for sale to friendly shareholders (to block takeovers) that constituted the major blow to cross-shareholding.[195]

Following the onset of recession in the early 1990s, the Japanese merger environment changed even further:

> The interesting feature of the new wave of Japanese M&A during the 1990s is that the nature of M&As has changed in face of the current micro- and macroeconomic situation in Japan. The economic conditions facing many firms today have fostered a climate where M&As based on due diligence and future strategic advantage, rather than based on network affiliations, have become common. In addition, the resistance towards takeovers by competitors and especially foreign firms seeking a foothold in Japan through M&As has started to diminish. In other words, the changing pattern of Japanese M&As is mirrored on multiple levels, including purely economic considerations and perceptions among individuals in the organizations.[196]

The steady increase of merger activity in Japan beginning in the early 1990s can be attributed largely to economic stagnation and the institutional change it produced. The old economic system of stable shareholders and lifetime employment had led Japan to recession; both economic actors and policy makers recognized the need for changes. Main banks could no longer play their role in the economy, and so began the disintegration of the cross-shareholding system. Firms were faced with increasing losses and greater pressure from shareholders, and saw mergers and acquisitions as a route to revitalization. The Japanese government recognized the need to facilitate corporate reorganization with new legislation. In essence, these changes reflected the delegitimization of previously ingrained economic norms, such as "cross-ownership, main bank system, and employee-centered corporate governance."[197]

For the purpose of understanding the onset of the merger boom, the first point to consider is the impact of the economic downturn on the main bank system, and by consequence, the cross-shareholding system. The main banks were adversely impacted by the stock market crash due to the large amount of unprofitable investment that had been readily offered to members of the bank's corporate group. This new economic reality meant that these banks were unable to play their accustomed role at the centre of their business groups. Banks were forced to call in outstanding loans and decrease their cross-shareholding to avoid failure.[198] As the cross-shareholding system began to unwind, another impediment to mergers and acquisitions was removed when several major Japanese banks merged in 1998. These mergers confirmed the decline of the old system, as the new banks rapidly decreased their cross-shareholding commitments.[199] With the influx of foreign capital following the financial deregulation of the same year, the role of the main banks further faded, as did the government guarantee against bank failure implicit in the system.[200]

It should be noted that foreign institutional investors purchased the vast majority of the stock that was sold by the main banks. These shareholders had very different perceptions from the previous stable shareholders, in that they demanded a reasonable rate of return on their investment.[201] As losses mounted and pressure from shareholders grew, firms found that corporate reorganization (through mergers and acquisitions) was an effective way of adapting to the demand for profits.

Japanese policy makers understood that legislative changes were needed in light of the economic stagnation. Beginning in 1997, the prohibition on holding companies was lifted from the AML to facilitate corporate reorganization. A year later, the "Big Bang" financial deregulation dramatically increased merger activity[202] by introducing the reality of financial sector reform.[203] Revision of corporate law began in earnest in 1999, when the *Commercial Code* was changed to allow share-for-share swaps between firms for the first time, enabling reorganization through holding companies or stock swap mergers and acquisitions. Further amendments to commercial legislation in 2001 permitted "corporate division," enabling firms to better manage subsidiaries and joint ventures. Another revision to the *Commercial Code* was introduced in 2002, providing firms with two options for the structure of their boards of governors and their systems of corporate governance.[204] More recently, changes in corporate law have permitted "triangular mergers" between Japanese and foreign firms. The new legislation allows foreign firms to acquire Japanese firms through the formation of a Japanese subsidiary, followed by a stock swap between the subsidiary and the target firm (whereby the Japanese subsidiary trades shares of the foreign parent company). Implementation was delayed, however, due to a series of hostile takeover attempts that worried policy makers and businesspeople. In particular, the attempted hostile acquisition of Fuji TV by Livedoor (a Japanese firm backed by American capital) in 2005 struck the public consciousness and created widespread alarm over unsolicited foreign acquisitions. Nonetheless, the new triangular merger law came into effect in May 2007, becoming part of Japan's strategy for attracting foreign investment and promoting growth.

The increasing numbers of mergers through the 1990s prompted the JFTC to issue a series of merger guidelines. In 1998, it introduced the factors that regulators would consider when evaluating a merger.[205] The guidelines added transparency to the process, but there was still uncertainty about how the JFTC would weight the various factors in a decision.[206] In this regard, the 1998 guidelines preserved elements of the previous approach to merger regulation, which had thrived in a bureaucratic regulatory culture and relied heavily on informal consultations between business and bureaucrats.

The JFTC revised the merger guidelines again in 2004, increasing transparency by clarifying exactly how decisions would be reached based on gathered information and economic measures.[207] These guidelines appear to greatly limit bureaucratic discretion and the practice of industrial policy through merger policy.

The guidelines were revised again in March 2007. The process for defining the relevant market was sharpened, safe and unsafe harbours were stipulated in terms of concentration levels, the efficiency exemption was more clearly defined and thereby constrained, and the roles of foreign competition and the condition of market entry in the evaluation were set out. Policy today, insofar as it is reflected in these guidelines, is strikingly similar to merger control in the United States.

The Selective Adaptation of Merger Policy

The development of merger policy within the context of a competition policy in Japan is markedly different from the evolution of anti-cartel policy. At the end of the Second World War, regulatory norms as reflected in bureaucratic guidance viewed horizontal agreements positively. Foreign rules hostile to such agreements were perceived as misguided and illegitimate; consequently, adoption of the foreign rules was resisted and adaptation in the early years was significant. Foreign rules hostile to horizontal mergers were not seen in the same light because local norms were also hostile to disruptive takeovers. In effect, there was little need for the authorities to deal with anti-competitive mergers because there were so few of them.

With the passage of time, policies that insulated firms from takeovers came into disrepute. Most importantly, the prolonged recession of the 1990s was blamed in part on crony capitalism, which was supported by the main bank system and extensive cross-shareholding. Public policies that protected firms from unwanted takeovers were reversed or moderated, and this opened the door to an upsurge in merger and acquisition activity. In effect, the prevailing anti-merger rules were seen as impairing economic performance. As with horizontal agreements, change came because of a perceived lack of complementarity between two social goals: harmony (as manifested by an absence of disruptive mergers) and economic performance.

Japan has only recently been witnessing the type of merger activity seen in North America and Western Europe. It appears that policy makers have accepted the legitimacy of merger controls that focus on protecting competition as opposed to controls that focus on maintaining the status quo.

Conclusions

As global economic integration proceeds, developing and transitional economies are implementing Western-style economic policies. Sometimes adoption of specific policies is the price of admission to a trade group or organization and is, in a sense, forced on the recipient. In other cases, the policies are willingly and voluntarily adopted because they are seen as a necessary condition for a well-functioning market economy. In many instances, regardless of whether or not adoption is voluntary, the adopting country is unfamiliar with the liberal economic norms that underlie the policy. There can be conflict when foreign rules or polices are incompatible with local economic and social norms and practices. Identification of the causes of such conflicts is a step towards their resolution.

Selective adaptation theory reasons that local norms will play a central role in the manner in which foreign ideas are integrated into the local context. Rather than blindly accepting foreign norms and practices (and the rules accompanying them), nations will adapt the foreign practices so that they serve local policy imperatives. Through this adaptation process, the dominant foreign practices are subject to modification by local norms. This modification and adaptation depends upon the local perspective of the foreign practice, the legitimacy of the foreign practice in the local context, and the extent to which the foreign practice complements local norms. Conflicts emerge when foreign and local perceptions as to the purpose and effects of the policy diverge, when local stakeholders view the policy as illegitimate, and when the foreign practice is seen to be at odds with local economic norms and goals.

This essay has employed the selective adaptation framework to explain the development of Japan's *Antimonopoly Law*. Application of the theory provides an evolutionary case study of a foreign policy that underwent adaptation according to local norms and priorities. The *Antimonopoly Law* was imposed on Japan by an occupying power, and the law was a reflection of that power's economic and social values. American belief in freedom from concentrations of economic power and anti-statism were the basis for antitrust in the United States, and they were also at the core of the imposed *Antimonopoly Law*. When the law came into being, Japan's sole concern was postwar recovery. Based on its prewar experience with rapid development using bureaucratic guidance that relied upon cooperation, and sometimes outright cartelization, among competing firms, it is unsurprising that Japanese policy makers looked to these methods to rebuild their country after the Second World War. For many Japanese, the AML was perceived as illegitimate and inconsistent with extant regulatory norms and economic goals, so when the opportunity arose, Japan amended the competition laws to better reflect local norms and priorities. In effect, adaptation (of both the law and the enforcement process) was such that Japan had no real competition policy for thirty years following passage of the AML. This adaptation process began to change direction only during the period of high inflation in the late 1970s, when the need for a stronger competition policy became apparent, and it was not until the onset of recession in the 1990s that the policy was made truly effective.

Based upon this review of the evolution of Japan's competition policy, it is our view that the selective adaptation model shows considerable promise as a tool to explain the speed of adoption and the extent of adaptation of foreign regulatory norms in local environments.

From the perspective of capacity building, we believe that, although important, the power relationship between the source of the foreign regulatory norms and the recipient is not the overriding consideration. Similarly, the written rule and the structure of the enforcement agency are important but not paramount. The critical factors are perception, legitimacy, and complementarity. The acceptance of the regulatory norms underlying an effective competition policy can require a wholesale change in business and regulatory cultures, and this does not happen quickly. "[The] 'Harmonization culture' that dominated Japanese business thinking need[s] to experience culture shock in order to concede to the new one, 'competition culture.' Needless to say, any culture requires a long time to change, and [the] Japanese business community is in the midst of such cultural changes."[208]

The lesson from the Japanese experience is that capacity builders should focus on perception, legitimacy, and complementarity issues, and of these, complementarity is the key. In Japan, it was only when stakeholders became convinced that competitive markets would deliver economic prosperity that competition policy became effective.

ACKNOWLEDGMENT
An earlier version of this chapter was published as: Richard Schwindt and Devin McDaniels, "Competition Policy, Capacity Building, and Selective Adaptation: Lessons from Japan's Experience" (2008) 7 Washington University Global Studies Law Review 35. The authors gratefully acknowledge support from the Asia Pacific Dispute Resolution Project for this work.

NOTES
1 The term "comprehensive" is used to indicate an explicit, unified set of rules intended to protect competition. Nearly all economies have long had rules, generally scattered among multiple pieces of legislation, that reflected certain elements of competition policy.
2 John Owen Haley, "Competition Law for the Asia-Pacific Economic Cooperation Community: Designing Shoes for Many Sizes" (2002) 1 Washington University Global Studies Law Review 1 at 2.
3 Russell W. Damtoft (Counsel for International Technical Assistance, Bureau of Competition, United States Federal Trade Commission), "Lessons Learned in the Delivery of Technical Assistance: The United States Experience" (Paper presented at the International Competition Network Second Annual Conference, Merida, Mexico, June 2003) at 2, online: International Competition Network <http://www.

internationalcompetitionnetwork.org/media/library/conference_2nd_merida_
2003/merida_speech6.pdf>.

4 See, *e.g.*, "Competition Policy Implementation Working Group," online: International Competition Network <http://www.internationalcompetitionnetwork.org/index.
php/en/working-groups/competition-policy-implementation>.

5 Pitman Potter, "Globalization and Economic Regulation in China: Selective Adaptation of Globalized Norms and Practices" (2003) 2 Washington University Global
Studies Law Review 119.

6 Akinori Uesugi, "Enforcement of Competition Laws in Japan" (Paper presented at
the International Competition Enforcement Conference, Tokyo – updated transcript
reflecting amendment of the AML on 20 April 2005) at 1, online: Japan Fair Trade
Commission <http://www.jftc.go.jp/e-page/policyupdates/speeches/050420uesugi.
pdf>.

7 Potter, *supra* note 5, at 119-21.

8 *Ibid.* at 120.

9 See, *e.g.*, *ibid.* at 122-24 (describing the case of China's accession to the WTO).

10 *Ibid.* at 120-21.

11 For the purposes of this essay, the third core (but less frequently enforced) set of
antitrust rules, those dealing with "abuse of a dominant position," are ignored.

12 Here and throughout this essay, the notion of efficiency is meant to include achievement of allocative efficiency (*i.e.*, production and consumption of the optimal quantity and mix of products and services), technical or productive efficiency (*i.e.*,
production of the optimal quantity and mix of products and services at the lowest
resource cost), and dynamic efficiency (*i.e.*, the optimal introduction over time of
new products and processes).

13 See, *e.g.*, Alex Y. Seita and Jiro Tamura, "The Historical Background of Japan's Antimonopoly Law" (1994) University of Illinois Law Review 115; Harry First, "Antitrust
in Japan: The Original Intent" (2000) 9 Pacific Rim Law and Policy Journal 1 at 6-16
["Antitrust in Japan"]; Richard E. Caves and Masu Uekusa, *Industrial Organization
in Japan* (Washington, DC: The Brookings Institution, 1976); Eleanor M. Hadley,
Antitrust In Japan (Princeton, NJ: Princeton University Press, 1970) at 3-106; Hiroshi
Iyori and Akinori Uesugi, *The Antimonopoly Laws and Policies of Japan* (New York:
Federal Legal Publication, 1994) at 1-10; Yoshio Kanazawa, "The Regulation of
Corporate Enterprise: The Law of Unfair Competition and the Control of Monopoly
Power" in Arthur Taylor von Mehren, ed., *Law in Japan: The Legal Order in a
Changing Society* (Cambridge, MA: Harvard University Press, 1963) 480; Saburo
Okita, comp., *Postwar Reconstruction of the Japanese Economy*, ed. by Special Survey
Committee, Japan Ministry of Foreign Affairs (1946) (Tokyo: University of Tokyo,
1992); Hugh T. Patrick, "The Economic Muddle of the 1920s" in James William Mor-
ley, ed., *Dilemmas of Growth in Prewar Japan* (Princeton, NJ: Princeton University
Press, 1971) 211; Arthur T. Tiedemann, "Big Business and Politics in Prewar Japan" in
Morley, *ibid.*, 267; Masayo Ohara, *Democratization and Expansionism: Historical
Lessons, Contemporary Challenges* (Westport, CT: Praeger, 2001) at 13-165.

14 Kanazawa, *ibid.* at 480-82.

15 Hadley, *supra* note 13 at 37.

16 First, "Antitrust in Japan," *supra* note 13 at 8-16.

17 Mark Tilton, *Restrained Trade: Cartels in Japan's Basic Materials Industries* (Ithaca, NY: Cornell University Press, 1996) at 27-29.

18 Kanazawa, *supra* note 13 at 480-82.

19 *Ibid.* at 482.

20 Hadley, *supra* note 13 at 363.

21 *Ibid.* at 365.

22 *Ibid.*

23 Kanazawa, *supra* note 13 at 483.

24 Michael L. Beeman, *Public Policy and Economic Competition in Japan: Change and Continuity in Antimonopoly Policy, 1973-1995* (London: Routledge, 2002) at 14 [*Public Policy*].

25 Tilton, *supra* note 17 at 28.

26 Kanazawa, *supra* note 13 at 480-82; Hadley, *supra* note 13 at 21 and 35.

27 Hadley, *supra* note 13 at 28-29.

28 Kanazawa, *supra* note 13 at 482.

29 First, "Antitrust in Japan," *supra* note 13 at 12-14.

30 *Ibid.* at 21-29.

31 Ulrike Schaede, *Cooperative Capitalism: Self-Regulation, Trade Associations, and the Antimonopoly Law in Japan* (New York: Oxford University Press, 2000) at 73 [*Cooperative Capitalism*].

32 Hadley, *supra* note 13 at 372.

33 Joe Staten Bain, *International Differences in Industrial Structure: Eight Nations in the 1950s* (New Haven, CT: Yale University Press, 1966) at 81-90.

34 Caves and Uekusa, *supra* note 13 at 16-28.

35 Richard Hofstadter, *The Paranoid Style in American Politics and Other Essays* (Cambridge, MA: Harvard University Press, 1965) at 199-200.

36 William E. Kovacic and Carl Shapiro, "Antitrust Policy: A Century of Economic and Legal Thinking" (2000) 14 Journal of Economic Perspectives 43 at 58.

37 Hadley, *supra* note 13 at 372.

38 It is an incomplete consensus because some observers take issue even with this conventional wisdom. For example, Fukuyama observes that much of the literature on national competitiveness of the late 1980s and early 1990s made the assumption that Japan is a "group-oriented" society and the US is the epitome of an individualistic society. He contends that the US is less individualistic than Americans believe it to be, but does accept that Americans are much more anti-statist than the Japanese: Francis Fukuyama, *Trust: The Social Virtues and the Creation of Prosperity* (New York: Free Press, 1995) at 269-81.

39 See, *e.g.,* Hadley, *supra* note 13 at 372; Caves and Uekusa, *supra* note 13 at 1-2 and 47-48; Douglas E. Rosenthal and Mitsuo Matsushita, "Competition in Japan and the West: Can the Approaches Be Reconciled?" in J. David Richardson and Edward M. Graham, eds., *Global Competition Policy* (Washington, DC: Institute for International Economics, 1997) 313 at 319; Kanji Ishizumi, *Acquiring Japanese Companies: Mergers and Acquisitions in the Japanese Market* (Cambridge, MA: Blackwell, 1990) at 13; J. Mark Ramseyer, "The Costs of the Consensual Myth: Antitrust Enforcement

and Institutional Barriers to Litigation in Japan" (1985) 94 Yale Law Journal 604 at 638; Leszek Leszczynski, "Economic Guidance and the Antimonopoly Law: Tradition versus Legal Changes" in Sarah Metzger-Court and Werner Pascha, eds., *Japan's Socio-Economic Evolution: Continuity and Change* (Sandgate, Folkestone, Kent, UK: Japan Library, 1996) 221 at 222; Steven K. Vogel, "Can Japan Disengage? Winners and Losers in Japan's Political Economy, and the Ties That Bind Them" (1999) 2 Social Science Japan Journal 3 (aversion to liberalization in an effort to maintain societal stability).

40 First, "Antitrust in Japan," *supra* note 13 at 5-6; *cf.* Harry First, "Antitrust Enforcement in Japan" (1995) 64 Antitrust Law Journal 137 at 138-45 ["Antitrust Enforcement"].

41 First, "Antitrust in Japan," *supra* note 13 at 6.

42 Tilton, supra note 17 at 27.

43 Schaede, *Cooperative Capitalism, supra* note 31 at 17-18.

44 First, "Antitrust in Japan," *supra* note 13 at 4.

45 Iyori Hiroshi, "Antitrust and Industrial Policy in Japan: Competition and Cooperation" in Gary Saxonhouse and Kozo Yamamura, eds., *Law and Trade Issues of the Japanese Economy: American and Japanese Perspectives* (Seattle: University of Washington Press, 1986) 56 at 62.

46 Ramseyer, *supra* note 39 at 638.

47 First, "Antitrust in Japan," *supra* note 13 at 67.

48 *Ibid.* at 1.

49 Caves and Uekusa, *supra* note 13 at 142.

50 Hideaki Kobayashi, "Competition Policy Objectives: A Japanese View" (Paper presented at the Competition Workshop, Florence, Italy, 13-14 June 1997), online: Japan Fair Trade Commission <http://www.jftc.go.jp/e-page/policyupdates/speeches/97-0613.html>.

51 Hadley, *supra* note 13 at 11.

52 First, "Antitrust in Japan," *supra* note 13.

53 Okita, *supra* note 13.

54 First, "Antitrust in Japan," *supra* note 13 at 16-21.

55 Saburo Okita, an electrical engineer by training, became interested in economic planning after analyzing possibilities for the development of power resources and industrial development in occupied China, where he served from 1939 to 1941. In the immediate postwar years, he held research positions in the Ministry of Foreign Affairs and the Economic Stabilization Board. In 1956, he was named Director of the Planning Bureau of Japan's Economic Planning Agency. He ultimately served as Japan's Foreign Minister. In 1992, he compiled an English version of the Special Survey Committee's report.

56 Okita, *supra* note 13 at 115-16.

57 Tetsuji Okazaka, *Government-Firm Relationship in Postwar Japan: Success and Failure of Bureau-Pluralism,* University of Tokyo Discussion Paper, CIRJE F-69 (April 2000), online: Graduate School of Economics, Faculty of Economics, University of Tokyo <http://www.e.u-tokyo.ac.jp/cirje/research/dp/2000/2000cf69.pdf>.

58 Okita, *supra* note 13 at 117-18.

59 Mitsuo Matsushita, *International Trade and Competition Law in Japan* (New York: Oxford University Press, 1993) at 78. (The exemption for cartels that have a "negligible" effect on competition does move the prohibition slightly away from a strict *per se* status. Apparently, a completely ineffective cartel could escape censure.)

60 First, "Antitrust in Japan," *supra* note 13 at 63.

61 Leonard H. Lynn and Timothy J. McKeown, *Organizing Business: Trade Associations in America and Japan* (Washington, DC: AEI Press, 1988) at 26-27.

62 Schaede, *Cooperative Capitalism, supra* note 31 at 77. See, *e.g.,* "Glorious Boren," a cotton spinning association that was dissolved by SCAP in 1947, but re-formed directly with the same firms and staff; it was later (1952) able to successfully cartelize cotton spinning production and output.

63 Tilton, *supra* note 17 at 31.

64 Schaede, *Cooperative Capitalism, supra* note 31 at 77.

65 First, "Antitrust in Japan," *supra* note 13 at 58.

66 James Fry, "Struggling to Teethe: Japan's Antitrust Enforcement Regime" (2001) 32 Law and Policy in International Business 825 at 835.

67 Yoshiro Miwa and J. Mark Ramseyer, "Toward a Theory of Jurisdictional Competition: The Case of the Japanese FTC" (2005) 1 Journal of Comparative Law and Economics 247 at 251-55; Harry First and Tadashi Shiraishi, *Concentrated Power: The Paradox of Antitrust in Japan,* New York University Law and Economics Working Paper 11 (2005) at 16-21, online: NELLCO Legal Scholarship Repository <http://lsr.nellco.org/nyu/lewp/papers/11>; Michael L. Beeman, "Japan's Flawed Antitrust Regime" (Working paper presented at the Friendship Commission Public Policy Series, 28 October 1999; revised 11 November 1999), online: Asia Policy Point <http://www.jiaponline.org/whatsnew/events/2000/june5/FinalJapansFlawedAntitrustRegime1199.pdf> ["Japan's Flawed Antitrust Regime"].

68 Beeman, *ibid.*

69 First, "Antitrust in Japan," *supra* note 13 at 68-70.

70 Ramseyer, *supra* note 39 at 643.

71 First, "Antitrust in Japan," *supra* note 13 at 70.

72 Fry, *supra* note 66 at 831.

73 Kanazawa, *supra* note 13 at 487.

74 Beeman, *Public Policy, supra* note 24 at 16; Fry, *supra* note 66 at 832; Kanazawa, *supra* note 13 at 487-88.

75 Schaede, *Cooperative Capitalism, supra* note 31 at 77.

76 Beeman, *Public Policy, supra* note 24 at 16-18.

77 Matsushita, *supra* note 59 at 80.

78 Lynn and McKeown, *supra* note 61 at 40.

79 Tilton, *supra* note 17 at 31.

80 Schaede, *Cooperative Capitalism, supra* note 31 at 80.

81 Beeman, *Public Policy, supra* note 24 at 18.

82 Kanazawa, *supra* note 13 at 497.

83 Franz Waldenberger, "The Changing Role of Competition Policy in Japan" in Metzger-Court and Pascha, *supra* note 39, 191 at 208.

84 Kotaro Suzumura, "Formal and Informal Measures for Controlling Competition in Japan: Institutional Overview and Theoretical Evaluation" in Richardson and Graham, *supra* note 39, 439 at 450; Matsushita, *supra* note 59 at 145; Kanazawa, *supra* note 13 at 496-97; Beeman, *Public Policy, supra* note 24 at 16-21.

85 Schaede, *Cooperative Capitalism, supra* note 31 at 82.

86 *Ibid.* at 83.

87 See *supra* note 62.

88 Schaede, *Cooperative Capitalism, supra* note 31 at 84; Tilton, *supra* note 17 at 33.

89 Schaede, *Cooperative Capitalism, supra* note 31 at 85.

90 Beeman, *Public Policy, supra* note 24 at 18.

91 Seita and Tamura, *supra* note 13 at 181-82; Suzumura, *supra* note 84 at 445; Waldenberger, *supra* note 83 at 215.

92 Michael E. Porter and Mariko Sakakibara, "Competition in Japan" (2004) 18 Journal of Economic Perspectives 27; Waldenberger, *supra* note 83 at 209.

93 Seita and Tamura, *supra* note 13 at 184.

94 First, "Antitrust Enforcement," *supra* note 40 at 148-53.

95 Beeman, *Public Policy, supra* note 24 at 16-17.

96 Waldenberger, *supra* note 83 at 198.

97 *Ibid.* at 201; Fry, *supra* note 66 at 854-56.

98 Kenji Sanekata and Stephen Wilks, "The Fair Trade Commission and Competition Policy in Japan" in G. Bruce Doern and Stephen Wilks, eds., *Comparative Competition Policy: National Institutions in a Global Market* (New York: Oxford University Press, 1996) 102 at 104; Beeman, *Public Policy, supra* note 24 at 40-41.

99 Beeman, *Public Policy, supra* note 24 at 46.

100 *Ibid.* at 46-47.

101 Matsushita, *supra* note 59 at 48.

102 Beeman, *Public Policy, supra* note 24 at 47-51.

103 Sanekata and Wilks, *supra* note 98 at 104.

104 Matsushita, *supra* note 59 at 147.

105 *Ibid.* at 83; Waldenberger, *supra* note 83 at 213.

106 Beeman, *Public Policy, supra* note 24 at 67.

107 James Sameth and John Owen Haley, "Guidelines Concerning the Activities of Trade Associations under the Antimonopoly Law" (English translation) (1979) 12 Law in Japan (Annual) at 118.

108 *Ibid.* at 125-29.

109 *Ibid.* at 143-49.

110 Beeman, *Public Policy, supra* note 24 at 131.

111 Waldenberger, *supra* note 83 at 198. These laws were the *Depressed Industries Law* (1978) and the *Structurally Depressed Industries Law* (1983).

112 *Ibid.* at 215-17.

113 Beeman, *Public Policy, supra* note 24 at 96-112.

114 James R. Lincoln and Michael L. Gerlach, *Japan's Network Economy: Structure, Persistence, and Change* (Cambridge, UK: Cambridge University Press, 2004) at 3.

115 Sadaaki Suwazono, "The Features of the Newly Revised Anti-Monopoly Act: Japan's Experience of Making Competition Policy Stronger" (Paper presented to

the Competition Policy Deregulation Group of APEC, Jeju, Korea, 24 May 2005) at 2-3 and 13, online: Japan Fair Trade Commission <http://www.jftc.go.jp/e-page/policyupdates/speeches/ 050524suwazono.pdf>.

116 Suwazono, the director of the Competition Policy Planning Office of the JFTC, identified two such studies: Porter and Sakakibara, *supra* note 92, and OECD, "Economic Survey of Japan, 2003," OECD Policy Brief (2003).

117 Porter and Sakakibara, *supra* note 92 at 45-47.

118 Sanekata and Wilks, *supra* note 98 at 107.

119 Leonard J. Schoppa, "Two Level Games and Bargaining Outcomes: Why *Gaiatsu* Succeeds in Japan in Some Cases but Not Others" (1993) 47 International Organization 353 at 362-64.

120 *Ibid.* at 379-82 and 383-86.

121 Beeman, *Public Policy, supra* note 24 at 141-43.

122 *Ibid.* at 148.

123 Sanekata and Wilks, *supra* note 98 at 118.

124 Schaede, *Cooperative Capitalism, supra* note 31 at 126.

125 Uesugi, *supra* note 6.

126 Ulrike Schaede, "The Japanese Model in the 1990s" (2004) 12 Review of International Economics 277 at 280-84 ["The Japanese Model"].

127 Curtis J. Milhaupt, "Creative Norm Destruction: The Evolution of Non-Legal Rules in Japanese Corporate Governance" (2001) 149 University of Pennsylvania Law Review 2083 at 2093.

128 Ishizumi, *supra* note 39 at 13.

129 Kelly Charles Crabb, "The Reality of Extralegal Barriers to Mergers and Acquisitions in Japan" (1987) 21 International Law Review 97 at 116.

130 Milhaupt, *supra* note 127 at 2088.

131 *Ibid.* at 2091-92 and 2098-99.

132 Ishizumi, *supra* note 39 at 15-17.

133 Hiroyuki Odagiri, "Mergers and Acquisitions in Japan and the Anti-Monopoly Policy" in Leonard Waverman, William S. Comanor, and Akira Goto, eds., *Competition Policy in the Global Economy: Modalities for Cooperation* (London: Routledge, 1997) 69 at 75.

134 See *supra* notes 39-40.

135 Hadley, *supra* note 13 at 28-29; Kanazawa, *supra* note 13 at 482.

136 Kanazawa, *supra* note 13 at 486.

137 Hadley, *supra* note 13 at 164.

138 *Ibid.* at 61-124.

139 First, "Antitrust in Japan," *supra* note 13 at 67-70.

140 Beeman, *Public Policy, supra* note 24 at 16.

141 Kanazawa, *supra* note 13 at 487.

142 *Ibid.*

143 Mark Scher, *Bank Cross-Shareholding in Japan: What Is It, Why Does It Matter, Is It Winding Down?* United Nations Economic and Social Affairs Discussion Paper No. 15 (February 2001) at 4, online: United Nations <http://www.un.org/esa/desa/papers/2001/esa01dp15.pdf>.

144 Hadley, *supra* note 13 at 163.

145 Scher, *supra* note 143 at 5.

146 Milhaupt, *supra* note 127 at 2087.

147 *Ibid.* at 2105.

148 Crabb, *supra* note 129 at 108.

149 Odagiri, *supra* note 133 at 71.

150 *Ibid.* at 70.

151 Hiroyuki Odagiri and Tatsuo Hase, "Are Mergers and Acquisitions Going to Be Popular in Japan Too?" (1989) 7 International Journal of Industrial Organization 49 at 49-50.

152 Curtis J. Milhaupt and Mark D. West, *Institutional Change and M&A in Japan: Diversity through Deals*, Working Paper No. 193, Columbia Law School: The Center for Law and Economic Studies (2001) at 15, online: Social Science Research Network <http://papers.ssrn.com/abstract=290744>.

153 Odagiri, *supra* note 133 at 74.

154 *Ibid.* at 77.

155 *Ibid.* at 74-75.

156 Scher, *supra* note 143, at 7.

157 Milhaupt, *supra* note 127 at 2087-88 and 2097.

158 *Ibid.* at 2114-17.

159 Scher, *supra* note 143 at 4.

160 Milhaupt, *supra* note 127 at 2100.

161 Scher, *supra* note 143 at 4.

162 Milhaupt, *supra* note 127 at 2088, 2091-92, and 2098-99.

163 Odagiri, *supra* note 133 at 75.

164 Milhaupt and West, *supra* note 152 at 16; Milhaupt, *supra* note 127 at 2095-99.

165 Todd S. Huckaby, "Defensive Action to Hostile Takeover Efforts in Japan: The Shuwa Decisions" (1991) 29 Columbia Journal of Transnational Law 439 at 440-41.

166 Scher, *supra* note 143 at 4-5; Ronald J. Gilson and Mark J. Roe, "Understand the Japanese *Keiretsu:* Overlaps between Corporate Governance and Industrial Organization" (1993) 102 Yale Law Journal 871 at 897.

167 Odagiri, *supra* note 133 at 74.

168 *Ibid.* at 79.

169 *Ibid.* at 86.

170 Matsushita, *supra* note 59 at 127.

171 Odagiri, *supra* note 133 at 86.

172 *Ibid.* at 49-50 and 70-71.

173 *Ibid.* at 75.

174 Dan F. Henderson, "Foreign Takeovers and Acquisitions in Japan" (1994-95) 39 St. Louis University Law Journal 897 at 902-3.

175 Mitsuru Misawa, "Mergers and Acquisitions in Japan: The Present and the Future" (1986) 19 Vanderbilt Journal of Transnational Law 785 at 786.

176 *Ibid.* at 791.

177 Henderson, *supra* note 174 at 902-3.

178 Odagiri, *supra* note 133 at 74-75 and 77.

179 Ishizumi, *supra* note 39 at 15-17.
180 Beeman, *Public Policy, supra* note 24 at 23-24.
181 Matsushita, *supra* note 59 at 129-30.
182 Caves and Uekusa, *supra* note 13 at 151.
183 Ishizumi, *supra* note 39 at 118-21.
184 Schaede, *Cooperative Capitalism, supra* note 31 at 59.
185 *Ibid.* at 119; Ishizumi, *supra* note 39 at 120.
186 Odagiri, *supra* note 133 at 85.
187 Huckaby, *supra* note 165 at 462.
188 Milhaupt and West, *supra* note 152 at 19.
189 Scher, *supra* note 143 at 8-9.
190 Beeman, *Public Policy, supra* note 24 at 75.
191 Misawa, *supra* note 175 at 786.
192 Odagiri and Hase, *supra* note 151 at 56.
193 Odagiri, *supra* note 133 at 78-85.
194 *Ibid.* at 80.
195 Huckaby, *supra* note 165 at 451-52.
196 H. Richard Nakamura, "Attitudes, Structure and the Partner Selection of Japanese M&As" (Paper presented at the First Nordic Association for the Study of Contemporary Japanese Society, Gothenburg University, April 2004) at 2-3.
197 *Ibid.* at 6.
198 Scher, *supra* note 143 at 6.
199 *Ibid.* at 13.
200 M. Diana Helweg, "Japan: A Rising Sun?" (2000) 79 Foreign Affairs 26 at 30; Milhaupt, *supra* note 127 at 2088.
201 Hiroyuki Itami, *Revision of the Commercial Code and Reform of the Japanese Corporate Governance,* Japan Institute for Labour Policy and Training Working Paper; online <http://www.jil.go.jp/english/documents/JLR05_itami.pdf>.
202 Nakamura, *supra* note 196 at 5.
203 Helweg, *supra* note 200 at 30.
204 Milhaupt and West, *supra* note 152 at 23.
205 Salil K. Mehra, "Same Plant, Different Soil: Japan's New Merger Guidelines" (2006) 26 Northwestern Journal of International Law and Business 515 at 517.
206 *Ibid.* at 523.
207 *Ibid.*
208 Akinori Uesugi, "Recent Developments in Japanese Competition Policy: Prospect and Reality" (Paper presented at the International Antitrust Forum, Antitrust Section, American Bar Association, 24 January 2005) at 5, online: Japan Fair Trade Commission <http://www.jftc.go.jp/e-page/policyupdates/speeches/050124uesugi.pdf>.

Selective Adaptation of Economic Governance Norms in China
Transparency and Autonomy in Local Context

PITMAN B. POTTER

In the People's Republic of China (PRC), economic development policies and practice involve a tension between local development goals and participation in the international economic order. This in turn suggests a dynamic of managing compliance with international rule regimes on transparency and autonomy. Transparency focuses on procedural limitations on central government decision making, while autonomy addresses questions about local government initiative. Thus, China's approach to participation in the world political economy can be appreciated in light of engagement with the rule regimes of the *General Agreement on Tariffs and Trade* (GATT) and the World Trade Organization (WTO) on transparency and autonomy, and in light of development experiences elsewhere.

Approaches to Economy and Development

As a matter of context, approaches to economy and development provide useful perspectives on China's engagement with the GATT/WTO system. To the extent the international trade liberalization regime is associated with particular approaches to economic development, it is useful to compare China's economic development project with international approaches.

Conceptual and Policy Approaches to Economic Development

Policy approaches to economic development have generally tended to focus on questions of agency, method and measurement, and boundaries of development.[1] Agency issues relate to factors of responsibility for development. State-led development models are still powerful exemplars for developing economies,[2] not least because these also tend to validate the legitimacy of strong, active central governments. A legacy of Keynesian liberal economics, state-led development models focus on the capacity of central governments to manage monetary and fiscal policy, engage international economic relations through trade policy, and allocate resources for social and physical infrastructure.[3] State-led development programs were pursued successfully in postwar Japan[4] and subsequently in each of East Asia's "four dragons."[5] A growing body of empirical scholarship suggests, however, that although central government support is important, successful development policies give significant authority to local agency.[6] The role of local government in tailoring policies to local development needs has been particularly important in large economies such as Indonesia[7] and India.[8] Agency questions also invite consideration of the role of civil society in setting development goals.[9]

Questions about methods for development emerge from questions about the meaning of development. Factors of sustainability, social well-being, and environmental protection are increasingly acknowledged as fundamental to development.[10] Although it seems axiomatic that development can no longer be couched purely in terms of economic accumulation, indicators of development issued by national governments and supra-national organizations continue to place considerable weight on economic accumulation as an indicator of development. Questions about the meaning of development are closely linked to how indicators of development are selected and disseminated. Indicators focusing on accumulation of goods or portraying macro-indicators of socioeconomic change reflect particular policy priorities. Conversely, measures of development that focus on human needs, social well-being, and particular local conditions suggest alternative approaches to development.

The discourse of economic efficiency tends to work as a trump card that imposes an almost insurmountable burden on public goods analysis of development.[11] Public goods essential to sustainable development – such as safe and secure employment, housing, health care, education, and environmental protection – are considered merely as adjustable cost components of the calculus of efficiency. This has the effect of equalizing the treatment of public and private goods, which, in the context of disparities of political power that privilege private interests, results in public goods being consigned to a secondary role. As well, norms about efficiency that inform much conventional thinking about development are often inapplicable to the broad intersections of interests that actually characterize the world economy. Efficiency perspectives grounded on liberal norms of individualism and property rights often overlook the extent to which local communities have different norms – such as collective interests and property relations – by which they organize their affairs. This not only has the potential to ignore the calculus of efficiency among local economic actors[12] but also to marginalize the perspectives of communities whose interests are not measured by their ownership of property. Although the consideration of sustainability and human well-being appears to be a natural and much-needed corrective to economic accumulation as a measure of development, it also challenges deeply embedded political and economic interests, and is therefore controversial and often challenged by established governance institutions and interests.

China's Policies on Local Economic Development

Viewed in terms of broad questions of agency, method, and indices of achievement, China's national policies on development are oriented generally towards state-centric, economic, and quantifiable approaches to development. China has expressly adopted the ideal of state-led development, both in its constitutional and legislative enactments and through support for academic and policy discourses extolling the central government's indispensable role in promoting development.[13] Indeed, many of China's national policy successes – such as agricultural responsibility systems and family planning – were first tested in local contexts and then adjusted for national application.[14] Although the question remains as to whether these were truly local initiatives that went national or were the result of central decisions to experiment locally, China's record suggests that local initiative and experimentation have been important factors in policy success. In China's tightly controlled political economy, the concept of civil society remains highly contested, although there is growing evidence of increasingly autonomous collections of intellectuals and community leaders serving as sources for policy initiative.[15] China's campaign in late 2004 to curb the activities of "public intellectuals" suggested both the budding influence of emerging communities of relatively autonomous policy actors and the government's apprehension about this. The government's emphasis on quantitative measures of development is evident in its reliance on statistical reporting, whose accuracy is highly contested and whose selectivity and reach are seemingly designed to validate state policy decisions.

China's approach to economic relations and development also reflects the influences of globalization. On the one hand, many in China have expressed apprehension about participation in economic globalization (as expressed most prominently through membership in the WTO);[16] on the other hand, the central government also places considerable emphasis on the role of international trade and investment as mechanisms for furthering development in China generally. These general approaches are particularly evident in Beijing's approach to economic relations along its border regions. China's economic reforms are tied closely to legal reform, particularly in the areas of contract and property law and in foreign economic relations.[17]

Thus, China's economic development project depends heavily on the initiative of the state. Although local participation and initiative are accepted and in many cases have led to reform of central programs, the central government retains primacy in determining economic development goals and programs. This places the central government in the position of balancing the demands of the international trade regime with the requirements of local development. Such a position has compliance implications as the government faces the challenges of meeting the requirements of GATT/WTO rules on transparency and autonomy.

Transparency Requirements of the GATT/WTO and the China Context

Boundaries of development reflect perspectives about economic governance. The dimensions of transparency and autonomy are particularly important. Transparency reflects normative positions on the agency of the state and its accountability to society. Autonomy reflects issues about allocation of authority within political systems. A key issue in the dissemination of GATT principles is the question of regulatory norms. Regulatory norms affect virtually all aspects of the relations between state and society, but are particularly important in economic relations. The GATT/WTO system provides rule regimes for transparency under Article X of the GATT,[18] while Article XXIV addresses issues of local autonomy. The operation of these provisions in the context of China's participation in the WTO provides insights into the operation of selective adaptation.

Enforcement of GATT rules is also dependent on the provisions of Article X requiring publication of trade regulations and uniform, impartial, and reasonable administration of laws and regulations.[19] The contracting parties are required to establish judicial, arbitral, or administrative tribunals or procedures for review and correction of administrative action regarding customs matters (which include virtually all aspects of trade regulation). Thus, the transparency and enforcement provisions of Article X provide the framework for implementing the substantive norms expressed elsewhere in the agreement. This is because in the absence of transparency about the content and application of trade regulations, trading partners and their businesses cannot know whether or not the central GATT principles of free trade are being granted or denied. The substantive and operational norms complement each other and set the tone for the GATT's regulatory culture.

Questions arise, however, about whether China's acceptance of the GATT/WTO rule regime is accompanied by assimilation of related norms. The WTO Working Party's Draft Protocol on China (1997)[20] sets forth the general terms for China's accession to the WTO and suggests the extent to which China's regulatory ethos remains at odds with GATT principles. Section I.2.A.2 of the Protocol requires China to administer in a uniform, impartial, and reasonable manner all its laws, regulations, and other measures governing trade in goods, services, trade-related aspects of intellectual property rights, and foreign exchange. Section I.2.A.4 requires China to establish a mechanism by which non-uniform application of the trade regime may be brought to the attention of the national authorities – implying the availability of a system of administrative review. Section I.2.C requires China to undertake significant transparency reforms, including publication of laws and regulations, while Section I.2.D requires China to establish a system of judicial review. In effect, the 1997 Protocol sets forth a program for bringing the Chinese regulatory system into compliance with the terms and principles of the GATT regime, while also suggesting that China has some distance to go in this regard.

GATT/WTO principles of transparency derive from liberal principles of accountability of government. Proceeding from tenets about human equality and natural law, the liberal tradition of political ideology asserts that government should be an agency of popular will.[21] Such an agency requires accountability from political leaders through democratic elections and from administrative agencies acting within the limits of lawfully delegated authority. Responsible agency is thus a typology by which regulators and their political superiors are accountable to the subjects of regulation and, as a result, are expected to exercise regulatory authority broadly in accordance with norms of transparency and the rule of law.[22] Thus, the accountability of political and administrative agents may be described in terms of their responsibility *to* society. Norms of responsible agency constitute a belief system driven by changing historical conditions of socioeconomic and political relations in Europe and North America. The essentially one-way nature of the dissemination of these norms around the world reflects the imbalances in political and economic power between developed and developing economies that characterize the current dynamic of globalization. The capacity of the liberal industrial economies to promote their preferred regulatory norms as an essential element of globalization derives as much from political and economic power as from the inherent wisdom of the ideas themselves.[23]

Local norms informing China's official regulatory culture may be described, however, in terms of patrimonial sovereignty.[24] Drawing on traditional norms of Confucianism combined with ideals of revolutionary transformation drawn from Marxism-Leninism and Maoism, regulatory culture in China tends to emphasize governance by a political authority that remains largely immune to challenge.[25] During the first thirty years of the PRC, law and regulation served primarily as instruments for enforcing policies of the Communist Party of China (CPC) and the state. Norms and processes for accountability were dismissed as bourgeois artifacts inappropriate to China's revolutionary conditions. By the turn of the twenty-first century, even after twenty years of legal reform, the supremacy of the Party/state remains a salient feature in the regulatory process.[26] Whether the policy aim is military restrengthening, economic growth, or social welfare, accountability is determined nearly exclusively by Communist Party and governmental leaders rather than through popular participation. The patrimonialism of Confucianized Marxist-Leninist Mao Zedong thought combines with the doctrine of Party/state supremacy to establish a powerful mode of governance in the PRC. Patrimonial sovereignty is thus a typology by which regulators are accountable only to their bureaucratic and political superiors and, as a result, have few obligations to heed the subjects of rule in the process or substance of regulation. Under the dynamic of patrimonial sovereignty, political leaders and administrative agencies have responsibility *for* society but are not responsible to it.

These tensions in political culture affect China's efforts to comply with the transparency requirements of the GATT and the WTO. China has begun a wide-ranging campaign to revise existing legislation and administrative regulations in most economic sectors, including customs, foreign exchange, taxation, intellectual property, enterprise law, bankruptcy, pricing, and other areas. These reforms reflect both the effects of selective adaptation and the challenge to transform a regulatory culture of patrimonial sovereignty into one of responsible agency. The intersection of property rights, administrative law, and corporate governance provides useful insights into this process in the context of changing approaches to economic regulation.

Recent efforts to establish systems of administrative hearings in anticipation of legislation – most recently on property law and previously on contract law – suggest increased efforts to build popular participation in rule making. This is complemented by regional experimentation with public participation in municipal governance. Whether these experiments will take on national significance remains uncertain – particularly in light of the central government's recent White Paper denouncing the application of liberal democratic values in China and in light of calls for a "Beijing Consensus" that departs from the Washington Consensus on trade liberalization and development.[27] Nonetheless, support for greater accountability in government is expanding in both intellectual and popular circles, which may open the door to increased compatibility with GATT/WTO rules on the rule of law and transparency and the norms upon which these rest.

GATT/WTO Provisions on Autonomy and the China Context

WTO provisions on local autonomy are addressed in Article XXIV, which provides that central governments are responsible for ensuring compliance with GATT (and by extension WTO) disciplines by their political subdivisions.[28] The GATT places significant emphasis on state responsibility for compliance and on regulatory transparency as the basis upon which the GATT's substantive free trade principles rely. Compliance with GATT rules by signatory states is in part a matter of internal administration. Accordingly, Article XXIV (12) requires each contracting party to take "necessary measures" to ensure observance of the GATT by regional and local governments and authorities. This provision has been amplified by the "Understanding on the Interpretation of Article XXIV of the General Agreement on Tariffs and Trade" attached to the Uruguay Round,[29] providing that signatory states are "fully responsible ... for the observance of all provisions of GATT 1994" and are required to "take such reasonable measures as may be available ... to ensure such observance by regional and local governments and authorities." These requirements are linked to the enforcement of provisions on dispute resolution coming out of the Uruguay Round. In response to the requirements of Article XXIV (12), federal states adopt various approaches to ensure that their political subdivisions remain in compliance with GATT principles. In the United States, constitutional provisions accord the federal government exclusive jurisdiction over international trade and interstate commerce, and thus provide authority to bind states to GATT principles. Even after Congress approved the GATT 1994 following the

Uruguay Round, however, wariness over accession to the GATT still affects the dynamics of US compliance, which remains subject to the 1947 Protocol of Provisional Application.[30] In Canada, the exclusive authority of the federal government to regulate international trade is less clear; as a result, Canada's participation in GATT negotiations entails significant consultations with provincial authorities to obtain their commitments to comply.[31]

Beijing has already drawn upon provisions of Article XXIV as justification for asserting greater control in order to resolve the long-standing tensions between central and local authority and power. Arriving at a productive balance between central and local authorities that ensures WTO compliance while still encouraging local initiative and policy diversity will be a major challenge. The PRC Constitution[32] provides overall guidance on issues of local autonomy. Article 2 addresses possibilities for autonomy through local people's congresses, which are augmented by a range of formal legislation. Article 3 articulates the principle of "democratic centralism," by which central mandates may be adjusted to local conditions. These broad principles are given specific application through Section V of the Constitution, which governs the powers of local people's congresses and local people's governments. Viewed in light of CPC policy dictates and broader official discourses on governance autonomy in nationality areas, these provisions reveal features of particular interest in the context of selective adaptation.

Article 95 and subsequent articles affirm the functions and powers of local governance organs but qualifies these by the limitations of the Constitution and other laws. These limitations, particularly in light of the unitary state ideal, effectively prohibit local governments from directly opposing policy directions from higher levels, although local governance departments are permitted to adapt state laws and policies to local conditions. The tension between a formal autonomy that is subject to higher-level direction and local adaptability in the course of enforcing state law and policy means that the extent of local autonomy in practice is unclear. This, in turn, has the potential to ensure that local officials hoping to adapt state law and policy to local conditions will continually be restrained by the content of the very laws and policies they are attempting to interpret. Thus, Article 100 permits local people's congresses to enact regulations in light of local characteristics, but still subject to the broad limitations of the Constitution and national laws. Although local legislation is not subject to formal approval by the centre, local people's congresses must submit enacted legislation to the National People's Congress Standing Committee for the record.

Article 107 extends significant authority to local provincial governments in the areas of economic development, education, science, culture, public health, physical culture, urban and rural development, finance, civil affairs, and a range of administrative activities, but these remain subject to policy interpretation in light of central CPC and government priorities. Financial autonomy is generally limited to autonomy in the management of local financial resources, but must still adhere to centrally directed policies and plans. Local development plans must also operate under the guidance of state plans. Thus, state initiatives such as the Western Development Programme (*Xibu da kaifa*) remain outside the purview of local autonomy, while local development efforts must continually defer to priorities issued from the centre. Constitutional grants of local autonomy over administration of education, science, and culture are qualified by the requirement of compliance with central policies.

The Western Development Programme: A Template for Managing Local Autonomy

China's Western Development Programme provides a template for understanding the central government's policies for balancing central programs on economic development with local needs. It echoes themes and aspirations of Chinese governments dating back at least to the Qianlong Emperor. During the post-Mao reform period in the early 1980s, the central government recognized the importance of border development and began to develop regional planning processes to facilitate internal and external trade in China's western hinterlands.[33] Despite the impressive economic growth rates achieved in China's coastal areas, the western areas continued to lag. A 1999 report by the National Conditions (*guoqing*) Research Institute in the Chinese Academy of Sciences indicated that the development gap between ethnic minority regions and the coastal areas had widened, and attributed this to steady population increases coupled with inadequate educational facilities, poor infrastructure, poverty, slow progress in developing foreign trade and investment relations, and lingering effects of the planned economy.[34] This was a major agenda item at the 1999 Central Nationalities Work Conference, which prioritized the process of bringing all nationalities onto the socialist road and accelerating economic and social development for all of them, especially ethnic minorities.[35] In operational terms, this meant diminishing disparate preferences for minorities under the theme of socialist equality between minority nationalities and Han Chinese, and relying on economic development as the basis for the assimilation of minorities into the broader Chinese state.

Not surprisingly, this combination of political and economic factors became a salient feature of the Western Development Programme.[36] The Programme was announced in 1999, and the leading small group was established
early in 2000. The Sixteenth Party Congress affirmed commitments to increase support for western development through investment in fixed assets
(primarily infrastructure projects), tax incentives, and financial transfer payments. Energy development has been a key priority in the Western Development Programme, reflecting China's growing energy needs and Beijing's
drive to secure foreign capital and technology.[37] These build on principles
set out in the governing regulations for implementation of the Programme.
The focus of the Programme is on economic development priorities that
suggest far-reaching changes in local socioeconomic arrangements:[38]

- Increasing construction investment through allocation of central financial resources, augmented by special-purpose construction funds, bank
  loans, foreign funds, and enterprise funds. This offers the prospect of
  significant increased investment by the central government in construction projects. Although expansion of the built environment will provide
  significant opportunities for improved living standards, questions remain
  about its effect on traditional cultural conditions and the distribution of
  benefits to local people.
- Priority allocation of construction projects in water conservancy, high-
  ways, railways, airports, pipelines and telecommunications facilities,
  ecological and environmental preservation, specialized agriculture, energy (particularly hydro, coal, petroleum, and natural gas) and mineral resources, urban infrastructure, tourism, and technology. The scope of
  construction suggests that imported construction workers from China
  proper will be needed, and, indeed, this is what has occurred. There are
  also questions regarding the impact on local social structures and how
  resulting economic changes will be received and distributed locally.
- Increasing general financial transfers to the western regions (especially
  minority nationality areas). Funding from the central government demonstrated state support for local development in the western regions, but
  questions regarding process, conditions, and implications remain.
- Increased credit supports. Financial support from the state indicates a
  high level of commitment, but there are questions about how local ethnic
  minorities will be able to share in this process in light of differences between local cultural expectations and the formalized financial and commercial norms implicit in the credit support scheme.

- Improvement of the investment environment. Outside investors have already welcomed these commitments. Questions about implementation, process, and local effects remain, however.
- Preferential tax policies. Again, commitments have been welcomed by the business sector, but there are uncertainties over the distribution of benefits and the long-term impacts on local society.
- Preferential land-use policies (especially conversion of marginal farmland to forest and grasslands, protection of basic farmlands, and streamlining of the processes for approval of conversion of land to "economic construction"). These provisions herald potentially far-reaching changes in local social and economic structures and behaviour. Questions of process arise in connection with decisions on land-use conversion. Questions about local cultural traditions arise in connection with planned changes in land use, particularly conversion of pastoral land to economic construction.
- Preferential policies for mining. Resource development may provide employment opportunities and increase local GDP growth rates. Questions have been raised, however, regarding how to balance resource depletion with local social development, particularly the issue of ensuring that mining royalties are retained to benefit local social well-being.
- Price reform, particularly increased reliance on market pricing and rationalization of pricing for energy, water, and rail transport. Improved pricing structures can benefit local social and economic well-being, although questions arise over issues of process and content and distribution of benefits.
- Expansion of foreign investment, foreign trade, and economic cooperation. Increasing investment in the region may create employment opportunities and other benefits. Issues arise over distribution of benefits and effects on local social and cultural traditions.
- Regional cooperation and technology transfer. Establishing the West as a regional commerce centre has been a long-sought goal of successive Chinese governments. Problems of distance, communication, transport, and international and regional tensions remain, however.
- Expansion of training and recruitment of specialized and professional personnel. Giving preferential treatment to trained specialists has generally worked against the interests and well-being of local peoples, who are disadvantaged in the areas of education and technical proficiency.
- Enhancing the leading role of science and technology. Although improvements to productivity and economic growth from science and technology

are expected, questions arise regarding local participation and the impacts on local culture.

- Expansion of education. This is a much sought-after goal, particularly as it has the potential to improve the capacity of local people to participate and compete in the changing economies being created through western development. Questions arise, however, about the level of state commitment to educational funding and the extent to which education will be used to assimilate local minorities and suppress local cultural norms and aspirations.
- Development of social services in culture and health. This is a key element in ensuring that the Western Development Programme supports local social well-being. Questions arise about the sustainability of state commitments, particularly since this item was listed last in the range of policy priorities.

Thus, the Western Development Programme offers a mixed array of potential benefits to economic growth and challenges to local sociocultural well-being. Although aware that local cultural systems rooted in nomadic pastoralism and small-scale economies might be threatened by the industrial orientation of the Programme, Chinese planners at the central and local levels appear to be committed to the national benefits of economic growth regardless of local cultural resistance.[39] Allowances for local initiative were made in the early years of the program, although national coordination under the rubric of "macro-economic control" has become a cornerstone of the Programme.[40] Some national planners have noted the importance of sustainability and balanced development that raises local living standards,[41] but the measures of living standards tend to focus on consumption and accumulation rather than qualitative measures of social well-being. In any case, the obstacles to substantially revising national planning to accommodate local identities and cultural perspectives make it unlikely these will be included as measures of development under the Western Development Programme.

Reflecting the broad relationship between legal and economic reform programs in the post-Mao period, the imperative of supporting economic development in the minority areas of the western regions has been an important factor in efforts to formalize local governance autonomy and to establish legal regulatory regimes for the nationality autonomous regions.[42] Efforts to build civil law systems for the nationalities areas to support economic development focus on responsibilities of state organs and departments to support the Western Development Programme, while enterprises in nationalities areas are accorded the lawful rights and responsibilities of legal persons under the national legal system, and members of minority nationalities themselves are to be protected as consumers under fair competition regimes and to receive special accommodation with regard to the cultural requirements of their nationality status.[43] This bespeaks notions of formalism in authority and equality rights, such that legal provisions entrenching the authority of government agency and the legal rights of economic actors serve as foundational principles against which minor adjustments for nationality culture are made, but no provisions are made that would allow preferential opportunities for minorities. The use of legal institutions to ensure that members of local ethnic groups comply with state policies in areas of environmental use and religion has tended to underscore the disengagement of law from local sociocultural practices and expectations.[44] Some specialists criticize the policy-centred nature of the Western Development Programme, however, finding that its general lack of legal provisions and restrictions invites abuse on the part of decision makers who are not accountable, and by economic actors who engage in extra-legal or unlawful activities.[45]

Thus, the Western Development Programme reflects the ways in which central policy objectives have the potential to conflict with local socio-economic conditions and needs. Even as the central government takes measures to support economic growth in China's western regions, these may not succeed in raising living standards unless local conditions are respected in a meaningful way. The question of autonomy thus becomes critical, for even as the central government reserves to itself legal authority to determine the parameters for local economic change (including by imposing legal institutional arrangements), these may ultimately thwart the government's own objectives. Thus, the limitations on autonomy suggested in GATT Article XXIV should be contextualized to local conditions. Mandating local compliance with GATT disciplines may be required under the GATT/WTO system, but this does not necessarily mean that centrally imposed economic development programs will succeed in meeting the needs of the localities in China.

Conclusion

International approaches to economic development present a range of policy options for China. Although the conventional approaches to accumulation are attractive in the short term, serious questions about sustainability and human well-being invite consideration of development policies of distribution and social justice. China's efforts to create economic development policies informed by these issues are complicated by GATT/WTO requirements on transparency and autonomy. Transparency requirements confront conflicting perspectives of legal culture, while limitations on local autonomy are often interpreted to support centralized approaches to economic development. As China pursues an independent path to development, balancing the imperatives of GATT/WTO compliance with the needs of local development will require attention to the selective adaptation of transparency and autonomy rules.

NOTES

1 Charles E. Lindblom, *Politics and Markets: The World's Political-Economic Systems* (New York: Basic, 1977).
2 Stephan Haggard, *Pathways from the Periphery: The Politics of Growth in the Newly Industrializing Countries* (Ithaca, NY: Cornell University Press, 1990).
3 Mario Monti, ed., *Fiscal Policy, Economic Adjustment, and Financial Markets* (Washington, DC: International Monetary Fund, 1989); José Antonio Ocampo and Juan Martin, eds., *Globalization and Development: A Latin American and Caribbean Perspective* (Palo Alto, CA: Stanford Social Sciences; Washington, DC: World Bank, 2003).
4 Chalmers Johnson, *MITI and the Japanese Miracle: The Growth of Industrial Policy, 1925-1975* (Stanford, CA: Stanford University Press, 1982).
5 Haggard, *supra* note 2; Kanishka Jayasuriya, ed., *Law, Capitalism and Power in Asia: The Rule of Law and Legal Institutions* (London: Routledge, 1999).
6 Bob Evans, Marko Joas, Susan Sundback, and Kate Theobald, "Governing Local Sustainability" (2006) 49 Journal of Environmental Planning and Management 849; Lucy De Groot, "Generating Improvement from Within: The Role of the Improvement and Development Agency for Local Government" (2005) 31 Local Government Studies 677.
7 Bruce Mitchell, "Sustainable Development at the Village Level in Bali, Indonesia" (1994) 22 Human Ecology 189.
8 Adrian Martin and Mark Lemon, "Challenges for Participatory Institutions: The Case of Village Forest Committees in Karnataka, South India" (2001) 14 Society and Natural Resources 585.
9 Philip Lewis, *Law and Technology in the Pacific Community* (Boulder, CO: Westview Press, 1994).
10 United Nations Development Programme, *Human Development Report 2001: Making New Technologies Work for Human Development* (New York: Oxford University Press, 2001).
11 Janice Gross Stein, *The Cult of Efficiency* (Toronto: House of Anansi Press, 2001).
12 Louis G. Putterman, *Dollars and Change: Economics in Context* (New Haven, CT: Yale University Press, 2001).

13 John Wong, *Understanding China's Socialist Market Economy* (Singapore: Times Academic Press, 1993); Dwight Perkins, "The Lasting Effect of China's Economic Reforms, 1979-1989" in Kenneth Lieberthal, Joyce Kallgren, Roderick MacFarquhar, Frederic Wakeman Jr., eds., *Perspectives on Modern China: Four Anniversaries* (Armonk, NY: M.E. Sharpe, 1991) 341.

14 Lynn White III, *Unstately Power.* Vol. 1: *Local Causes of China's Economic Reforms* (Armonk, NY: M.E. Sharpe, 1998).

15 He Qinglian, "The Development Trap: Economic and Social Problems in Contemporary China" in Xu Ming, ed., *Zhongguo wenti baogao* [Report on China's problems] (Beijing: China Today Publishers, 1998).

16 Kong Qingjiang, *China and the World Trade Organization: A Legal Perspective* (Singapore: World Scientific Publishing, 2002).

17 Pitman B. Potter, "Globalization and Economic Regulation in China: Selective Adaptation of Globalized Norms and Practices" (2003) 1 Washington University Global Studies Law Review 119.

18 *General Agreement on Tariffs and Trade,* 30 October 1947, 55 U.N.T.S. 187, Can. T.S. 1947 No. 27 (entered into force 1 January 1948).

19 *Ibid.*

20 World Trade Organization, Ministerial Conference, Fourth Session, "Draft Protocol on the Accession of the People's Republic of China" in *Report of the Working Party on the Accession of China* (Doha, 2001), WT/MIN(01)/3.

21 Roger Cotterrell, *The Politics of Jurisprudence: A Critical Introduction to Legal Philosophy* (London: Butterworths, 1989) at 112; Lindblom, *supra* note 1 at 126-30; Will Kymlicka, *Liberalism, Community and Culture* (New York: Oxford University Press, 1991).

22 Potter, *supra* note 17 at 119-50.

23 R.H. Wagner, "Economic Interdependence, Bargaining Power and Political Influence" (1988) 42 International Organization 461.

24 Potter, *supra* note 17 at 119-50.

25 Kenneth Lieberthal, *Governing China* (New York: W.W. Norton, 1995); Kenneth Lieberthal and Michel Oksenberg, *Policy-Making in China: Structures and Processes* (Princeton, NJ: Princeton University Press, 1988); Pitman B. Potter, "Legal Reform in China: Institutions, Culture, and Selective Adaptation" (2004) 29 Law and Social Inquiry 465; State Council Information Office, *Progress in China's Human Rights Cause* (Beijing: State Council Information Office, 2001); William Theodore deBary and Tu Weiming, eds., *Confucianism and Human Rights* (New York: Columbia University Press, 1998).

26 Pitman B. Potter, "The Chinese Legal System: Continuing Commitment to the Primacy of State Power" (1999) 159 China Quarterly 673.

27 State Council Information Office, "White Paper on Political Democracy" (19 November 2009), online: *China Daily* <http://www.chinadaily.com.cn/english/doc/2005-10/19/content_486206.htm>; Joshua Cooper Ramo, *The Beijing Consensus* (London: Foreign Policy Centre, 2004).

28 *General Agreement on Tariffs and Trade, supra* note 18.

29 *Understanding on the Interpretation of Article XXIV of the General Agreement on Tariffs and Trade 1994*, 15 April 1994, *Marrakesh Agreement Establishing the World Trade Organization*, Annex 1A, Legal Instruments – Results of Uruguay Round, 33 I.L.M. 1161.

30 Detlev Vagts, *Transnational Business Problems*, 2d ed. (New York: Foundation Press, 1998) at 35-40.

31 J.G. Castel, A.L.C. DeMestral, and W.C. Graham, *The Canadian Law and Practice of International Trade, with Particular Emphasis on Export and Import of Goods and Services*, 2d ed. (Toronto: Emond Montgomery Publications, 1997) at 21-26.

32 National People's Congress of the People's Republic of China, Fifth Congress, Fifth Session, *Constitution of the People's Republic of China* (1982), online: <http://www.npc.gov.cn/englishnpc/Constitution>.

33 Xie Junchun and Ma Kelin, *Xibu renwen huanjing youhua yanjiu* [Study of improving the human environment in the west] (Lanzhou: People's Press, 2002) at 134-35.

34 Fei Yu, "Science, Education Gap in Minority Regions," Analyst's Note, Xinhua (HK) FBIS Daily Report – China (21 May 1999); Lang Sheng and Tao Ying, *Zhongguo xibu da kaifa zhong de renkou yu kechixu fazhan* [Population and sustainable development in China's western development] (Beijing: People's Press, 2002).

35 Li Dezhu, *Xibu dakaifa yu woguo minzu wenti* [Western development and our nationalities issues] (2000) 288 Qiushi [Seeking Truth] 22.

36 Y.M. Yeung and Shen Jianfa, eds., *Developing China's West: A Critical Path to Balanced National Development* (Hong Kong: The Chinese University Press, 2004); David S.G. Goodman, ed., *The Campaign to "Open Up the West": National, Provincial and Local Perspectives* (Cambridge, UK: Cambridge University Press, 2004) at 178; Abigail Sines, "Civilizing the Middle Kingdom's Wild West" (2002) 21 Central Asian Survey 5; Lai Hongdah Harry, "China's Western Development Program: Its Rationale, Implementation, and Prospects" (2002) 28 Modern China 432; Yasuo Onishi, ed., *China's Western Development Strategy: Issues and Prospects* (Tokyo: Institute of Developing Economies, 2001).

37 Mehmet Ogutcu, "Foreign Direct Investment and Importance of the "Go West" Strategy in China's Energy Sector" in *Foreign Direct Investment in China: Challenges and Prospects for Regional Development* (Paris: OECD, 2002).

38 "Opinion on the Implementation of Certain Policy Measures on the Great Development of the Western Regions" in *China Laws for Foreign Business – Special Zones and Cities*, looseleaf (North Ryde, NSW: CCH Australia, 2001).

39 Ni Guoliang, *Zhongguo xibei diqu xiandaihua zhong de jingji yu wenhua guanxi* [Relations between economy and culture in the modernization of China's northwest] (Lanzhou: People's Press, 1998) at 201-15.

40 Zhibin Li, Deputy Director of the Office of the Leading Group for Western Regional Development of the State Council and Vice Minister of National Development and Reform Commission, Speech (14 October 2004), Xinhua (English version) FBIS Daily Report – China (FBIS-CHI- 2004-1014).

41 Shantong Li, ed., *Xibu dakaifa yu diqu xietiao fazhan* [Western development and regional coordinated development] (Beijing: Commercial Press, 2003).

42 Shenglong Yang, *Minzu wenti minzu wenhua lunji* [Collection of essays on national-
    ities issues and nationalities culture] (Beijing: Nationalities Press, 2004).
43 Zhanrong Li, *Minzu jingji fa yanjiu* [Research on nationalities economic law] (Bei-
    jing: Nationalities Press, 2003) at 181-94.
44 Wang Tianjin, *Xibu huanjing ziyuan chanye* [Environmental and resource industries
    of the western region] (Dalian: Dongbei University of Finance and Economics Press,
    2002) at 303-12.
45 Xie Junchun and Ma Kelin, *supra* note 33 at 134-35.

PART 3

CASE STUDIES ON DISPUTE RESOLUTION

International Dispute Resolution in Japan
A Combination of Judicial and Other Systems

MAOMI IWASE

There are many forms of dispute resolution in Japan, such as litigation and conciliation in courts and alternative dispute resolution (ADR) in public or private organizations. Some ADR organizations cover international disputes, but these organizations have received only a limited number of cases. Traditionally, arbitration cases have been extremely rare in Japan because of the former arbitration law, which was enacted in 1890 as part of the former *Code of Civil Procedure* (CCP). To improve both dispute resolution and the business environment, a judicial reform was initiated in 1999. A new arbitration law, based on the United Nations Commission on International Trade Law (UNCITRAL) Model Law on International Commercial Arbitration, was passed in 2003 and came into force in 2004. The legal framework for ADR was also scrutinized by the government, and a new ADR law was passed in 2005. The state of the Japanese judicial system has influenced the handling of legal disputes, affecting both the parties engaged in a dispute and ADR organizations.

The purpose of this essay is to introduce the current state of international dispute resolution in Japan and present some of the main aspects of the dispute resolution system. First, we review the civil dispute resolution system. Second, we analyze dispute resolution in the courts and in other settings. Third, we briefly discuss recent changes to the dispute resolution system. Finally, we present our opinion with regard to dispute resolution in Japan.

In this essay, the term "international dispute" refers to disputes in which one of the disputing parties is a foreigner. In other words, international disputes are between people from different countries.

Overview of the Japanese Civil Dispute Resolution System

In Japan, the judicial system is the major dispute resolution system for civil cases. There are also other systems, run by neutral third parties.[1]

Litigation and ADR in the Courts

The civil cases in the courts consist of civil litigation cases, civil conciliation cases, civil execution cases, bankruptcy cases, and so forth. These cases are dealt with through different judicial settlements: settlement-in-court (settlement-in-litigation and settlement prior to filing), civil and family conciliations, umpiring, and procedures for decisions in non-litigation cases. In other words, mediation has been made a part of court procedure in Japan, where it has played a very important role within the judicial system. When they recommend conciliation during litigation, judges participate in these procedures as one of the mediators or conciliators.[2]

Civil Litigation

The court can resolve civil disputes by passing a judgment through the litigation procedure. In civil litigation procedures, however, the court is authorized to recommend that the parties enter into settlement (resolution by negotiation) at any time while the case is pending (CCP,[3] Article 89). This is known as settlement-in-litigation, a type of *de facto* conciliation by the judge where the resulting settlement is as enforceable as a judgment.[4] Many cases are resolved through this procedure.[5] The court often sets several dates for settlement hearings. During these hearings, it suggests appropriate terms of settlement and persuades the parties to make concessions. When the settlement is reached, it is entered into the court records; the record has the same effect as a final and binding judgment.[6]

Alternatively, before commencing a civil suit, the disputing parties may file the settlement with a summary court (CCP, Article 275). In this case, when the settlement is reached, it becomes as enforceable as a judgment.

Civil Conciliation

Conciliation is a system unique to Japan and is regulated under the *Law on Civil Conciliation* (LCC).[7] The special feature of this system is that it resolves disputes by ensuring concessions from the concerned parties through the intervention of either the judge or the Conciliation Committee, which is composed of one judge and two or more Conciliation Commissioners appointed from outside the court. Since these proceedings are simple and inexpensive, they are widely utilized. The aim of conciliation is to resolve the civil dispute in a reasonable manner while taking account of the actual circumstances.[8] Under the LCC, the procedure for conciliation proceedings can be commenced according to either of the following scenarios: (1) one of the parties to the dispute makes an application (LCC, Article 2); or (2) the court considers conciliation an appropriate remedy and exercises its authority by issuing a court order. Both parties, however, must agree to engage in conciliation (LCC, Article 20).[9]

This procedure is available for settling all types of civil disputes. According to the LCC, the conciliation procedure covers civil disputes as well as general and specific disputes, such as agriculture, commerce, environmental pollution caused by mining, traffic, and environmental pollution in general. As a result of amendments to the LCC in 1992, conciliation proceedings must be exhausted before a case is filed in a district court when the case concerns an increase or decrease in rent for housing or land (LCC, Article 24-2). In 1999, the *Law Concerning Specific Conciliation*[10] was enacted to help debtors on the verge of financial collapse negotiate a reduction in debt or a grace period.[11]

When conciliation is successfully accomplished, the terms of conciliation are entered in the court records, and they have the same force and effect as a final binding judgment. On the other hand, if the conciliation has been unsuccessful, the proceedings end with the dispute remaining unsettled. In this event, if the court deems it necessary, it may adjudicate the case by a ruling (LCC, Article 17). The concerned parties or any interested third person may make an objection to the adjudication within two weeks from the date of the adjudication. If an objection is made, the adjudication loses its effect (LCC, Article 18).[12] If no objection is made, the adjudication has the same effect as a judicial settlement.

In commercial conciliation and other special conciliation cases (requested by the parties in writing), the Conciliation Committee decides the terms of conciliation (LCC, Article 24-3). There are only a few practical instances of this, however.[13]

ADR Organizations Other Than the Courts

In Japan, there are many types of ADR, such as administrative hearings and arbitration, conciliation, intermediary arrangement, and so forth. These can be administered by public or private organizations.

Administrative Hearings
The following Japanese quasi-judicial organizations conduct administrative hearings:

- the Japanese Patent Office, which conducts patent hearings
- the Marine Accidents Inquiry Agency, which conducts marine accident hearings.

ADR Systems Other Than Administrative Hearings
Both public and private organizations are engaged in arbitration, conciliation, intermediary arrangements, and so forth. The following is a list of such public organizations:

- the Environmental Disputes Coordination Commission[14]
- the Central Labour Relations Commission (CLRC)[15]
- the Construction Work Disputes Committee (CWDC)[16]
- the National Consumer Affairs Center of Japan (NCAC) (the former Japan Consumer Information Centre).[17]

The following is a list of such private organizations:

- the Japan Commercial Arbitration Association (JCAA)[18]
- the Tokyo Maritime Arbitration Commission (TOMAC), a part of the Japan Shipping Exchange, Inc. (JSE)[19]
- the Japan Center for Settlement of Traffic Accident Disputes (JCSTAD)[20]
- the Japan Credit Counseling Association (JCCA)[21]
- the arbitration centres[22] established by local bar associations[23]
- the Japan Intellectual Property Arbitration Center (JIPAC) (the former Arbitration Center for Industrial Property).[24]

Among these Japanese ADR organizations, the JCAA and TOMAC deal with both domestic and international disputes. JIPAC also deals with both domestic and international disputes, such as disputes related to patents owned by a Japanese party in foreign countries[25] or disputes related to the use of the JP domain name by foreigners.[26] According to a survey conducted by the Institute for Socioeconomic Dispute Studies (ISDS), in addition to the abovementioned organizations, the CWDC[27] and most of the arbitration centres managed by local bar associations also deal with both international and domestic disputes.[28] It can be said, therefore, that most ADR organizations in Japan handle international disputes. As will be explained, however, this does not imply that these organizations have actually settled international disputes.

Moreover, as mentioned earlier, the synthesis of conciliation and adjudication is a long-standing tradition in Japanese courts. The same is true of arbitration. Conciliation led by arbitrators has frequently been used during the arbitration process for both domestic and international disputes.[29] According to a survey by the ISDS,[30] the JCAA, TOMAC, JIPAC, and five of the seven arbitration centres managed by the local bar associations utilize a hybrid type of ADR that combines arbitration with conciliation or mediation.[31]

There is no legal provision that directly authorizes the JCAA to engage in hybrid procedures, but Rule 39 of the *Commercial Arbitration Rules* includes a provision regarding an arbitrator's authority to mediate a settlement. In 2003, however, the JCAA amended its arbitration rules to correspond with the new Japanese *Arbitration Law* (to be discussed later). Rule 47 of the amended *Commercial Arbitration Rules* provides for the "Settlement of Disputes by the Arbitral Tribunal."

With regard to the JSE, Article 8 of the *Commercial Arbitration Rules* states that after an application for arbitration has been accepted, the secretariat can suggest conciliation to both parties in order to resolve the dispute between them in a prompt, simple, and non-acrimonious manner.

With regard to JIPAC, the ability to conduct continuous conciliation and arbitration in order to settle a dispute is provided for by its Rule 29.

Most arbitration centres managed by the local bar associations do not have formal authorization to perform hybrid procedures, so these centres appear to be doing so without any oversight.[32]

Hybrid Dispute Processing in Japan
Historically, conciliation has been the basic practice in dispute processing. Hence, it was given a high level of importance among the various litigation practices that were established following the modernization of the nation's judicial system. Even after the enactment of modern statutes and the changes in the judicial system, this particular tradition continues to exist.[33] Hybrid dispute processing in Japan, such as a combination of litigation and conciliation, has been primarily based on court procedure.[34] It has also been applied by practising lawyers to resolve disputes outside of court, albeit through intervention by a judge. In Japan, when conciliation by a third party fails, the third party itself is given the authority to make a binding decision. In such cases, the third party serves as both the conciliator and

umpire, resulting in paternalistic dispute processing, which is often a target of criticism. The use of negotiation and conciliation as the basic tools of dispute processing, with the potential for a third party to force a solution, satisfies the needs of dispute resolution; however, from the perspective of promoting the autonomy of the concerned parties and taking into account the international orientation of a dispute, it is important that natural justice be ensured.[35]

The Contemporary State of International Dispute Resolution in Japan

We turn now to the state of international dispute resolution in Japan.

Courts

International Cases Filed in the Courts

Generally, civil litigation cases can be categorized as follows: common action (*tsujô soshô jiken*),[36] bills and cheques action,[37] personal affairs action (*jinji soshô jiken*),[38] and administrative action (*gyôsei soshô jiken*).[39] The Supreme Court publishes an *Annual Report of Judicial Statistics* that summarizes statistics for the different types of cases, such as civil and administrative cases, criminal cases, family affairs cases, and juvenile delinquency cases.[40] Based on this report, the different types of civil litigation cases can be summarized as follows:

- disputes related to personal affairs
- disputes related to money (purchases, loans, damages for traffic or other accidents, payment of bills and cheques, and so forth)
- disputes related to building
- disputes related to land
- others.

International cases,[41] however, are not analyzed in the section on civil and administrative cases in the official statistics report.[42] The different types of international cases typically seen in Japanese courts are:

- *Private versus private case,* usually filed to claim damages on account of an airline accident, the failure to fulfill a shipping contract, the ill treatment of foreign labourers and war victims (forced labour), and so forth[43]
- *Private versus state case,* usually filed by foreign war victims against a state. Examples include claims filed by foreign war victims regarding their exploitation as forced labour, claims by Japanese labourers against

the US Army, claims by refugees (pension claims by Koreans living in Japan), and so forth.

Based on the purpose of the relevant laws, court-led civil conciliation appears to be intended to cover domestic disputes. Conciliation cases, therefore, rarely involve the settling of international disputes or disputes involving foreigners.

The Number of Civil Cases Filed and Procedures in the Court

It has been argued that Japan's low incidence of litigation is due to the country's socioeconomic system.[44] The cases of litigation and conciliation in the courts have gradually increased since 1990 and have almost doubled since 1997,[45] but this upward trend changed in 2004.

Litigation. According to the annual Supreme Court report,[46] the number of newly filed civil litigation cases in the district courts has continued to increase or has remained high. It has increased by approximately 19 percent since 1997. A similar trend is visible in the summary courts, with an increase of approximately 30 percent since 1997. These figures do not imply, however, that all the cases filed in these courts ended in a judgment.[47]

As mentioned earlier, in the overview of the Japanese civil dispute resolution system, during the litigation process, the court may encourage the parties to settle the case at any point. Because of this, many cases are resolved through settlement-in-litigation. In reality, there are many cases where a judge may effect a settlement at the request of the parties or on his or her own initiative; approximately half of the lawsuits in Japan end through such a settlement.[48] According to the *Annual Report of Judicial Statistics for 2003* published by the Supreme Court,[49] 46 percent of all the cases in the summary courts (excluding the small claims procedure) were resolved by judgment, 26 percent by settlement, and 25 percent by withdrawal. In the district courts, 50 percent of all the cases were resolved by judgment, 33 percent by settlement, and 14 percent by withdrawal. In 2004,[50] 45 percent of all the cases in the summary courts (excluding the small claims procedure) were resolved by judgment, 25 percent by settlement, and 22 percent by withdrawal. In the district courts, 48 percent of all cases were resolved by judgment, 35 percent by settlement, and 14 percent by withdrawal. Thus, since withdrawal can technically be interpreted as a "settlement,"[51] settlement as a means of resolving civil disputes has been used for approximately 50 percent of all the cases in both summary and district courts. It is reported that certain judges prefer to transfer cases so that they can be resolved through a civil conciliation procedure, instead of attempting a settlement-in-litigation. If the litigation process fails to yield a settlement and the same judge were to render judgment, this would lead to misgivings about natural justice. Certain judges therefore prefer to transfer cases in order to ensure natural justice.[52]

Conciliation.   Since 1997, the number of newly filed civil conciliation cases in the district courts has remained at approximately the same level. In contrast, the number of newly filed civil conciliation cases in the summary courts has increased rapidly, and by 2003 it was approximately three times higher than in 1997. In 2004, however, the number of cases in both the district and summary courts declined from 2,047 to 1,545 (approximately 35 percent) and from 613,260 to 439,173 (approximately 30 percent), respectively.[53]

In 2003, with regard to the conciliation cases in the summary courts, 13 percent of all the disposed of cases were successful,[54] while 5 percent were unsuccessful;[55] 18 percent were resolved by withdrawal and 64 percent by other means.[56] The corresponding figures for 2004 were 9, 5, 17, and 69 percent, respectively.[57] In 2003, 55 percent of all the disposed of cases in the district courts were successful, while 26 percent were unsuccessful; 5 percent were resolved by withdrawal and 14 percent by other means. The corresponding figures for 2004 were 52, 30, 6, and 12 percent, respectively.

International Commercial Dispute Cases Filed with the ADR Organizations

No official statistics are provided by the government for international dispute cases. The total number of cases in litigation is rather low, however, so the number of cases dealing with international issues or involving foreigners that are settled in the courts is also low. This situation is identical to that in the ADR organizations.

ADR Organizations Other Than Those Managed by the Bar Associations

According to an ISDS survey, the total caseload of newly filed international arbitrations that were handled by the JCAA, TOMAC, and JIPAC from 1996 to 2000 was 58, 28, and 1, respectively.[58]

During the same period, the JCAA disposed of a total of 55 cases. Of these, 34 were resolved by award, and 12 of these were based on either settlement or conciliation. Twenty-one cases were resolved by withdrawal, and 18 of these were withdrawn as a result of either settlement or conciliation. The types of disputed contract in which an arbitration clause was stipulated and the dispute was disposed of are as follows:

- long-term product sales based on an agency or distributorship contract (export)
- long-term product sales based on an agency or distributorship contract (import)
- licence or technology transfer
- individual or spot product sales (export)
- individual or spot product sales (import)
- construction
- others (service agreements, such as design, work/commission, franchise, etc.)

The TOMAC disposed of a total of 34 cases. Of these, 18 were resolved by award, and none were based on either settlement or conciliation. Sixteen cases were resolved by withdrawal, and 5 of these were based on either settlement or conciliation.

The JIPAC had disposed of no cases as of the end of February 2003.

Arbitration Centres Managed by the Local Bar Associations

According to the annual arbitration report by the Japan Federation of Bar Associations (JFBA) (*Nihon Bengoshi Rengôkai*), the number of newly filed cases in all the arbitration centres managed by the local bar associations has continued to increase[59] – by approximately 160 percent from 1997 to 2008. The total number of cases filed in these centres since 1997 was estimated at 10,840 in 2008.

According to an ISDS survey, from 1996 to 2000, only one case pertaining to an international commercial dispute was filed in a bar association arbitration centre – a mediation case filed in the arbitration centre managed by the Nagoya Bar Association.[60] With the recent surge of interest in ADR, however, there has been a rapid increase in the number of cases received by all arbitration centres and in the number of cases disposed of by these centres.[61] It is therefore likely that there are other reasons for the limited number of international and domestic dispute cases handled by Japanese ADR organizations.[62]

International Dispute Resolution and Judicial Reform

Judicial Reform

In 1994, the government established the Japan Investment Council (JIC) as a ministerial-level council that could promote foreign direct investment in Japan. The government also adopted several measures to make the business environment more favourable for corporations, such as introducing reforms in the systems related to business management, initiating deregulation, and lowering the effective tax rate for corporations. With regard to foreign investment, investors tend to focus on the dispute resolution system of the host country.[63] Improvement of its dispute resolution system has therefore been one of the policies adopted by the Japanese government in order to promote investment.[64]

In 1999, the government began implementing judicial reform. In 2001, the Justice System Reform Council, which was established under the Cabinet,[65] submitted its recommendations to the Cabinet, stating:

> In addition to making special efforts to improve the function of adjudication ... efforts to reinforce and vitalize ADR should be made so that it will become an equally attractive option to adjudication for the people ... Comprehensive consultation windows concerning dispute resolution, including litigation and ADR, should be improved and cooperation should be promoted by utilizing information technology, such as Internet portal sites, in order to realize a system to provide information at one stop ... In order to respond to the increasing number of international civil cases, the civil justice system should be further reinforced and speeded up, beginning with strengthening of comprehensive response to cases related to intellectual property. The arbitration system (including international commercial arbitration) should be coordinated quickly, paying heed to international trends.[66]

In 2001, the Office for Promotion of Justice System Reform was established within the Cabinet based on the *Justice System Reform Promotion Law*, Law No. 119 of 2001. In 2002, the Cabinet decided on a "Program for Promoting Justice System Reform." Based on the program, eleven groups of consultation experts were established.[67]

The New Arbitration Law

The Consultation Group on Arbitration began debating potential changes to arbitration in 2002, and an *Arbitration Law* was passed on 1 August

2003,[68] replacing an older statute.[69] The new law came into force on 1 March 2004.[70] In principle, it is based on the UNCITRAL Model Law. As with the German *Arbitration Act,* this new law applies to both domestic and international arbitration and makes no distinction between commercial and non-commercial arbitration. The topics of the new *Arbitration Law* are:[71]

- Arbitrability[72]
- Multiparty Arbitration[73]
- Court Assistance in Written Communications[74]
- Arb-Med[75]
- Costs of Arbitration[76]
- Criminal Penalties for an Arbitrator's Corruption[77]
- Special Provisions for Consumer Arbitration and Individual Employment Arbitration.[78]

In response to the new *Arbitration Law,* a number of arbitration practitioners, lawyers, and professors established the Japan Association of Arbitrators (JAA) on 16 October 2003.[79] Education and training is one of the chief activities of the JAA.[80]

The ADR Law

The *Law for Promotion of Utilization of ADR (ADR Law)* was passed on 1 December 2004.[81] It provided the basis for ADR and outlined the responsibilities of the central and local governments. Under the *ADR Law,* "out-of-court dispute resolution (ADR) procedures" are stipulated as "dispute resolution procedures conducted by a third party impartially, for disputing parties aiming to solve the civil disputes other than the litigation procedure" (Article 1). Further, "private dispute solution procedures" are defined as "ADR procedures conducted by private businesses, to mediate the settlement of a civil dispute that may be resolved by settlement between the parties, based on a request by both the disputing parties under their contract" (Article 2[i]). According to this definition, the *ADR Law* is not applicable to ADR conducted by the state, local governments, and other independent administrative agencies because they are not "private businesses." It also does not apply to arbitration regarding whether the award determined by the arbitrators is binding because the arbitrators do not "mediate settlement." Only Chapter 1 of the *ADR Law,* which provides general provisions such as the duties of the state and local government, and so on, applies to all types of ADR, that is, ADR by courts, administrative organizations, and private organizations, including arbitration, conciliation, mediation, and so forth. Other sections of the *ADR Law* deal with a certification system for organizations that will engage in ADR, application of the ADR system, and acceptance of arbitration by private businesses.[82] Determining a certification system (*Ninsyô Seido*) for the organizations that will undertake ADR procedures was one of the major issues debated by the Consultation Group on ADR, and some members of the public voiced their concern that such a system would be tantamount to governmental intervention.[83] Such a system is stipulated in the law that was passed, however.

Conclusion: Japan and International Dispute Resolution

Although there are various types of alternative dispute resolution in Japan, the number of cases – particularly those related to international commercial disputes – that are filed for resolution through such means is extremely low. In contrast, for example, numerous international commercial disputes are submitted to the China International Economic and Trade Arbitration Commission (CIETAC) in the People's Republic of China.[84] For several years, China has promoted arbitration as the preferred method for dealing with commercial disputes. It is the most popular means of settling disputes between Chinese and foreign parties, and in recent years, the CIETAC has emerged as a world heavyweight in terms of the number of cases heard each year. In addition, arbitration has a clear advantage over litigation because of near-global enforceability of arbitration awards under the 1958 United Nations *Convention on the Recognition and Enforcement of Foreign Arbitral Awards* (the *New York Convention*), to which China is also a signatory.[85] Another reason that foreign businesses prefer to settle disputes in the CIETAC rather than in the courts is that the Chinese courts are viewed as tending to favour local parties over foreigners.[86] Both the CIETAC and the Chinese courts have been criticized with regard to the facilities for and approach towards international dispute settlement, however.

There are also many reasons that foreign companies may wish to avoid both the courts and arbitration centres in China, making professional mediation a more attractive option. As in many developing countries, China's court system still suffers from corruption and a lack of competence on the part of some judges. Furthermore, although arbitration through the CIETAC is generally considered to be fair, parties have recently complained about the limited number of arbitrators with adequate expertise in Chinese foreign investment and commercial law. Concern has also been expressed about confidentiality, outside influence, and *ex parte* communications between arbitrators and the lawyers or the parties involved. A study in the late 1990s regarding foreign and CIETAC arbitration award enforcement cases found that only 52 percent of the foreign awards and 47 percent of the CIETAC awards were enforced. Of these, only 34 percent of the applicants recovered 100 percent of the award.[87]

Despite its problems, the CIETAC is certain to be one of the important ADR organizations for foreigners in China. Thus far, it has received and settled far more disputes than the Japanese ADR organizations. With the changes in the Japanese system, however, not only the government but also private ADR organizations have been attempting to improve their dispute resolution systems. Accordingly, the new *Arbitration Law* has been enforced and the *ADR Law* has been enacted. Toshio Matsumoto, executive director of the JSE, states: "Before the new *Arbitration Law* was enacted, some Japanese people said that there were very few arbitration cases in Japan because of the old *Arbitration Law*. But that may be a mere excuse for their being idle. I think that we have to aim at arbitration of high quality."[88]

At present, London and New York are considered the centres of international arbitration. I believe that under the new *Arbitration Law*, Japan should be developed as the centre of international arbitration in Asia.[89] As Tatsuya Nakamura, general manager of the International Arbitration Department at the JCAA, states: "The new *Arbitration Law*, which adopts the UNCITRAL Model Law, will contribute to activating international commercial arbitration in Japan. Therefore, we should attempt to play a central role in international commercial arbitration in Asia."[90]

The new law has adopted most of the UNCITRAL Model Law, signifying Japan's joining of the international arbitration community. It is expected to make Japan a more attractive place for international arbitration. It is important to note, however, that the law contains no provisions on important issues such as confidentiality in arbitration and the immunity of arbitrators. These issues should be addressed in amendments to the law.[91]

Reinhard Neumann, a German attorney-at-law, holds a different position.[92] He believes that the limited number of international arbitration cases in Japan is due to the fact that foreign parties are not well acquainted with Japan, its language, customs, and laws. This makes them feel uneasy about arbitration in Japan. Therefore, based on his opinion, if this uneasiness is dispelled by enactment of the new *Arbitration Law* and the *ADR Law*, there could be a rise in the number of cases filed with the Japanese

ADR organizations. If we study the discussions of the ADR Council and the Japan Federation of Bar Associations, however, it appears that only Japanese lawyers can qualify as attorneys or arbitrators, even with regard to international arbitration procedures. Considering the current state of the Japanese legal system, where only a few lawyers are trained to handle international trade issues and/or can speak English, it is difficult to imagine that foreign parties would prefer international arbitration in Japan, even if new and improved laws were enacted in the future.[93] In fact, the total caseload of newly filed international arbitrations that were handled by the JCAA is not so high. The JCAA disposed of a total of 98 cases from 2001 to 2007,[94] 17 in 2008,[95] and 19 in 2009,[96] respectively.

Many Japanese businesses have their own model contracts that include arbitration clauses. Generally, they tend to frame specific contracts based on these models. It is reported that both Japanese and foreign businesses include arbitration clauses in many contracts and stipulate that these clauses specify the method of dispute resolution.[97] At this point, we need to consider the recent state of, and changes in, the international dispute resolution system. We should bear in mind that the current legal system reflects both the Japanese business consciousness as well as the dispute resolution system. We must also note that these changes to the legal system could effect changes in international trade. The current situation describes not only the features of dispute resolution for international trade disputes but also the adequate system for that.

ACKNOWLEDGMENT
An earlier version of this chapter appeared in Pitman B. Potter and Gu Xiaorong, eds., *Establishment of Selective Adaptation and Implementation of Rule of Law in China* (Shanghai: Shanghai Academy of Social Sciences Press, 2009).

NOTES
1 For a general outline of the judicial system in Japan, see Secretariat of the Justice System Reform Council, "The Japanese Justice System" (1999), online: Prime Minister of Japan and His Cabinet <http://www.kantei.go.jp/foreign/policy/sihou/singikai/990620_e.html>.
2 Rieko Nishikawa, "Judges and ADR in Japan" (2001) 18 Journal of International Arbitration 361.
3 *Minji Soshô Hô* [Code of Civil Procedure], Law No. 109 of 1996, amended in 2005 [CCP]. This law was introduced after the revision of the old CCP. It was enacted on 26 June 1996 and entered into force on 1 January 1998. It was enacted in order to further rectify and expedite the procedures and facilitate the use of civil litigation.

4   Yasunobu Sato, "3 Hybrid Dispute Processing in Japan: Linking Arbitration with Conciliation (Regional Report for the Second Symposium)" in *Final Report to the Project "Conditions and Policies for the Enhancement of International Commercial Arbitration in Asia and Oceania,"* Vol. II (Nagoya: Meijo University, Institute for Socioeconomic Dispute Studies, 2004) at 461 ["Hybrid Dispute Processing"]; Yasunobu Sato, "Hukugôteki Hunsô Shori (Chôtei to Chusai no Renkei) wo meguru Chusaihô Kaisei Shinan (2)" [A proposal for modifying the draft Arbitration Law with regard to the clauses related to hybrid dispute processing (2)] (2001) 48(9) JCA Journal 23 at 25-26 ["Modifying the draft Arbitration Law (2)"]. For more details, see Yasunobu Sato, *Commercial Dispute Processing and Japan* (The Hague: Kluwer Law International, 2001) at 37-129.
5   With regard to the current scenario, see art. 89, sec. 3.1.1 of the CCP.
6   Supreme Court of Japan, "Guide to Judicial Proceedings in Japan: Outline of Civil Litigation in Japan," online: Supreme Court of Japan <http://www.courts.go.jp/english/proceedings/civil_suit_index.html> ["Guide to Judicial Proceedings"]. Basically, the settlement is reached and effected with the appearance of both parties in the court on a set date. If it is difficult for one party to appear, for example, if the party lives far from the court, the party may instead file with the court a document in which he or she accepts the terms for settlement proposed in advance by the court. In this case, a settlement is considered to have been reached in accordance with the terms for settlement shown in the proposal, provided that the opposing party appears on a subsequent date and accepts the same proposal (art. 264). On the other hand, the court may award, upon both parties' joint submission in writing, proper settlement by notifying both parties of the terms of settlement by an appropriate means of communication at any time (art. 265). In addition, the pre-trial stage procedures for specifying issues and evidence (*Benron Junbi Tetsuzuki*) are provided in the CCP (arts. 168 through 178). These procedures specify the court practices that were known as "argument and settlement" (*Benron ken Wakai*) but were not specified in the old CCP. Under the old CCP, the judges took initiatives to improve the quality of the hearings and reduced the duration of the proceedings, and the courts attempted to put into practice several legal devices that were at their disposal. The "argument and settlement" were virtually endorsed in the measures for improving civil proceedings that were proposed by the Tokyo District Court and the Osaka Court in 1985. Thereafter, they prevailed in all the courts. For a more detailed discussion, see Sato, *Commercial Dispute Processing and Japan, supra* note 4 at 159-64 and 167-73; Yasunobu Sato, "Implications of the 1998 Civil Procedure Reform" (2000) 19 Civil Justice Quarterly 224 at 245-49 and 251-56.
7   *Minji Chôtei Hô* [Law on Civil Conciliation], Law No. 222 of 1951, amended in 2004.
8   Article 1 of the LCC "aims at a resolution that matches the actual environment in a manner that prevails in *jôri* (reason) and through mutual concession by the parties concerned."
9   Supreme Court of Japan, "Guide to Judicial Proceedings," *supra* note 6. The proceeding in conciliation cases commences, as a rule, on application of the parties concerned (art. 2), but the courts "*ex officio*" occasionally refer cases pending before them to conciliation (art. 20). As a rule, conciliation should be made by the Conciliation

Committee, but the judge may make conciliation if he or she deems it adequate, although the disposition by the Conciliation Committee becomes mandatory upon the parties' application (art. 5). On the date of conciliation, the committee or the judge in charge, as the case may be, summons the parties concerned and endeavours to settle the dispute by persuading the parties to make concessions or by suggesting proper terms of settlement.

10 *Tokutei Saimu Chôsei Sokushin Tokutei Chôtei Hô* [Law Concerning Specific Conciliation], Law No. 158 of 1999, amended in 2003. This law was enacted to promote the adjustment of specific debt and so on.

11 Supreme Court of Japan, *supra* note 6.

12 Sato, "Hybrid Dispute Processing," *supra* note 4 at 456-57; Sato, "Modifying the draft Arbitration Law (2)," *supra* note 4 at 25. According to Sato, Akira Ishikawa reported that, in practice, the ratio of cases where an objection is filed stands at approximately only 10 percent in recent years: Akira Ishikawa and Kajimura Taichi, eds., *Chukai Minji Chôtei Hô (Kaitei)* [Commentary on the Law on Civil Conciliation (revised ed.)] (Tokyo: Seirin Shoin, 1996) at 272-74.

13 Sato, "Hybrid Dispute Processing," *supra* note 4 at 456-57; Sato, "Modifying the draft Arbitration Law (2)," *supra* note 4 at 25. For more details, see Sato, *Commercial Dispute Processing and Japan, supra* note 4 at 37-129.

14 Environmental Dispute Coordination Commission, "Short History: Establishment of Environmental Disputes Settlement System," online: Ministry of Internal Affairs and Communications <http://www.soumu.go.jp/kouchoi/english/about_us/short.html> and <http://www.soumu.go.jp/kouchoi/english/index.html>. The Environmental Dispute Coordination Commission was established in 1972 as an external agency of the Prime Minister's Office. It was established by consolidating the Land Coordination Commission and the General Pollution Examination Commission. The government enacted the *Basic Law for Environmental Pollution Control* in 1967 in consideration of the following issues: (1) aggravation of environmental pollution and the damage caused by it; (2) awakening of the public's environmental consciousness; and (3) the characteristics of environmental disputes. This law states that "the Government must take necessary measures to establish an environmental dispute settling system." Based on this law, the *Environmental Disputes Settlement Law* was enacted in 1970. This system is unique in that it provides for a dispute settlement system by administrative agencies and the Environmental Dispute Coordination Commission, which is uncommon in other countries. Because of the *Environmental Disputes Settlement Law*, conciliation, mediation, arbitration, and adjudication systems were established, and the Environmental Dispute Coordination Commission was created at the national level while the Pollution Examination Commissions were established at the prefectural level.

15 Ministry of Health, Labour and Welfare, "Central Labour Relations Commission," online: Ministry of Health, Labour and Welfare <http://www.mhlw.go.jp/english/org/policy/central-labour.html>. The CLRC was established in March 1946 following the enactment of the *Trade Union Law*. The CLRC is an extra agency of the Ministry of Health, Labour and Welfare. As an independent administrative agency, it is neither directed nor supervised by any other government agency.

16 "Concerning Construction Work Disputes Committees," online: Ministry of Land, Infrastructure, Transport and Tourism (MLIT) <http://www.mlit.go.jp/sogoseisaku/ 1_6_hf_000127.html>. The CWDC was established to resolve disputes concerning construction contracts between MLIT and each prefecture, under the *Law on Construction Business*, Law No. 100 of 1949.

17 National Consumer Affairs Center of Japan, "What Is NCAC?" online: NCAC <http:// www.kokusen.go.jp/e-hello/ncac_hello.html>. The NCAC was established by the government in October 1970 as a special-status organization, and was reorganized into an independent administrative agency in October 2003. The mission of the NCAC is to improve and stabilize people's lives. Since its founding in 1970, the NCAC has answered consumer inquiries; published a wide variety of information, including the results of product testing; and has come to play an important role in aiding consumer choice. As the core of a network of approximately 490 consumer centres run by local governments across the country, the NCAC gathers information, analyzes it, and provides it to the public. The major changes in daily living and lifestyles brought about by globalization, the current advances of the information society, and deregulation in Japan demand that consumers be more self-reliant. The NCAC works to gather and provide information on a wide range of issues in order to respond to economic and social changes as they arise and to establish consumer networks.

18 Japan Commercial Arbitration Association, "History," online: JCAA <http://www. jcaa.or.jp/e/jcaa-e/history.html>. The International Commercial Arbitration Committee, the former body of the JCAA, was established in 1950 within the Japan Chamber of Commerce and Industry, with the support of six other business organizations, including the Japan Federation of Economic Organizations, the Japan Foreign Trade Council, and the Federation of Banking Associations of Japan, to serve as an organization to settle commercial disputes and promote international trade, thereby contributing to the development of the Japanese economy. In 1953, with the further growth of international trade, the arbitration committee was reorganized as the JCAA to become independent from the Japan Chamber of Commerce and Industry in order to expand and streamline its business activities.

19 Japan Shipping Exchange, "What Is JSE?" online: JSE <http://www.jseinc.org/en/jse/ whatis.html>. The JSE was established in 1921 along the lines of the Baltic Mercantile and Shipping Exchange of London to provide the facilities for establishing a freight and/or charter contract in Japan. Nevertheless, the JSE does not strictly function as a shipping exchange.

Japan Shipping Exchange, "Main JSE Activities," online: JSE <http://www.jseinc. org/en/jse/activities.html>. The JSE is involved in every aspect of maritime business. The TOMAC is thus uniquely capable of dealing with arbitrations involving problems arising in the field. The TOMAC resolves disputes arising under bills of lading, charter parties, contracts relating to the sale and purchase of ships, shipbuilding, ship financing, manning, and so forth.

20 Japan Center for Settlement of Traffic Accident Disputes, "Enkaku" [History], online: JCSTAD, <http://www.jcstad.or.jp/about/enkaku.htm>. The Committee on Traffic Accidents Adjudication, a former body of the JCSTAD, was established in 1974 for consulting on settlements. In 1978, the committee was reorganized as the

JCSTAD in order to strengthen its fair and neutral position as a dispute resolution organization. The JCSTAD aims to undertake all the activities necessary to complete the procedures for disputes concerning traffic accidents, to attempt to provide fair and appropriate protection of the concerned parties, and to contribute to the improvement of common welfare. In order to achieve these goals, the JCSTAD provides diversified services and information free of charge.

21 Japan Credit Counseling Association, "Goaisatsu – Setsuritsu Shushi" [Greetings and our purpose], online: JCCA <http://www.jcca-f.or.jp/business/foundation.html>. The Japan Credit Counseling Association (JCCA) was established in 1987 with the support of various groups, such as the Japan Federation of Bar Associations (JFBA), the Consumers Union, journalists, academics, the credit industry, etc., and with the permission of the Ministry of International Trade and Industry. In 2002, with the support of the lending and banking businesses, the JCCA was authorized as a counselling organization across the consumer credit industry by the Ministry of Economy, Trade and Industry and the Financial Services Agency. The JCCA aims to counsel consumers or the so-called multiple debtors in order to restore their lives.

22 They are known as the "arbitration center" (*Chusai Center*), the "mediation/arbitration center" (*Assen-Chusai Center*), the "compromise and mediation center" (*Jidan-Assen Center*), the "dispute resolution center" (*Hunsô Kaiketsu Center*), the "civil dispute resolution center" (*Minji Hunsô Shori Center*), the "legal consultation center" (*Hôritsu Sôdan Center*), and the "ADR Center" in each bar association.

23 Japanese Federation of Bar Associations, "Hunsô Kaiketsu Center" [The dispute resolution center], online: JFBA <http://www.nichibenren.or.jp/ja/legal_aid/consultation/houritu7.html>. At present, there are fifty-two bar associations in Japan. According to the JFBA (*Nichibenren*), as of November 2004, nineteen bar associations (including branch offices) have established arbitration centres: Tokyo, Dai-ichi [First] Tokyo, Dai-ni [Second] Tokyo, Yokohama, Saitama, Yamanashi-ken, Niigata-ken, Nagoya, Nishi-Mikawa branch of Nagoya, Gifu-ken, Osaka, Kyoto, Hyogo-ken, Nara, Hiroshima, Okayama, Shimane-ken (in Iwami), and Fukuoka-ken (in Tenjin and Kita-Kyusyu) Bar Associations.

24 Japan Intellectual Property Arbitration Center, "Center no Enkaku" [History of the center], online: JIPAC <http://www.ip-adr.gr.jp/enkaku/index.html>. The JIPAC was jointly established by the JFBA and the Japan Patent Agents Association in 1998.

25 Japan Intellectual Property Arbitration Center, "Q.26 Gaikoku no Tokkyoken Shingai" [Infringement of patent owned in foreign countries] in "Q & A (JP Domain wo Nozoku)" [Q&A, excluding the JP domain name disputes], online: JIPAC <http://www.ip-adr.gr.jp/qa/qa.html#%90¥%97%A7%82%CC%91%CE%8F%DB>.

26 Japan Intellectual Property Arbitration Center, "Q.6" in "JP Domain Mei Hunsô Shorino Q & A" [Q & A about JP domain name disputes management], online: JIPAC <http://www.ip-adr.gr.jp/jp_adr/jpdomain_qa.html#mousitate>. For information on all the domain name dispute cases handled by the JIPAC, see Japan Intellectual Property Arbitration Center, "Domain Name Hunsô Shori Zen Jiken Ichiran" [List of all domain name dispute cases], online: JIPAC <http://www.ip-adr.gr.jp/jp_adr/jpdomain_jikenitiran.html>.

27 In particular, the CWDC handles disputes pertaining to construction.

28 "Questionnaire A: Institutional Arbitration" in *Final Report to the Project "Conditions and Policies for the Enhancement of International Commercial Arbitration in Asia and Oceania,"* Vol. II (Nagoya: Meijo University, Institute for Socioeconomic Dispute Studies, 2004) at 472-533 ["Questionnaire A"]. In this survey, the following centres answered the questionnaires: the arbitration centres managed by the Daini Tokyo Bar Association, Hyogo-ken Bar Association, Kyoto Bar Association, and Okawaya Bar Association; the Iwami Law Centre supported by the Shimane-ken Bar Association, the Chugoku Area Federation of Bar Associations, and the JFBA; and the mediation and arbitration centres of both the Nagoya Bar Association and its Nishi-Mikawa (former Okazaki) Branch. Among these, only the arbitration centre of the Kyoto Bar Association handles domestic disputes.

29 Sato, *Commercial Dispute Processing and Japan, supra* note 4 at 261.

30 "Questionnaire A," *supra* note 28 at 493-95.

31 The arbitration centre managed by the Kyoto Bar Association and the Iwami Law Centre do not utilize the hybrid type of ADR.

32 Sato, *Commercial Dispute Processing and Japan, supra note* 4 at 250-51.

33 Sato, "Hybrid Dispute Processing," *supra* note 4 at 456-57; Sato, "Hukugôteki Hunsô Shori (Chôtei to Chusai no Renkei) wo meguru Chusaihô Kaisei Shinan (1)" [A proposal for modifying the draft Arbitration Law with regard to the clauses related to hybrid dispute processing (1)] (2001) 48(8) JCA Journal 2 at 3-4 ["Modifying the draft Arbitration Law (1)"]. For more details, see Sato, *Commercial Dispute Processing and Japan, supra* note 4 at 37-129.

34 Sato, "Hybrid Dispute Processing," *supra* note 4 at 463; Sato, "Modifying the draft *Arbitration Law (2),"* *supra* note 4 at 25-26. By contrast, in the common law countries, hybrid dispute processing has evolved mainly as agreements among the concerned parties without any court intervention, a practice later introduced in court practice and arbitration procedure. In the common law jurisdictions, although a third-party recommendation is sought for facilitating settlement by the parties, this recommendation should be given as a result of adversarial procedure and should be separated from the process of the decision to bind the parties. For more details, see Sato, *Commercial Dispute Processing and Japan, supra* note 4 at 37-129.

35 Sato, "Hybrid Dispute Processing," *supra* note 4 at 463-64; Sato, "Modifying the draft Arbitration Law (2)," *supra* note 4 at 25-26.

36 Supreme Court of Japan, "Guide to Judicial Proceedings," *supra* note 6. "Common action" is a suit seeking resolution between individuals. It is chiefly related to property rights, such as suits seeking repayment of a loan, eviction, or damages for injuries sustained from falls. This suit is tried in accordance with the provisions of the *Code of Civil Procedure.*

37 Supreme Court of Japan, "Guide to Judicial Proceedings," *supra* note 6. A "bills and cheques action" is a suit seeking payment of bills and cheques, and it is tried in accordance with special provisions in the *Code.* This suit was originally adopted as a result of the amendments to the old *Code of Civil Procedure* in 1964. In this type of suit, evidence is restricted to documentary evidence and examination of the parties to enable the court to render a speedy judgment. There is an opportunity to demand a retrial in accordance with the "common action" procedure in the court of

first instance, however. A plaintiff seeking payment of bills or cheques has the option of bringing a lawsuit of this type or as a "common action."

38 Supreme Court of Japan, "Guide to Judicial Proceedings," *supra* note 6. "Personal affairs action" pertains to disputes among family members, such as suits for divorce and for recognition of paternity. In 1949, the family court was established to mediate family affairs cases, including these types of cases, through an informal discussion called conciliation proceedings. According to the law regulating family cases, the conciliation proceedings in family court must be exhausted before a case can be filed with the district court. Such cases are tried according to the CCP and the *Code of Procedure Concerning Personal Affairs*. This *Code* provides for special rules necessary for the disposition of personal actions in accordance with the interests of the general public. The total number of such cases filed with the courts of first instance was 11,021 in 2006.

39 Supreme Court of Japan, "Guide to Judicial Proceedings," *supra* note 6. The main types of administrative action provided in the *Administrative Case Litigation Law*, Law No. 1962 of 1962, are: (1) suits for revocation of acts of administrative agencies stemming from the exercise of public power; (2) litigation for the declaration of illegality of inaction of administrative agencies; and (3) special kinds of litigation aimed at the application of laws or orders for the protection of the public interest rather than for the relief of individual rights and interests (for example, actions demanding the declaration of nullity of an illegal election). Hearings for all these types of litigation are conducted according to the *Administrative Case Litigation Law*. In the case of matters not covered in this law, the relevant provisions of the *Code of Civil Procedure* are applied *mutatis mutandis*. The total number of administrative actions filed with the courts of first instance was 2,081 in 2006.

40 Supreme Court of Japan, *Shihô Tôkei Nenpô* [Annual report of judicial statistics], online: Supreme Court of Japan <http://courtdomino2.courts.go.jp/tokei_y.nsf>. This report has been reprinted in Statistics Bureau and Statistical Research and Training Institute, Ministry of Internal Affairs and Communications, "Chapter 25: Justice and Police" in *Japan Statistical Yearbook*, online: Ministry of Internal Affairs and Communications <http://www.stat.go.jp/english/data/nenkan/1431-25.htm>.

41 As mentioned at the beginning of this chapter, "international disputes" refers to disputes in which one of the parties is a foreigner.

42 In the annual report, the section on family affairs cases analyzes the international elements in such cases. Cases handled by the family courts are categorized as domestic cases and international cases. With regard to international cases, an "international case in family affairs" implies that one or all of the disputing parties, such as the applicant, adversary party, principal, participant, deceased, testator, etc., are foreigners for both determination cases and conciliation cases.

43 For more details, see Masato Dogauchi, "Litigation and Arbitration in International Business Disputes in Japan," paper presented at *the International Symposium: Development of International Economic Law from an Asian Perspective* (Japanese Association of International Economic Law and Nagoya University's Research Project on "Legal Technical Assistance in Asia," 1 November 2003) at 50-64.

44 Sato, *Commercial Dispute Processing and Japan, supra* note 4 at 95-129 and 133.

45 Sato, "Implications of the 1998 Civil Procedure Reform," *supra* note 6 at 255.

46 Supreme Court of Japan, *Shihô Tôkei Nenpô, supra* note 40.

47 Civil litigation cases can be concluded in any of the following ways: "conclusion by judgment" (*Hanketsu*), "order" (*Kettei and Meirei*), "settlement" (*Wakai*), "waiver by the plaintiff of the claim" (*Hôki*), "recognition by the defendant of the claim" (*Nindaku*), "voluntary dismissal of the case by the plaintiff" (*Torisage*), and others.

48 Sato, "Hybrid Dispute Processing," *supra* note 4 at 461; Sato, "Modifying the draft Arbitration Law (2)," *supra* note 4 at 25-26. For more details, see Sato, *Commercial Dispute Processing and Japan, supra* note 4 at 37-129.

49 Supreme Court of Japan, *Shihô Tôkei Nenpô (Heisei 15-Nen)* [Annual report of judicial statistics for 2003], online: Supreme Court of Japan <http://www.courts.go.jp/sihotokei/nenpo/pdf/15DDF694BB70AE5349256EDD0006DBB1.pdf>; <http://www.courts.go.jp/sihotokei/nenpo/pdf/B69CD6B1EB53CF2549256EDD0006DC11.pdf>.

50 Supreme Court of Japan, *Shihô Tôkei Nenpô (Heisei 16-Nen)* [Annual report of judicial statistics for 2004], online: Supreme Court of Japan <http://www.courts.go.jp/sihotokei/nenpo/pdf/7612D18BAFD1250249257059001897EB.pdf>; <http://www.courts.go.jp/sihotokei/nenpo/pdf/451D66A8EC4AA63E492570590018984B.pdf>.

51 Moreover, as a result of the settlement provision (art. 265 of the CCP, which was introduced during the 1996 reform of the CCP), if all the parties make a request in written form, the terms stipulated by the court or judge in charge of the settlement attempt for the litigation case will be deemed to be settlement-in-litigation. This can be interpreted as a form of arbitration following conciliation by the court.

52 Sato, "Hybrid Dispute Processing," *supra* note 4 at 461; Sato, "Modifying the draft Arbitration Law (2)," *supra* note 4 at 25-26. For more details, see Sato, *Commercial Dispute Processing and Japan, supra* note 4 at 37-129.

53 Supreme Court of Japan, *Shihô Tôkei Nenpô (Heisei 16-Nen), supra* note 50, online: Supreme Court of Japan <http://www.courts.go.jp/sihotokei/nenpo/pdf/B59A5A0DF9B76470492570590018980E.pdf>.

54 Achievement in a settlement agreement (LCC, art. 16).

55 No achievement in a settlement agreement (LCC, art. 14).

56 This includes "adjudication of the case by the court" (LCC, art. 17), "termination of the case by the Conciliation Committee" (LCC, art. 13), and so on: Supreme Court of Japan, *Shihô Tôkei Nenpô (Heisei 15-Nen), supra* note 49, online: Supreme Court of Japan <http://www.courts.go.jp/sihotokei/nenpo/pdf/E5E248E559DCC6A949256EDD0006DBA4.pdf>; <http://www.courts.go.jp/sihotokei/nenpo/pdf/3C89630C05E6750749256EDD0006DBF1.pdf>.

57 Supreme Court of Japan, *Shihô Tôkei Nenpô (Heisei 16-Nen), supra* note 50, online: Supreme Court of Japan <http://www.courts.go.jp/sihotokei/nenpo/pdf/1DCD976069BEAE1F49257059001897DE.pdf>; <http://www.courts.go.jp/sihotokei/nenpo/pdf/8F6ECB8BC0DD2508492570590018982B.pdf>.

58 "Questionnaire A," *supra* note 28.

59 For general information regarding this annual report, see Japan Federation of Bar Associations, "Chusai Tôkei Nenpô" [Annual report of arbitration statistics], online: JFBA <http://www.nichibenren.or.jp/ja/legal_aid/consultation/tyusaitoukei_nenpou.html>.

60 "Questionnaire A," *supra* note 28, at 495-500.

61 Sato, *Commercial Dispute Processing and Japan, supra* note 4 at 250-51; see also Hiroshi Okawa, "Chusai Center – Ima Zenkoku deha!" [Arbitration center in Japan now], *Niben News,* No. 208 (2000), online: *Niben News* <http://www.niben.jp/07frontier/news/news00/208/news20806.html>.

62 The following are the reasons for the low number of arbitration cases in Japan: (1) People are not well informed about the arbitration system; (2) the social system supporting arbitration – for instance, the availability of qualified arbitrators – is not well developed; (3) arbitration has not been needed in society. See Takakuwa Akira, "Aratana Chusaihô to Syôgaiteki Chusai" [Choice of problems in Japanese new Arbitration Act] (2004) 56 *Hôsô Jihô* 1589 at 1591-92, n3.

63 For instance, UNCTAD states: "Significant efforts to implement financial, administrative, and judicial reforms would be necessary for the subregion to enhance its attractiveness to investors and increase FDI inflows, in keeping with its size and economic significance." United Nations Conference on Trade and Development, *The World Investment Report 2005,* UNCTAD/WIR/2005 at 87, online: UNCTAD <http://www.unctad.org/en/docs/wir2005_en.pdf> ("Apart from establishing a legal framework for the IPRs, it is clear that many developing countries need to build the capacity for its implementation – including an efficient patent office and judicial system"). With regard to the Japanese situation, see Japan Investment Council, "Tai-Nichi Tôshi Kankyou Seibi nikansuru Syogaikoku karano Yôbô no Jôkyô" [Requests by foreign countries for constructing foreign investment condition in Japan], online: JIC <http://www.investment-japan.net/jp/meeting/2002/1219item3.pdf>.

64 With regard to dispute resolution, the JIC stated the following:

> (1) Activities of foreign lawyers
> Because of the globalization of the world economy and increasing interdependence in trade and investment, the OTO Advisory Council undertook a review of Japanese systems and regulations with a view to achieving international harmonization. In accordance with the Council's report, the law has been amended to relax regulations concerning the work experience requirements of foreign lawyers and to allow joint enterprises between foreign and Japanese lawyers.
>
> As to the issue of representation of parties by foreign lawyers in international arbitration, the Market Access Ombudsman Council of the OTO has delivered a recommendation that a conclusion which has logic acceptable internationally should be reached soon at the Study Commission on the Representation of Parties in International Arbitration established by the Ministry of Justice and the JFBA and necessary measures including the adjustment of law should be taken promptly on the basis of the conclusion. The Office of Market Access meeting has decided the measures respecting the recommendation to the maximum extent.
>
> (2) Shortening the time required for legal procedures
> The issue of lawsuit procedures is inseparably linked to the execution of the judiciary's powers, and from the viewpoint of separation of the three powers, it is inappropriate to take this matter up in the Japan Investment Council, which is a

government body. However, since 1990, the Legislative Council of the Ministry of Justice has been undertaking a comprehensive review of civil lawsuit procedures and if the laws on such procedures are amended based on its findings, this will contribute to shortening the time required to examine cases.

For more information, see *Yearbook of the Japan Investment Council* (No. 1, June 1995), online: JIC <http://www5.cao.go.jp/e-e/doc/tainichi-e-e.html>.

65 On 30 November 2004, the Office for Promotion of Justice System Reform was dissolved. See Office for Promotion of Justice System Reform, "Kongo no Shihô Seido Kaikaku no Suishin nitsuite" [Future promotion of justice system reform], online: Prime Minister of Japan and His Cabinet <http://www.kantei.go.jp/jp/singi/sihou/kouhyou/041126kongo.html>.

66 Justice Reform Council, "Recommendations of the Justice System Reform Council – for a Justice System to Support Japan in the 21st Century" (June 2001) online: Prime Minister of Japan and His Cabinet <http://www.kantei.go.jp/foreign/judiciary/2001/0612report.html>.

67 The eleven groups of consultation experts are:

- Consultation Group on Labour: Strengthening of comprehensive response to labour-related cases
- Consultation Group on Access to the Justice System: Expansion of access to the courts
- Consultation Group on ADR: Broadening and revitalization of alternative dispute resolution
- Consultation Group on Arbitration: Establishment of arbitration schemes
- Consultation Group on Administrative Litigation: Reinforcement of the checking function of the justice system vis-à-vis the administration
- Consultation Group on "*Saiban-in*" System and Criminal Affairs: Introduction of a new participation system in criminal proceedings and improvement and speeding up of criminal trials
- Consultation Group on a Public Defence System: Introduction and establishment of a public criminal defence system
- Consultation Group on Internationalization: Responses to internationalization
- Consultation Group on Legal Training: Reform of the legal training system
- Consultation Group on the System for the Legal Profession: Reform of the system for lawyers, public prosecutors, and judges
- Consultation Group on Intellectual Property Litigation: Improvement and speeding up of intellectual property-related litigation.

See "The Formulation of Consultation Groups of Experts," online: Prime Minister of Japan and His Cabinet <http://www.kantei.go.jp/foreign/policy/sihou/kentou/index_e.html>.

68 Law No. 138 of 2003 (entered into force 1 March 2004). The structure of the *Arbitration Law* is as follows:

- Chapter I: General Provisions (arts. 1-12)
- Chapter II: Arbitration Agreement (arts. 13-15)
- Chapter III: Arbitrator (arts. 16-22)
- Chapter IV: Special Jurisdiction of Arbitral Tribunal (arts. 23-24)
- Chapter V: Commencement and Conduct of Arbitral Proceedings (arts. 25-35)
- Chapter VI: Arbitral Award and Termination of Arbitral Proceedings (arts. 36-43)
- Chapter VII: Setting Aside of Arbitral Award (art. 44)
- Chapter VIII: Recognition and Enforcement Decision of Arbitral Award (arts. 45-46)
- Chapter IX: Miscellaneous (arts. 47-49)
- Chapter X: Penalties (arts. 50-55)
- Supplementary Provisions.

An English translation of the *Arbitration Law* by the Arbitration Law Follow-up Research Group, which has been established within the Secretariat of the Office for Promotion of Justice System Reform, is available at <http://www.kantei.go.jp/foreign/policy/sihou/arbitrationlaw.pdf>.

69 The former *Arbitration Law* was enacted in 1890 with insufficient provisions, whereas the new law contains many non-compulsory and practical provisions. Whereas the former law cited the articles concerning civil procedure, the new law does not in principle refer to other Japanese laws. Accordingly, arbitrators and other concerned persons hardly need to research the *Code of Civil Procedure* and other Japanese laws in order to conduct the arbitral procedure. See Toshio Matsumoto, "Development in Arbitration in Japan" (2004) 48 Japan Shipping Exchange Bulletin 1 at 1, online: Japan Shipping Exchange <http://www.jseinc.org/en/bulletin/issues/Vol.48.pdf>.

70 For general information, see Masaaki Kondo, Takeshi Goto, Kotatsu Uchibori, Hiroshi Maeda, and Tomomi Kataoka, *Arbitration Law of Japan* (Tokyo: Shoji Homu, 2004).

71 Reiko Nishikawa, "Arbitration Law Reform in Japan" (2004) 21 Journal of International Arbitration 303; Tatsuya Nakamura, "Salient Features of the New Japanese Arbitration Law Based upon the UNCITRAL Model Law on International Commercial Arbitration" (2004) 17 JCAA Newsletter 1, online: Japan Commercial Arbitration Association <http://www.jcaa.or.jp/e/arbitration-e/syuppan-e/newlet/news17.pdf>. For further details, see Kondo *et al., supra* note 70.

72 Art. 13(1).

73 Art. 17(4).

74 Art. 12.

75 Art. 38(4).

76 Arts. 47-49.

77 Arts. 50-55.

78 Arts. 3, 4 in the Supplementary Provisions of the new law. These issues are essentially national in nature.

79 For general information, see Japan Association of Arbitrators < http://arbitrators.jp/>.

80 Matsumoto, *supra* note 69 at 1.

81 Law No. 151 of 2004. The structure of the *ADR Law* is as follows:

- Chapter I: General Provisions (arts. 1-4)
- Chapter II: Affairs in the Certified Dispute Resolution Procedures
  - Section I: Certification of Affairs in the Private Dispute Resolution Procedures (arts. 5-13)
  - Section II: Affairs of the Certified Dispute Resolution Businesses (arts. 14-19)
  - Section III: Reports (arts. 20-24)
- Chapter III: Exception Related to Utilizing the Certified Dispute Resolution Procedures (arts. 25-27)
- Chapter IV: Miscellaneous (arts. 28-31)
- Chapter V: Penalties (arts. 32-34)
- Supplementary Provisions.

The text in Japanese is available at <http://www.moj.go.jp/KANBOUR/ADR/adr01-01.pdf >.

82 Toru Kobayashi, "Saibangai Hunsô Kaiketsu Tetsuzuki no Riyô no Sokushin nikansuru Hôritsu no Gaiyô" [Outline of the ADR Law] (2005) 52(3) JCA Journal 9 at 10.

83 For example, see American Chamber of Commerce in Japan, "Harmonize Japan's Proposed Out-of-Court Dispute Resolution System with International Standards by the Arbitration and ADR Task Force (Valid through October 2005)," online: ACCJ <http://www.accj.or.jp/document_library/Viewpoints/ADR.pdf>.

84 China International Economic and Trade Arbitration Commission, "Works of CIETAC," online: CIETAC <http://www.cietac.org.cn/english/introduction/intro_2. htm>. For example, from 1995 to 1997, the total caseload of the CIETAC was 2,404 cases, and 2,301 cases were concluded. The total caseloads for 1998 and 1999 were 678 and 669 cases, respectively. In 1999, 609 cases of the total caseload involved an international element.

85 *Convention on the Recognition and Enforcement of Foreign Arbitral Awards*, 10 June 1958, 330 U.N.T.S. 38, 7 I.L.M. 1046 (entered into force 7 June 1959); Eu Jin Chua and Kathryn Sanger, "Arbitration in the PRC" (May 2005) 19(4) China Law and Practice 19.

86 For example, with regard to the perspective of Japanese businesses, see Yukio Kajita, *Ni-Chu no Kokusai Shôji Chusai Seido niokeru Kyôryoku no Kanôsei nitsuite* [The possibility of cooperation on international arbitration system by Japan and China], CDAMS Discussion Paper 05/7J (May 2005) at 4-6, online: Center for Legal Dynamics of Advanced Market Societies (CDAMS), Graduate School of Law, Kobe University <http://www.cdams.kobe-u.ac.jp/archive/dp05-7j.pdf>.

87 Randall Peerenboom and Kathleen Scanlon, "An Untapped Dispute Resolution Option" (2005) 32 China Business Review 36 at 38.

88 Matsumoto, *supra* note 69 at 4.

89 Secretariat of the Office for Promotion of Justice System Reform, "Chusai Kentôkai Dai 13 Kai Kaigô, Heisei 15-Nen 3-Gatsu 6-Nichi" [The minutes of the third meeting of the Consultation Group on Arbitration held on 6 March 2003], online: Prime Minister of Japan and His Cabinet <http://www.kantei.go.jp/jp/singi/sihou/kentoukai/tyuusai/dai13/13gijiroku.html>. This was the final meeting of the group.

90 *Ibid.*
91 Nakamura, *supra* note 71 at 6.
92 Reinhard Neumann, "Hôkoku 4: Gaikoku Chusainin kara Mita Nihon niokeru Kokusai Chusai" [Report 4: international arbitration in Japan from the perspective of a foreign arbitrator], in Ikukazu Hnamizu and Takeshi Kojima, eds., *Nihon Chusainin Kyôkai Symposium: Panel Discussion – Shin Chusaihô no Seitei to Kongo no Chusai Jitsumu (Jô)* [The Japan Arbitrators Association symposium: panel discussion – The enactment of the new Arbitration Act and the future of arbitration practices (1)] (2004) 51(4) JCA Journal 72 at 80-82.
93 At discussions during the drafting the *ADR Law,* the ACCJ expressed similar concerns regarding the certification of ADR neutrals. See ACCJ, *supra* note 83.
94 Tatsuya Nakamura, "Wagakuni niokeru Kokusai Chusai no Genjô to Mondaiten" [Current situation and issues of international arbitration in Japan], presented at the Symposium on Transparency of Japanese Law: "Koko ga Hen dayo Nihonhou" (Kyushu University's Research Project on "The Transparency and Enrichment of Japanese Laws Concerning International Transactions in the 21st Century: Doing Cross-Border Business with/in Japan" [Transparency of Japanese Law Project], 28 November 2008), online: Transparency of Japanese Law Project <http://www.tomeika.jur.kyushu-u.ac.jp/sympo2008/rejume/nakamura_rejume.pdf >.
95 JCAA, "Heisei 20-Nendo Jigyô Hôkokusho" [Annual business report for 2008], online: JCAA <http://www.jcaa.or.jp/jcaa/docs/h20_1.pdf>.
96 JCAA, "Heisei 21-Nendo Jigyô Hôkokusho" [Annual business report for 2009], online: JCAA < http://www.jcaa.or.jp/jcaa/docs/h21_1.pdf>.
97 With regard to a cross-border/transnational joint venture agreement, see Kazuo Iwasaki and Takashi Kubota, "Dai 10 Syô, Joint Venture to Hunsô Jirei" [Chapter 10, The joint venture and dispute cases: Introduction of English and American precedents], in Toshio Sawada, Noboru Kashiwagi, Tetsuo Morishita *et al.,* *Kokusaitekina Kigyô Sen-Ryaku to Joint Venture* [Transnational business strategies and the joint venture] (Tokyo: Shoji Homu, 2005) at 269.

Introduction to International Trade Dispute Settlement in China

WANG SHULIANG

In 1979, following the "reform and openness" policy, China began liberalizing its economy, moving away from the older Soviet-style planned economy into a "socialist market economy." China's accession to the World Trade Organization (WTO) and its increasingly active role in the global economy are a direct result of its "opening to outside" agenda. The effects of liberalization are clearly visible. From 1979 to 2004, China's gross domestic product (GDP) increased by 9.6 percent annually, reaching US$1.93 trillion and ranking sixth in the world. In terms of international trade, China's total imports and exports in 2005 totalled US$1,422.12 billion, over seventy times the 1978 figure.[1] A rapid increase in foreign investment, trade, and GDP has inevitably led to an increased number of trade-related disputes, both domestic and foreign. Disputes not resolved by direct negotiation between the parties are resolved through China's domestic mechanism for dispute settlement. Since most disputes are primarily concerned with the implementation of contracts, this essay will focus on the Chinese mechanism for contractual disputes involving implementation. It will begin with an introduction to the Chinese judiciary and then address the relevant laws and the available options for legal representation.

Legal Mechanisms for Dispute Resolution

The Chinese Legal System

China is a civil law country with codified statutes.[2] According to Chinese law, the Constitution is the highest authority, followed by laws, administrative regulations, local regulations, administrative rules, and local rules. Judicial interpretation plays a major role in lawmaking and adjudication. The Supreme People's Court of China (hereinafter Supreme Court of China) always provides detailed explanations and interpretations of new laws and regulations. These interpretations are considered binding rules that all levels of court must follow. Similarly, high courts of every province may interpret certain laws and regulations. These interpretations are to be followed by that high court and all lower courts in the province. The effectiveness of such judicial interpretations is still controversial, especially when some interpretations stray from the original law and appear to be "re-legislation." Despite this, judicial interpretations made by the Supreme Court are very important rules, which lower courts use to make decisions.[3]

In China, disputes related to international trade are often referred to as foreign-related economic disputes.[4] The Supreme Court of China has interpreted "foreign-related" to mean those cases where: (1) one or both parties are foreign or with no nationality, or foreign legal persons or other economic organizations; and (2)(a) the civil legal relationship between the two parties has been established, changed, or terminated in a foreign country, or (b) the subject of the litigation is overseas.[5]

The Chinese Court System

China is a unitary state with a total of thirty-four provincial-level administrative regions: twenty-three provinces, five autonomous regions, four municipalities, and two special administrative regions. The court system has four levels: primary courts, intermediate courts, high courts, and the Supreme Court. The Supreme Court serves as the highest judicial authority in the country, but every provincial-level administrative region has a high court, every city has an intermediate court, and every county or district has a primary court. In China's judicial hierarchy, "second instance as the final instance" is the overarching principle. According to *Civil Procedure Law*, if a party refuses to accept the decision made by the local court in the first instance, they have the right to appeal to the next highest court, but decisions of the second instance are final.[6]

Jurisdiction

In international trade disputes, Chinese courts accept jurisdiction over a matter by considering: (1) the location of the defendant's property or the object of litigation; (2) the location of the signing or implementation of the contract; and (3) any agreement made by the parties.[7] If a Chinese court is chosen by the parties, Chinese laws and regulations will apply.[8] In some cases, Chinese courts assume jurisdiction over a dispute: (1) if the defendant does not raise any objection to the jurisdiction of Chinese courts, or has made replies to the court, in which cases it will be considered that the defendant has accepted the jurisdiction; (2) subject to review by the Supreme Court of China, when matters pertain to invalidity or expiry of arbitration clauses or agreements; and (3) where both Chinese and foreign courts have jurisdiction, and one party brings suit in a foreign court while the other brings suit in a Chinese court, in which cases whether or not to accept jurisdiction will be determined on a case-by-case basis.[9]

Most of the foregoing rules are similar to rules governing domestic litigation between Chinese citizens, with some exceptions. For example, whereas Chinese citizens can bring a lawsuit only in a court in whose jurisdiction they have real estate, foreign merchants can bring a lawsuit in a court in whose jurisdiction either the object of the litigation or the property of the defendant is located.[10]

China has well-defined jurisdictions for the four levels of court. According to Chinese law, only important foreign-related cases should be brought to intermediate courts,[11] although there is no clear definition of "important foreign-related cases." China's large size and regional variation affect the consistency and reliability of primary courts. In order to ensure uniform judicial practice, therefore, intermediate courts are usually responsible for the first instance, especially in most interior regions, although some competent primary courts deal with small claims foreign-related cases. Except for the coastal region, most areas have intermediate courts or economic-zone courts that are responsible for the first instance of international trade and other foreign-related cases, whereas high courts are in charge of the second instance. In Shanghai, for example, primary courts have first instance jurisdiction to deal with foreign civil cases of claims less than 1 million Yuan RMB, intermediate courts handle first instance cases with a claim between 1 million and 80 million Yuan RMB, and the Shanghai High Court handles first instance cases with a claim of over 80 million Yuan RMB. The determination of jurisdiction based on the claim amount is a controversial issue, but the unique nature of each case makes it hard to set any other standard.

Options for Dispute Settlement

When contractual conflicts take place in China, Chinese law provides four legal approaches that parties in international trade disputes can use to protect their interests: consultation, mediation through a third party, arbitration, and litigation.[12]

Consultation

In contractual conflicts, traders in China prefer negotiation (consultation) because of the costs involved with other methods of dispute settlement. Consultation involves direct communication between parties after a contractual dispute arises. It is a voluntary method of dispute resolution based on mutual understanding, and should be done in accordance with the provisions provided in law or in the contract. Consultation also involves voluntary acceptance of a resolution. Coercion violates the prerequisite that the consultation be voluntary and renders any solution invalid. Alternatively, the parties may jointly apply to an arbitration institution to cancel their agreement.

Legality is another prerequisite for consultation. Any agreement must comply with the applicable laws and regulations. An agreement should not infringe the interests of the country, the group, or third parties. In addition, it should not breach social or public interests.[13]

Mediation

Mediation is a process where a neutral third party assists in reaching an acceptable solution. The third party can be a government organ, such as the Administration of Industry and Commerce, the Administration of State Assets, or the Foreign Investment Administration Commission. The third party can also be any appropriate economic organization, group, or individual who is not a party to the contract, except arbitration institutions and courts. The prerequisites for mediation are the same as those for negotiation. Mediation should be voluntary and any agreement must comply with laws and regulations.

In China, there is also something called administrative mediation. A document called "Administrative Mediation Rules for Contractual Disputes" (AMRCD) was issued by the State Administration of Industry and

Commerce of China on 3 November 1997. It specifies the scope, procedures, and principles for mediating contractual disputes through the industry and commerce administrative authority.

According to the AMRCD, industry and commerce administrative authorities may, upon request by the parties, appoint mediators to organize and participate in mediation of contractual disputes. Such administrative mediation should also be in accordance with the principles of voluntariness and legality. Industry and commerce administrative authorities are required to reject mediation applications if one of the parties is not willing to accept mediation, or if the dispute has already been brought to a court or arbitration institution. If at any point during the mediation one party does not want to continue, the mediation must be terminated. Mediation is not open to the public unless otherwise requested by the parties. Industry and commerce administrative authorities should complete the mediation process within two months after accepting the application. This time limit can be extended for up to one month under special circumstances. If the mediation is completed successfully, the parties sign a mediation agreement or a new contract. This mediation process is different from mediations occurring at courts or arbitration institutions as a part of litigation or arbitration.

In practice, traders usually agree in the contract that there should be negotiations when conflicts arise, and that arbitration or litigation should take place only when the negotiation is unsuccessful. Any such clause, however, does not make it a prerequisite of arbitration or litigation that the parties go through the negotiation process first. Some contracts specify a particular time or period for negotiation or mediation. Such a clause can be understood only as a suggestion, and not as a prerequisite for arbitration or litigation.

The Legal Effects of the Reconciliation and Mediation Agreement

At the end of a successful negotiation or mediation, parties usually have the choice of either accepting changes or replacing their contract. An agreement is also considered to be a contract, however, and must comply with all the prescribed requirements of Chinese contract law.

An important issue that needs to be addressed here is whether the reconciliation or mediation agreements can be enforced through state enforcement agencies. In other words, can one party appeal to a court for direct enforcement of the agreement if the other party does not abide by it? The answer is no, and this distinguishes mediation from arbitration (including mediation done by the courts). If one party does not abide by the mediation or reconciliation agreement, the innocent party can only bring the case to the arbitration institution or court to resolve the dispute.[14]

Ordinarily, non-judicial solutions are automatically excluded from state enforcement mechanisms. Depending on the format and content of the reconciliation or mediation agreement, however, I believe that state enforcement can be availed of in two circumstances.

First, according to the Procedures for Trial Supervision, a creditor may apply to the court for a payment warrant if the dispute between traders involves only payment of debt and if the amount owed and the repayment date are indicated in the agreement. After accepting the application, assuming that the relationship between the parties is definite and legitimate, the People's Court that has jurisdiction will examine the facts and evidence provided by the creditor and issue a payment warrant to the debtor to comply within a prescribed period. The debtor can either repay his debts or submit a written objection to the People's Court within a certain period of time. If the debtor neither submits an objection nor complies with the payment warrant, the creditor may apply to the People's Court for execution.[15] In other words, creditors can apply to the court for payment warrants based on their mediation or consultation agreements. Only if the debtor is not in the territory of China or cannot be found in China will the Procedures for Trial Supervision not apply.

The second method is through notarization. If the dispute involves only the payment of debts, the parties can include a compulsory enforcement clause in their agreement, which, if notarized, will be granted legal effect for compulsory implementation.[16] As with other litigation matters, the validity and accuracy of the notarized document are required for court enforcement. The process of arbitration or litigation can therefore be bypassed in these situations.

Legal effect is indirectly granted to mediation or reconciliation agreements under the Procedures for Trial Supervision, while compulsory implementation is directly applicable to notarized mediation or reconciliation agreements under China's notarization law.

Arbitration

If traders in China cannot solve their contractual disputes through mediation or negotiation, they may choose arbitration. Compared with litigation, arbitration is often considered preferable because it is efficient and confidential, and can help maintain the business relationship between the parties.

Arbitration is available to citizens, legal persons, and organizations for disputes over contracts or property rights only. Disputes related to personal or family issues cannot be submitted for arbitration. Similarly, administrative disputes, which fall within the jurisdiction of government agencies, are barred from arbitration.[17] Before proceeding to international trade arbitration, the parties must select a Chinese arbitration institution through either an arbitration clause in the contract or an arbitration agreement between the parties. The ability to go to arbitration has a time limit of four years, calculated from the date on which a party knows or ought to know that its contractual rights were infringed.[18]

According to Chinese arbitration law, there are no geographical restrictions on arbitration and no special restrictions on the choice of an arbitration institution.[19] The China Maritime Arbitration Commission (CMAC), under the China Council for the Promotion of International Trade (CCPIT), will usually be selected for maritime cases. Other disputes can be brought to the local arbitration commission in each province (such as the Shanghai Arbitration Commission) or to the China International Economic and Trade Arbitration Commission (CIETAC), which is also under the CCPIT. Headquartered in Beijing, the CIETAC has arbitrators not only from China but also from other countries. It deals with more foreign-related cases (arbitration cases in 2004 numbered 850, of which 462 were foreign-related cases) than do local arbitration commissions.[20] The costs associated with the CIETAC are relatively high, but it has a reputation for meeting international standards.

According to China's *Arbitration Law*, mediation is part of the arbitration procedure. The arbitration tribunal may first attempt to get the parties to negotiate an agreement. If an agreement is reached, the parties may apply to the arbitration tribunal for an award based on the agreement, and/or they may withdraw the arbitration application. A reconciliation statement sets forth the arbitration claims and the results of the agreement between the parties. The reconciliation statement is signed by the arbitrators, sealed by the arbitration commission, and served on both parties. An arbitration ruling made by the tribunal based on the reconciliation agreement has the same legal force as a judicial ruling. If the parties do not fulfill their obligations after the conclusion of a reconciliation agreement and the withdrawal of the arbitration application, the parties may reapply for arbitration. If reconciliation is unsuccessful, an arbitration ruling is promptly made.[21]

Litigation

The last resort available to traders in China is litigation. To begin litigation, a trader must apply to a court with proper jurisdiction. Determining the applicable law is an important consideration in settling international trade and other foreign-related civil disputes. In terms of the application of law, there are two aspects: substantive law and procedural law.

Substantive Law

In China, substantive law includes the general principles of civil law, contract law, maritime law, and some relevant judicial interpretations. The sources of law include foreign laws, treaties, and international customary law.

According to Chinese law, parties in international trade and other foreign-related disputes can usually choose the law they wish to apply in settling contractual disputes. If parties have not chosen the applicable law in the contract, the law of the country to which the contract has the closest connection applies.[22]

Chinese courts review any foreign law chosen by the parties to ensure that it complies with China's social and public interests. If the intention of the parties in choosing foreign law was to avoid restrictive Chinese laws and regulations, Chinese courts will reject the parties' choice and apply Chinese law.[23]

In China, the application of law conforms to a specific order (hierarchy). International treaties are given first preference (the 1980 *United Nations Convention on Contracts for the International Sale of Goods*[24] [CISG] being the most common), followed by Chinese law and then any applicable international customary law. Any international agreement signed by China prevails over contradictory Chinese laws, except where reservations have been made. International law is given preference as long as it does not conflict with the social or public interests of China.[25]

China signed the CISG on 30 September 1981. It was ratified on 11 December 1986 with two reservations: (1) China is not restrained by s. (b) of Articles 1 and 11, and (2) China agrees to apply the convention only to contracts of parties belonging to other CISG member states. Also, only contracts evidenced in writing are recognized. According to a Supreme Court memo, "from January 1st, 1988, the United Nations Convention on Contracts for the International Sale of Goods should be directly applied to settle contractual disputes, unless other laws are chosen by the parties to the contract."[26]

Although China declared reservations to the CISG, no reservations are allowed for any provision of the WTO Agreement,[27] and each Member must ensure the conformity of its laws, regulations, and administrative procedures with its WTO obligations. Upon its accession to the WTO, China stated:

> [China] has been consistently performing its international treaty obligations in good faith. According to the Constitution and the Law on the Procedures of Conclusion of Treaties, the WTO Agreement falls within the category of "important international agreements" subject to the ratification by the Standing Committee of the National People's Congress. We will ensure that its laws and regulations affecting trade are in conformity with the WTO Agreement. For this purpose, China has commenced a plan to systematically revise its relevant domestic laws. The WTO Agreement will, therefore, be implemented in an effective and uniform manner through revising its existing domestic laws and enacting new ones in full compliance with the WTO Agreement.[28]

A relevant question to ask is what the procedure would be if China were to violate its commitment to the WTO. In this case, foreign traders could not bring the case to a Chinese court. They could only request that their home government solve the dispute under the WTO dispute resolution mechanism.

Procedural Law

Civil litigation law, arbitration, and some relevant judicial interpretations fall under the heading of procedural law. In international trade disputes, the procedures followed for arbitration and litigation are quite different in China.

If the parties choose arbitration, submission of the case to the arbitration commission (the arbitration commission is that to which both parties agree to submit the case) is usually regarded as acceptance of the commission's rules, unless otherwise agreed by the parties and approved by the commission.

If the parties choose litigation, the laws of the country where the court is located are usually applied. If the case is accepted by a Chinese court, specific Chinese rules governing foreign-related litigation (including jurisdiction, delivery of documents, investigation, time limit, and recognition and enforcement of court judgments) will be followed.[29] The time limit for Chinese courts to deal with foreign-related civil cases is more flexible than for cases between Chinese citizens. For example, the time limit for the latter is six months for the first instance and three months for the second instance,[30] but there is no time limit for dealing with foreign-related cases.[31] Similarly, whereas domestic parties have the right to appeal within fifteen days from the delivery of a judgment or ten days from the delivery of a decision,[32] foreign parties have the right to appeal within thirty days from the delivery of a judgment or decision.[33]

China adheres to the "counter-treatment" principle, which imposes the same restrictions on a foreign nation's citizens, enterprises, and organizations as the foreign nation places on Chinese citizens, enterprises, and organizations in their civil litigation rights. Foreign merchants, however, enjoy national treatment in China as far as litigation procedures are concerned. In both arbitration and litigation cases, the principle of "second instance as the final instance" applies, and the same litigation procedures apply for foreign-related cases and cases between Chinese citizens. Chinese laws and regulations prescribe guidelines for Chinese courts to follow when dealing with foreign-related cases, which primarily include rules regarding applicable laws and the "counter-treatment" principle.

Legal Representation

When parties in foreign-related disputes choose a Chinese arbitration institution, Chinese laws do not explicitly prohibit foreign lawyers from acting as legal agents for the parties. Restrictions have been imposed, however, to prevent foreign lawyers from making comments on Chinese law and its application. Any interpretation or explanation of Chinese law made by a foreign lawyer must be made in cooperation with a Chinese lawyer.[34]

For litigation, foreign citizens, people with no nationalities, or foreign enterprises and organizations must retain Chinese lawyers to act as their agents.[35] According to rules made by the Chinese Ministry of Justice on 1 January 2004, residents of Hong Kong or Macau who are called to the Chinese bar may apply to practise law on the mainland, but they are restricted to non-litigation work.[36]

Foreign parties involved in such disputes can use foreign individuals or lawyers to act as their attorneys, along with officials in foreign embassies or consulates, but the officials cannot enjoy diplomatic privileges during litigation.

Enforcement

If arbitration awards or court decisions are not implemented, an aggrieved party can apply to a Chinese court for enforcement. If Chinese arbitration rulings are not implemented by one party, the other party may apply to the intermediate court where the residence or property of the obligor is located. The ruling will not be implemented, however, if obligors can prove one of the following: (1) the parties do not have an arbitration clause in the contract and did not reach a written arbitration agreement; (2) obligors were not informed by the appointed arbitrators to attend arbitration, or obligors could not present their side for reasons beyond their control; (3) the composition of the arbitration panel or the arbitration procedures were not in accordance with arbitration rules; (4) the substantive issue is beyond the scope of the arbitration agreement. Also, if Chinese courts deem the arbitration award to be in violation of social or public interests, it may be struck down.[37]

If one party refuses to implement a civil judgment or decision made by a Chinese court, the other party may apply to the court of first instance for enforcement, or the judge may directly forward the case to the enforcement division.[38]

If a party applies to a Chinese court for recognition and enforcement of a foreign arbitration award, they should apply directly to the intermediate court where the residence or property of the obligor is located (following any relevant international treaty).[39] In cases where there are no applicable international treaties or agreements, Chinese courts determine whether or not to recognize and enforce the award based on reciprocity principles.[40] Among all international treaties regarding the recognition and enforcement of foreign arbitration awards, the United Nations *Convention on the Recognition and Enforcement of Foreign Arbitral Awards*[41] (the *New York Convention*) is the most important. China placed two reservations on the *New York Convention*: (1) China recognizes and enforces foreign arbitration awards based only on reciprocity; and (2) only commercial relationships (contractual or non-contractual) can be applied to the convention.[42] China does not recognize or enforce foreign arbitration awards unless they are related to commercial disputes. When a party applies to a Chinese court for enforcement of an arbitration award, the application is examined to see whether ss. 1 and 2 of Article 5 of the *New York Convention* apply. Any arbitration award covered by these sections is not enforceable under Chinese law.

If judgments or decisions made by foreign courts require recognition and enforcement by Chinese courts, an application for enforcement can be made to Chinese intermediate courts by either the interested parties or by the foreign courts. China grants such applications based on international treaties or the reciprocity principle, as long as enforcement does not violate Chinese national security, sovereignty, or social and public interests.[43]

Similarly, for arbitration awards made by Chinese arbitration agencies, if the assets subject to enforcement are not in China, the party should apply for recognition and enforcement to a foreign court where the assets are located, or Chinese courts may directly request the same.[44]

As mentioned earlier, in some cases, one party brings a lawsuit in a foreign court while the other party brings the same lawsuit in a Chinese court. If a ruling has been made by the Chinese court, requests for recognition or enforcement of the foreign ruling will not be accepted, unless otherwise prescribed in an international treaty that both China and the foreign country have signed.

Conclusion

This essay introduced China's international trade dispute resolution mechanisms. As a developing country, China has a legal system that is still evolving. For example, Chinese laws governing foreign-related arbitration and foreign arbitration awards are too general and too simple, and judicial interpretations made by the Supreme Court are of large number, which makes them difficult to follow. In order to appropriately deal with, and improve judicial review of, foreign-related arbitration and foreign arbitration awards (a foreign-related arbitration award is issued by a Chinese arbitration institution, and a foreign arbitration award is issued by a foreign arbitration institution), the Supreme Court issued a document entitled "Some Rules Governing Foreign-Related Arbitrations and Foreign Arbitration Cases (Draft)."[45] The draft version provides detailed rules, procedures, and requirements for recognizing and enforcing foreign arbitration awards (arbitration cases in Hong Kong, Macau, and Taiwan are also covered). This draft is still under scrutiny but it shows that the Supreme Court is paying close attention to the issue. Chinese courts are also carrying out reforms in the litigation system in which relevant laws will be revised to meet the requirement of social development. Although China is still a developing country in both an economic and legal sense, its rapidly changing economy is having a marked effect on its legal system.

NOTES

1 See "China Statistics Yearbook 2005" and "China Statistics Yearbook 2006," online: National Bureau of Statistics of China < http://www.stats.gov.cn/tjsj/ndsj/>.

2 See generally Pitman B. Potter, *Chinese Legal System: Globalization and Local Legal Culture* (New York: Routledge, 2001). Also see generally Chen H.Y. Albert, *An*

Introduction to the Legal System of the People's Republic of China (Hong Kong: Lexis/ Nexis, 2004).

3 The effectiveness and applicable range of judicial interpretation is controversial. For example, it is unclear whether arbitration institutions should follow judicial interpretations.

4 See, *e.g., Civil Procedure Law of the People's Republic of China* (as adopted on 9 April 1991 at the Fourth Session of the Seventh National People's Congress, and revised according to the Decision of the Standing Committee of the National People's Congress on Amending the *Civil Procedure Law of the People's Republic of China* as adopted at the Thirtieth Session of the Standing Committee of the Tenth National People's Congress), arts. 235-67 [*Civil Procedure Law*]. Also see, *e.g., China International Economic and Trade Arbitration Commission Arbitration Rules* (revised and adopted by the China Council for the Promotion of International Trade/China Chamber of International Commerce on 11 January 2005, effective as from 1 May 2005), art. 3 [*CIETAC Arbitration Rules*].

5 See the Supreme People's Court's *Opinions on Several Issues Concerning the Application of the Civil Procedure Law of the PRC* (as adopted on 14 July 1992 at the 528th Session of the Supreme People's Court's Judicial Committee), art. 304 [*Application of the Civil Procedure Law*].

6 See *People's Court Organization Law of the People's Republic of China* (as adopted on 1 July 1979 at the Second Session of the Fifth National People's Congress, and revised on 2 September 1983 at the Second Session of the Sixth National People's Congress, on 2 December 1986 at the Eighteenth Session of the Sixth National People's Congress, and on 31 October 2006 at the Twenty-fourth Session of the Standing Committee of the Tenth National People's Congress), arts. 2, 11, and 17-32. See also *Civil Procedure Law, supra* note 4, arts. 18-39 and 147-59.

7 See *Civil Procedure Law, supra* note 4, art. 241.

8 *Ibid.,* art. 235.

9 *Ibid.,* arts. 241 and 243; see also *Application of the Civil Procedure Law, supra* note 5, art. 306.

10 See *Civil Procedure Law, supra* note 4, arts. 34 and 241.

11 *Ibid.,* art. 19.

12 See generally Moser J. Michael and Yu Fu, *Doing Business in China,* vol. 3 (Huntington, NY: Juris Publishing, 2009) at iv-1.3–iv-5.69.

13 See *Contract Law of the People's Republic of China* (adopted at the Second Session of the Ninth National People's Congress on 15 March 1999), art. 7 [*Contract Law*].

14 See the State Administration for Industry and Commerce's *Administrative Mediation Rules for Contractual Disputes* (the 79th Order Issued by State Administration for Industry and Commerce of PRC on 3 November 1997), art. 20.

15 See *Civil Procedure Law, supra* note 4, arts. 191-94.

16 See *Notarization Law of the People's Republic of China* (adopted at the Seventeenth Meeting of the Standing Committee of the National People's Congress of the People's Republic of China on 28 August 2005), art. 37. Also see *Notarization Procedure Rules of the People's Republic of China* (adopted by the Ministry of Justice of PRC at the Executive Meeting on 10 May 2006), arts. 39 and 55.

17 See *Arbitration Law of the People's Republic of China* (adopted by the Ninth Meeting of the Standing Committee of the Eighth National People's Congress of the People's Republic of China on 31 August 1994), arts. 2 and 4 [*Arbitration Law*].

18 See *Contract Law, supra* note 13, art. 129. This time limitation concerns only disputes involving international trade contracts and technology import and export contracts.

19 See *Arbitration Law, supra* note 17, art. 6.

20 See "Statistic Figures 2009" (in Chinese), online: CIETAC <http://cn.cietac.org/AboutUS/AboutUS4Read.asp>.

21 See *Arbitration Law, supra* note 17, arts. 51 and 52.

22 See *Contract Law, supra* note 13, art. 126.

23 *Ibid.*, art. 127. Also see *Rules of the Supreme People's Court on Related Issues Concerning the Application of Law in Hearing Foreign-Related Contractual Dispute Cases Related to Civil and Commercial Matters* (adopted at the 1,429th Meeting of the Judicial Committee of the Supreme People's Court on 11 June 2007), arts. 6 and 7.

24 *United Nations Convention on Contracts for the International Sale of Goods*, Vienna, 11 April 1980, UN Doc. A/CONF 97/19, 1489 U.N.T.S. 3 [CISG].

25 See *Civil Procedure Law, supra* note 4, art. 236.

26 CISG, *supra* note 24.

27 *Marrakesh Agreement Establishing the World Trade Organization*, 15 April 1994, 1867 U.N.T.S. 3, 33 I.L.M. 1144 [WTO Agreement].

28 See *Report of the Working Party on the Accession of China* (1 October 2001), art. 67.

29 See *Civil Procedure Law, supra* note 4, arts. 135 and 159.

30 *Ibid.*, art. 235.

31 *Ibid.*, art. 284.

32 *Ibid.*, art. 260.

33 *Ibid.*, art. 247.

34 See *Regulations on Administration of Foreign Law Firms' Representative Offices in China* (adopted at the Fifty-first Executive Meeting of the State Council on 19 December 2001, promulgated by Decree No. 338 of the State Council of the People's Republic of China on 22 December 2001, and effective as of 1 January 2002), art. 15.

35 See *Civil Procedure Law, supra* note 4, art. 239.

36 See *Administration Rules on the Practice of Law in the Mainland China by Residents of Hong Kong Special Administrative Region and Macau Special Administrative Region Who Have Obtained Legal Profession Qualifications in the Mainland China* (issued by the Ministry of Justice of PRC on 11 November 2003 as 81st Order, and revised on 28th December 2005 as 99th Order, on 22nd December 2006 as 105th Order, and on 1 September 2009 as 117th Order), art. 4, and according to which, a resident of Hong Kong or Macau who has obtained legal profession qualification in mainland China and practices in a law firm in mainland China is allowed to be an attorney in Hong Kong- and Macau-related marriage and heritage litigation work, and other non-litigation work.

37 See *Civil Procedure Law, supra* note 4, art. 258.

38 *Ibid.*, art. 212.

39 *Ibid.,* arts. 256 and 267.
40 *Ibid.,* art. 266.
41 *Convention on the Recognition and Enforcement of Foreign Arbitral Awards,* 10 June 1958, 330 U.N.T.S. 38, 7 I.L.M. 1046 (entered into force 7 June 1959) [*New York Convention*].
42 *Ibid.*
43 See *Civil Procedure Law, supra* note 4, arts. 258 and 266.
44 *Ibid.,* art. 264.
45 The Supreme Court of China issued the document on 31 December 2003: <http://www.people.com.cn/GB/shehui/2273973.html>.

Alternative Dispute Resolution in Japanese Legal Education
Preliminary Evidence from the 2003 and 2004 Curricula

MAYUMI SAEGUSA AND JULIAN DIERKES

For the first time in Japan's history, seventy-four American-style graduate law schools were opened between 2004 and 2005. This reflects a massive shift in legal education from undergraduate law faculties (*hougakubu*) to graduate-level professional law schools (*houka daigakuin*).[1] Among more than ninety universities with undergraduate law faculties in Japan, seventy-three universities immediately responded to the new system and established graduate law schools from scratch.[2] Prior to the introduction of graduate law schools in 2004, Japanese legal training looked very different from the American system. Law was taught in undergraduate programs in Japan, yet this undergraduate education did not truly prepare graduates for legal practice. Unlike in European countries, where law is also taught at the undergraduate level, the completion of undergraduate legal education was not a prerequisite for taking the bar exam in Japan. Under the new legal training system, undergraduate law faculties continue to exist in Japan, but the emphasis in legal education has shifted to graduate law schools. A JD degree from a Japanese graduate law school is now a requirement for taking the bar exam.[3] In principle, the undergraduate law faculties are geared more towards general legal studies, whereas the new graduate law schools are responsible for training future legal professionals.[4]

This legal education reform in Japan represents a massive exogenous institutional shock. The implementation of the reform thus offers opportunities to advance theory development within the neo-institutional paradigm in sociology and organizational analysis, as it represents a case of the whole-sale restructuring of an entire organizational field, rather than the mere in-stitutionalization of organizational innovation or the de-institutionalization of existing practices. We propose to examine the teaching of alternative dis-pute resolution (ADR) in Japanese legal education before and after this ex-ogenous shock in order to test the prediction of pervasive isomorphism in the context of the adoption of a foreign/international model (American law schools) in a substantially different local institutional environment. This es-say presents preliminary analyses of processes that are in flux and occurring in Japan. While contributing broadly to a sociological understanding of in-stitutions and legal education, our research also illuminates the diffusion of particular dispute resolution mechanisms from North America to Japan and possibly around the world.

Neo-Institutionalism: Why Are Organizations So Similar in Structure and Substance?

The neo-institutional perspective in sociology grew out of organizational analysis in the 1980s and has come to be a widely applied theoretical per-spective across sociology's subdisciplines and in neighbouring social sci-ences.[5] Neo-institutionalism is grounded in the insight that many organizations in a given organizational field share a wide variety of struc-tural and substantive features – that is, are characterized by isomorphism.

One of the first hypotheses suggested within the neo-institutional per-spective was that isomorphism[6] would prevail particularly in situations of great uncertainty. Under such conditions, three mechanisms can be distin-guished: (1) normative isomorphism, (2) coercive isomorphism, and (3) mimetic isomorphism.[7] Among these three types, North American organ-izational researchers tend to place considerable weight on mimetic iso-morphism and disproportionately neglect isomorphism caused by power and coercion.[8]

One of the major criticisms of the neo-institutional paradigm has been that it tends to ignore variation in organizational responses to institutional pressures towards conformity.[9] Several organizational researchers have taken up the study of variation in organizational practices. Edelman explains that organizations that are subject to normative pressure from their environ-ment elaborate their formal structures to create visible symbols of their in-stitutional adoption.[10] Westphal, Gulati, and Shortell note that economic causes govern early adoption and normative causes govern later adoption.[11] Oliver proposed a typology of organizational responses that vary according to the degree of active agency and resistance exerted by the organization.[12]

Status Hierarchies and Organizational Innovation

Few organizational studies have emphasized status hierarchies as a key component of institutional isomorphism. Status hierarchies are important because uncertainty is often associated with a struggle to gain or maintain status while simultaneously engaging in efforts to construct a new set of rules.[13]

Status hierarchies have been examined by researchers working on the diffusion of innovations and by social psychologists. Both literatures typically have classified organizations into three groups based on their status (high, middle, and low), and have illustrated that organizations of different statuses adopt innovations at different rates and with different scopes.[14] Research on the diffusion of innovations has tested a U-shaped relationship between status and innovation; that is, high-status actors are more likely to adopt innovations that conform to institutionalized behavioural norms, whereas low-status actors create counter-normative innovations. In contrast, sociopsychological researchers presented an inverted U-shaped relationship between status and conformity.[15] High-status actors feel confident in their social acceptance, so they are emboldened to deviate from conventional behaviour, and low-status actors feel free to deviate from accepted practices because they are excluded regardless of their actions. Middle-status actors, however, tend to become conservative because of their insecurity: they aspire to a higher social status but fear disenfranchisement.[16]

Legal Education Reform: Radical but Vague

An examination of the recent reform of legal education in Japan offers an interesting field for the application of the neo-institutional perspective. While most institutional changes have been relatively ill defined in existing studies, the case of state-initiated legal education reform makes for a very clear delineation of the scope of uncertainty and the timing of its arrival, particularly in a situation like that in Japan, where reform has been mandated but has not been prescribed in very specific terms. This situation is akin to a number of organizational analyses that have examined relatively vague legal mandates for affirmative action for US corporations and the institutionalization of a small number of highly legitimated responses to this vagueness.[17] Japanese legal education is being reshaped much more radically and rapidly by the current reforms, however, leading to more "existential uncertainty" rather than policy-implementation uncertainty among the organizations effected.

The fact that the current Japanese reforms are not only remoulding institutionalized behavioural norms but are in fact reshaping an entire organizational field is of particular relevance to the continued development of neo-institutional theory and to the examination of the emergence and process of institutionalization. While state-credentialed legal education by universities is continuing, it is continuing under very different circumstances, utilizing very different structural forms. In Japan, legal education as an organizational field had continued with only minor changes for over a hundred years, but it is now being rebuilt from the ground up, although some existing organizational shells and templates are being reused. This wholesale reconstruction of an organizational field creates uncertainty about actors' choices for specific organizational models and about the institutionalized ordering of the organizational field itself. Aspects of legal education that have been highly legitimate up to now (for example, the exceedingly small number of lawyers, the dominance of the Legal Training and Research Institute operated by the Supreme Court in the training of lawyers, and so on) have thus lost some of their legitimacy and would appear to need reinstitutionalization if they are not to be supplanted by alternative institutions.

As the universe of organizations that are subject to this institutional change is bounded (only current Japanese law schools would be at immediate "risk" of adopting the dominant modes of organization that will emerge from the current institutional uncertainty), legal reform in Japan offers an ideal field for data collection and analysis for several reasons. First, we are examining shifts in legal education from the inception of reforms onward. This opens the possibility of great variability in organizational responses. As we continue to examine the adoption of organizational innovations, we may pinpoint a rate of adoption over time but fail to understand why such an adoption has occurred, or what it substantively means for legal education and legal practice. Second, few other cases of institutional change take place with such remarkable scope and speed. Third, US organizational scholars often examine institutional change driven by technology, professionalization, and ambiguous regulation. Outside the US, states are major initiators of institutional change because the influence of Americanization is so significant that foreign governments often need to adopt American practices intentionally and immediately. In many polities, state-initiated reforms are a historically dominant response to the perceived need to respond to challenges.[18] State-initiated legal reform in Japan is an ideal case with which to illustrate how institutional isomorphism takes place when a state deconstructs

an old institution and constructs a new one in response, or at least in reference, to perceived Americanization.

   We examine how organizations of different status respond to institutional pressure towards conformity. We focus on the teaching of alternative dispute resolution mechanisms in Japanese legal education. ADR is a relatively
new subject and has been emphasized by the recent legal reform. ADR
began to be addressed in the early 1980s in courses on dispute resolution,
court law, and sociology of law at universities,[19] but it was considered a min-
or and "trivial" subject in Japanese legal education. This conception has
gradually changed in the 1990s and in the course of the current legal reforms. ADR is now regarded as a minor but "important" subject.[20] When the
Ministry of Education provided model course syllabi for new law schools,
ADR was used as an item in the syllabus for Civil Procedure.[21] Given its relative newness and the emphasis placed on it during the legal reform process,
ADR is a prism for viewing change in legal education.

Globalization of Law: Diffusion of ADR across Nations

Because of the place of the United States in the world economy and the
globalization of legal practice, certain North American legal practices are
being diffused throughout the world, and ADR is no exception to this international trend.[22] ADR began receiving attention in the US in the 1970s as a
possible response to a significant increase in the incidence of litigation.[23]
The term "alternative dispute resolution" generally refers to conflict resolution among disputants through means other than a trial, such as mediation,
conciliation,[24] or arbitration. The use of ADR mechanisms is seen in many
countries, but the reasons behind the evolution of ADR differ from one
jurisdiction to another.[25] In contrast to practice in the US, ADR has been
preferred to litigation in Japan because of a presumed antipathy to litigation
and/or inadequate legal infrastructure.[26] In the United Kingdom, ADR has
been utilized in response to the delays in and the increasing cost of litigation. In Germany, the demand for ADR has increased since the unification
of East and West Germany. When the former East Germany needed to
adopt the West German judicial system, the shortage of judges and other
court staff was so serious that ADR was considered as a supplement.[27]

   In response to these various pressures, legislation promoting the use of
ADR was introduced in several jurisdictions in the 1990s. Two federal ADR
laws were introduced in the US, one in 1990 and the other in 1998. The *Alternative Dispute Resolution Act of 1998*[28] requires federal district courts to
authorize the use of ADR in all civil actions and to encourage litigants to use

ADR. In the UK, the use of ADR was included in a recommendation by a reform committee on the civil judicial system in 1996, and a new civil procedure act in 1999 requires courts to encourage litigants to use ADR. Similar laws were introduced in Germany and France in the late 1990s.

American law schools gradually responded to the rise of ADR, and training in ADR has become a growth industry.[29] The concept of teaching negotiation and related skills was endorsed by the 1979 American Bar Association Task Force on Lawyer Competency.[30] Since 1983, the American Bar Association Section on Dispute Resolution has periodically surveyed law schools in regard to ADR offerings. The first survey listed 43 law schools as offering ADR courses, which equalled roughly a third of all US law schools. By the next survey, in 1986, a majority of the ABA-approved law schools offered courses on ADR. The survey described it as "a significant achievement in a field that was barely known a decade ago."[31] In the 1997 survey, 714 courses in 177 law schools were listed. Besides ADR-related courses, some 21 law schools offered clinical programs focusing on the use of dispute resolution as an alternative to litigation in resolving clients' problems. Several elite law schools, including those at Stanford University, Harvard University, and the University of Wisconsin, have established centres for dispute resolution that encourage research, writing, and advanced training in this field. Three law journals are now published by law schools with a focus on dispute resolution: the *Journal of Dispute Resolution* at the University of Missouri at Columbia, the *Ohio State Journal of Dispute Resolution,* and the *Journal of Negotiation* from the Program on Negotiation at Harvard Law School.[32]

ADR in Japan

The concept of out-of-court dispute resolution has existed for centuries in Japan and has often been used to explain why Japanese disputants are reluctant to resort to the formal court system.[33] Even within the court system, conciliation has been integrated as an important court procedure. Civil and family conciliation made up almost three-quarters of the number of civil litigations in 1998; there were 356,000 of these conciliation procedures, whereas the incidence of civil litigation in a first trial was 476,000.[34] Thus, conciliation has been commonly practised in the Japanese legal system. When reintroduced under the new name of "alternative dispute resolution," however, the old concept was seen as an innovation based on foreign models. ADR has received much attention in the current legal reform process. In legal education, until the 1990s, ADR had been mainly taught by scholars of Sociology of Law and Dispute Resolution, but because of its development internationally, it has been transformed from being considered a minor and trivial subject to one that is seen as minor but important.

Since the late 1990s, the diffusion of ADR has been one of the central issues for Japan's judicial reform. New ADR legislation, entitled the *Law for Promoting the Use of Out-of-Court Dispute Resolution Procedures,*[35] was proclaimed in December 2004 and enacted by June 2007. The ADR law has drawn criticism because a person must be a licensed legal or technical expert to engage in the field.[36] The law is implicitly intended to ensure that ADR is primarily initiated by government agencies. It makes it difficult for private and grassroots ADR agencies to participate. After in-court ADR, the next significant form of ADR is conducted by government agencies, including the Environmental Dispute Coordination Commission (*kogaito chosei iinkai*), the Committee for Adjustment of Construction Work Disputes (*kensetsu koji funso shinsakai*), and the National Consumer Affairs Center of Japan (*kokumin seikatsu center*). Unlike in the US, ADR initiated by the private sector is very rare.[37]

Tracing the Teaching of ADR in Japanese Legal Education

In order to examine the institutionalization of specific models of legal education under conditions of extreme uncertainty created by a sudden shift in policy, we examine a specific aspect of legal education, the teaching of ADR. This focus enables us to trace continuities and changes through the institutional disruption created by the establishment of graduate law schools. In turn, the content of courses offers unique possibilities for tracing substantive changes associated with graduate law schools, because the main thrust of this shift to graduate professional education is seen to be a reform of teaching methods. We asked all sixty-eight graduate-level professional law schools for their 2004 course catalogues, as well as their 2003 and 2004 undergraduate law faculties' course catalogues. Two law schools do not have undergraduate law faculties. In terms of the undergraduate law faculties, we looked for 2003 and 2004 course catalogues in order to examine both structural and substantive isomorphism before and after the exogenous shock of the introduction of graduate-level professional law schools. In those course catalogues, we searched for the coverage of ADR. As explained earlier, conciliation and mediation have been widely practised in Japan, and those concepts began to be known as ADR in the 1980s. Many practitioners and researchers, however, still prefer to use the terms "conciliation" and "mediation" rather than "ADR." Because we intend to test isomorphism in Japanese legal education in response to the exogenous shock of the introduction of a new law school system, we specifically focused on the term "ADR."

We investigated several research questions. How many courses include coverage of ADR? How is ADR placed within the context of courses? What are those courses? Who teaches those courses? We coded the collected materials in order to trace any emerging models of curricular content that might be institutionalized as legitimate responses to the current uncertainty.

For our analysis, we classified the sixty-eight law schools into three prestige groups: high-status, middle-status, and low-status. This status ordering was based on how graduates of each school did on the bar exam over the last six years. Among high-status schools, we included the five schools that had been most successful in having their graduates pass the bar, middle-status schools included the sixth to the twentieth school in this ranking, and the rest were classified as low-status schools. For high-status schools, the average number of applicants who successfully passed the bar exam per year ranged from 90 to 220, whereas middle-status schools had an average number from 10 to 45. Low-status schools averaged up to 9 successful applicants per year, but many such schools had never had students who passed the bar exam.

Is ADR Taught in New Law Schools?
We collected 62 catalogues from law schools, a response rate of 91.2 percent. Of the 62 law schools, 48 schools (77.4 percent) offered 111 distinct courses covering ADR. This number was high compared with the first survey on ADR offerings at US law schools (25 percent). In the first year of the Japanese law schools' operation, over three-quarters of the schools included ADR in their curricula. The higher a law school's status, the more likely the school was to include ADR in the curriculum. All high-status schools included ADR, compared with 78.6 percent of middle-status schools and 74.4 percent of low-status schools. National low-status schools had the lowest rate of adoption, at 54.5 percent. Private low-status schools had an adoption rate of 81.3 percent. A similar tendency was found in the average number of ADR-related courses: high-status schools offered 4.6 courses on average, middle-status schools 2.6, and low-status schools 1.8.

Who Teaches ADR?
According to the law school establishment standards set by the Ministry of Education,[38] at least 20 percent of faculty members hired should be

practitioners, including lawyers, judges, and public prosecutors (so-called *jitsumuka kyoin*). The new law school system envisions a clear division of labour between academics and practitioners: academics teach core legal theory courses, including Constitutional Law, Civil Law, Commercial Law, and Criminal Law, while practitioners teach legal practice courses, including Legal Writing and Lawyering. In other words, practitioners are not allowed to teach legal theory courses, and academics are discouraged from teaching legal practice courses. Some courses are not assigned clearly, such as Civil Procedure, Criminal Procedure, and International Law. The courses that are not assigned clearly at the graduate law schools exist in the under-graduate law faculties. The assignment of instructors for those courses is at the discretion of the schools. Since ADR is more likely to be taught in such "grey-zone" courses,[39] both academics and practitioners can be expected to teach ADR. We believe, however, that national law schools have more academics than practitioners to cover ADR courses, because they can draw upon the staff used for their undergraduate law programs. We believe that private universities, especially low-status ones, use more practitioners to teach ADR. In general, national universities have smaller classes than private universities. This gap in class size creates a large difference in the faculty/student ratio of undergraduate law faculties of national and private universities. For example, the average ratio for an undergraduate law faculty of a national university is approximately 1:30. The ratio for private universities is 1:50 or even 1:80. Among private universities, the faculty/student ratio tends to become more skewed in lower-status universities. Since the law school establishment standard prohibits younger academics with less than five years of teaching experience from teaching at new law schools, we can assume that lower-status private universities are likely to assign practitioners to the grey-zone courses. ADR, therefore, can be predicted to be taught by practitioners more than academics at lower-status private universities.

Our research showed that of the 111 courses covering ADR, roughly a third (35 courses) are taught by practitioners, while most of the courses are taught by academics (61.3 percent). The remaining 8 courses are taught jointly by academics and practitioners. Among high-status schools, about 60 percent of the courses are taught by academics and about 30 percent by practitioners. Middle-status schools have the lowest rate of courses taught by practitioners, 10.3 percent. Low-status schools have the highest rate of courses taught by practitioners, 42.4 percent. At all levels, as we predicted, private schools had greater numbers of practitioners teaching ADR courses. Among private low-status schools, the rate of practitioners (44.9 percent) was the highest of all categories. This figure was the same as that for academics and was lower than we expected. We assumed that at private low-status schools, more practitioners than academics would teach ADR.

What Courses Include Coverage of ADR?

Of the 111 courses covering ADR, 12 were actually entitled "Alternative Dispute Resolution." Six of the 12 courses were taught at high-status schools, 2 at middle-status schools, and 4 at low-status schools; 8 courses were offered by academics. Other courses covering ADR included Civil Procedure (18 courses), Lawyering (14), Judicial System (12), International Law (9), and Sociology of Law (9). Civil Procedure was the most common course covering ADR. We assume that this is because conciliation has traditionally been practised as an element of civil proceedings in Japan. Unlike "ADR"-titled courses, which are dominated by high-status schools, about 80 percent of the Civil Procedure courses are offered at low-status schools, and none at high-status schools. Overall, 66 percent of Civil Procedure courses are taught by academics and 33 percent by practitioners. This difference is the smallest at low-status schools (academics, 57.1 percent; practitioners, 42.9 percent). The second most common course covering ADR is Lawyering. As we expected, 10 of the 14 Lawyering courses (71 percent) were taught by practitioners (2 of the remaining 4 were taught jointly, and 2 by academics).

Adoption of ADR in Undergraduate Law Faculties

The data collection rates for undergraduate law faculties were 65.2 percent for 2003 catalogues and 81.8 percent for 2004 catalogues. The rates of ADR inclusion in the curriculum are almost the same for the two years: 46.5 percent in 2003 and 46.3 percent in 2004. This shows that the introduction of graduate law schools had little impact on the inclusion of ADR in undergraduate legal education. When we look at inclusion by status levels, however, a different picture emerges. Middle-status schools showed a significant decrease in inclusion of ADR, from 57.1 percent in 2003 to 27.3 percent in 2004, whereas high-status and low-status schools showed an increase from 50 percent to 60 percent, and from 43.8 percent to 50 percent, respectively. When we divide middle-status schools between national and private, the picture becomes even clearer. The rate for national middle-status schools decreased from 66.7 percent in 2003 to 14.3 percent in 2004, whereas private middle-status schools had the same adoption rate in both years (50%). We assume that this considerable decrease at national middle-status schools had something to do with the mobility in the academic labour market caused by the introduction of a law school system. It was essential and urgent for each law school to secure qualified instructors. Unlike Japan's typically non-mobile academic labour markets, there was a large-scale shift among legal scholars from undergraduate law faculties to graduate law schools, as well as across universities. We can assume that undergraduate faculties at national middle-status schools were hurt the most by competition for qualified scholars.

Of the ADR-related courses offered at undergraduate law faculties, Sociology of Law, Civil Procedure, and Dispute Resolution were the major areas. Both Sociology of Law and Dispute Resolution courses decreased in number from 2003 to 2004 (from 10 to 6 and from 5 to 3, respectively), but Civil Procedure courses increased from 6 to 9. Unlike graduate law schools, undergraduate law faculties are not required to hire practitioners, and thus the number of practitioners is very small.

Discussion

Our research indicates that the teaching of ADR has been adopted by new Japanese law schools. The overall adoption rate is high, particularly compared with the early stage of ADR adoption at US law schools. This radical ADR adoption is unique to the graduate law schools and is not seen in undergraduate law faculties. Teaching of ADR is not mandated by the ministerial law school guidelines, but the development of ADR in the legal system was recommended by the Justice System Reform Council. Despite the absence of any requirement to introduce ADR into the legal education curriculum, many law schools did so immediately.

Although ADR has been widely dispersed across law schools, there is variation among schools of different status. Higher-status schools have included ADR in their curricula to a greater degree. In our study, the relationship between status and ADR adoption is linear, not a U-shape or an inverted U-shape: the higher a law school's status, the more likely ADR is to be included in the school's curriculum. Middle-status law schools do not appear to face legitimacy pressures at this point. Given their lack of resources compared with higher-status schools, low-status schools must struggle to adjust to a new institution in order to survive. In fact, whereas all high-status schools offer ADR-titled courses, low-status schools are more likely to address ADR in other courses, such as Civil Procedure and Judicial System. As is seen in studies of the diffusion of innovations, high-status schools adopt changes, but we assume that such adoption is not due to meshing with prevailing group norms. Instead, it appears to be related to a status competition. According to media coverage and our interviews with Japanese law scholars, there appears to be keen competition among the top five schools for the number one ranking.

It remains to be seen, of course, how durable the integration of ADR into the Japanese legal education curriculum will be. Courses on ADR have been integrated into legal education curricula in other countries, but they have frequently been marginalized as a specialization that a law school should offer, but not necessarily address, across the curriculum. The prevalence of ADR-titled courses at high-status law schools in Japan suggests that they could become segregated into a subspecialty in the future, whereas the more prevalent inclusion of ADR in Civil Procedure and Lawyering courses suggests an integration of ADR across the curriculum. The eventual outcome will also depend in large part on the availability of teaching personnel qualified to offer ADR-courses. Professor Yoshitaka Wada, a leading scholar in ADR, states that there is almost no one in Japan who can teach both theoretical and practical aspects of ADR. Another law school professor also explained that a shortage of scholars to teach ADR was due to students' limited interest in the subject. In this sense, the diffusion of ADR-titled courses to middle- and low-status law schools may not take place until ADR receives more recognition as an effective means of dispute resolution. Furthermore, we noticed that the terms "conciliation" and "mediation" have not been fully replaced by "ADR" in many courses on civil procedure and international business law. We need to examine the reasons behind the preference for the older terminology. Since we conducted this research in 2004, there has not been a major reshuffle of course offerings at the graduate law schools. Some law schools had only a very small number of students who passed the bar exam, however, and because this is now seen as a problem,[40] law schools tend to focus on the subjects tested on the bar exam. Under these circumstances, we see no clear evidence that ADR has been included to a greater extent in the law school curriculum today.

Conclusion

This essay is a snapshot of our preliminary research on ADR adoption in Japanese legal education. We have presented several suggestive findings. When the Japanese government initiated the transformation of legal education by creating new graduate law schools, many of these schools immediately responded to the government's ambiguous recommendation on teaching ADR. Such isomorphism may not be an unexpected outcome of state-initiated institutional change, but the remarkable scope and speed of ADR adoption into the curriculum of Japanese law schools was unexpected. We conclude that an institutional shock initiated by a state gives organizations an impetus for the immediate adoption of innovations.

In our analysis, status emerges as a key variable impacting the response of organizations to institutional pressure towards conformity. Our study shows that the relationship between status and conformity is a linear one: higher-status organizations are more likely to adopt new institutional components.

ACKNOWLEDGMENT

This article reproduces significant portions of Mayumi Saegusa and Julian Dierkes, "Integrating Alternative Dispute Resolution into Japanese Legal Education" (2005) 10 Journal of Japanese Law 101. We are grateful to the editors of the Journal of Japanese Law for their permission to reprint these portions.

NOTES

1 M. Saegusa, "Why the Japanese Law School System Was Established: Co-optation as a Defensive Tactic in the Face of Global Pressures" (2009) 34 Law and Social Inquiry 365.
2 Among seventy-four graduate law schools, Omiya Law School is a brand-new graduate school.
3 Those who pass a preliminary exam will be qualified to take the bar exam, but the number of those passing the preliminary exam will be small.
4 These two institutions overlap to a large extent in providing legal theory courses, however. As a solution, the graduate law schools have two different courses: a two-year course and a three-year course. The two-year course is designed for graduates of the undergraduate law programs or those who have equivalent legal knowledge. Saegusa, *supra* note 1.
5 W. Powell and P. DiMaggio, eds., *The New Institutionalism in Organizational Analysis* (Chicago: University of Chicago Press, 1991).
6 Isomorphism is defined as the tendency for the structures of organizations to become similar to each other. P. DiMaggio and W. Powell, "The Iron Cage Revisited: Institutional Isomorphism and Collective Rationality in Organizational Fields" (1983) 48 American Sociological Review 147.
7 P. DiMaggio and W. Powell, *supra* note 5.
8 M. Mizruchi and L. Fein, "The Social Construction of Organizational Knowledge: A Study of the Uses of Coercive, Mimetic, and Normative Isomorphism" (1999) 44 Administrative Science Quarterly 653.
9 M. Lounsbury, "Institutional Sources of Practice Variation: Staffing College and University Recycling Programs" (2001) 46 Administrative Science Quarterly 29; M. Lounsbury, "Institutional Transformation and Status Mobility: The Professionalization of the Field of Finance" (2002) 45 Academy of Management Journal 255.

10 L. Edelman, "Legal Ambiguity and Symbolic Structures: Organizational Mediation of Civil Rights Law" (1992) 97 American Journal of Sociology 1531.
11 J. Westphal, R. Gulati, and S. Shortell, "Customization or Conformity? An Institutional and Network Perspective on the Content and Consequences of TQM Adoption" (1997) 42 Administrative Science Quarterly 366.
12 C. Oliver, "Strategic Responses to Institutional Processes" (1991) 16 Academy of Management Review 145.
13 N. Fligstein, "Markets as Politics" (1996) 61 American Sociological Review 656; W. Powell, "Expanding the Scope of Institutional Analysis" in Powell and DiMaggio, *supra* note 5.
14 D. Phillips and E. Zuckerman, "Middle-Status Conformity: Theoretical Restatement and Empirical Demonstration in Two Markets" (2001) 107 American Journal of Sociology 379.
15 P. Blau, "Patterns of Deviation in Work Groups" (1960) 23 Sociometry 245; J. Dittes and H. Kelley, "Effects of Different Conditions of Acceptance upon Conformity to Group Norms" (1956) 53 Journal of Abnormal and Social Psychology 100.
16 Phillips and Zuckerman, *supra* note 14.
17 Edelman, *supra* note 10; J. Sutton and F. Dobbin, "The Two Faces of Governance: Responses to Legal Uncertainty in American Firms, 1955-1985" (1996) 61 American Sociological Review 794; E. Kelly and F. Dobbin, "How Affirmative Action Became Diversity Management: Employer Response to Antidiscrimination Law, 1961-1996" (1998) 41 American Behavioral Scientist 960; J. Burk, *Values in the Marketplace: The American Stock Market under Federal Securities Law* (New York: Aldine de Gruyter, 1988); W. Clune, "A Political Model of Implementation and the Implications of the Model for Public Policy, Research, and the Changing Role of Lawyers" (1983) 69 Iowa Law Review 47; K. Hawkins, *Environment and Enforcement: Regulation and the Social Definition of Pollution* (New York: Oxford University Press, 1984).
18 F. Dobbin, *Forging Industrial Policy: The United States, Britain, and France in the Railway Age* (New York: Cambridge University Press, 1994).
19 Y. Hayakawa, Y. Taniguchi, R. Hamano, H. Takahashi, *et al.*, *ADR no kihonteki shiza* [Fundamental perspectives on ADR] (Tokyo: Fuma Shobo, 2004).
20 *Ibid.*
21 Houkadaigakuin ni okeru kyouiku naiyou houhou ni kansuru kenkyukai [Research group on the contents and teaching methods of graduate law school], Japan, Ministry of Education, Culture, Sports, Science and Technology, "Houkadaigakuin ni okeru minjiho curriculum no arikata" [Model curriculum on civil law at graduate law schools] (24 April 2001), online: Japan Ministry of Education, Culture, Sports, Science and Technology <http://www.mext.go.jp/b_menu/shingi/chousa/koutou/003/toushin/010401/minzi/00.htm>.
22 M. Shapiro, "The Globalization of Law" (1993) 1 Indiana Journal of Global Legal Studies 37; A. Kawamura, "WTO taiseika ni okeru bengoshigyo no houteki wakugumi" [Legal service systems under the WTO] in Japan Federation of Bar Associations, ed., *Atarashi seiki heno bengoshizo* [Lawyers in a new century] (Tokyo: Yuhikaku 1997).
23 L. Riskin and J. Westbrook, *Dispute Resolution and Lawyers,* 2d ed. (St. Paul, MN: West Group, 1998); L. Edelman and M. Suchman, "When the 'Haves' Hold Court:

Speculations of Organizational Internalization of Law" (1999) 33 Law and Society 941.

24 The term "mediation" is preferred in common law jurisdictions, whereas "concilia-
    tion" is used more frequently in continental law jurisdictions, including Japan, as well
    as in the United Nations Commission on International Trade Law (UNCITRAL). See
    Yasunobu Sato, "Hybrid Dispute Processing in Japan: Linking Arbitration with Con-
    ciliation (Regional Report for the Second Symposium)" in Vijay K. Bhatia et al., eds.,
    Legal Discourse across Cultures and Systems (Hong Kong: Hong Kong University
    Press, 2008).

25 Reference materials provided by Office for Promotion of Justice System Reform
    (2002), online: <http://www.kantei.go.jp/jp/sihouseido/kentoukai/adr/dai1/1siryou1_
    2_08.html>.

26 T. Kawashima, *Nihonjin no Hoishiki* [The legal consciousness of the Japanese]
    (Tokyo: Iwanami Shoten, 1967); J. Haley, "Saiban girai no shinwa I" [The myth of
    antipathy toward trials I] (1978) 902 Hanrei Jiho 14, and "Saiban girai no shinwa II"
    [The myth of antipathy toward trials II] (1979) 907 Hanrei Jiho 13.

27 H. Pruetting, "ADR in Germany" in A. Ishikawa and T. Mikami, eds., *Hikaku saiban-
    gai funso kaiketsu seido* [Comparison of the out-of-court dispute resolution system]
    (Tokyo: Keio Gijuku Daikagu Shuppan, 1997).

28 *Alternative Dispute Resolution Act of 1998*, Pub. L. No. 105-315, [1998] 112 Stat.
    2993.

29 R. Moberly, "ADR in the Law School Curriculum: Opportunities and Challenges," on-
    line: Mediate.com <http://www.conflict-resolution.net/articles/moberly.cfm?plain=t>.

30 American Bar Association, *Report and Recommendation of the Task Force on Lawyer
    Competency: The Role of the Law Schools*, ABA Section of Legal Education and Ad-
    missions to the Bar (Chicago: American Bar Association, 1979).

31 American Bar Association, *Law School Directory of Dispute Resolution Programs*
    (Chicago: American Bar Association, 1986).

32 J. Boskey, "Alternative Dispute Resolution in the Law Schools" (1995) 55 The Fourth
    R, Newsletter of the National Association for Mediation in Education.

33 Kawashima, *supra* note 26; Haley (*supra* note 26) countered that the inadequacy of
    the legal system, including the low number of legal professionals, high legal costs, and
    long delays in litigation, have prevented Japanese disputants from using litigation.

34 Supreme Court of Japan, "Shiho tokei nenpo" [The annual report of the justice system]
    (1999), online: Supreme Court of Japan <http://courtdomino2.courts.go.jp/tokei_y.
    nsf>.

35 *Law for Promoting the Use of Out-of-Court Dispute Resolution Procedures* (*ADR Pro-
    motion Law*), Law No. 151 of 2004, online: Ministry of Internal Affairs and Com-
    munications < http://tinyurl.com/2fb8or3>.

36 *Ibid.*

37 Various product liability centres are often included as a type of private ADR, but
    such centres are initiated by Ministry of Economy, Trade, and Industry (Hayakawa *et
    al.*, *supra* note 19).

38 Central Council for Education, Ministry of Education, Culture, Sports, Science and
    Technology, "Houkaidaigakuin no secchi kijyun tou ni tsuite" [Japanese law school

standards] (5 August 2002), online: <http://www.mext.go.jp/b_menu/shingi/chukyo/chukyo0/toushin/020803.htm>.

39 We can assume that ADR is more likely to be taught in Civil Procedure (Houka-daigakuin ni okeru kyouiku naiyou houhou ni kansuru kenkyukai, *supra* note 21) and in International Law, where arbitration has been traditionally used.

40 Central Council for Education, Law School Committee, Ministry of Education, Culture, Sports, Science and Technology, "Houka daigakuin kyouikyu no shitsu no koujyou no tameno kaizen housaku nit tsuite (houkoku)" [Report on the improvement of the quality of law school education] (2009), online: <http://www.mext.go.jp/b_menu/shingi/chukyo/chukyo4/houkoku/1261059.htm>.

A Comparative Study of Olympic Marks Protection and Beyond
The United States, Canada, and China

WENWEI GUAN

The research of the Asia Pacific Dispute Resolution (APDR) project of the Institute of Asian Research at the University of British Columbia reveals the dynamics between the international regime and local legal systems in the areas of international trade, human rights, and cross-cultural dispute resolution in Canada, China, and Japan. The theoretical paradigm of selective adaptation explains the dynamics of the interplay between global norms and local practices, contributing to scholarship on the jurisprudence of international compliance. China's international integration is a good example. As Pitman Potter argues, the last two decades of development of the legal system in China before its accession to the World Trade Organization (WTO) was a process of "selective adaptation" by which "conditions of local legal culture" constantly mediated the application of foreign norms, in particular in the fields of "legal institutions, contract, property, human rights, and foreign economic relations."[1] Potter suggests that China's selective adaptation to foreign norms indicates a "consistent pattern by which foreign legal norms and institutional arrangements are adjusted to meet local political and ideological imperatives."[2] The question of how China can "achieve compliance with GATT/WTO requirements" and yet remain "true to its local cultural and developmental imperatives" presents a challenge for China.[3] This challenge will be examined here through a comparative study of Olympic marks protection in the United States, Canada, and China. This essay provides a case study illustrating the dynamics of selective adaptation between global norms and local practices. In particular, selective adaptation is demonstrated in China's compliance with the WTO *Agreement on Trade-Related Aspects of Intellectual Property Rights* (the TRIPS Agreement).

The protection of intellectual property rights reflects a tension between private interests and the public good. In general, intellectual property rights are recognized as private rights.[4] This has long been recognized by judicial practice. In the case of *James v. Campbell* in 1882, the US Supreme Court recognized that patent rights are inviolable private property rights.[5] This was reiterated in *Hollister v. Benedict & Burnham Mfg. Co.*[6] Copyrights are also recognized as private property rights. The "sweat of the brow" doctrine developed from the *Jeweler's Circular Pub. Co.* case suggests that individual labour makes produced materials copyrightable and, thus, exclusive private property.[7] Similarly, the protection of databases in the EU under the "*sui generis* rights" doctrine under copyright law also illustrates the private rights protection given to copyrights.[8] Trademark rights are also recognized as private rights, the significance of which has been given constitutional protection. In the *San Francisco Arts & Athletics* cases, trademarks were clearly recognized as private property.[9] In these cases, the word "Olympic" and its associated marks were clearly recognized as the US Olympic Committee's private property or its own distinctive "goods in commerce" under US trademark law.[10]

On the other hand, the protection of intellectual property rights also reflects the need to promote public welfare. According to the TRIPS Agreement, the protection of intellectual property contributes to the "mutual advantage of producers and users" and promotes the "transfer and dissemination of technology" in a manner "conducive to social and economic welfare."[11] The private/public tension, therefore, is intrinsic to the protection of intellectual property rights.[12] For example, the "intellectual property bargain" underlying the US federal framework for intellectual property law, a trade-off between "private incentives and social benefits," reflects this private/public dynamic.[13] This essay examines how the private/public dynamic reveals itself in the differences between protection of Olympic marks in the US, Canada, and China. This will illustrate the dynamics between global norms and local practices during the process of selective adaptation.

Through a comparative case study of Olympic marks protection in the three nations, and a further examination of China's protection mechanism, this research seeks to reveal the how and the why of the dynamics between global norms and local practices and the related theoretical implications. The comparative case study of Olympic marks protection in the next section indicates that whereas the US and Canada display a clear private-oriented rights approach, China's protection of Olympic marks reveals a clear public-oriented perspective, as China relies heavily on the aggressive *ex officio* action of the administration. This public-oriented perspective differentiates China from the private-oriented mechanism in the US and Canada. At the same time, however, China still exceeds the requirements of the TRIPS Agreement. A brief historical account of the protection of intellectual creations follows the case study, and reveals that imperial China also relied heavily on administrative and criminal protection of intellectual property. This administration-dependent mechanism was a socially derived product of China's public-oriented culture, which significantly shaped local practices. The public-oriented cultural imperative plays a key role, therefore, in China's selective adaptation to TRIPS. Building on these findings, I offer some concluding remarks on the policy implications of the theory of selective adaptation, suggesting that selective adaptation is a dynamic process between global norms and local practices. The private-oriented rights approach in the US and Canada and the public-oriented perspective in China shape the global protection of intellectual property rights differently. Looking at China's compliance with the TRIPS Agreement by reference to the theory of selective adaptation, it is apparent that both international compliance and domestic legal reform need to pay more attention to the public-oriented cultural imperative.

Olympic Marks Protection: One World, Different Dreams

The United States and Canada: Private Rights with Private Enforcement
It is well recognized that intellectual property theory in the West is firmly built on Hegel and Locke's private property theory.[14] Building on the long tradition of the protection of private property rights, intellectual property rights have been strongly protected in the contemporary legal system.[15] To some extent, this is because private property in the West is as vital as, if not more vital than, life and liberty. For example, in the US Constitution, private property is given the same significance as life and liberty, and is protected from unfairly compensated appropriation by government.[16] In this type of framework, intellectual property as a private right has been well recognized and strongly protected in the West. The discussion below of the protection of Olympic marks in the US and Canada provides us with an illustration.

In the US, the 1981 *San Francisco Arts & Athletics* case indicates a clear tension between public and private in intellectual property protection.[17] In

1981, San Francisco Arts & Athletics (SFAA) started promoting an international "Gay Olympic Games," and it planned to sell posters, T-shirts, buttons, and stickers. SFAA's plans were in conflict, however, with the *Amateur Sports Act of 1978,*[18] which authorized the United States Olympic Committee (USOC) to prohibit promotional and commercial use of the word "Olympic." When this case was heard in the courts, the district court granted the USOC a permanent injunction prohibiting SFAA from using the word "Olympic," and the Ninth Circuit Court affirmed this decision.[19] This was further supported by the US Supreme Court. The Supreme Court stated that the word "Olympic" and its associated slogans and symbols merited protection as "goods in commerce" under US trademark law.[20] Relevant to our examination here is the fact that the USOC was recognized as a non-governmental, private corporation by the Supreme Court. In addition to its challenge of the unconstitutionality of granting exclusive use of generic words to the USOC, SFAA argued that the USOC's enforcement of the exclusive right was discriminatory and in violation of the Fifth Amendment of the US Constitution. The Supreme Court rejected this, however, and stated that the USOC was a private corporation set up under federal law instead of a governmental actor to whom the prohibitions in the Constitution apply.[21] The Supreme Court stated:

> The fact that Congress granted it a corporate charter does not render the USOC a government agent. All corporations act under charters granted by a government, usually by a State. They do not thereby lose their essentially private character. Even extensive regulation by the government does not transform the actions of the regulated entity into those of the government. Nor is the fact that Congress has granted the USOC exclusive use of the word "Olympic" dispositive. All enforceable rights in trademarks are created by some governmental act, usually pursuant to a statute or the common law. The actions of the trademark owners nevertheless remain private. Moreover, the intent on the part of Congress to help the USOC obtain funding does not change the analysis. The Government [sic] may subsidize private entities without assuming constitutional responsibility for their actions.[22]

Furthermore, the Supreme Court stated that how the USOC decided to "enforce its exclusive right to use the word 'Olympic'" was not a governmental decision: "There is no evidence that the Federal Government coerced or encouraged the USOC in the exercise of its right. At most, the

Federal Government, by failing to supervise the USOC's use of its rights, can be said to exercise 'mere approval of or acquiescence in the initiatives' of the USOC. This is not enough to make the USOC's actions those of the Government."[23]

This case provides a good example of how "the expenditure of labor, skill, and money" of a private corporation (the USOC) can make something from the public domain (the word "Olympic") into private property. The expressive instead of purely commercial use of these terms by SFAA is characterized by the Supreme Court as "appropriat[ing] to itself the harvest of those who have sown."[24] Justice Brennan disagreed, however, and stated in his dissenting opinion:

> The statute [the *Amateur Sports Act*] is overbroad on its face because it is susceptible of application to a substantial amount of noncommercial speech, and vests the USOC with unguided discretion to approve and disapprove others' noncommercial use of "Olympic." Moreover, by eliminating even noncommercial uses of a particular word, it unconstitutionally infringes on the SFAA's right to freedom of expression. The Act also restricts speech in a way that is not content neutral. The Court's justifications of these infringements on First Amendment rights are flimsy.[25]

This case reveals a tension between the protection of the USOC's private property rights and the public's right to freedom of expression. In this case, the Supreme Court favoured the private over the public.

Certain Olympic logo cases in Canada show some similarity in this regard. Canada hosted the 1976 Summer Olympics in Montreal, the 1988 Winter Olympics in Calgary, and the 2010 Winter Olympics in Vancouver. Protection of the Olympic logo stirs up legal issues every time. In *Organizing Committee of the 1976 Olympics Games (COJO) v. Exclusive Leather Products Corp.*, COJO was the exclusive licensee of two trademarks containing the words "Montreal 76" of which the City of Montreal was the proprietor. Exclusive Leather Products was a private company specializing in producing sport and flight bags. Finding that Exclusive was making flight bags displaying the phrase "Olympic Montreal 1976," COJO brought the case to court and sought an injunction to prohibit Exclusive from infringing on COJO's trademarks. Exclusive submitted that it applied for the registration of the trademark "Olympic Montreal 1976 – Olympique Montréal 1976" with a design of two men engaged in athletic pursuit in 1974, before COJO's application for the mark "Montreal 76." The Quebec Superior Court found that COJO's use of "Montreal 76" was prior to Exclusive's use of "Montreal 1976,"[26] and concluded that the mark used by Exclusive was likely to be mistaken for the mark to which COJO had acquired the exclusive rights. The action was maintained, and the Court ordered the injunction. COJO was entitled to restrain Exclusive from using the mark "Montreal 1976" or any other marks that were so similar as to be mistaken for the marks COJO had exclusive rights to. The Court stated that:

> [T]he matter which Defendant added to the expression Montreal 1976 ... is not sufficient to remove the possibility of confusion between its wares and those manufactured under licence from Plaintiff. On the contrary the word "Olympic" and a figure bearing the internationally known Olympic torch add to the confusion. Not only do they add to the confusion but it is clear from the evidence that the confusion is deliberate. Defendant; [sic] having failed to obtain a licence from Plaintiff to manufacture flight bags identified with the Olympic games and thus ostensibly barred from participation in what is expected to be a profitable trade in Olympic souvenirs, decided to market flight bags obviously identified with those games. In marketing articles marked with the expression "Montreal 1976" Defendant intended to deceive a substantial number of potential purchasers of souvenir flight bags.[27]

On 11 July 1975, the Canadian House of Commons passed Bill C-63, *An Act to Amend the Olympic (1976) Act.* The Act states that "[t]he Olympic Corporation is and always has been a public authority in Canada for the purpose of the *Trade Marks Act.*"[28] According to this Act, "Montreal 1976" or "Montreal 76" were marks of the Olympic Corporation and others were prohibited from using them unless licensed to do so.[29] The Act also prohibited any unauthorized use of Olympic-related symbols during the six months before the time of the Olympic Games, even if the symbols had been used before that time:

> Where before June 14, 1975, a person adopted any mark, word, abbreviation, expression, symbol, emblem, insignia or design described in paragraph (2)(*a*) or (*b*), as a trade mark or otherwise, in association with goods or services or in connection with any business or any establishment or premise in which a business is carried on, that person shall not, after June 13, 1975, and before January 1st, 1977, use such mark, word, abbreviation, express, symbol, emblem, insignia or design, as a trade mark or otherwise,

in association with goods or services or in connection with any business or any establishment or premise in which a business is carried on, except in accordance with the terms and conditions set forth in any licence issued by the Olympic Corporation in that behalf or except as permitted by any by-law of the Olympic corporation.[30]

Bill C-63 was passed by the House of Commons after the dispute between the parties occurred but before the Court had rendered its judgment. The Court mentioned the Act in the judgment, and although it did not claim to follow the Act,[31] the Court did follow its spirit.

In the 1987 case *Canadian Olympic Assn. v. Hipson*, the Canadian Olympic Association (COA) sought a permanent injunction prohibiting the defendant, William Hipson, from manufacturing, distributing, and selling six lapel pins that were claimed to infringe on the COA's trademarks. The COA owned official marks such as "Calgary 88," "Olympic Torch," "Winter Games," and the "Interlocking ring design." Some of the pins Hipson distributed had a white bear holding a torch with the number 88 resembling the interlocking rings, and the word "Calgary" appeared above the numerals. The plaintiff sent an application to Hipson in January 1985 and brought the case to court when it received no response. The injunction was granted because Hipson's pins so closely resembled the official marks of the COA that they could have been mistaken for the official marks. The Alberta Court of Queen's Bench stated:

> In my view a word as general as "winter" standing alone should not be protected as an official mark and no public authority should be able to gain the protection of an official mark of the name of a season of a year. I hold the same view with respect to a year (i.e. 1988) standing alone – that is to say a year not preceded or succeeded by the name of a city or a word or words descriptive of a particular event. Certainly Winter Olympics or Winter Olympic Games merit protection as an official mark of the public authority. If a year is preceded by the name of a city such as Calgary 1988 or Calgary '88, then in my view the numerals read in conjunction with the name of the city clearly suggest an event or a special meaning that will obviously take place in that particular year and merit protection.[32]

Something relevant to our analysis and worth mentioning is that the Court clearly recognized the COA as a "public authority."[33] This is consistent with Bill C-63, passed by the Canadian House of Commons in 1975. The internal logic of the judgment was similar to that of the earlier judgment. Things changed somewhat, however, when Canada was granted the right to host the 2010 Winter Olympic Games in Vancouver.

In December 1998, Vancouver was chosen as the Canadian candidate city to take part in the competition to host the 2010 Winter Games, and it won the bidding contest at the 115th International Olympic Committee session in July 2003 in Prague. Right away, Olympic logo protection and small businesses using names similar or related to the Olympics became important issues.[34] The downtown Olympia Pizza & Pasta Restaurant and Olympic First-Aid Services were the two most famous cases. Olympia Pizza is a long-established family business in downtown Vancouver. Olympic First-Aid Services is relatively new but was set up before Vancouver won the right to host the 2010 Winter Olympics. Both were contacted by the Vancouver Organizing Committee (VANOC) and asked to change their names. On 25 January 2006, VANOC issued a press release stating that companies that were set up before January 1998 using the Olympic name might have to change their names, and companies that were established after January 1998 would face lawsuits if they did not change their names. VANOC declared in its release that "intentional and unintentional steps taken to make false associations with the Olympic Games, and unauthorized use of the Olympic Brand, undermines the rights of Canadian companies that have committed significant financial resources to become Olympic sponsors and support the ambitions of Canadian athletes."[35]

In 2007, the Government of Canada introduced new legislation to protect the Olympic trademarks. The proposed legislation, Bill C-47, was described as "aggressive," and its expansion of the protection that is available under current copyright law and trademark laws is thought to be "running the risk of violating freedom of expression rights" as the roots of the Olympic Games "lie in a common culture, a common shared experience."[36] The *Olympic and Paralympic Marks Act* was passed by Parliament and came into effect on 17 December 2007.[37]

Compared with Bill C-63 in 1975, this Act was obviously trying to accommodate public needs while still giving VANOC the ability to protect Olympic trademarks. According to the Act, besides approved or licensed users, trademarks used before 2 March 2007, public authorities, wine or spirit labels, personal names or addresses, news criticism and reporting, and artistic works on a non-commercial scale were allowed to use the Olympic or any resembling marks.[38] For example, the use of a trademark by an owner or licensee of the trademark if the owner/licensee used it before

2 March 2007 could continue under the Act, provided that the subsequent use is in association with the "same wares or services" or "any other wares or services of the same general class" that it was used with before.[39] This obviously left room for the owners of resembling marks that used them before the Vancouver Winter Olympics. If *Canadian Olympic Assn. v. Hipson* had been tried under this Act, it would not have been surprising if the result had been different.

Whether or not the Act treated VANOC as a public authority is unclear. What is clear is that this legislation "gives the Vancouver Organizing Committee of the 2010 Olympics ... considerable powers to prevent the use of Olympic marks by businesses or individuals seeking to profit from an unauthorized association with the 2010 Games."[40] According to Colin Carrie, Parliamentary Secretary to the Minister of Industry (the sponsor of Bill C-47): "Bill C-47 will give VANOC the authority it needs to deal with people and business that are using marks they do not have the right to use. It gives VANOC the authority to deal with companies or organizations that try to link themselves to the Olympics without having earned that privilege as others have."[41]

The Act also substantially amended the test one must meet to obtain an interim injunction under Canada's current *Trade-marks Act;*[42] this was done to privilege VANOC. Under the *Trade-marks Act*, satisfactorily meeting a three-part test is necessary before a court will grant an interim injunction: a serious issue to be tried, irreparable harm, and the balance of convenience must be in the plaintiff's favour. The Act, however, waived the onus on VANOC to prove the second, most difficult part of the test – proving irreparable harm.[43] This made VANOC at least a quasi-, if not full, public authority.

China: Public Protection for Private Rights

The law on Olympic marks protection in China might at first glance not seem very different from the law in the US and Canada. In July 2001, Beijing won its bid to host the 2008 Summer Olympic Games. Because of this, China enacted a specific regulation to "strengthen the protection of Olympic logo, protect rights holder's legal interest in Olympic logo, and defend the dignity of the Olympic Movement."[44] On paper, the *Olympic Logo Protection Act* does not look very different from the related Canadian acts discussed above. The regulation clearly states that those who had used logos resembling the Olympic logo before the law was enacted could continue to use them: "Any organization or individual who has already used Olympic logo in accordance to law before the implementation of this regulation may continue to use within the original scope."[45]

Several things are made clear in this provision. First, the *Olympic Logo Protection Act* did not have any retroactive effect. Second, for continued use to be allowed, the prior use of the Olympic logo or resembling marks must have been legal. Third, continued use must not exceed the original scope. Thus, it would appear that VANOC's argument against Olympic First-Aid Services and Olympia Pizza might not have been valid under this Chinese law. Illegal use of the Olympic logo would not have been permitted even if use began before the law was enacted, as was amply demonstrated in a famous trademark infringement case, *Chinese Olympic Committee v. Shantou Jinwei Food Ltd.*[46]

In the *Jinwei* case, the Chinese Olympic Committee (COC) claimed that Shantou Jinwei Food had used the "Olympic five-ring interlocking mark" on its cereal products and in outdoor and cable TV advertisements without the COC's authorization, and even after the COC contacted the company and tried to stop the infringement. The COC brought the case to the First Intermediate People's Court of Beijing. The action was allowed, and the Court ordered Jinwei to pay compensation of 5 million Yuan RMB for trademark infringement. Jinwei appealed to the High People's Court of Beijing. It questioned the COC's standing and argued that the owner of the Olympic marks was the IOC instead of the COC, and that the personal letter from the Legal Department of the IOC that the COC provided did not constitute a valid authorization. Even if the authorization were valid, the respondent (the COC) should only be representing the IOC rather than filing the action on its own behalf. Jinwei also argued that no trademark infringement occurred according to trademark law because using the mark on cereal packages did not fall into the exclusive range of rights related to use of the Olympic marks. Also, Jinwei paid 65,000 Yuan RMB to the Revenue Committee of the Chinese Gymnastic Representative Group of the Twenty-Sixth Olympic Games and was licensed to use the Olympic interlocking mark.

The Court rejected Jinwei's appeal of the COC's standing, stating that under Chinese law and according to the Olympic Charter and the Charter of the Chinese Olympic Committee, the COC was also the proprietor of Olympic marks, which justified the COC's standing in the case. The Court asserted that what Jinwei got from the authorization of the Revenue Committee of the Chinese Gymnastic Representative Group of the Twenty-Sixth Olympic Games was the right to use the representative group's marks instead of Olympic marks, and that this did not constitute any type of authorization from the COC. The injunction was granted, and Jinwei was ordered to pay damages of 5 million Yuan RMB.

In the *Jinwei* case, the COC's property rights regarding the Olympic interlocking logo were recognized and protected. The protection mechanism – proprietors resorting to civil procedures – was not at all different from the Canadian or American approaches, but the 2002 *Olympic Logo Protection Act* takes a big step forward. The Act differs significantly from the Canadian approach, which gives the Organizing Committee and the Canadian Olympic Committee power to protect the Olympic logo. In contrast, the Chinese *Olympic Logo Protection Act* assigns a government branch to protect the Olympic logo:

> The department of industrial and commercial administration of the State Council will be responsible for nation-wide protection of Olympic logo under the stipulation of the Regulation. The local department of industrial and commercial administration above the county level will be responsible for the protection of Olympic logo of the administrative area under the stipulation of the Regulation.[47]
>
> Where import or export goods are suspected of infringing the exclusive rights of Olympic symbols, the Customs shall investigate into and deal with the case, with reference to the powers and procedures laid down in PRC Customs Law and PRC Regulations on the Customs Protection of Intellectual Property Rights.[48]

According to this Act, the national or local Industry and Commerce Administration Bureau has the right to initiate investigations, carry out on-the-spot checkups, and detain wares that violate the intellectual property rights of the Olympic logo.[49] Customs Authorities in China are responsible for these border measures. A Customs Authority also has the right of *ex officio* action of suspension of release, and the right to confiscate detained goods if it determines that the goods infringe patents. According to the *Implementing Rules of PRC Regulations on Customs Protection of Intellectual Property Rights* issued by the General Administration of Customs, when a Customs Authority launches an *ex officio* action ordering suspension of release of goods:

> Where the consignor or consignee lodges a request, which is in conformity with the preceding paragraph, to the Customs for releasing the goods suspected of infringing a patent, the Customs shall handle the matter in

accordance with Article 19 of PRC Regulations on the Customs Protection of Intellectual Property Rights [to release the goods]. While the goods are determined to be infringing the patent by the Customs investigation, the Customs shall handle the matter in accordance with Article 27 of PRC Regulations on the Customs Protection of Intellectual Property [to confiscate the infringing goods].[50]

This is made clear in a notice issued by the General Administration of Customs in 2002 regarding customs protection of Olympics-related intellectual property rights.[51] According to this notice, as of April 2002, Customs Authorities had begun implementing protection of rights holders' exclusive rights to Olympic symbols that had been registered according to the *Olympic Logo Protection Act:*

> When it is suspected that the import and export of goods are involved with violations of the Olympic symbols, the Customs should detain the goods.[52]
> After Customs Authority's investigation, the import and export of goods that violate the exclusive rights of the Olympic symbols shall be confiscated and the consignee or consigner shall be fined.[53]

The power of *ex officio* action by the Industry and Commerce Administration Bureau and the Customs Authorities indicates that China takes a clear public rights approach while still recognizing the private ownership of the Olympic marks. In Canada, however, in the case of prohibited use or ambush marketing, court orders for injunctions, compensation, destruction, exportation, and disposition of infringing wares can be initiated only upon application from the Canadian Olympic Committee, the Organizing Committee, or a private party authorized by the Canadian Olympic Committee or the Organizing Committee.[54] This reveals an interesting and significant difference between Chinese and Canadian approaches to intellectual property rights to the Olympic logo. China's *Olympic Logo Protection Act* clearly recognizes the Chinese Olympic Committee and the Organizing Committee as the proprietors of the intellectual property rights to the logo.[55] The Chinese Olympic Committee and the Organizing Committee are legal persons under Chinese corporate law, and neither of them is a public authority. The automatic initiation of protection by government branches indicates, therefore, that the law considers intellectual property rights as public rights. This is different from the Canadian approach, in which the intellectual property rights to the Olympic logo are clearly recognized as private rights yet are protected by a strong quasi-public group. Furthermore, both the Chinese approach and the Canadian approach are quite different from the American approach, that of private rights protected by private groups.

Ex Officio Action under the TRIPS Agreement

Under the system of *ex officio* action, China's administration gained strong powers of enforcement in the area of Olympic marks protection. This type of pre-emptive protection is not limited to intellectual property rights to Olympic logos, nor is it limited to border measures. To comply with WTO entry commitments, China amended its *Foreign Trade Law* in 2004 to include a whole chapter on "intellectual property protection related to foreign trade."[56] According to the *Foreign Trade Law* (as amended in 2004), the State "shall protect intellectual property rights related to foreign trade, in accordance with laws and administrative regulations on protection of intellectual property rights."[57] The law states: "Where goods which are produced and sold by a party in violation of intellectual property rights are imported and undermine the order of foreign trade, the foreign trade department of the State Council may adopt measures to prohibit the import of such goods for a specific period of time."[58]

This indicates that *ex officio* action covers a broad range of intellectual property products, and provides strong and active protection. As long as *prima facie* infringement is found and the criteria for undermining the order of foreign trade are met, the Ministry of Commerce can launch the *ex officio* action of an embargo on the importation of goods for a certain period of time. Compared with the suspension of release or confiscation of goods, this provision provides more aggressive protection. This protection of "foreign trade related" intellectual property rights has a clear public interest aspect: protection of foreign trade.

The 2004 amendment to the *Foreign Trade Law* also added a new provision to comply with Article 40 of the TRIPS Agreement, "control of anti-competitive practices in contractual licenses."[59] The law grants the power of *ex officio* action to the Ministry of Commerce to enable the Ministry to limit abuses of intellectual property rights and ensure fair competition.[60] The combination of the active and aggressive power of the Ministry of Commerce, the power of *ex officio* action of the State Administration for Industry and Commerce and its local branches, and the powers of border measures of the General Administration of Customs and local customs authorities constitutes a seamless web of protection that aggressively defends intellectual property rights under China's contemporary regime and clearly shows China's public-oriented approach towards such rights. This approach differs from the TRIPS Agreement requirements under the WTO framework, while at the same time surpassing those requirements.

The TRIPS regime takes a private-oriented rights approach that is similar to those of the US and Canada. The TRIPS Agreement has a whole section devoted to protection of intellectual property rights.[61] It stipulates that all methods to remedy a violation – regardless of whether they are "civil and administrative procedures and remedies," "provisional measures," or "border measures" – are to be initiated by the rights holders. For civil and administrative procedures and remedies related to enforcement of intellectual property rights, the TRIPS Agreement states: "Members shall make available to rights holders civil judicial procedures concerning the enforcement of any intellectual property right covered by this Agreement."[62] This clarifies to some extent that it is the rights holders instead of others who have the right to initiate the procedures. As for provisional measures to prevent the entry of intellectual property infringement into the channels of commerce and to preserve relevant evidence of infringement, the TRIPS Agreement states:

> The judicial authorities shall have the authority to require the applicant to provide any reasonably available evidence in order to satisfy themselves with a sufficient degree of certainty that the applicant is the right holder and that the applicant's right is being infringed or that such infringement is imminent, and to order the applicant to provide a security or equivalent assurance sufficient to protect the defendant and to prevent abuse.[63]

For border measures of "suspension of release by customs authorities," the TRIPS Agreement states:

> Members shall ... adopt procedures to enable a right holder, who has valid grounds for suspecting that the importation of counterfeit trademark or pirated copyright goods may take place, to lodge an application in writing with competent authorities, administrative or judicial, for the suspension by the customs authorities of the release into free circulation of such goods. Members may enable such an application to be made in respect of goods which involve other infringements of intellectual property rights, provided that the requirements of this Section are met.[64]

Under the TRIPS Agreement, the only situation in which public authorities can initiate an action upon their own (*ex officio* action) is a border measure to "suspend the release of goods" if: (1) the authorities "have acquired prima facie evidence that an intellectual property right is being infringed"; (2) the importer and the rights holder are promptly notified of the suspension; and (3) the action is "taken or intended in good faith."[65] Furthermore, the TRIPS Agreement places strict limitations on the duration of *ex officio* actions (ten working days in a normal situation). After this time period, the *ex officio* action to suspend the release of goods is either revoked or ceases to have effect, or must be carried forward to a judicial proceeding.[66] Moreover, customs authorities have the power only to order the suspension of the release of goods. It is worth mentioning that the TRIPS Agreement explicitly does not require Members to provide stronger protection:

> It is understood that this Part [Part III: Enforcement of Intellectual Property Rights] does not create any obligation to put in place a judicial system for the enforcement of intellectual property rights distinct from that for the enforcement of law in general, nor does it affect the capacity of Members to enforce their law in general. Nothing in this Part creates any obligation with respect to the distribution of resources as between enforcement of intellectual property rights and the enforcement of law in general.[67]

This has been made even clearer in the TRIPS Agreement's basic principles. While all Members are required to "give effect to the provisions of this [TRIPS] Agreement," they remain free to choose the appropriate means of implementation.[68] As discussed above, however, China's law goes beyond the requirements of the TRIPS Agreement and provides intellectual property rights strongly protected by public bodies.

History and Culture: Roots of the Public-Oriented Imperative

Administration-Oriented Yet Limited Protection in Ancient China

Relying on the government to protect intellectual property rights is not unique to modern China; it has historical roots in Imperial China. China is one of the oldest continuous civilizations in the world. Imperial China's technology and economic development led the world for several centuries. Some of the inventions first developed in China, such as printing techniques and the use of paper, made significant contributions to the social development of the world. Over time, Imperial China developed mechanisms to recognize and protect intellectual creations. These mechanisms to a certain extent resemble our contemporary intellectual property regime. In almost all of these protection mechanisms, we also see a clear public-oriented perspective towards intellectual creations.

In the areas of trademark and patent, Imperial China developed basic protections that are similar to ours today. For example, the first well-documented trademark was used 800 years ago in the Song Dynasty, a mark of a white rabbit used by a needle manufacturer in Jinan, Shandong Province.[69] The first case dealing with the wrongful use of a trademark was documented in 1736, in the mid-Qing Dynasty. It was a criminal case in which a cloth manufacturer was punished for selling his goods under another's trademark.[70] Certain business associations established rules of horizontal competition restraints for the protection of trademarks in Shanghai as early as 1825.[71] In the field of patent production, royal monopolies over production and trade in iron and salt, resembling the monarch-granted privileges in some medieval European countries, were granted in China in the Western Han Dynasty about 2,300 years ago.[72] The patent system in its modern form is believed to have been set up in China by Hong Rengan in 1859, during the Taiping Heavenly Kingdom movement.[73] The capitalist entrepreneur Zheng applied for a patent for his textile machine technology in 1881, and was granted a ten-year patent right by the Qing Emperor the following year.[74]

Probably due to the early development of printing techniques and paper, the mechanism that developed in Imperial China to deal with copyrights is closer to the modern intellectual property regime than these precursors of patents and trademarks. The earliest documentation of the protection of a book producer's right against unauthorized reproduction that is close to the modern copyright can be found in the Song Dynasty.[75] In 1068, the central government issued an order to prevent unauthorized reprints of the Nine Classics and stated that any reprint of the "Nine Classics" would need permission from the *Guozijian* – the Imperial Academy in the Chinese dynasties after the Sui (581-618 AD).[76] Most of the prohibitions on reprinting enacted during the Song Dynasty were intended to protect the original printers of the books rather than the authors. One historical record, however, also shows that the *Guozijian* of the Song Dynasty indicated that the protection covered both the printer and the author for his intellectual endeavours. This resembles the protection given in the famous "Statute of Anne" in the United Kingdom in 1710.[77] In another book from the Song

Dynasty, the author attached a government notice prohibiting unauthorized reprinting and indicating the author's right to prosecute the offender,
destroy the printing tools, and stop the infringement when unauthorized
reprints were found.[78] The first law in Imperial China for the purpose of
controlling publishers was not promulgated, however, until the early Qing
Dynasty in 1779.[79]

The foregoing mechanisms did not carry over into modern China as the
Qing Dynasty – the last empire of China – was defeated by foreign powers.
The public-oriented perspective is seen, however, in protection mechanisms
in both Imperial and contemporary China. Both Zheng and Alford point
out that Imperial China relied heavily on criminal and administrative laws,
and the management of the printing business was mainly for purposes of
political order and social harmony instead of protection of private rights.[80]
This suggests that Imperial China would protect privately owned copyrights
only to the extent that it would benefit public order and social harmony. The
imperial copyright protection of the Song Dynasty is a good example. Instead of existing to promote commerce, it was for those books related to the
calendar, agriculture, codifications of law, and canonical books of Confucianism – clearly directed towards public order.[81] To protect copyright for
purposes of public order instead of for commercial purposes or promotion
of private rights indicates a public-oriented perspective regarding intellectual property.

The Public-Oriented Cultural Imperative Travels
from Ancient to Modern Times

The mechanisms for protecting intellectual property rights in Imperial
China have ceased to have effect and have been replaced by a fairly Western-
ized regime in modern China, yet the heavy dependence on administrative
and criminal procedure remains. This indicates a cultural continuity between Imperial and modern China, and the existence of a culture encouraging a public-oriented approach to intellectual property.

In their discussions of why technological advances did not lead to a
strong intellectual property mechanism in Imperial China, both Zheng and
Alford mention the linkage between perceptions of the importance of commerce and the development of intellectual property protection. Zheng suggests that the underdevelopment of the commodity economy in Imperial
China might have led to the underdevelopment of intellectual property protection. Alford also suggests that the "Confucian disdain for commerce" led

to less importance being placed on intellectual and imaginative endeavours.[82] This presents us with a puzzle: the disassociation between technological advances and strong intellectual property protection in Imperial China. Given Imperial China's impressive technological advances over several hundred years, what caused the underdevelopment of commerce in ancient China? A Weberian analysis of religious influence on the rise of capitalism suggests that an answer may lie in cultural influences.

The Weberian analysis of the linkage between the Protestant ethic and the spirit of capitalism is a classic study of how culture can influence economic development. According to Weber, the Protestant ethic made an independent and important contribution to the rise of capitalism in the West through religious asceticism's facilitation of the accumulation of capital and the encouragement of skilled, disciplined labour.[83] By reference specifically to English Puritanism and German Pietism, Merton suggests that the values of ascetic Protestantism were strongly compatible with scientific enterprise, thus providing a powerful impetus to the development of modern science.[84] The Protestant ethic, therefore, contributed significantly to the pursuit of science and technology and the rise of capitalism. As for China, Weber acknowledges that in terms of material conditions, Chinese social structure contained a mixture of elements both favourable and unfavourable to the development of a capitalist economy, and thus material conditions could not have been a decisive factor in China's failure to develop capitalism. Rather, it was the consistently traditionalist nature of Confucianism that was the main contributor to such failure.[85] This was because Confucianism enjoined adaptation to the given world, and not the transformation of it. For the classical Puritan, who was characterized by a religiously determined and rational method of life, economic success was not an ultimate goal or end in itself but it was still a valid means of proving oneself.[86] In contrast, for the Confucian, wealth was insecure and could upset the equilibrium of the genteel soul.[87] Whereas Protestant asceticism contributed to the rise of capitalism in the West, Confucianism's corresponding ethic of adjustment was the cause of the failure of capitalism to appear in China.

The difference between Protestant- and Confucian-inspired cultural traits also has fundamental implications for our current research, as it provides the key to why technological advances were not accompanied by a strong intellectual property protection mechanism in Imperial China. From a transformative perspective, intellectual and imaginative endeavours should serve primarily as the means of proving the self instead of serving society, thus requiring individualization or privatization of the intellectual endeavour. The commercialization of the privatized intellectual creation then provides a powerful driving force for the development of capitalism. Capitalist development and commercial success in turn prove the success of the self and strengthen the private ownership of the intellectual creation. From a Confucian perspective, however, making the intellectual endeavour for the public will facilitate the adaptation of the self to society and to the world, thereby avoiding the isolation of the self. Protection of intellectual property for the maintenance of social order and harmony thus becomes a reasonable choice as seen in Imperial China. To make intellectual creations in the service of the public instead of the self, however, limits the commercial success of the self and constrains the development of capitalism. The underdevelopment of commerce and capitalism in turn undermines the importance given to the private ownership of intellectual endeavours, which leads to the underdevelopment of the intellectual property regime.

Culturally induced public- and private-oriented perspectives are linked, respectively, to weak and strong intellectual property regimes. The dependence on administrative and criminal procedures, the underdevelopment of commerce, the weak intellectual property protection, and the "adaptive perspective" are all interconnected and linked to culture. They are all socially derived cultural processes.

Selective Adaptation and the Public-Oriented Cultural Imperative

Our examination of Imperial China's protection of intellectual creations and its aggressive administrative enforcement through the mechanism of *ex officio* action reveals the public-oriented cultural traits of China's intellectual property regime. It has long been recognized that different legal systems are deeply embedded in the cultures from which they evolve. Montesquieu argued that the laws of each nation "should be adapted in such a manner to the people for whom they are framed that it should be a great chance if those of one nation suit another."[88] For him, different social and geoenvironmental conditions set the bounds of different systems and cultures. For example, Montesquieu indicates that those people who do not cultivate the land enjoy great liberty as they are not fixed.[89] Both political systems and religions are products of the natural selection process in response to distinctive social geo-environmental conditions. Montesquieu suggests that this is the reason that Islamism developed in the Middle East but not in Europe, and why Christianity is maintained in Europe but is almost impossible to establish in China.[90]

China's legal system is a socially derived product, a product of China's distinct culture. As socially derived products, legal cultures shape different legal systems in different countries. Collectivistic or individualistic cultures will have different preferences for the norms of tradition and religion on the one hand and formal procedures and guidelines on the other.[91] Many contemporary legal researchers, such as Stanley Lubman, William Alford, and others, have stated that China's legal tradition perceives individual rights through their collective embedment and perceives private interests as being inextricably embedded in the public good.[92] The distinctive perspective of perceiving private rights from a public-oriented social context is a product of natural selection in response to the social and geo-environmental conditions of China.

The public-oriented cultural imperative that distinguishes China's legal regime from the private rights-oriented liberal legal tradition has long been studied by the fields of sociology and cultural psychology.[93] In his examination of China's traditional social structure, Fei Xiaotong argues that the Chinese agriculture-based tradition, in which the people are attached to the cultivation of the land, is a non-floating culture from the perspective of human/environment relationships. This results in groups being isolated into family-like rural units.[94] According to Fei, this fosters a collectivist-oriented and *Gemeinschaft*-like social structure, where social relations between individuals are based on kinship or geo-proximity, and individuals are valued through their collective embedment and contribution.[95] This agriculture-based tradition necessitates substantial cooperation with neighbours to carry out economic activities in an effective way. Harmony, social order, and collective orientation are central to this cultural tradition. Social scientists since Marx have observed that economic and social arrangements such as these are generally associated with "collectivist" or "interdependent" social orientations, as distinguished from the "individualistic" or "independent" social orientations that are characteristic of societies with economies based on hunting, fishing, trading, or the modern market economy.[96] Research in cultural psychology over the last two decades also suggests that, in contrast to the West, Chinese tend to perceive the individual through inter-relations and social embedment.[97]

Deriving from this public-oriented cultural imperative, the Chinese Confucian tradition shows quite a different perspective from the West with regard to considering individual intellectual endeavours as private rights. Not only are private interests believed to be inextricably embedded in the public good in Confucianism, but Confucianism is also against indulgence in material pleasures and considers material profit as something dangerous, something only for the "small man."[98] Chinese tradition not only considers the private rights of intellectual endeavours to be socially embedded but also considers them historically embedded, constituting a part of a historically continuous whole.[99] This means that there is nothing completely new at any time in our society, and any innovation must be based on exploitation of our old knowledge. An innovator must at the same time be a copier of the past. This describes to us a clear collective-oriented perspective on intellectual property, one that recognizes individual intellectual endeavours as something inextricably embedded in a social as well as historical context.

This research challenges our "common" understanding of the future development of the Chinese legal system in general and China's intellectual property regime in particular. Foreign critics often suggest that besides the cultural and historical obstacles mentioned above (Confucian ethics of knowledge in particular), the absence of top leadership involvement, the negative effects of bureaucratic politics, and a fragmented political structure also significantly hinder intellectual property protection in China.[100] Mertha argues that the "direct impact of exogenous pressure on the organizational and institutional structure of the State" has significantly contributed to the development of China's intellectual property regime, and the three US-China memoranda of understanding (MOUs) in the 1990s are a successful result of "top-down external pressure" on the Chinese government.[101]

Our analysis here indicates, however, that resorting to a powerful and aggressive administration for private rights protection has stemmed from China's public-oriented cultural imperative, which is in sharp contrast to the private-oriented rights perspective underlining the TRIPS Agreement. Foreign pressures on the Chinese government to strengthen the government's involvement will also strengthen China's public-oriented approach, which in turn strengthens China's cultural and historical obstacles to effective intellectual property protection. The three bilateral MOUs in the 1990s resulted from strong American pressure on the Chinese government to enhance intellectual property protection. This has created an ironic dilemma. The private rights-oriented US government has been unstinting in its efforts to push the Chinese administration to strengthen its administrative influence through a public approach, which in turn facilitates China's public-oriented approach. This pushes China further away from the private rights-oriented goal of the US government. The harder the US government pushes, and the more the Chinese government accepts, the further China's intellectual property regime moves away from the US regime.

Conclusion

The private/public dynamics that exist in the area of intellectual property rights are manifested differently in the US, Canada, and China. This indicates the dynamics between global norms and local practices during selective adaptation. As the cases involving Olympic marks protection in the US and Canada have shown, the private rights-oriented approach has significantly shaped the intellectual property protection mechanism in both countries. The dynamics between global norms and local practices have led to a different balance in China, however: in complying with the TRIPS Agreement, China adapted the private-oriented international intellectual property norms to its local public-oriented imperative. We also found a striking similarity between Imperial China and modern China in their reliance on a strong administration in protecting intellectual property rights. The public-oriented cultural imperative has travelled from ancient to modern China, and plays an important role in China's selective adaptation of the TRIPS Agreement. China's compliance with its requirements confirms the theory of selective adaptation and contributes to our understanding of the dynamics of international compliance.

For the development of China's domestic regime or the international regime under the TRIPS Agreement, more attention should be paid to the significant role of local cultural imperatives in the process of selective adaptation. China's attempt to integrate with the international regime needs to take account of the dynamics of selective adaptation. Establishing an omnipotent administrative power to protect private rights in intellectual property is in the interest of neither China nor the international regime. China's efforts to embrace the private rights-oriented regime amounts to cutting off one's toes to make a shoe fit. Central to the issue of China's compliance with the TRIPS Agreement is the private/public dynamic. Regardless of what stage of economic development China is in, its perspective regarding intellectual property will always be mediated by the public-oriented cultural imperative. We can predict that public concerns will still arise in China even if China eventually crosses the development threshold. The domestic and international regimes should not ignore the public concerns in China during the process of constructing, enforcing, and developing an intellectual property regime.

Furthermore, the dynamics between global norms and local practices in the US, Canada, and China indicate that the theory of selective adaptation has greater implications, going far beyond China's legal reform and development, and can enrich the jurisprudence on international compliance. As we have seen, whereas the private rights-oriented approach significantly shapes legal practices in the US and Canada, the public-oriented cultural imperative deeply characterizes China's administration-dependent enforcement mechanism. The private/public dynamics and the tension between global norms and local practices are manifested differently in different countries. International compliance has, therefore, never been a one-way process but rather a two-way dynamic process of selective adaptation. During this process, where local cultural imperatives mediate global norms, both the international framework and local regimes evolve, and the paradigm of selective adaptation significantly enriches the jurisprudence on international compliance. The dynamics between global norms and local practices as revealed in the process of selective adaptation provide the basic driving force for the evolution of law internationally and domestically.

NOTES

1 Pitman B. Potter, *The Chinese Legal System: Globalization and Local Legal Culture* (London: Routledge, 2001) at 2-3.
2 *Ibid.* at 137.
3 *Ibid.* at 142.
4 *Agreement on Trade-Related Aspects of Intellectual Property Rights*, 15 April 1994, *Marrakesh Agreement Establishing the World Trade Organization*, Annex 1C, 1869 U.N.T.S. 299, 33 I.L.M. 1197 [TRIPS Agreement]. The TRIPS Agreement's Preamble states that WTO Members recognize that "intellectual property rights are private rights."
5 *James v. Campbell*, 104 U.S. 356 at 357-58 (1881).
6 *Hollister v. Benedict & Burnham Mfg. Co.*, 113 U.S. 59 at 67 (1885). The Supreme Court stated "that the right of the patentee, under letters patent for an invention granted by the United States, was exclusive of the government of the United States as well as of all others, and stood on the footing of all other property the right to which was secured, as against the government, by the constitutional guarantee which prohibits the taking of private property for public use without compensation."
7 *Jeweler's Circular Pub. Co. v. Keystone Pub. Co.*, 281 F. 83 at 88 (2d Cir. 1922). See also Peter Drahos, *A Philosophy of Intellectual Property* (Aldershot, UK: Dartmouth Publishing, 1996) at 208.
8 Hasan A. Deveci, "Databases: Is *Sui Generis* a Stronger Bet Than Copyright?" (2004) 12 International Journal of Law and Information Technology 178. The protection of databases under *"sui generis* rights" doctrine has been characterized as a "reinvention" of the "sweat of the brow" doctrine. See Drahos, *supra* note 7 at 208.
9 *San Francisco Arts & Athletics, Inc. v. United States Olympic Committee*, 483 U.S. 522 (1987) [*San Francisco Arts & Athletics*].
10 *International Olympic Commitee v. San Francisco Arts & Athletics, Inc.*, 781 F .2d 733 at 737 (9th Cir. 1986); *San Francisco Arts & Athletics, supra* note 9 at 534-35.

11 TRIPS Agreement, *supra* note 4, art. 7.

12 See, *e.g.,* G. Dutfield, *Intellectual Property Rights and the Life Science Industries: A 20th Century History* (Hampshire, UK: Ashgate, 2003) at 29; Jeffrey L. Harrison and Jules Theeuwes, *Law and Economics* (New York: W.W. Norton, 2008) at 143. The private/public dynamic is commonly categorized as an inherent tension in protecting intellectual property. See also Mira T. Sundara Rajan, *Copyright and Creative Freedom: A Study of Post-Socialist Law Reform* (New York: Routledge, 2006) at 165. In her examination of the conflict between copyright and free expression, Sundara Rajan recognizes that copyright as a "hybrid sphere of law" combines "private and public-law concepts, individual and social interests, and commercial and cultural dimensions."

13 US Congress, Office of Technology Assessment, *Finding a Balance: Computer Software, Intellectual Property, and the Challenge of Technological Change,* OTA-TCT-527 (Washington, DC: US Government Printing Office, 1992) at 20. This book points out that "U.S. patent and copyright laws define limited monopoly rights granted to creators of certain classes of 'works and inventions.' *In this country, these monopoly rights are not viewed as 'natural' or 'inherent' rights of creators; rather, they are granted by the government in order to promote the public interest and are designed within a framework involving an economic tradeoff between private incentives and social benefits*" [emphasis in original].

14 J. Hughes, "The Philosophy of Intellectual Property" (1988-89) 77 Georgetown Law Journal 287. Hughes examines the justifications of intellectual property based on an analysis of Lockean "labor theory" and Hegelian "personality theory." See also S. Balganesh, "Copyright and Free Expression: Analyzing the Convergence of Conflicting Normative Frameworks" (2004) 4 Chicago-Kent Journal of Intellectual Property 45. Balganesh claims that "the most commonly advocated philosophical justifications for intellectual property are the Lockean labor theory and the Hegelian personality theory." Drahos, however, examines the contemporary theory of intellectual property beginning with interpretations of Locke and Hegel, and Marx's writings on property: *supra* note 7 at 1.

15 See Wenwei Guan, "The Poverty of Intellectual Property Philosophy" (2008) 38 Hong Kong Law Journal 359.

16 The Fifth Amendment to the US Constitution states: "No person shall be held to answer for a capital, or otherwise infamous crime, unless on a presentment or indictment of a Grand Jury, except in cases arising in the land or naval forces, or in the Militia, when in actual service in time of War or public danger; nor shall any person be subject for the same offence to be twice put in jeopardy of life or limb; nor shall be compelled in any criminal case to be a witness against himself, nor be deprived of life, liberty, or property, without due process of law; nor shall private property be taken for public use, without just compensation."

17 *San Francisco Arts & Athletics, supra* note 9.

18 *Amateur Sports Act of 1978,* Pub. L. No. 95-606, [1978], 92 Stat. 3045.

19 *International Olympic Commitee. v. San Francisco Arts & Athletics, Inc.,* 219 U.S.P.Q. (BNA) 982 (N.D. Cal. 1982), aff'd 781 F .2d 733 (9th Cir.), reh'g denied and opinion amended, 789 F .2d 1319 (9th Cir. 1986), aff'd sub nom. *San Francisco Arts & Athletics, Inc. v. United States Olympic Committee,* 483 U.S. 522 (1987).

20 *San Francisco Arts & Athletics, supra* note 9 at 534-35.
21 Justice Brennan, joined by Justice Marshall, dissented, however. They argued that the action concerned constituted government action because what the USOC performs are important governmental functions and also because of the sufficient and close "nexus between the government and the challenged action of the USOC": *ibid.* at 548-60.
22 *Ibid.* at 543-44.
23 *Ibid.* at 547. The Supreme Court states that "a government normally can be held responsible for a private decision only when it has exercised coercive power or has provided such significant encouragement, either overt or covert, that the choice must in law be deemed to be that of the government": *ibid.* at 546.
24 *Ibid.* at 541.
25 *Ibid.* at 561.
26 *Organizing Committee of the 1976 Olympics Games (COJO) v. Exclusive Leather Products Corp.*, Q.J. No. 113 at para. 34 (1976) [*COJO*].
27 *Ibid.* at para. 46.
28 Canada, Bill C-63, *An Act to Amend the Olympic (1976) Act,* 1st Sess., 13th Parl., 1975, art. 13.
29 *Ibid.,* art. 14.
30 *Ibid.,* art. 15(5).
31 *COJO, supra* note 26 at para. 23.
32 *Canadian Olympic Assn. v. Hipson,* A.J. No. 576 (Alta. Q.B. 1987).
33 *Ibid.* The Court stated: "It is true that by adopting an official mark the *public authority* (COA) prevents that mark from becoming the trade mark of a person to be used exclusively or monopolistically in association with that person's particular wares and services" [emphasis added].
34 Sasha Nagy, "Olympic Trademark Battle Snares Small Businesses" *Globe and Mail* (24 February 2006), online: <http://www.theglobeandmail.com/report-on-business/article814075.ece>.
35 *Ibid.*
36 Canadian Press, "Bill Introduced Restricting Use of Olympic Words" (2 March 2007).
37 *Olympic and Paralympic Marks Act,* S.C. 2007, c. 25.
38 *Ibid.,* s. 3.
39 *Ibid.,* s. 3(4)(*b*) and (*c*).
40 Andrew Kitching and Marc-André Pigeon, "Bill C-47: The Olympic and Paralympic Marks Act" (LS-555E) (26 September 2007), online: Parliament of Canada <http://www2.parl.gc.ca/Sites/LOP/LegislativeSummaries/bills_ls.asp?lang=E&ls=c47&source=library_prb&Parl=39&Ses=1>.
41 Canada, *House of Commons Debates,* No. 171 at 1255 (14 June 2007) (Mr. Colin Carrie).
42 *Trade-marks Act,* R.S.C. 1985, c. T-13.
43 Section 6 of the *Olympic and Paralympic Marks Act, supra* note 37, states: "If an interim or interlocutory injunction is sought during any period prescribed by regulation in respect of an act that is claimed to be contrary to section 3 or 4, an applicant is not required to prove that they will suffer irreparable harm."

44 *Regulations on the Protection of Olympic Logo*, State Council Order No. 345 (approved by the State Council in the fifty-fourth council meeting on 30 January 2002, promulgated on 4 February 2002, and came into force on 1 April 2002), art. 1 [*Olympic Logo Protection Act*].

45 *Ibid.*, art. 9.

46 *Chinese Olympic Committee v. Shantou Jinwei Food Ltd.*, 32 GaoZhiZhongZi (PRC Beijing High Court 1999). Case number: GaoZhiZhongZi 32(1999) [*Jinwei*]. The case was judged on 10 April 2001.

47 *Olympic Logo Protection Act*, supra note 44, art. 6.

48 *Ibid.*, art. 12.

49 *Ibid.*, art. 11.

50 *Implementing Rules of PRC Regulations on Customs Protection of Intellectual Property Rights*, Decree No. 114 (adopted by the General Administration of Customs of the People's Republic of China on 25 May 2004, effective as of 1 July 2004), art. 24.

51 Notice No. 6 issued by the General Administration of Customs of the People's Republic of China on 3 April 2002.

52 *Ibid.*, art. 3.

53 *Ibid.*, art. 4.

54 *Olympic and Paralympic Marks Act, supra* note 37, s. 5.

55 *Olympic Logo Protection Act*, supra note 44, arts. 3 and 4. The Act states that "the right holder of the Olympic Logo in this law refers to International Olympic Committee, Chinese Olympic Committee, and the Organization Committee of the 29th Olympic Games," and "under this Act, the right holder has exclusive rights over the Olympic Logo."

56 Ministry of Commerce, "Legislative Introduction to the Amendments of PRC *Foreign Trade Law*" (2003).

57 *Foreign Trade Law of the People's Republic of China* (adopted at the Seventh Meeting of the Standing Committee of the Eighth National People's Congress on 12 May 1994, revised at the Eighth Meeting of the Standing Committee of the Tenth National People's Congress and promulgated by Order No. 15 of the President of the People's Republic of China on 6 April 2004), art. 29 [*Foreign Trade Law*].

58 *Ibid.*

59 Article 40(2) of the TRIPS Agreement, *supra* note 4, states: "Nothing in this Agreement shall prevent Members from specifying in their legislation licensing practices or conditions that may in particular cases constitute an abuse of intellectual property rights having an adverse effect on competition in the relevant market. As provided above, a Member may adopt, consistently with the other provisions of this Agreement, appropriate measures to prevent or control such practices, which may include for example exclusive grantback conditions, conditions preventing challenges to validity and coercive package licensing, in the light of the relevant laws and regulations of that Member."

60 Article 30 of China's *Foreign Trade Law, supra* note 57, states: "Where an intellectual property rights owner prevents a licensee from querying the validity of intellectual property rights contained in a license contract, implement compulsory blanket licensing, or stipulate exclusive grant back conditions in a license contract and thus

creating a negative impact on fair competition and the order of foreign trade, the foreign trade department of the State Council may adopt necessary measures to eliminate such impact."

61 See TRIPS Agreement, *supra* note 4, Part III (arts. 42-61), "Enforcement of Intellectual Property Rights."

62 *Ibid.*, art. 42.

63 *Ibid.*, art. 50(3).

64 *Ibid.*, art. 51.

65 *Ibid.* Art. 58.

66 *Ibid.*, art. 55, which states: "If, within a period not exceeding 10 working days after the applicant has been served notice of the suspension, the customs authorities have not been informed that proceedings leading to a decision on the merits of the case have been initiated by a party other than the defendant, or that the duly empowered authority has taken provisional measures prolonging the suspension of the release of the goods, the goods shall be released, provided that all other conditions for importation or exportation have been complied with; in appropriate cases, this time-limit may be extended by another 10 working days. If proceedings leading to a decision on the merits of the case have been initiated, a review, including a right to be heard, shall take place upon request of the defendant with a view to deciding, within a reasonable period, whether these measures shall be modified, revoked or confirmed."

67 *Ibid.*, art. 41(5).

68 *Ibid.*, art. 1(1), which states: "Members may, but shall not be obliged to, implement in their law more extensive protection than is required by this Agreement, provided that such protection does not contravene the provisions of this Agreement. Members shall be free to determine the appropriate method of implementing the provisions of this Agreement within their own legal system and practice."

69 Zheng Chengsi with Michael D. Pendleton, *Chinese Intellectual Property and Technology Transfer Law* (London: Sweet and Maxwell, 1987) at 21.

70 *Ibid.* The local government also carved the notice prohibiting unfair use in stone to inform the public. See Chengsi Zheng, *Zhishi Chanquan Lun* [On Intellectual Property] (Beijing: Law Press, 1998) at 12.

71 Zheng with Pendleton, *supra* note 69. See also Zheng, *supra* note 70 at 14.

72 Zheng with Pendleton, *supra* note 69 at 51.

73 *Ibid.* The "Taiping Heavenly Kingdom Movement" is also known as the "Taiping Rebellion."

74 Zheng, *supra* note 70 at 9-10.

75 In the West, the German Gutenberg is commonly credited with the invention of the type printing technique in the fifteenth century, but Bi Sheng in Song Dynasty China developed type printing as early as the eleventh century. Moreover, long before Bi Sheng, books had been printed in China through block printing (the technique of printing with carved wooden blocks) since the Sui Dynasty (about 1,400 years ago), and ownership of books was protected against theft by criminal law. See Zheng with Pendleton, *supra* note 69 at 86-87.

76 Zheng, *supra* note 70 at 17. In ancient China, the "Nine Classics" refers to nine ca-
    nonical books of Confucianism: *Book of Changes, Book of History, Book of Odes,
    Zuoqiu's Commentary, Gongyang's Commentary, Guliang's Commentary, Book of
    Rites, Book of Ritual,* and *Rites of Chou.*
77 *Ibid.* at 18-19 and 23.
78 *Ibid.* at 23-24. The book, *Fanyu Lanshen,* is a local geographical record of the Zhe-
    jiang area published in 1239. See also Tan Ye, "The Press Business and Copyright
    Protection in the Song Dynasty" (1996) 2.2 Zhongguo Yanjiu [China Studies] 57.
79 Zheng with Pendleton, *supra* note 69 at 87.
80 Zheng, *supra* note 70 at 24; William P. Alford, *To Steal a Book Is an Elegant Offense:
    Intellectual Property Law in Chinese Civilization* (Stanford, CA: Stanford University
    Press, 1995) at 10 and 24.
81 Jianpeng Deng, "The Copyright Issue in the Song Dynasty: Comment on Debates
    between Zheng Chengsi and William Alford" (2005) 1 Huanqiu Falu Pinglun [Global
    Law Review] at 71-80. See also Tan Ye, *supra* note 78.
82 Alford, *supra* note 80 at 28-29.
83 Max Weber, *The Protestant Ethic and the Spirit of Capitalism,* trans. Talcott Parsons
    (New York: Charles Scribner's Sons, 1958).
84 G. Becker, "Pietism's Confrontation with Enlightenment Rationalism: An Examina-
    tion of the Relation between Ascetic Protestantism and Science" (1991) 30 Journal
    for the Scientific Study of Religion 139.
85 Max Weber, *The Religion of China: Confucianism and Taoism,* trans. Hans H. Gerth
    (New York: Free Press, 1968) at 248.
86 *Ibid.* at 243-44.
87 *Ibid.* at 245-46.
88 Baron de Montesquieu, *The Spirit of Laws,* vol. 1, trans. Thomas Nugent (New York:
    Hafner Press, 1949) at 6.
89 *Ibid.* at 277.
90 *Ibid.* at 252 and 302.
91 Gunter Bierbrauer, "Toward an Understanding of Legal Culture: Variations in Indi-
    vidualism and Collectivism between Kurds, Lebanese, and Germans" (1994) 28 Law
    and Society Review 243.
92 Alford, *supra* note 80; Barden N. Gale, "The Concept of Intellectual Property in the
    People's Republic of China: Inventors and Inventions" (1978) 74 China Quarterly
    344; Stanley B. Lubman, *Bird in a Cage: Legal Reform in China after Mao* (Stanford,
    CA: Stanford University Press, 1999).
93 Fei Xiaotong, *Xiangtu Zhongguo* [Rural China] (Beijing: Joint Publishing, 1985); Mi-
    chael H. Bond, "Chinese Values and the Search for Culture-Free Dimensions of Cul-
    ture" (1987) 18 Journal of Cross-Cultural Psychology 143; Gu Hongming, *The Spirit
    of the Chinese People* (Beijing: Foreign Language Teaching and Researching Press,
    1988); Geert Hofstede and Michael Harris Bond, "The Confucius Connection: From
    Cultural Roots to Economic Growth" (1988) 16 Organizational Dynamics 5; Geert
    Hofstede, *Cultures and Organizations: Software of the Mind* (Maidenhead, UK:
    McGraw-Hill, 1991); Qian Mu, *Zhongguo Wenhuashi Daolun* [An Introduction to

the History of Chinese Culture] (Beijing: the Commercial Press, 1994); Geert Hof-
stede, *Culture's Consequences: Comparing Values, Behaviors, Institutions, and Organizations across Nations*, 2d ed. (Thousand Oaks, CA: Sage, 2001); Richard E.
Nisbett, K. Peng, I. Choi, and A. Norenzayan, "Culture and Systems of Thought:
Holistic versus Analytic Cognition" (2001) 108 Psychological Review 291; Richard E.
Nisbett, *The Geography of Thought: How Asians and Westerners Think Differently ...
and Why* (New York: Free Press, 2003).

94 Fei, *supra* note 93.
95 *Ibid.* at 5-6.
96 Nisbett *et al., supra* note 93 at 303.
97 Nisbett, *supra* note 93.
98 Lau, D.C., trans., *Confucius: The Analects*, 2d ed. (Hong Kong: Chinese University
Press, 1992) at 31, 33. According to the *Analects:* "If one is guided by profit in one's
actions, one will incur much ill will. The gentleman is versed in what is moral, while
the small man is versed in what is profitable."
99 This is evident from a well-known phrase, "*wen gu zhi xin*" [new knowledge acquired
through reviewing what has been learned before], from one of the canonical books
of Confucianism, *The Book of Rites: The Doctrine of Mean.* See also Alford, *supra*
note 80 at 19 and 20. He argues that at the heart of traditional Chinese society's view
of intellectual property is "the dominant Confucian vision of the nature of civilization and of the constitutive role played therein by a shared and still vital past." In this
vision, the past serves "dual functions" through which, on one hand, individual
moral development was attained, and on the other hand, power legitimacy was born
and guidance of social structure was constituted, which justifies "broad access to the
common heritage" as well as "demanding more controlled access."
100 Michel Oksenberg, Pitman B. Potter, and William B. Abnett, "Advancing Intellectual
Property Rights: Information Technologies and the Course of Economic Development in China" (1996) 7 NBR Analysis 1.
101 Andrew Mertha, *The Politics of Piracy: Intellectual Property in Contemporary China*
(Ithaca, NY, and London: Cornell University Press, 2005).

Conclusion
Reaching Normative Consensus in International Trade Law

LJILJANA BIUKOVIC

This volume grew out of a series of examinations – by a group of scholars from Australia, Canada, China, and Japan involved in the Cross-Cultural Dispute Resolution project – of the "selective adaptation" paradigm that provides a unique perspective on how the rules of international law are contextualized locally. The Vancouver workshop in November 2004 was a forum for generating ideas to address cultural differences in international trade and conflict resolution. Starting with the baseline that in certain cases a member state's legal culture leads to different perceptions of the norms and values that underlie World Trade Organization (WTO) rules, the workshop ended with a call for WTO member states to assess the adaptability of WTO norms to their own local environments, and the influence of such norms on local economic growth. The forum also suggested that further collaborative research should develop empirical methodology to assess the relationship between rule compliance and legal culture and to examine the manner and circumstances under which selective adaptation affects the dynamics of WTO rule enforcement.

Pitman Potter, the principal investigator of the project, refers elsewhere to selective adaptation as a coping strategy that states and societies in transition utilize to balance local needs against the requirement for compliance with external rules.[1] Selective adaptation offers an analysis of compliance in the context of the socially grounded theory of normative consensus.[2] The general hypotheses of selective adaptation that inspired all the contributions in this volume are that: (1) the sharing of international practice rules does not necessarily indicate consensus on the normative order underlying those rules, and (2) the behaviour of people who are involved in the interpretation and application of international practice rules is informed by their *perception* of the purpose, content, and effect of non-local rules and the norms underlying those rules.[3] An additional hypothesis is that *complementarity* between local and non-local practice rules and norms depends on the historical background, political ideology, policy priorities, structural and organizational environments, substantive and procedural precedents, and other factors particular to specific rules and norms. The final hypothesis, which is yet to be tested in this project, is whether compliance with non-local practices and norms depends in part on the degree of *legitimacy* accorded by the affected communities to the processes and results of interpretation and application.

How the meaning of international laws changes in the context of different cultures and local practices has been examined by many scholars whose discourses were reflected in many of the contributions in this volume. Two such discourses, developed by law and society and international law scholarship, appear to be of particular importance here. The first is the theory of legal transplantation rooted in the sociology of legal adaptation. The second discourse is the norm-based compliance theory of international law. Both use culture as a metaphor for locality, and locality as a further metaphor for change.

Both the workshop in Vancouver and this volume are in a way complementary to the theme of "Changing Legal Cultures" developed in Spain by the Oñati Institute for the Sociology of Law and its follow-up publications. The central concept of that project is legal transplants, commonly described as "borrowing other people's law as a method of speeding up the process of finding legal solutions to similar problems," or the process that facilitates convergence of laws brought about by globalization.[4] Nelken and Feest's volume *Adapting Legal Cultures*[5] focuses on the sociology of legal adaptation and elaborates on the concept of legal transplants. It studies the complex and almost impossible legal adaptation of Western legal concepts in Asia, a difficult process due to Asia's deep historical and cultural roots.[6] The Appelbaum, Felstiner, and Gessner volume *Rules and Networks: The Legal Culture of Global Business Transactions*[7] suggests that global legal convergence of the rules on conflict prevention and dispute resolution may not immediately parallel global economic interaction, but, rather, develop in less formal mechanisms that allow .flexible normative understanding. Their project identifies four ways in which conflict resolution laws and rules may converge and normative understanding of business practices may develop: (1) an international legal order in which international formal legal institutions, such as the United Nations Commission on International Trade Law (UNCITRAL), the International Institute for the Unification of Private Law (UNIDROIT), or WTO foster application of unified law and practice; (2) the development of a private normative order based on common business practices, such as the *lex mercatoria,* which appears as a decentralized form of lawmaking; (3) through the efforts of internationalized law firms, whose practice generates some sort of international law; and (4) by means of extensive, thick personal relationships often referred to by the Chinese term *guanxi.*

The contributions in this volume encompass all four manners of legal convergence identified at the Spain workshop. The mere topic of this volume, "Globalization and Local Adaptation in International Trade Law," indicates that convergence of trade laws is at the centre of these individual contributions and that the themes analyzed include both international legal order, as contextualized in the GATT/WTO agreements, and *lex mercatoria,* or law that converged through harmonious merchant practice.

Most of the essays in this volume focus on adaptability of principles or disciplines of the *General Agreement on Tariffs and Trade* (GATT) and WTO trading regimes, such as transparency, nondiscrimination, and rule-based dispute resolution systems (see, for instance, the essays by Pitman Potter, Kathrine Richardson, Maomi Iwase, and Liao Zhigang). In addition, two articles address the substantive issues of competition law and policy, which are explicitly included in neither the WTO agreements nor the traditional *lex mercatoria,* but are considered to be of utmost importance for the functioning of the global international trade order, and which are the subject of numerous bilateral and international trade and investment treaties to which WTO Members are signatories (see the essays by Ljiljana Biukovic and by Richard Schwindt and Devin McDaniels). Richardson's article discusses regional international treaties, labour mobility within member states, and the development of professional culture and common institutional practices, and how these restrict the number of disputes that trigger formal dispute settlement procedures. Yoshitaka Wada analyzes the contribution of the legal profession to convergence of legal norms through commercial practice of relational contracts based on trust and network rather than on elaborate written provisions; his empirical research includes Japanese companies represented in Thailand. Mayumi Saegusa and Julian Dierkes provide preliminary evidence on how Japanese legal education reform is becoming a tool for facilitating the convergence of legal practices by matching Japanese law school curricula with Western, especially American, curricula. This is achieved not only by the implementation of a far-reaching reform of legal education but also by the introduction of courses related to alternative dispute resolution (ADR).

The selective adaptation hypotheses rest on a premise similar to that utilized by various norm-based theories on compliance with international law – that perception and legitimacy inform the way in which foreign norms influence local behaviour. In brief, norm-based theories argue that commitment to international norms depends on the norms' substantive character, on how well they are incorporated into the domestic legal system, and on the degree of legalization.[8] Franck's legitimacy theory,[9] Chayes' managerial theory,[10] and Koh's transnational process theory[11] all make an important link between the norms of behaviour and the social context in which compliance and/or noncompliance takes place, suggesting a correlation between the implementation, interpretation, and internalization (or socialization) of international norms.[12] These three theories argue that the manner of integration of international treaties in the domestic legal system influences the extent of compliance with these treaties. The emphasis by Koh on the contextualization of international norms implies that norms have an internal aspect that cannot be achieved solely through institutional enforcement but requires "volitional commitment" of individuals and groups as well as of the nation state. In their focus on this internal aspect of norms, norm-based compliance theories rely on disciplines such as sociology and sociopsychology, which analyze individuals' attitudes about the law and assert that individuals' perceptions of a law's fairness, legitimacy, and justice are the basis for compliance.[13]

Clearly, there are several points at which selective adaptation hypotheses intersect with norm-based theories. One part of this volume deals with what Koh calls legal internalization; that is, it analyzes data on the textual implementation of WTO disciplines and on domestic case law related to the issues of transparency and noncompliance (Schwindt and McDaniels, Liao Zhigang, Wenwei Guan, and Iwase, to name a few). The other part suggests the shift towards social internalization (Potter, Biukovic, Emma Buchtel, and Richardson, for example). Thus, the project proposes to use selective adaptation as the context of social internalization of international norms that underpin WTO agreements, and looks into perception, complementarity, and legitimacy as the factors indicating the dynamics of such internalization. This makes an interesting methodological and analytical addition to the two previously mentioned discourses of law and society and international law.

In his contribution, Potter argues that differences between the normative settings of international treaties and the domestic implementation context could determine the effectiveness of various compliance and enforcement instruments. Indeed, his analysis of economic governance norms in China and the Chinese interpretation of principles of transparency and autonomy echoes in the most direct way the major argument of selective adaptation that has been carried over by other authors of the volume. The argument is that the level of compliance with WTO rules and norms depends, among other factors, on people's understanding of both the foreign rules and the local norms and practices, on the degree of support that members of the local community give to the reception of the foreign norms, and on the extent to which the international norms and local norms are complementary or capable of coexisting and operating together in non-conflicting and effective ways, although they might substantively contradict each other. Hence, the level of compliance depends on perception, legitimacy, and complementarity.[14]

In Potter's own words, selective adaptation helps us to understand that noncompliance involves issues of political will and institutional capacity as well as the issue of legal culture. It also helps to explain the extent to which "compliance with international norms [is] contextualized to domestic conditions and local imperatives."[15] In his other writings, he discusses how selective adaptation helps to limit the scope of the claim that cultural relativism is the explanation for noncompliance with international norms, and supports the acceptance of normative diversity only in cases where there is an obvious lack of consensus between international rule regimes and local popular norms.[16] Selective adaptation does not deny the fact that local legal culture, concepts, and vocabulary are powerful filters applied to the perception and interpretation of foreign law. It proposes, however, that legal cultures are no longer so isolated that it is impossible for lawyers and persons educated in one legal culture to learn and interpret the norms of foreign legal systems and foreign legal concepts. Widespread application of *lex mercatoria* and homogenized commercial practice gives merit to Potter's claim.

Similarly, Twining argues that commercial laws can "travel" better than non-commercial ones, can be easier to borrow due to their more technical character, and can be applied in a very wide range of normative systems.[17]

It is possible to conclude that the common thread in this volume is an attempt to resolve the problem of identifying the normative framework of international trade by accepting the WTO agreements as a coherent system of international trade built on norms of liberalism. At most, however, the GATT and WTO have identified a few of their principles, such as trade liberalization, transparency, and nondiscrimination. As a result of this vague wording in the GATT and WTO agreements, and the fact that the meaning of "norms" and "principles" is a subject of academic debate, explanations of the theoretical foundations of international trade norms and values vary – from equality, justice, and morality, as advanced by the liberalists, to economic efficiency, as endorsed by economists. Thus, it is worthwhile to explore this volume to find out the extent to which selective adaptation is applied to certain concepts, and what determines the extent of adaptation.

The principles of nondiscrimination, transparency, and fair trade (which are not explicitly mentioned in the GATT and WTO agreements) and the underlying norm of economic efficiency are essential for both trade and competition. Several essays in this volume illustrate how those principles are perceived differently by different WTO member states. Richardson eloquently describes the labour mobility principle as being interpreted and understood differently in Canada and the United States, despite the fact that these two countries are NAFTA partners, share a common law-based legal tradition, and "similar overall cultural norms regarding rules and laws." What creates this difference, argues Richardson, is the interpretation of those norms and principles through a lens of narrow, local norms. Nondiscrimination, transparency, and fair trade principles protect the equality of competitive opportunities between domestic and foreign companies and products and services. In her contribution on the development of global competition law, Biukovic convincingly argues that developing and developed countries differ in their interpretations of the basic principles of trade and competition because the two groups of countries have different objectives, particularly with respect to transparency and fair trade. In her opinion, it is possible to notice a trend towards Europeanization rather than globalization of competition laws. Biukovic explains how the European Union's proactive policy of exporting its competition laws found a mechanism for transplantation through the inclusion of competition clauses in association agreements signed with third countries. Schwindt and McDaniels describe the evolution of Japan's competition policy and use selective adaptation to explain the degree of Japan's adaptation of the transplanted US model and the influence of surrounding local regulatory norms on the functioning of the transplanted rules in the context of a power relationship between the source of foreign norms and the recipient. These authors find that, initially, Japan adopted the foreign (US) regulatory model of competition policy, and then tried to adapt it. That tendency was caused by postwar political constraints, such as the country's occupation. As autonomous lawmaking ability increased and the Japanese became able to restore their local regulatory norms, the level of adaptation increased.

Wenwei Guan uses the discourse of selective adaptation to compare China's legal rules on the protection of Olympic marks in particular and intellectual property more broadly with relevant legal rules in Canada and the US. His analysis of local conditions in China is comprehensive in scope and complex in methodology. Guan weaves his argument that China's attempt to comply with TRIPS Agreement[18] rules centres on the dynamics of interaction between that country's inherited public-oriented cultural imperatives of Confucianism and its international obligations to protect private rights in intellectual property based on imperatives of Western constitutional traditions. Consequently, the Chinese intellectual property protection regime has become dependent on the ever increasing administrative power of the state and its enforcement mechanism. As a result of this selective adaptation of TRIPS Agreement obligations, he argues, Chinese continue to consider private and individual intellectual property rights in a public-oriented social context.

Iwase argues that the most substantive changes in Japanese dispute resolution rules occurred with the adoption of the UNCITRAL Model Law on International Commercial Arbitration as the basis for new Japanese legislation on international commercial arbitration. The Model Law itself is a flexible framework designed by international experts to encourage selective adaptation. According to Iwase, however, Japanese selective adaptation does not appear to be unique and closely tailored to Japanese local conditions, but, rather, follows the path of the German adaptation of the same model!

Further discussion of the scope of legislative change referred to by Iwase is provided in an essay on the reform of legal education in Japan. An empirical study by Saegusa and Dierkes establishes that the extent of internalization of international ADR rules in Japan is broad. The authors explain that it includes the introduction, with unprecedented speed, of ADR courses in

high-status Japanese law schools – even surpassing the speed of introduction of ADR courses in schools in the US, which have been the models for
Japanese law school reform.

Chinese arbitration law departs from the Model Law on International
Commercial Arbitration to such an extent that Wang Shuliang's review of
Chinese dispute resolution mechanisms for international trade disputes
does not even make reference to it. One may assume that the departure
from the Model Law is triggered by the Chinese disagreement with the
broad concept of party autonomy, which is the paramount principle of
the Model Law. Chinese adherence to the United Nations *Convention on the
Recognition and Enforcement of Foreign Arbitral Awards*[19] (the *New York
Convention*) and the growth of the China International Economic and Trade
Arbitration Commission (CIETAC) are not remedies for this departure
from the Model Law's core principles.

Liao Zhigang's contribution discusses the direction and the extent of selective adaptation to the TRIPS Agreement. He claims that the scope and
direction of selective adaptation of the TRIPS Agreement are dependent on
the legal status of the treaties under the constitutional law of each adopting
country. China internalizes international treaties, including the TRIPS
Agreement, in a monistic way, without any need for transposition of international rules by introduction of domestic legislation. His study indirectly
suggests that the remaining problems of compliance with the TRIPS Agreement are then at the level of social internalization. Although he remarks that
some concepts, such as the notion of private rights, are no longer alien to
Chinese government and ordinary people, the fact that he calls for further
improvements in the enforcement of intellectual property rights still indicates a lack of normative consensus at the level of social internalization. If
there were a higher level of normative consensus, the application of imported norms would be voluntary and the enforcement mechanisms would
not be needed, even if some disputes relating to interpretation arise, as
shown by Richardson's analysis of the infrequent invocation of formal dispute resolution mechanisms in the context of Chapter 16 of the *North
American Free Trade Agreement*.[20]

In conclusion, this volume is a collection of essays that contribute to an
ongoing debate on the possibilities of establishing a balanced, workable
international legal system that is also flexible enough to accommodate particularities of local rules and practices. It does not provide the formula for
success, but it does show that social dimensions undeniably dictate the extent of selective adaptation and that understanding the local concepts is

essential for comprehending the directions of adaptation. It is thus worthwhile to restate Buchtel's suggestion that if we accept that the international rules and conflict resolution methods (including the rules and methods of the WTO) do change their meanings when brought into different cultures, then further lawmaking has to be culturally sensitive before trying to be culturally neutral.

NOTES

1 Pitman Potter, "Legal Reform in China: Institutions, Culture, and Selective Adaptation" (2004) 29 Law and Social Inquiry 465 at 478.
2 Pitman Potter and Lesley Jacobs, "Limits to Cultural Relativism: Selective Adaptation and Human Rights to Health" (2006) 9 Health and Human Rights 113 at 114.
3 Potter, *supra* note 1 at 480.
4 David Nelken, "Towards a Sociology of Legal Adaptation" in David Nelken and Johannes Feest, eds., *Adapting Legal Cultures* (Oxford: Hart Publishing, 2001) 7 at 7.
5 Nelken and Feest, *ibid.*
6 *Ibid.* at 3.
7 Richard P. Appelbaum, William F. Felstiner, and Volkmar Gessner, *Rules and Networks: The Legal Culture of Global Business Transactions* (Oxford: Hart Publishing, 2001).
8 K. Raustiala and A.M. Slaughter, "International Law, International Relations and Compliance" in Walter Carlsnaes, Thomas Risse, and Beth A. Simmons, eds., *Handbook of International Relations* (Thousand Oaks, CA: Sage Publications, 2002) 538 at 546.
9 Thomas M. Franck, *The Power of Legitimacy among Nations* (Oxford: Oxford University Press, 1990); Thomas M. Franck, *Fairness in International Law and Institutions* (Oxford: Clarendon Press, 1995).
10 Abram Chayes and Antonia Handler Chayes, *The New Sovereignty: Compliance with International Regulatory Agreements* (Cambridge, MA: Harvard University Press, 1995).
11 Harold Hongju Koh, "Transnational Legal Process" (1996) 75 Nebraska Law Review 181.
12 Raustiala and Slaughter, *supra* note 8 at 544.
13 See, *e.g.*, Tom Tyler, *Why People Obey the Law* (New Haven, CT: Yale University Press, 1990).
14 Potter, *supra* note 1 at 478-79.
15 *Ibid.* at 480.
16 Potter and Jacobs, *supra* note 2 at 3.
17 William Twining, "Have Concepts, Will Travel: Analytical Jurisprudence in a Global Context" (2005) 1 International Journal of Law in Context 5 at 9. In this article, he argues that concepts such as legal education, legal profession, and lawyer do not travel particularly well, whereas concepts of health law are quite cosmopolitan. See, in particular, 33-34.

18 *Agreement on Trade-Related Aspects of Intellectual Property Rights,* 15 April 1994, *Marrakesh Agreement Establishing the World Trade Organization,* Annex 1C, 1869 U.N.T.S. 299, 33 I.L.M. 1197 [TRIPS Agreement].

19 *Convention on the Recognition and Enforcement of Foreign Arbitral Awards,* 10 June 1958, 330 U.N.T.S. 38, 7 I.L.M. 1046 (entered into force 7 June 1959).

20 *North American Free Trade Agreement between the Government of Canada, the Government of Mexico and the Government of the United States,* 17 December 1992, Can. T.S. 1994 No. 2, 32 I.L.M. 289 (entered into force 1 January 1994).

Contributors

Ljiljana Biukovic
Associate Professor, Faculty of Law, University of British Columbia.

Emma E. Buchtel
Assistant Professor, Department of Psychological Studies, Hong Kong Institute of Education.

Julian Dierkes
Associate Professor and Keidanren Chair in Japanese Research, Institute for Asian Research, University of British Columbia.

Wenwei Guan
Assistant Professor, School of Law, City University of Hong Kong.

Maomi Iwase
Associate Professor, Institute for Policy Analysis and Social Innovation, University of Hyogo.

Liao Zhigang
Professor, Southwest University of Political Science
and Law, Chongqing, China.

Devin McDaniels
Research Associate, Haskayne School of Business,
University of Calgary.

Pitman B. Potter
Hong Kong Bank Chair in Asian Research, Institute of
Asian Research; Professor, Faculty of Law, University
of British Columbia.

Kathrine Richardson
Assistant Professor, Department of Geography, San José
State University.

Mayumi Saegusa
Researcher and Lecturer, Centre for East and South-East
Asian Studies, Lund University.

Richard Schwindt
Associate Professor, Department of Economics and
Faculty of Business Administration, Simon Fraser
University.

Yoshitaka Wada
Professor, Waseda Law School and Chair, Centre for
Dispute and Negotiation Research, Waseda University.

Wang Shuliang
Law Institute, Shanghai Institute of Social Sciences;
Research Assistant, Shanghai Academy of Social Sciences.

Index